WRIGHT'S BOOK

OF

3000 PRACTICAL RECEIPTS,

OR

COMPLETE BOOK OF REFERENCE,

CONTAINING

VALUABLE AND IMPORTANT RECEIPTS

FOR

MEDICINE,

COOKERY,
PASTRY,
PRESERVING,
PICKLING,
CONFECTIONARY,
DISTILLING,
PERFUMERY,
VARNISHING
CHEMICALS,
DYEING,

AND

AGRICULTURE.

BY

A. S. WRIGHT.

NEW YORK:
DICK & FITZGERALD, PUBLISHERS.

1869

ADVERTISEMENT.

In preparing the following pages for the public, the intention of the publishers has been to furnish, within a small compass, and at a reasonable rate, a work comprehending the most recent discoveries of science, in a form convenient for practical use. With this view, the editor has drawn freely upon the most distinguished and universally received Pharmacopœias and Dictionaries of Science, including those of London and Edinburgh, as well as the most authentic works of the kind published in this country. From all these sources he has taken whatever could be of practical use to the Manufacturer, the Tradesman, the Agriculturist, or the Housekeeper. It is even hoped that the general reader, debarred by the want of means or leisure from consulting the more voluminous and expensive works, may draw both instruction and amusement from these pages.

No exertion has been spared to make the work as comprehensive and accurate as possible. Many receipts will be found in it that have never before appeared in print in this country. Some idea may be formed of its value in this latter respect, when it is stated that the compiler has been for many years engaged in collecting rare and valuable receipts from numerous languages besides the English.

The apparent want of arrangement in the subjects is fully compensated by the copious Index at the end; and some advantages are derived from it, which could not be so well obtained in a strictly regular arrangement. Under its present form, the work will admit the addition of new matter from time to time, so as to enhance the value of the whole, and to keep pace with the progress of general scientific discovery.

Care has been taken to avoid, as much as possible, difficult technical terms, and so to simplify the language that the general reader shall not be embarrassed by expressions unfamiliar to any one ordinarily acquainted with his native tongue; and it is thus presented in the confident hope that it may prove, as intended, a work of practical utility.

WRIGHT'S AMERICAN

PRACTICAL RECEIPT-BOOK.

Powder of Cassius.

By adding a little nitro-muriate of gold, to a fresh solution of muriate of tin, both being much diluted with water, the gold will be precipitated of a purple colour, forming that beautiful pigment called powder of Cassius.

Ring Worm,

May be, in most cases, simply cured by scratching around the outer surface with the point of a sharp pin. The disease will not pass the line, if the skin is thus cut.

Growth of Hair increased and Baldness prevented.

Take 4 ounces of castor oil, 8 do. good Jamaica rum, 30 drops oil of lavender, or 10 do. oil of rose, anoint occasionally the head, shaking well the bottle previously.

To prevent the Hair falling off.

Wash the head once a day with good old Jamaica rum.

Black Ink improved.

To a pint of common black ink add one drachm of impure carbonate of potassa, and in a few minutes it will be a jet black. Be careful that the ink does not run over, during the effervescence caused by the potassa.

To give Iron the colour of Copper.

Take 1 oz. of copper-plates, cleansed in the fire; 3 ozs. of *aqua fortis;* dissolve the copper, and when it is cold use it by washing your iron with it by the help of a feather; it is presently cleansed and smooth, and will be of a copper colour; by much using or rubbing it will wear off, but may be renewed by the same process.

A way of Gilding with Gold upon Silver.

Beat a ducat thin, and dissolve in it two ounces of *aqua regia;* dip clean rags in it and let them dry; burn the rags, and, with the tinder thereof, rub the silver with a little spittle; be sure first that the silver be cleansed from grease.

Grafting.

Melt beeswax and tallow together, stirring in a little chalk if handy; while hot dip in some strips of rags; then tear them into strips suitable to envelope the stock and scion. Let the stock and scion be so covered as to prevent the escape of the sap or the introduction of water, and the work is finished.

To make Copper into a Metal like Gold.

Distilled verdigris four ounces; Tutiæ Alexandrinæ præparatæ two ounces; saltpetre one ounce; borax half an ounce; mix all together with oil, till they be as thick as pap; then melt it in a crucible, and pour it into a fire-shovel, first well warmed.

To make transparent Silver.

Refined silver, one ounce; dissolve it in two ounces of *aqua fortis;* precipitate it with a *pugil* (a quantity that may be taken up between the thumb and finger) of salt, then strain it through a paper, and the remainder melt in a crucible for about half an hour, and pour it out, and it will be transparent.

To whiten Copper throughout.

Take thin plates of copper, as thin as a knife, heat them six or seven times, and quench them in water; then melt them, and to each pound add 4 ounces of saltpetre and 4 ounces of arsenic, well powdered and mixed, and first melted apart in another crucible, by gentle degrees; then take them out, and powder them; then take Venetian borax and white tartar, of each an ounce and a half; then melt these, with the former powder, in a crucible, and pour them out into some iron receiver; it will appear as clear as crystal, and is called *crystallinum fixum arsenicum.* Of this clear matter, broken into little pieces, throw into the melted copper (by small pieces at a time, staying five or six minutes between each injection) 4 ounces; when all is thrown in, increase the fire, till all be well melted together for a quarter of an hour; then pour it out into an ingot.

Ward's Paste for the Piles.

Powder of elecampane 4 ounces; black pepper 4 ounces; fennel seed 6 ounces; honey 8 ounces; sugar 8 ounces; mix and take a spoonful two or three times a day.

Ward's White Drops.

Bichloride of mercury 90 grains; hydrochloric acid 10 drachms; and water 24 ounces. Dissolve.

Wash Balls, No. 1.

White soap 4 pounds; white pipe-clay 4 pounds; and Scotch soda half a pound; mix with water, perfume and form to taste.

Wash Balls, No. 2.

Take white soap 7 pounds; pearlash 6 ounces; orris powder 8 ounces; bergamot 1 ounce; oil of lavender half an ounce; cassia oil quarter of an ounce; oil of cloves 1 drachm; caraway half a drachm; mix with water to a paste, and finish to taste.

Watchmaker's Oil, which never corrodes or thickens.

Take olive oil and put it into a bottle, then insert coils of thin sheet lead. Expose it to the sun for a few weeks, and pour off the clear

Water Colour Cakes.

1st. Take the colours and grind them to a proper consistence with gum water, then mould. 2d. Isinglass 1 ounce ; water 10 ounces ; as before.

Varnish for Water Colour Drawings.

Take Canada balsam 1 part ; oil of turpentine 2 parts, mixed ; size the drawing before you apply the varnish.

Vanilla Chocolate.

Ten pounds of prepared nuts, ten pounds of sugar, vanilla two ounces and a half, cinnamon one ounce, one drachm of mace, and two drachms of cloves ; or the vanilla may be used solely.

Having prepared the nuts by carefully heating them over a moderate fire in an open iron vessel, stirring them until the skins begin to separate, remove them from the fire for the purpose of thoroughly winnowing them, when they must be replaced over the fire, and very lightly scorched. Then pounding them in a heated iron mortar until they are reduced to an oily paste, into which the pestle will sink by its own weight, cut the vanilla in small bits, pound it fine with part of the sugar, and mix it with the paste ; boil about one-half of the sugar before you add it ; and pour into moulds.

Waffles.

Milk, 1 quart ; eggs, 5 ; flour, 1¼ pound ; butter, ½ pound ; yeast, 1 spoonful. When baked, sift sugar and powdered cassia on them.

To choose Water for Brewing.

Use soft water, or if it cannot be procured, expose hard water in the coolers to the air for two or three days, and throw a handful of soda into each hogshead.

Potter's Patent Water-proof Cloth.

Isinglass, alum, soap, equal parts ; water sufficient. Dissolve each separately, and mix the solution, with which imbue the cloth on the wrong side ; dry and brush the cloth well, first with a dry brush, and afterwards (lightly) with a brush dipped in water.

Wainscot Varnish.

Gum animé, 32 parts ; pale oil, 100 parts ; litharge (in powder), 1 part ; sugar of lead (in powder), 1 part ; boil, until stringy, then cool a little, and add spirits of turpentine, 170 parts. Mix well and strain.

To hasten the ripening of Wall Fruit.

Paint the wall black.

Walnut Catsup.

Walnut-shell juice, 3 gallons ; salt, 7 pounds ; ginger, 8 ounces ; shallots, 8 ounces ; garlic, 8 ounces ; horse-radish, 8 ounces , essence of anchovies, 1 quart. Mix.

To Pickle White Walnuts.

Pare them, until the white appears, then simmer for ten minutes in salt and water, drain, and put them into the bottles with a little mace and sliced nutmeg; lastly, pour on the vinegar (hot) and cork immediately.

Walnut Wine.

Honey, 100 pounds; water 30 gallons; walnut liquor, 1 gallon; ferment, and add spirit, 2 gallons; cream of tartar, 8 ounces.

To make fine Black Writing Ink.

Take 2 gallons of a strong decoction of logwood, well strained, and then add 1½ pounds blue galls in coarse powder; 6 ounces sulphate of iron; ounce acetate of copper; 6 ounces well ground sugar; and 12 ounces gum arabic. Set the above on the fire until it begins to boil, then set it away until it has required the desired black.

Red Ink for Writing.

Boil over a slow fire 4 ounces of Brazil-wood, in small raspings or chips, in a quart of water, till a third part of the water is evaporated. Add during the boiling, 2 drachms of alum in powder. When the ink is cold, steam it through a fine cloth. Vinegar or stale urine is often used instead of water. In case of using water, adding a very small quantity of salammoniac would improve this ink.

Blue Ink.

Take sulphate of indigo, dilute it with water till it produces the colour required. It is with sulphate very largely diluted, that the faint blue lines of ledgers and other account books are ruled. If the ink were used strong, it would be necessary to add chalk to it to neutralize the acid. The sulphate of indigo may be had of the woollen dyers.

Fire and Water-proof Cement.

To half a pint of milk put an equal quantity of vinegar, in order to curdle it; then separate the curd from the whey, and mix the whey with four or five eggs, beating the whole well together. When it is well mixed, add a little quicklime through a sieve, until it has acquired the consistence of a thick paste. With this broken vessels may be united. It resists water, and, in a measure, fire.

To Whiten Beeswax.

In March or April melt yellow wax without boiling; then having several pewter dishes ready, dip the outside bottom of each dish in fair water; then dip them into the wax, and take up a very thin plate of wax, the thinner the better: take them off, and expose them upon the grass to the sun, air, and dews, until they be milk-white, turning them often. Try some of them by sprinkling water on them with a cloth. *Query*, whether white lead may not in this way be made with very thin plates.

Yellow Wash.

Lime-water, 1 pound; bichloride of mercury, 40 grains. Rub together, Shake the bottle before use. Used for syphilitic ulcers.

Treatment of Acute Rheumatism with Large Doses of the Nitrate of Potass.

Dr. Brocklesby seems to have been the first to point out the curative efficacy of saltpetre in the treatment of acute articular rheumatism. In his economical and medical observations, published in 1764, he has explained the practice which he found to be most useful. After taking a free bleeding from the arm, when the patient is young and robust, he orders a very copious allowance of warm gruel, in which from one to two drachms of the salt have been dissolved ; the patient is to take large draughts of this drink at short intervals. He has given as much as from six to ten drachms of the nitrate, dissolved in from three to six quarts of the gruel, during the course of twenty-four hours. This mode of treatment rarely fails in producing a great relief of all the symptoms in two or three days : and very often a complete cure of the disease is effected, without having recourse to any other mode of treatment, within a week from commencing the treatment. The nitred diluent usually causes very profuse perspiration, and generally also acts upon the bowels ; if it does not, an aperient enema should be given occasionally.

It is to be observed that Dr. Brocklesby's remarks are drawn from practice in military hospitals, where the patients are usually robust and healthy.

In 1772, Dr. Macbride, in his introduction to the theory and practice of medicine, recommended the same mode of treatment. Two years later Dr. William White (Observations on the use of Antimonial Preparations) makes the following remarks on the effects of large doses of saltpetre :

"The employment of this salt, after bloodletting, is very useful in the treatment of acute rheumatism ; but it must be given to the extent of an ounce in the twenty-four hours, if the vascular irritation be considerable ; small doses are of little service. In many cases of chronic rheumatism also, it is of great efficacy. Administered in the dose of from one ounce to an ounce and a half in twenty-four hours, it often cures the most severe cases of the disease, which may have resisted every other mode of treatment."

The use of the nitrate, notwithstanding such decided recommendations, fell into neglect, and although noticed by M. Bosquillon in his translation of Cullen, was not till 1832 when it was again brought to notice by M. Gendrin. One of his *internes* at the Beaujon Hospital, M. Aran, has brought together the reports of a dozen of cases treated with the nitrate of potash in full doses, dissolved in copious draughts of a mild demulcent diluent, very nearly according to the directions of Dr. Brocklesby. The dose of the salt varied from four to eight or ten drachms in the course of the twenty-four hours. The average duration of the treatment seems to have been about a week. In many of the cases there were well marked symptoms indicating disease of the heart : these symptoms usually subsided with the suffering in the joints.

The *modus operandi* of the remedy was usually as a powerful diuretic and diaphoretic : occasionally too it acted on the bowels.

Another for Rheumatism.

One of the most generally useful of all remedies, in a large proportion of rheumatic cases, is the mistura guaiaci of the London Pharmacopœia and it is observed that it is usually most beneficial when it acts on the bowels and kidneys. The vinum colchici, or the Dover's powder, may often be added with much advantage to it. Moderate bloodletting, and the exhibition of calomel at bed time, with or without opium, should seldom be neglected at the same time.

Burnt Rhubarb in Diarrhœa.

It may be useful to know the value of burnt rhubarb in diarrhœa. It is more serviceable in the diarrhœa, attendant on the last stage of consumption, than the chalk-mixture and opium, or any other of the usual remedies.

It has been used, with the same pleasing effects, for more than twenty years, in incidental diarrhœas. After one or two doses, the pains quickly subside, and the bowels return to their natural state. The dose is from five to ten grains.

The manner of preparing it is to burn the rhubarb powder in an iron crucible, stirring it until it is blackened; then smother it in a covered jar.

It loses two-thirds of its weight by the incineration. It is nearly tasteless. In no one case where it has been given has it failed. It may be given in port-wine, milk, and water.

Improved Method of Preparing Vinum Ferri.

Take of the best hock, one pint; common rust of iron of the shops, well levigated, two ounces. Introduce both into a matrass, which plunge into a water bath maintained at the temperature of 100°. Constantly agitate the matrass for an hour; then remove it from the water, and the next day filter. The colour of this vinum ferri is a very deep greenish brown, almost black when the volume is great: its taste is ferruginous, agreeably and highly vinous; it produces a pleasant warmth in the stomach, and never sickens. In its effects it must be tonic, diuretic, emmenagogue, anthelmintic, and carminative. It does not, in a moderate dose, excite.

No other wine than hock will afford a preparation possessing these virtues. The dose for an adult may be three or four drachms thrice a day; in smaller doses it is of little use. If it is to be exhibited in combination with a bitter, it agrees well with colombo or gentian.

By this method, in one day, we obtain a far better preparation than is procurable by the processes of the pharmacopœias in two months. The iron exists in it, chiefly in the state of protoxide.

The Celebrated Brilliant French Varnish for Boots and Shoes.

Take ¾ of a pint spirit of wine; 5 pints white wine; ½ lb. gum senegal in powder; 6 oz. loaf sugar; 2 oz. powdered galls; 4 oz. green copperas. Dissolve the sugar and gum in the wine. When dissolved, strain; then put it on a slow fire, being careful not to let boil. In this state put in the galls, copperas, and the alcohol, stirring it well for five minutes. Then set off, and when nearly cool, strain through flannel, and bottle for use. It is applied with a pencil brush.

Note.—If not sufficiently black, a little sulphate of iron and ½ pint of a strong decoction of logwood may be added, with $\frac{1}{16}$ oz. pearlash.

Liquid Japan, for Boots and Shoes, Harness, &c.

Take treacle, 8 parts; lampblack, 1 part; sweet oil, 1 part: gum arabic, 1 part; isinglass, 1 part. Mix well in 32 parts of water. Apply heat; when cool, add one ounce of spirit of wine. You may add an ox's gall Place the bottle by the side of the fire before use, and apply with the tip of the finger or a sponge.

Liquid Sulphuretted Hydrogen.

Take sulphuret of iron, 1 part; dilute sulphuric acid, 3 parts. Pass the gas into a bladder or bag, then fasten it into the neck of a bottle quarter filled with water; agitate for ten minutes, applying pressure to the bag. Keep it in well-stopped bottles.

Liquodilla.

Take the peels of oranges and lemons, each, 1 dozen; steep them in spirit (brandy or rum), 3 gallons, for 3 days. Then add water, 2 gallons; sugar, 8 pounds. Mix and filter.

Liquorice Lozenges.

1. Take extract of liquorice, 1 pound; powdered white sugar, 2 pounds. Mix with mucilage made with rose-water.

2. Take lump sugar, 100 parts; liquorice, 150 parts; powdered starch, 40 parts; mucilage, to mix.

Liquor Opii Sedativus.

Take opium, 4 parts; soft water, 15 parts; verjuice, 1 part; spirit of wine, 1 part. Rub together in a mortar; then let them stand in a close corked bottle for ten days, and filter.

Litharge Plaster.

1. Take litharge, 5 parts; sweet oil, 13 parts; water, 3 parts. Mix. This is an excellent defensive plaster, and will stick well: it is particularly useful to repel the milk in women weaning children.

2. Take litharge, 35 parts; sweet oil, 63 parts; water, 18 parts. Mix.

Litharge Plaster with Gum.

Take simple diachylon, 32 parts; galbanum (reduced), 6 parts; thuris, 1 part; turpentine, 1 part. Mix.

Livers of Sulphur.

Take sulphur, 1 part; pearlash, 3 parts. Melt in a covered vessel.

Liquid Livers of Sulphur.

Take flowers of sulphur, 1 part; strong potass ley, 20 parts. Boil for a few minutes, filter, and keep it from the air.

Blue Litmus Paper.

Steep the paper in a decoction of litmus, and dry.

Reddened Litmus Paper.

Take common litmus paper, and brush it over with dilute acetic acid

Liquor of Libavius.

Take solution of muriate of tin, and transmit chlorine gas through it until saturated.

To manage Lisbon Wine.

If too dry, add calcavella; if too mild, add malaga sherry. Fine with white of eggs.

Lithographic Crayons.

1. Take white wax, 4 parts; gum lac, 2 parts. Melt over a gentle fire, then add dry tallow soap in shavings, 2 parts. Stir until dissolved. Next add white tallow, 2 parts; copal varnish, 1 part; lampblack, 1 part. Mix well, and continue the heat and stirring until, on trial by cooling a little, it appears of a proper quality, which should be that it will bear cutting to a fine point, and trace delicate lines without breaking.

2. Take dry white tallow soap, 6 parts; white wax, 6 parts; lampblack, 1 part. Fuse in a covered vessel.

3. Take lampblack, 1 part: tallow soap, 2 parts; shell lac, 2 parts· wax, 4 parts. Mix, with heat, and mould.

4, Take dried tallow soap, 5 parts; wax, 4 parts; lampblack, 1 part. Mix as before.

Lithographic Ink.

1. Take Venice turpentine, 1 part; lampblack, 2 parts; tallow, 6 parts; hard tallow soap, 6 parts; mastic in tears, 8 parts; shell lac, 12 parts; wax, 16 parts. Melt and pour it out on a slab.

2. Take dry tallow soap, 5 parts; mastic in tears, 5 parts; Scotch soda, 5 parts; shell lac, 25 parts; lampblack, 2 parts. Fuse the soap and lac, then add the remainder.

For use this ink must be rubbed down with water, in a saucer (warmed), until an emulsion is formed of a proper consistence to flow easily from a pen or pencil.

To check an immoderate Flow of the Menses.

1. Take infusion of roses, 8 ounces; laudanum, 50 drops. Dose; two table-spoonfuls, three times a day.

2. Take tincture of ergot, 1 ounce; liquor of ammonia, 3 drachms Mix. Dose; one tea-spoonful in water, three times a day.

3. Take tincture of iron, 1 drachm; water, 1 ounce. Dose; a table-spoonful, three or four times a day.

Pills to promote the Menstrual Secretion.

1. Take pills of aloes and myrrh, 1 drachm; compound iron pills, 70 grains. Mix and form into twenty-five pills. Dose; two, twice a day.

2. Take compound galbanum pill, 1 drachm; socotrine aloes, 1 drachm. Mix. As above.

Pills for obstructed Menstruation.

Take sulphate of iron, 30 grains; potassa (subcarb.), 30 grains; white sugar, 30 grains; myrrh, 1 drachm. Make them into 3½ grain pills; two to be taken three times a day, when there is no fever present.

Another, for same purpose.

Take pulv. myrrhæ, 1 drachm; pulv. rhei, 1 drachm; aloes spic. ext., 1 scruple; anthemid, 2 drachms; syrup to mix. Divide into moderate sized pills, and take two or three, or as many as will produce two or three healthy motions daily.

Pills for painful Menstruation.

Take pulv. rhei, 1 drachm; pulv. jalap. 1 drachm; pulv. opii, 1 drachm; syrup of poppies to mix. Divide into 100 pills, and take one night and morning.

Mercurial Liniment.

Take camphor, 1 ounce; powder it by using a little alcohol, then add, lard, 4 ounces; strong mercurial ointment, 4 ounces; liquor of ammonia, 4 ounces. Mix.

Mild Mercurial Ointment.

Take quicksilver, 1 pound; suet, 2 pounds; lard, 5 pounds. Mix, by patient rubbing. Used to kill insects on the body.

Strong Mercurial Ointment.

Take quicksilver, 6 pounds; lard, 8 pounds; suet, 4 pounds. Kill the silver with the suet by friction in a mortar, then add the lard. Used as a dissolvent or alterative, in syphilis, by rubbing in, once a day, from one to three scruples.

Mercurial Plaster.

1. Take quicksilver, 1 pound; liquid storax, 2 ounces; turpentine, 2 ounces. Kill the silver, then add diachylon, 2 pounds; gum ammoniac, 1 pound; sulphate of zinc, 1 ounce. Mix, with heat.

2. Take balsam of sulphur, 1 part; quicksilver, 25 parts; diachylon, 140 parts. Mix the balsam and silver together, and rub them until thoroughly mixed, then add the diachylon previously melted.

3. Take quicksilver, 1 pound; turpentine, 2 ounces. Kill the silver by rubbing in a mortar, then add diachylon, 1 pound; yellow resin, 12 ounces; sweet oil, 12 ounces. Mix, with heat.

Cerate of Mercury.

Take yellow wax, 1 pound; lard, 1 pound. Melt; and, when nearly cold, pour them into a mortar, and add quicksilver, 8 ounces; milk of sulphur, 4 drachms. Mix well.

Ointment of Protoxide of Mercury.

Take protoxide of mercury, 4 ounces, lard, 12 ounces. Mix.

Chaudet's Metal for Medals.

Take copper, 100 parts; tin, 4.17. Cast in moulds formed of cupel bone-ash.

Paste for cleaning Metals.

Take oxalic acid, 1 part; rotten stone, 6 parts. Mix with equal parts of train oil and spirits of turpentine to a paste.

Issue Plaster.

1. Take diachylon, 2 pounds; orris powder, 2 ounces. Mix with heat spread, and polish.

2. Take diachylon, 1 pound; Burgundy pitch, 2 ounces; sarcocoll, 1 ounce; turpentine, 1 ounce. Melt and spread.

Italian Varnish.

Take yellow resin, 4 pounds; turpentine, 1 gallon. Dissolve.

Lotion for Itching Chilblains.

Take hydrochloric acid, 1 part; water, 8 parts. Mix. Apply on going to bed. This must not be used if the skin is broken.

Itch Lotion.

Take a solution of chloride of lime, or a weak solution of bichloride of mercury, for this purpose. Both these articles possess the advantage of being free from smell, and are very efficacious.

Itch Ointment.

1. Take lard, 1 pound; suet, 1 pound; sugar of lead, 8 ounces; vermilion, 2 ounces. Mix. Scent with a little bergamot.

2. Take bichloride of mercury, 1 ounce; lard, 1 pound; suet, 1 pound; hydrochloric acid, 1½ ounce. Melt and well mix, and when perfectly cold, stir in essence of lemon, 4 drachms; essence of bergamot, 1 drachm.

3. Take powdered chloride of lime, 1 ounce; lard, 1 pound. Mix well, then add essence of lemon, 2 drachms.

4. Take bichloride of mercury, 1 part; lard, 15 parts. Mix *well* together.

5. Take white precipitate, 1 part; lard, 12 parts. Mix.

A portion of either of these ointments must be well rubbed on the parts affected, night and morning.

Jumbles.

Take flour, 1½ pound; sugar, 1 pound; butter, ¾ pound; four yolks and two whites of eggs; rose-water, one wine-glassful. Roll thin with fine powdered sugar, and bake on tins.

Juniper Berry Wine.

Take berries, 3 pounds: water, 25 gallons; honey 26 pounds; raisins, 26 pounds; red tartar, 4 ounces; cardamons, 2 ounces; cassia, 2 ounces; caraways, 1 ounce; ginger, 1 ounce. Boil and ferment, then add spirit, 3 gallons.

Juniper Water.

Take juniper berries, 56 pounds; water, 69 gallons. Distil off 65 gallons.

Powell's Diuretic Drops.

Take oil of juniper, 1 part; alcohol, 5 parts. Mix. Dose, a tea spoonful, in any warm liquid, twice a day. By simply placing these together in a bottle, and shaking them repeatedly during two or three days, the alcohol will retain the oil in solution.

The Roman Pomade.

Take apples of a good smell, pare and core them, and cut each into six pieces; then take hog's grease of the bowels, which has not been melted, wash it in orange and citron flower water *aa*; then add cloves, cinnamon, galinga, ligni santali *aa* ℥j.; ligni rosarum, sassafras, violarum radicum, Benjamin, storax calamita *aa* ʒj.; chop all into small pieces, and mingle them with the apples and the lard; pour over all rose-water a finger high, and let it boil on a gentle fire till all the moisture be gone; then strain it whilst hot through a cloth, and afterwards mix therewith six ounces of white wax melted, and well-stirred together; this must be done in a new earthen pot, and while you are stirring it, yet hot, pour in one after another of oil of cinnamon, of citrons, oranges, roses, and jasmine, *aa* six drops.

To Perfume Clothes.

Take dried red roses, and, to increase their smell, pour on them fresh rose-water, and still drying between in the shade; then take cloves, cinnamon, spikenard seed, storax, calamita, benjamin, violet roots, nutmegs *aa* ʒiij. to a pound of roses; beat them all into small pieces, and mix them with the roses, and put them into perfuming bags.

To Marble a Globe Glass.

Grind well on a stone, minium for red, turmeric, or rather cerussa citrina, for yellow, smalt for blue, verdigris for green, ceruse, or chalk, for white. Work each in oil separate, and with a hog's hair pencil, single or mixed, as you think fit, scatter the same into the glass, and roll it, or dispose the colours, as you like. Then, last of all, fling a little mead amongst them, which covers all. For the Magic Lanthorn, paint the glasses with transparent colours, tempered with oil of spike.

To gild Carps, Crawfish, &c.

Warm an earthen pot, till it receive as much white pitch as will stick round it within; then strew finely-powdered amber over the white pitch; when it is growing cold, pour into it *oleum lini*, 3 pounds; *oleum terebinth*, 1 pound, well mixed together. Close up all, and boil them an hour on a gentle fire. This is a varnish. Grind some of this on a painter's stone, throwing to it fine powder of pumice-stone, till it be as thick as ordinary paint; then take a live carp, or crawfish, out of the water, and dry it well with a linen cloth; then daub it over with this paint, it will presently dry, before which spread your leaf gold, and gently press it with a soft dry cloth, and then you may let it go into the water. For the more this varnish is in the water, the harder it dries and grows, and does the fish no hurt.

Cure for Headaches.

Liquor of ammonia (Qy. the strength?), 100 parts; distilled water, 900 parts; purified marine salt, 20 parts; camphor, 2 parts; essence of rose or some other scent, in the necessary proportion. The whole dissolved cold. A piece of linen is to be steeped in this solution and applied over the part of the head that the patient points out as the seat of pain, taking care, if it is on the forehead, to apply a thick bandage over the eyebrows, to prevent any drops of the fluid passing into the eyes.

Twenty-Five Experimental Receipts on Colours.

I.

Pour boiling water upon a little red cabbage sliced, and when cold decant the clear infusion. Divide the infusion into three wine-glasses. To one add a solution of alum, to the second a little solution of potash, and to the third a few drops of muriatic acid. The liquor in the first glass will assume a purple, the second a bright green, and the third a beautiful crimson. Here is an instance of three different colours from the same vegetable infusion, merely by the addition of three *colourless* fluids.

II.

Prepare a little tincture of litmus. Its colour will be a bright blue with a tinge of purple. Put a little of it in a phial, and add a few drops of diluted muriatic acid; its colour will change to a *vivid red.* Add a little solution of potash; the red will now disappear, and the *blue* will be restored. By these means, the liquor may be changed alternately from a red to a blue, and from a blue to a red, at pleasure. An instance of the effects of acids and alkalies in changing vegetable colours.

III.

Make an infusion of red roses, violets, or mallow flowers; treat it with solution of potash, and it will become *green;* the addition of diluted muriatic acid will convert it immediately to a *red.* This experiment may be as frequently varied as the last, and furnishes an excellent test for acids and alkalies.

IV.

Add a drop or two of solution of potash to tincture of turmeric. This will change its original bright *yellow* colour to a dark *brown:* a little colourless diluted acid will restore it. By this tincture we can detect the most minute portion of any alkali in solution.

V.

Into a wine-glass of water put a few drops of prussiate of potash, and a little dilute solution of sulphate of iron into another glass; by pouring these two colourless fluids together, a bright deep blue colour will be immediately produced, which is the true prussian blue.

VI.

Put some prussiate of potash into one glass; into another a little nitrate of bismuth. On mixing these colourless fluids a yellow will be the product.

VII.

Pour a little prussiate of potash into a glass containing a colourless solution of sulphate of copper, and a reddish brown will be produced being a true prussiate of copper.

VIII.

Pour a little tincture of litmus into a wine-glass, and into another some diluted sulphate of indigo; pour these two blue fluids together, and the mixture will become perfectly red.

IX.

Prepare a phial with pure water and a little tincture of galls; and another with a weak solution of sulphate of iron; then mix these transparent colourless fluids together, and they will instantly become black.

X.

Drop as much sulphate of copper into water as will form a colourless solution: then add a little ammonia, equally colourless, and an intense blue colour will arise from the mixture.

XI.

Take water holding carbonate of iron in solution, and add some diluted prussiate of potash: prussian blue will be formed by the mixture.

XII.

Take some of the same water as that used in the last experiment; boil it, and now add prussiate of potash. In this case no colour will be produced.

XIII.

Take some water impregnated with carbonic acid, and add to it a little blue tincture of litmus. The whole will be changed to a red.

XIV.

Take some of the same carbonated water and boil it. Then add a little tincture of litmus, and the blue colour will experience no change.

XV.

Take some of the black liquid described in Experiment IX., add by degrees muriatic acid to it, and the colour will be discharged. Now drop in a little solution of potash, and the black colour will be restored. Some nicety is requisite in adding the acid and alkali: for if they be given in excess the effects will not be so apparent.

XVI.

Take the blue solution formed by the Experiment No. X., and a little sulphuric acid, and the colour will disappear; pour in a little solution of caustic ammonia, and the blue colour will be restored. Thus may the liquor be alternately changed at pleasure.

XVII.

If a spoonful of good alcohol and a little boracic acid be stirred together in a tea-cup, and then set on fire, they will produce a very beautiful green flame.

XVIII.

If alcohol be inflamed in like manner with a little pure strontites in powder, or any of its salts, the mixture will give a carmine flame.

XIX.

If barytes be used instead of strontites, we shall have a brilliant yellow flame.

XX.

If alcohol contains muriate of magnesia, it has the property of burning with a reddish yellow flame.

XXI.

Evaporate to dryness a solution of gold, made with nitro-muriatic acid, and dissolve the crystals in a sufficiency of pure water to prevent the crystallization of the metallic salt. Thoroughly moisten a little magnesia with this aqueous solution, and place the mixture in the sun's rays. A change of colour will soon be apparent. It will first take a faint violet hue, and in a few hours the whole will have acquired a very deep purple.

XXII.

Moisten a little magnesia with some of the solution as before, and then dry the mixture in the dark. If it be then submitted to the action of the sun's rays, it will acquire only a faint violet, even by several hours' exposure.

XXIII.

If the mixture employed in the last experiment be now thoroughly wetted with pure water, and again placed within the rays of the sun, its colour will rapidly change, and it will acquire a deep purple approaching to crimson.

XXIV.

Moisten a piece of white riband with the aqueous solution of gold, and dry it thoroughly in the dark: then suspend it in a clean, dry, transparent phial, and cork it close with a dry cork. Expose the riband, thus secured, to the strong light of a bright sun, for half an hour, and only a faint appearance of change of colour will be perceived.

XXV.

Now take the riband out of the phial that was employed in the last experiment, and wet it well with distilled water. If it be now exposed to the sun's rays, it will instantly change colour, and will quickly be stained of an indelible purple.

Ink Powder.

Infuse a half pound of galls powdered, and 1½ ounces of pomegranate peels in half a gallon of soft water for a week, in a gentle heat, and then strain off the fluid through a cloth. After which, add to it 4 ounces of vitriol dissolved in a pint of water, and let them remain for a day or two, preparing in the mean time a decoction of logwood, by boiling half a pound of the chips in half a gallon of water, till one-third be evaporated, and then straining the remaining fluid while it is hot. Mix the decoction and the solution of galls and vitriol together, and add 2½ ounces of gum-arabic, or the whitest of gum-senegal, and then evaporate the mixture over a common fire to 1 quart, when the remainder must be put into a proper vessel, and reduced to dryness, by placing it in a sufficiently warm place, o letting it hang in boiling water. After the whole of the liquid is evaporated, the residue must be well powdered. When wanted for use, all that is needed, is to dissolve the powder in water.

On the Treatment of Worms.

1. *Ascarides.*—Aperient medicines, although they are not to be trusted to alone for the removal of these worms, are generally necessary. Strong drastic purgatives should be avoided. Rhubarb and aloes, with the addition of a small portion of some mercurial, may be given over night, and in the morning a draught of Epsom salts in a bitter infusion will be found to add to their efficacy. Instead of administering much medicine by the mouth, it is better to use enemata frequently. Common table salt, the muriate of soda, dissolved in chamomile or wormwood tea, to which some oil may be added, will often succeed admirably well. The sulphuret of potash may be used in the same way, or aloes dissolved in milk.

The tincture of the muriate of iron in water has been highly recommended by some writers; by others lime-water is much esteemed.

M. Martinet advises that three different kinds of enemata should be administered, one after the other, at short intervals; first, a common purgative injection to evacuate the bowels; then one to kill the worms and bring them away, consisting of common salt, or of vinegar with some bitter infusion; and lastly, an emollient oily one to soothe the irritation of the gut.

Bremser recommends an enema, consisting of the infusions of absinth, tansy, orange-peel, and valerian with a small portion of the empyreumatic oil of hartshorn, immediately after each alvine evacuation, as it is more likely then to be retained, and as it will also come more immediately in contact with the animalculæ.

Injections either of cold water, or of a few ounces of olive oil, to which several drops of laudanum or of hydrocyanic acid may be added, will generally relieve the irritation of the anus, which is often so distressing a symptom.

By some of these means, the worms may almost always be dislodged and removed. To prevent their reproduction, it is necessary that the use of a tonic aperient be continued for a considerable time. Pills, containing rhubarb, aloes, myrrh, and sulphate of iron, will answer very well in a number of cases.

A powder, consisting of rhubarb, worm seed (semina santonici) and carbonate of soda, is well suited for children. The patient should be recommended to use a good deal of salt with his food; and vegetables and fruit should on the whole be abstained from.

2. *Lumbrici.*—Stronger purgatives are necessary for the expulsion of these worms than of the ascarides. A powder, containing calomel, jalap, and rhubarb, is perhaps as good a formula as can be adopted. Rosenstein has recommended a combination of sulphate of iron, jalap, and wormseed powder and sugar, to be taken for three mornings successively; while Stork's favourite remedy was an electuary composed of sal polychrest, jalap, and valerian, a drachm of each, and four ounces of oxymel of squills —in doses of half an ounce three or four times a day to an adult.

Bremser tells us that he derived great benefit from a combination of wormseed, tansy, valerian, jalap, and sulphate of potash—an excellent formula, if the compound was not so nauseous. When the worms are expelled, he recommends a mixture containing tincture of aloes, steel, and elixir of vitriol.

The cowage (dolichos pruriens,) granulated tin, and steel filings have occasionally been used, made into an electuary with syrup or treacle, with advantage; but of late years they have generally been superseded by other remedies. A combination of carbonate of iron, powdered wormseed, and scammony makes a good formula. Equal parts of infusion of senna and of the infusion of the spigelia, or of the decoction of pomegranate bark, may be taken at the same time with benefit.

We have not yet alluded to two of the most powerful anthelmintic purgatives, viz: croton oil, and the spirit of turpentine. The former has the great advantage of being so easily administered; even the external application of a few drops, rubbed on the abdomen, will occasionally succeed in dislodging the worms. The turpentine may be either given by the mouth or administered in an enema; the oil may be suspended by means of gum arabic in milk or gruel.

Common table salt has been highly recommended against lumbrici by the late celebrated physician, Dr. Rush of Philadelphia, in doses of half a drachm every morning before breakfast for a length of time. A glassful of sea water may be usefully substituted.

The tolerably free use of somewhat salted meat for food, at the same time avoid fruits and vegetables, has often been observed to be attended with much benefit to persons subject to worms.

Friction of the abdomen with some liniment containing turpentine, ox-gall, absinth, aloes, and such like medicines, or the application of a plaster containing assafœtida galbanum, camphor, rue, &c., are certainly some times useful.

3. *Tænia.*—The spirit of turpentine has of late years almost quite superseded every other remedy for the expulsion of this kind of intestinal worm. In administering it, the physician must be especially attentive to secure its purgative action; otherwise the urinary organs are apt to suffer from excessive irritation. For this purpose the patient should always be instructed to take a full dose of castor oil, or of some other certain aperient, in the course of an hour or two after the turpentine has been swallowed, if the latter has not already acted on the bowels.

It is well known to cause in many instances vertigo and great disturbance of the head, amounting sometimes to a state of complete intoxication; but these symptoms will gradually subside. The essence of lemons is perhaps the best disguiser of the unpleasant taste of terebinthinate medicines. Chewing a piece of orange-peel immediately afterwards will often relieve the nausea.

The pomegranate bark, either in the form of powder or of a strong decoction, has been successfully used by several medical men. One or two scruples of the powder in a wine-glassful of cold water is to be repeated every hour to the fourth, fifth, or sixth dose. If the worm is not expelled, the same medication is to be repeated on the following day. The decoction is the form in which it is generally used by the French physicians; it is prepared by boiling two ounces of the bark in a pint of water; a wine-glassful is to be taken every half hour or so, till half the pint is swallowed it is well to follow it up with a purgative, in case it does not act on the bowels.

Most of the remedies, which we have alluded to as useful against *lumbrici*, have been employed by different practitioners against tape-worms.

A combination of tin filings, fern root, wormseed, scammony, gamboge, and sal polychrest, is a favourite remedy in some parts of Germany. Should the worm be partially extruded from the gut after a stool, the patient should continue to sit over the night-table, and swallow repeated doses of a solution of Epsom salts, or of any quickly-acting aperient, to induce further evacuations until the entire worm be expelled. Any attempts to pull it out with the fingers, or by affixing a portion of thread or tape to it, will almost always fail.

4. A course of vegetable and metallic tonics, with the addition of gentle aperients, should be continued for a length of time. The best are pills composed of aloes, rhubarb, and steel, along with some mucilage.

To dissolve Copal in Spirits of Turpentine.

Reduce two ounces of copal to small pieces, and put them into a proper vessel. Mix a pint of the best spirits of turpentine with one-eighth of spirits of sal ammoniac; shake them well together, put them to the copal, cork the glass, and tie it over with a string or wire, making a small hole through the cork. Set the glass in a sand-heat so regulated as to make the contents boil as quickly as possible, but so gently that the bubbles may be counted as they rise from the bottom. The same heat must be kept up exactly till the solution is complete.

It requires the most accurate attention to succeed in this operation. After the spirits are mixed, they should be put to the copal, and the necessary degree of heat be given as soon as possible, and maintained with the utmost regularity. If the heat abates, or the spirits boil quicker than is directed, the solution will immediately stop, and it will afterwards be in vain to proceed with the same materials: but if properly managed, the spirit of sal ammoniac will be seen gradually to descend from the mixture, and attack the copal, which swells and dissolves, excepting a very small quantity which remains undissolved.

It is of much consequence that the vessel should not be opened till some time after it has been perfectly cold; for if it contain the least warmth when opened, the whole contents will be blown out of the vessel.

Whatever quantity is to be dissolved should be put into a glass vessel capable at least of containing four times as much, and it should be high in proportion to the width.

This varnish is of a deep rich colour, when viewed in the bottle, but seems to give no colour to the pictures upon which it is laid. If it be left in the damp, it remains racky, as it is called, a long time; but if kept in a warm room, or placed in the sun, it dries as well as any other turpentine varnish, and when dry it appears to be as durable as any other solution of copal.

Copal may also be dissolved in spirits of turpentine by the assistance of camphor.

Turpentine varnishes dry more slowly than those made with alcohol, and are less hard; but they are not so liable to crack.

Lutes.

Lutes are compositions which are employed to defend glass and other vessels from the action of fire, or to fill up the vacancies which occur, when separate tubes, for the necks of different vessels, are inserted into each other during the process of distillation. Those lutes which are exposed to the action of fire, are usually called *fire-lutes.*

For a very excellent fire-lute, which will enable glass vessels to sustain an incredible degree of heat, take fragments of porcelain, pulverise and sift them well, and add an equal quantity of fine clay, previously softened with as much of a saturated solution of muriate of soda, as is requisite to give the whole a proper consistence. Apply a thin and uniform coat of this composition to the glass vessels, and allow it to dry slowly before they are put into the fire.

Equal parts of coarse and refractory clay mixed with a little hair, form a good lute.

Fat earth, beaten up with fresh horse-dung, Chaptal recommends as an excellent fire-lute, which he generally used, and the adhesion of which was such, that after the retort had cracked, the distillation could be carried on and regularly finished.

Lutes for the joining of such vessels as retorts and receivers, are varied according to the nature of the vapours which will act against them, in order not to employ a more expensive and troublesome composition than the case requires. For resisting watery vapours, slips of wet bladder, or slips of wet paper or linen, covered with stiff flour paste, may be bound over the juncture.

A closer and neater lute for more penetrating vapours, is composed of whites of eggs made into a smooth paste with quick-lime, and applied upon strips of linen. The quick-lime should be previously slacked in the air, and reduced to a fine powder. The cement should be applied the moment it is made; it soon dries, becomes very firm; and is in chemical experiments one of the most useful cements known.

Where saline, acrid vapours are to be resisted, a lute should be composed of boiled linseed oil intimately mixed with clay, which has been previously dried, finely powdered, and sifted. This is called fat lute. It is applied to the junctures, as the undermost layers, and is secured in its place by the white of egg lute last mentioned, which is tied on with pack-thread.

Blacking, to make.

Put one gallon of vinegar into a stone jug; add one pound of ivory-black, well pulverized; half a pound of loaf-sugar; half an ounce of oil of vitriol, and one ounce of sweet-oil; incorporate the whole by stirring. This is a blacking of very great repute.

Vases or Baskets, &c., in Spanish Candy.

Prepare some plaster moulds, as for grained sugar: soak them in water before you use them; prepare some sugar as for Spanish candy, and fill the moulds. When finished they may be ornamented with gum-paste, piping or gold-paper. They may also be made in copper or tin moulds, oiled.

Fly in Sheep.

Make a strong decoction from the leaves of tobacco, or from chewing-tobacco, and apply with a small squirt, or syringe, repeated several times during the fall months.

To preserve Fruit Trees from Mice and Insects.

Apply, early in the fall, around the root a thick layer of lime and ashes. It would be well to sink the earth around the tree about six or eight inches; throw in a few shovels-full of the lime and ashes, and then cover up with earth, tramping it well down.

Pine Boughs for Sheep.

Give to your sheep pine boughs once or twice a week; they will create appetite, prevent disease, and increase their health.

Grubs in Horses.

Take 1 pint strong vinegar, 1 ounce chalk in powder, stir it well and drench the animal.

To wash Woollens.

Always wash in very hot suds, and never rinse them.

Gapes in Chickens

May be easily cured by giving them small crums of dough impregnated with a little soft soap; once or twice is sufficient.

To improve the Wicks of Candles.

First steep the wicks in a solution of lime-water, in which saltpetre has been dissolved. To 1 gallon of water add 2 ounces saltpetre and ½ pound lime. Dry well the wicks before using. It improves the light, and prevents the tallow from running.

Horse-radish to have in keeping.

Grate a sufficient quantity during the season, while it is green, put it in bottles, fill up with strong vinegar, cork them tight, and set them in a cool place.

Powder for Hiccough.

Put as much dill-seed, finely powdered, as will lie on a shilling into two spoonsful of syrup of black cherries, and take it presently.

A Powder for Digestion.

Take galingal and setwal, of each 1 ounce; long pepper, mace, and nutmeg, of each 2 ounces; aniseeds, carraway-seeds, fennel-seeds, and angelica-seeds, of each ½ an ounce; put to these, all finely powdered, the weight in fine powdered sugar; take as much as will lie on a shilling after every meal, and drink a glass of simple carduus water after it. This has done mighty cures to weak, depraved stomachs.

A Present Remedy for Convulsion Fits.

Make a draught of an equal quantity of piony and simple black-cherry water, and for a man put 30, for a woman 20, for a child 5 drops of spirits of hartshorn; drink this in or before a fit.

Powder for a Dizziness in the Head, and to prevent Apoplectic Fits.

Take the seeds and roots of single piony, of each a like quantity; dry and beat them severally into a fine powder; take the weight in nutmeg, which you must beat, and dry, and beat again; mix fine-sifted sugar, and take as much as will lie on a shilling every morning for a month constantly.

Remedy for Sore Throat.

Take 5 spoonsful of syrup of elder-berries and mix with 1 spoonful of honey, and as much salt prunel (in powder) as will lie on a shilling: take a teaspoonful of this as often as you can.

To Cure Hams.

Cover the bottom of the cask with coarse salt, lay on the hams with the smooth or skin side down, sprinkle over fine salt, then another layer of hams, and so continue until the cask is full. This ought to be of the larger kind. A cask holding 64 gallons is small enough, and it would be better if it held 120 gallons. Make a brine in the following proportions 6 gallons water, 9 pounds salt, 4 pounds brown sugar, 3 ounces saltpetre, 1 ounce sal-eratus. Scald and skim, and when cold pour the brine into the cask until the hams are completely covered. The hams should remain in this pickle at least three months, and a little longer time would do them no harm.

Artificial Oysters.

Take young green corn, grate it in a dish; to one pint of this add one egg well beaten, a small teacup of flour, half a cup of butter, some salt and pepper, and mix them well together. A tablespoonful of the batter will make the size of an oyster. Fry them a light brown, and when done, butter them. Cream, if it can be procured, is better than butter.

Horn-ail.

When the animal is observed to be suffering from this disorder, 1 or 2 quarts of blood, according to the size of the animal, are to be drawn immediately from a neck vein. Then 2 tablespoonsful of the following powder are to be given 3 times every day, the powder being previously dissolved in a pint of lukewarm water; this to be continued until the animal recovers: Glauber salts, 6 ounces; cream of tartar, 2 ounces; purified saltpetre, 2 ounces; powdered root of althæ, 1½ ounce. Rub the animal frequently during the disease, principally on the back. If the animal should be costive, either of the following clysters is to be given:—Take a handful of chamomile flowers, 2 handsful of flaxseed; boil them in 2 quarts of water, strain them, and add 8 ounces of linseed oil and 3 tablespoonsful of common salt. This clyster is to be applied by means of a syringe. Should these articles not be at hand, take 1 quart of wheat bran, pour 2 quarts of boiling water on it, strain, and add 8 ounces of flaxseed oil and 2 ounces of common salt. This clyster is to be lukewarm when applied to the rectum or straight gut, by the means of a syringe or a fit funnel.

Cure for Botts.

Give the horse one ounce of slaked lime three times a week, mixed with his food, for two or three weeks.

To give Iron a temper to cut Porphyry.

Make your iron red-hot, and plunge it into distilled water from nettles, acanthus, and pilosella, or in the very juice pounded out from these plants.

To prevent Iron from rusting.

Warm your iron till you cannot bear your hand on it without burning yourself. Then rub it with new and clean white wax. Put it again to the fire till it has soaked in the wax. When done, rub it over with a piece of serge. This prevents the iron from rusting afterwards.

To dye in Gold, Silver Medals, or Laminas, through and through.

Take glauber salt, dissolve it in warm water, so as to form a saturated solution. In this solution put a small proportionate quantity of calx, or magister of gold. Then put and digest in it, silver laminas cut small and thin, and let them lay 24 hours over a gentle fire. At the end of this term you will find them thoroughly dyed gold colour, inside and out.

An Oil, one ounce of which will last longer than one pound of any other.

Take fresh butter, quick-lime, crude tartar, and common salt, of each equal parts, which you pound and mix well together. Saturate it with good brandy, and distil it in a retort over a gradual fire, after having adapted the receiver and luted well the joints.

To make Corks for bottles.

Take wax, hog's lard, and turpentine equal quantities, or thereabouts. Melt all together and stop your bottles with it.

An Oil to prevent Pictures from blackening. It may serve, also, to make cloth to carry in the pocket against wet weather.

Put nut or linseed oil into a phial, and set it in the sun to purify it. When it has deposited its dregs at the bottom, decant it gently into another clean phial, and set it again in the sun as before. Continue so doing till it drops no more fæces at all. And with that oil you make the above described compositions.

To gild on Calf and Sheep Skin.

Wet the leather with the white of eggs; when dry, rub it with your hand and a little olive oil, then put the gold leaf and apply the hot iron to it. Whatever the hot iron shall not have touched will go off by brushing.

To dye Wood Red.

Take chopped Brazil wood, and boil it well in water, strain it through a cloth. Then give your wood two or three coats, till it is the shade wanted. If wanted a deep red, boil the wood in water impregnated with alum and quick-lime. When the last coat is dry, burnish it with the burnisher and then varnish.

A Preparation for Tortoise-Shell.

Take orpine, quick-lime, pearl-ashes, and aqua fortis Mix well altogether, and put your horn or tortoise-shell in it to soak.

Another method to dye Wood Red.

Take vermilion and Spanish brown; make them thin with linseed oil and turpentine. Rub it on with a cloth in such a manner as to show the grain of the wood; when dry, varnish. The proportion of vermilion and Spanish brown, must be according to the fineness of the shade wanted.

To produce various undulations on Wood.

Slack some lime in chamber-ley. Then with a brush dipped in it, form your undulations on the wood according to your fancy. And, when dry rub it well with a rind of pork.

To soften Ivory.

In 3 ounces of spirits of nitre, and 15 of spring-water, mixed together, put your ivory a soaking. And in 3 or 4 days it will be soft so as to obey your fingers.

To dye Ivory thus softened.

1. Dissolve, in spirits of wine, such colours as you want to dye your ivory with. And when the spirit of wine shall be sufficiently tinged with the colour you have put in, plunge your ivory in it, and leave it there till it is sufficiently penetrated with it, and dyed inwardly. Then give that ivory what form you please.

2. To harden it afterwards, wrap it up in a sheet of white paper, and cover it with decrepitated common salt, and the driest you can make it to be; in which situation you shall leave it only 24 hours.

To whiten Ivory, even that which has turned a brown yellow.

1. Slack some lime in water, put your ivory in that water, after decanted from the ground, and boil it till it looks quite white.

2. To polish it afterwards, set it in the turner's wheel, and after having worked it, take rushes and pumice-stones, subtile powder with water, and rub it all till it looks perfectly smooth. Next to that, heat it by turning it against a piece of linen, or sheep-skin leather, and when hot, rub it over with a little whitening diluted in oil of olive; then with a little dry whitening alone, and finally with a piece of soft white rag. When all this is performed as directed, the ivory will look remarkably white.

To whiten Bones.

Put a handful of bran and quick-lime together, in a new pipkin, with a sufficient quantity of water, and boil it. In this put the bones, and boil them also till perfectly freed from greasy particles.

To petrify Wood, &c.

Take equal quantities of gem-salt, rock-alum, white vinegar, chalk, and pebbles powder. Mix all these ingredients together: there will happen an ebullition. If, after it is over, you throw in this liquor any porous matter, and leave it there a soaking four or five days, they will positively turn into petrifactions.

To restore Wine that has turned sour or sharp.

Fill a bag with leek-seed, or of leaves or twisters of vine, and put either of them to infuse in the cask.

Kalydor for the Complexion.

Take blanched bitter almonds, 1 part; rose-water, 16 parts. Mix and strain, then add five grains of bichloride of mercury to every eight-ounce bottle of the mixture, and scent with rose or violet.

Powell's Opium.

Take opium, 1 part; spirit, 9 parts. Macerate until the spirit will take up no more, decant, and reserve the tincture; then pour six parts of water on the residuum and repeat the process. Strain and mix the two solutions: next put them into a retort and distil over, spirit nine parts, and evaporate the remainder to a proper consistence.

Pradier's Cataplasm

Pradier's remedy for the gout was purchased by the Emperor Napoleon for £2500:—Take of balm of Mecca, 6 drachms; red bark, 1 ounce; saffron, half an ounce; sarsaparilla, 1 ounce; sage, 1 ounce; rectified spirit of wine, 3 pounds. Dissolve separately the balm of Mecca in one third of the spirit of wine: macerate the rest of the substances in the remainder for forty-eight hours, filter, and mix the two liquors for use. The tincture obtained is mixed with twice or thrice its quantity of lime-water: the bottle must be shaken in order to mix the precipitate settled at the bottom by standing.

Mode of application.—The following is the mode of employing the remedy:—A poultice must be prepared of linseed meal, which must be of good consistency and spread very hot, of the thickness of a finger, on a napkin, so as to be able completely to surround the part affected: if it be required for both legs, from the feet to the knees, it will take about three quarts of linseed meal. When the poultice is prepared, and as hot as the patient can bear it, about two ounces of the prepared liquor must be poured equally over the whole of the surface of each, without its being imbibed; the part affected is then to be wrapped up in it, and bound up with flannel and bandages to preserve the heat. The poultice is generally changed every twenty- four hours, sometimes at the end of twelve.

Dyes for Ivory.

Black.—Immerse the ivory in a boiling solution of logwood, take it ou and wash it in a solution of copperas.

Blue.—Immerse the ivory in a mixture of sulphate of indigo and water, partly neutralized with potash.

Green.—Steep blued ivory in a solution of nitromuriate of tin, and then in a decoction of fustic: or it may be at once dyed green by steeping it in a solution of acetate of copper.

Yellow.—Steep the ivory in a bath of neutral chromate of potash, and afterwards in a boiling solution of acetate of lead.

Red.—Steep the ivory for a short time in a solution of tin, then in a decoction of Brazil or cochineal.

Violet.—Moisten the ivory with a solution of tin, as before, then immerse it in a decoction of logwood.

Fluid for Marking Ivory.

Take nitrate of silver, 2 parts; nitric acid, 1 part; water, 7 parts. Mix

Etching Fluid for Ivory.

Take dilute sulphuric acid, dilute muriatic acid, equal parts. Mix.

Etching Varnish for Ivory.

Take white wax, 2 parts; tears of mastic, 2 parts. Mix.

To gild Ivory.

Immerse it in a solution of nitromuriate of gold, and then expose it to hydrogen gas whilst damp. Wash it afterwards in clean water.

To polish and soften Ivory.

To soften it, let it stand thirty-six or forty hours in a warm place. Polish with a rubber and putty and water.

Plum Pudding.

To make a rich plum pudding, take a pound of marrow, or suet, well chopped, a pound of fine flour dried, eight or ten eggs beaten well; half a nutmeg grated; as much mace, cinnamon, and ginger, all powdered very fine; a pinch of salt; mix these well together, and beat up into a batter; then add one pound of currants, one pound of raisins, stoned and chopped a little; the currants should be rubbed in a cloth, and well picked, or well wash and dry them; two ounces of candied citron peel, or part lemon, and orange, cut small; and two ounces of sweet almonds, blanched, and cut up in bits; two ounces of loaf-sugar grated; then add these to the batter, and put in a wine-glass of brandy; well mix them together. It may be boiled in a buttered basin or mould; if the batter should be too stiff, put a glass of white wine in it. It will take four or five hours' boiling. Strew over it powdered loaf-sugar; garnish with sliced lemon.—Sauce, containing half a glass of best brandy, a glass of white wine, a little rind of lemon grated, and a little powdered cinnamon, half an ounce of grated loaf-sugar, mixed with an equal quantity of very thick melted butter. It is a good plan to make and keep by you a little of this sauce, and then it is ready at any time. In a bottle containing a pint of sherry, and half a pint of best brandy, add two ounces of loaf-sugar, a quarter of an ounce of mace, half an ounce of shaved lemon rind, with kernels of apricots, peaches, and nectarines, and steep in a little white wine; when steeped, pour it off clear, and put to the wine and brandy: and add half a quarter of a pint of capillaire. Two table-spoonfuls of this sauce will flavour a boat-full of thick melted butter.

A National Plum Pudding is made by mixing suet, jar raisins, and currants, one pound each, four ounces of crumbs of bread, two table-spoonsful of sugar, one table-spoonful of grated lemon peel, half a nutmeg, a small blade of mace, a tea-spoonful of ginger, and six well-beaten eggs.—Boil it five hours.—N. B. If you want to keep plum puddings good for a long time, say some months, hang them in a cold place in the cloth in which they are boiled. When wanted to be used, take them out of the cloth, cover them with a clean one, and warm them through with hot water, they will then be fit for the table.

Prepared Chalk.

Take a solution of muriate of lime, and add a solution of carbonate of soda as long as it causes precipitation; wash the sediment, and dry it.

Hazlenut Kisses.

Beat one pound of pulverized white sugar with the whites of eight eggs, over a slow fire until they are light, then add four ounces of blanched filberts, cut fine; lay them out on paper, and bake in a slow oven.

Apple-Water Ice.

Pare and core some fine apples, cut them in pieces into a preserving pan with sufficient water for them to float, boil until they are reduced to a marmalade, then strain: to a pint of apple-water add half a pint of syrup, the juice of a lemon, and a little water; when cold, freeze.

Pear-Water Ice is also prepared in the same way.

Priming Powder, for Percussion Caps.

Take gunpowder, 40 parts. Reduce it to a fine powder, then mix it to a thin paste with water, next add chlorate of potass, 21 parts, previously reduced to a very fine powder. Make the paste rather thin, and deposit a small drop at the bottom of the cap. Care must be taken not to handle the mixture in quantity, when dry, lest it should explode.

Primrose Vinegar.

To 15 quarts of water put 6 pounds of brown sugar; let it boil ten minutes, and take off the scum; pour on it half a peck of primroses; before it is quite cold, put in a little fresh yeast, and let it work in a warm place all night. Put it in a barrel in the kitchen, and when done working close the barrel, still keeping it in a warm place.

To cure the Rot in Sheep.

It is the opinion of some that the rot in sheep is caused, in most instances, by *Tathy* herbage. If so, sheep should always be removed as soon as it is discovered that the disease has sprung from the above cause.

Take foxglove leaves, 2 ounces; boiling water, 1 quart. Pour the water on the leaves, cover up, and let stand in a warm place half a day; then strain through flannel. Give of this decoction two tea-spoonfuls, morning and evening, to each sheep, for two or three days, when an interval of two days should be allowed, the mixture being an active poison.

To prevent the Rot in Sheep.

Rot is often hereditary in sheep. Hence the great importance of *weeding* out from the flock all such ewes as exhibit the least appearance of unsoundness. Again—during winter every attention should be paid to sheep Study the kind of pasture that they thrive best on, the kind of hay, grain, &c. Keep them from exposure in bad weather, and keep them in as high health as possible, if you would preserve them from the rot.

Hair-curling Liquid for Ladies.

Take borax, 2 ounces; gum Senegal in powder, 1 drachm; add hot water (not boiling), 1 quart. Stir, and, as soon as the ingredients are dissolved, add 2 ounces of spirits of wine strongly impregnated with camphor On retiring to rest, wet the locks with the above liquid, and roll them on twists of paper as usual. Leave them till morning, when they may be unwrapt and formed into ringlets.

3*

To dye Bones any colour.

Boil the bones first for a good while; then in a ley of quick-lime mixed with chamber-ley, put either verdigris, or red or blue chalk, or any other ingredient fit to procure the colour you want to give to the bones. Lay the bones in the liquor, and boil them, they will be perfectly dyed.

To write on Silver with a Black which will never go off.

Take burnt lead and pulverize it. Incorporate it next with sulphur and vinegar, to the consistency of a painting colour, and write with it on any silver plate. Let it dry, then present it to the fire so as to heat the work a little, and it is finished.

To correct a bad taste and sourness in Wine.

Put in a bag the root of wild horse-radish cut in bits. Let it down in the wine, and leave it there two days: take this out, and put another, repeating the same till the wine is perfectly restored. Or fill a bag with wheat: it will have the same effect.

To cure those who are too much addicted to drinking Wine.

Put in a sufficient quantity of wine, 3 or 4 large eels, which leave there till quite dead. Give that wine to the person you want to reform, and he or she will be so much disgusted with wine, that though they formerly made use of it, they will now have an aversion to it.

To increase the sharpness and strength of Vinegar.

Boil two quarts of good vinegar till reduced to one; then put it in a vessel and set it in the sun for a week. Now mix the vinegar with six times its quantity of bad vinegar in a small cask: it will not only mend it, but make it strong and agreeable.

To make Vinegar with water.

Put 30 or 40 pounds of wild pears in a large tub, where you leave them three days to ferment. Then pour some water over them, and repeat this every day for a month: at the end of which it will make very good vinegar; the goodness of which may be increased by the above method.

A dry, portable Vinegar.

Wash well half a pound of white tartar with warm water, then dry it, and pulverize as fine as possible. Soak that powder with good sharp vinegar, and dry it before the fire or in the sun. Re-soak it as before with vinegar, and dry it as above, repeating this operation a dozen times. By these means you will have a very good and sharp powder, which turns water instantly into vinegar. It is very convenient to carry in the pocket, especially when travelling.

Ginger Beer.

One pint of molasses and two spoonfuls of ginger put into a pail to be half filled with boiling water; when well stirred together, fill the pail with cold water, leaving room for one pint of yeast, which must not be put in until lukewarm. Place it on a warm hearth for the night, and bottle it in the morning.

How to extract the Essential Oil from any Flower.

Take any flowers you like, which stratify with common sea-salt in a clean earthen glazed pot. When thus filled to the top, cover it well and carry it to the cellar. Forty days afterwards put a crape over a pan, and empty the whole to strain the essence from the flowers by pressure. Bottle that essence and expose it four or five weeks in the sun, and dew of the evening, to purify. One single drop of that essence is enough to scent a whole quart of water.

To make Mutton-Suet Candles, in imitation of Wax.

1. Throw quick-lime in melted mutton suet; the lime will fall to the bottom, and carry along with it all the dirt of the suet, so as to leave it as pure and as fine as wax itself.

2. Now, if to one part of the suet you mix three of real wax, you will have a very fine, and to appearance, a real wax candle, at least the mixture could never be discovered, nor even in the moulding way of ornaments.

Corn Plaster.

Yellow wax, 1 pound; Venice turpentine, 3 ounces; verdigris (finely powdered), 1 ounce. Mix, with heat.

Kermes Mineral.

Ground antimony, 20 parts; pearlash, 11 parts; sulphur, 1 part. Melt in a crucible, cool, powder, and boil in water; filter, and the kermes will precipitate as the water cools; wash the powder in two or three waters.

Kidder's Spice.

Cloves, cassia, mace, nutmegs, salt, pepper, turmeric, equal parts. Mix

German Kirsch-Wasser, (Cherry Brandy.)

Ripe cherries, 1 cwt.; water, 15 gallons. Bruise the cherries (kernels and all), then ferment the whole; lastly, draw off the liquid, express the remaining juice from the lees, and distil. Or put the whole of the mash into the still and draw over the liquid as much as is required.

Kidelano's Neutral Cerate.

Diachylon, 1 pound; sweet oil, ½ pound; prepared chalk, 7 ounces. Melt, and when nearly cold stir in vinegar, 8 ounces; sugar of lead, 6 drachms.

A Peculiar Sauce.

Claret or port, 1 gallon; mushroom catsup, 1 gallon; walnut pickle, 2 quarts; pounded anchovies, 2 pounds; lemon-peel, 8 ounces; eschalots (peeled and sliced), 8 ounces; scraped horse-radish, 6 ounces; black pepper, 3 ounces; cayenne, 1 ounce; celery seeds (bruised), 1 ounce; soy, 1 quart. Steep for a fortnight, then strain with expression.

Krumholz Oil.

Distil oil of turpentine in a glass retort, and reserve the red balsam that is left.

Labdanum Plaster.

Labdanum, 7 pounds; yellow wax, 56 pounds; palm oil, 50 pounds, resin, 40 pounds; Burgundy pitch, 20 pounds; oil of mace, 3 ounces; oil of caraway, 3 ounces; oil of peppermint, 4 ounces. Mix.

Lozenges of Lactate of Iron.

Lactate of iron, 30 parts; sugar, 360 parts; mucilage, sufficient quantity. Make into ten-grain lozenges.

Pills of Lactate of Iron.

Lactate of iron, 16 grains; marshmallow powder, 15 grains; honey to mix. Divide into two-grain pills, and silver them immediately.

Syrup of Lactate of Iron.

Lactate of iron, 8 parts; boiling distilled water, 400 parts; white sugar, 800 parts. Mix. This contains about four grains in the ounce.

Cheap Lac Varnish.

Shell lac, 9 parts; borax, 2 parts; water sufficient. Boil until dissolved and of a proper consistence.

Toothache Tincture.

Kreosote, 1 part; spirit of wine, 10 parts. Mix, and apply by means of a small piece of lint.

To give various Shades of colour to Lake.

A beautiful tone of violet, red, and even of purple red, may be communicated to the colouring part of cochineal, by adding to the coloured bath a solution of tin in nitro-muriatic acid. The effect will be greater, if, instead of this solution, one of oxygenated muriate of tin be employed.

Another.—The addition of arseniate of potash (neutral arsenical salt), gives shades which would be sought for in vain with sulphate of alumine (alum).

To judge of the Quality of Lamb.

If fresh, the vein in the neck of a fore-quarter is bluish; if green or yellow, stale. In the hind-quarter, if the knuckle is limp and the part under the kidney smells slightly disagreeable, avoid it. If the eyes are sunken, do not buy the head.

Factitious Lapiz Lazuli.

Plain paste, 1000 parts; calcined bones, 73 parts; Zaffre, 7 parts; magnesia, 5 parts. If it is desired to vein it with gold—gold-powder and borax, equal parts; vein the cakes to taste, and then heat them sufficiently hot for cementation.

Simple Recipe for Preserving Eggs.

Pack them during the summer and fall for winter. Take a stone crock or firkin, and put in a layer of salt, half an inch deep—insert your eggs on the *small end*, and cover each layer of eggs with a layer of salt. If the eggs are fresh when packed, and put into a cool, dry place, they will keep perfectly good until the following summer.

To Prevent the Smoking of Lamps.

Soak the wick in strong vinegar and dry it well. They will of course smoke, even after this preparation, if the wicks are put up too high.

Factitious Labdanum.

Yellow wax, 7 pounds; suet, 7 pounds; ivory black, 3 pounds. Mix.

Composition for Lances.

1. *White fire.*—Nitre, 16 parts; sulphur, 8 parts; meal powder, 4 parts. Mix.

2. *French white fire.*—Nitre, 16 parts; sulphur, 8 parts; antimony, 4 parts. Mix.

3. *Blue fire.*—Nitre, 16 parts; antimony, 8 parts. Mix.

4. *Yellow fire.*—Nitre, 16 parts; gunpowder, 16 parts; sulphur, 8 parts; amber, 8 parts. Mix.

5. *Green fire.*—Nitre, 16 parts; sulphur, 6 parts; verdigris, 6 parts; antimony, 6 parts. Mix.

6. *Pink fire.*—Nitre, 16 parts; gunpowder, 3 parts; lamp-black, 1 part. Mix.

Lardner's Prepared Charcoal.

Charcoal, prepared chalk, equal parts. Mix them, and sift through gauze.

To prepare Pure Lard.

Good white lard. Melt it in a water bath, then put it into warm water and agitate them well together, to wash out any salt; let them cool, then collect the lard from the top of the water, drain it, melt it again in a water-bath, let it remain melted for half an hour, and lastly, pour off the clearest portion and preserve it from the air.

Laurel Water.

Laurel leaves, 1 cwt.; water, 17 gallons. Distil off 15 gallons with a gentle heat.

Reduced Oil of Lavender.

Lavender oil, 2 parts; acetic acid (sp. 0·898), 3 parts. Mix.

Lavender Water for immediate Use.

One gallon of proof spirit, and one ounce of true English oil of lavender, which is all that will properly combine with the spirit, without injuring the colour by rendering it muddy. When the spirit and the oil are properly mixed, they are to be put into glass bottles, which are to be well stopped, and ought to be shaken before used.

Lozenges for the Heartburn.

Prepared chalk four ounces, crab's eyes prepared two ounces, bole ammoniac one ounce, nutmeg one scruple, or cinnamon half an ounce. Make into a paste with dissolved gum Arabic. When held in the mouth until they dissolve, they will afford effectual relief.

Acetic Ether.

1. Take strong alcohol, 3 parts; acetate of potass, 3 parts; concentrated sulphuric acid, 2 parts. Mix and distil; then take of the product 4 parts, and sulphuric acid 1 part, and draw over a quantity equal in weight to the alcohol employed.

2. Take acetate of lead, 40 parts; alcohol, 20 parts; strong sulphuric acid, 23 parts. Mix and distil into a large refrigerated receiver.

Silent spirit, flavoured with this ether and the other articles usually employed, forms the most wholesome substitute for foreign brandy that can be made, and at the same time has much of its flavour.

Acetic Lozenges.

Take white sugar, 7 pounds; strong vinegar to mix. A little gum may also be used.

Acidulous Water.

Take water, and force carbonic acid gas through it until saturated. Keep it in well-closed bottles, in a cool situation.

Aconitine (Aconitina).

Take sliced root of aconite, 1 pound; alcohol, 2 quarts. Boil in a retort, to which a receiver is adjusted, for one hour; pour off the liquor and pour on a second, 2 quarts of alcohol and the spirit in the receiver, and boil as before. Repeat the process a third time, then strain with expression. Mix all the liquors together, and distil off the spirit, until the remainder is of the consistence of an extract. Dissolve in distilled water, and filter; again evaporate to the consistence of a syrup, to this add water acidulated with sulphuric acid, sufficient to dissolve the aconitine, then precipitate with a solution of ammonia. Dissolve the precipitate as before, in water acidulated with sulphuric acid, and add two ounces of purified animal charcoal. Agitate and filter; lastly, precipitate the aconitine with water of ammonia; wash and dry. Never used internally.

Ointment of Aconitine.

Take pure lard, 1 ounce; aconitine, 8 grains. Mix with great care. Used in neuralgic affections.

Adhesive Plaster.

1. Take sweet oil, 84 pounds; litharge, 48 pounds; yellow resin, 20 pounds. Melt the oil and litharge together, then add the resin.

2. Take diachylon, 30 pounds; yellow resin, 5 pounds. Mix with heat.

Sulphuric Ether.

Take alcohol, sp. gr. 0.830; sulphuric acid, sp. gr. 1.842. Mix in a large tubulated retort, and distil into a large refrigerated receiver. A sand heat must be employed for this process, and great caution observed.

Æthiop's Mineral.

Take quicksilver, 1 part; sulphur, 2 parts. Unite with heat. Dose twenty to sixty grains. A much larger quantity of sulphur is used for a common article.

Acorn Coffee.

Take sound ripe acorns, peel them and roast them with a little butter, or fat, then, when cold, grind them with one third their weight of real coffee

To give Beer the appearance of Age.

Add a few handfuls of pickled cucumbers and Seville oranges, both chopped up. This is said to make malt liquor appear six months older than it really is.

Ague Drops.

Take arsenic, 1 grain; water, 1 ounce. Mix. Dose, one tea-spoonful night and morning.

To harden and polish Alabaster.

1. Take a strong solution of alum, strain it, and put it into a wooden trough sufficiently large to contain the figure, which must be suspended in it by means of a thread of silk; let rest until a sufficient quantity of the salt is crystallized on the cast, then withdraw it, and polish it with a clean cloth and water.

2. Take white wax; melt it in a convenient vessel, and dip the cast or figure into it; withdraw and repeat the operation of dipping until the liquid wax rests upon the surface of the cast; then let it cool and dry, when it must be polished with a clean brush.

Pure Albumen.

Take white of egg, 1 part; strong alcohol, 11 parts. Mix, agitate, and collect the precipitate.

Alcohol.

1. Take chloride of calcium, rectified spirit, equal parts. Mix and agitate in a well-stoppered bottle for some time, pour off the clear, and distil off one half at a gentle heat.

2. Take the bladder of an ox or calf, soak it for some time in water, then inflate it and carefully free it from the attached fat and vessels; this must be done on both sides. After it is again inflated and dried, smear over the outer surface twice, and the inner surface four times, with a solution of isinglass. Then nearly fill it with the spirit to be concentrated, leaving only a small space vacant; it is then to be securely fastened, and suspended in a warm temperature of about 122° Fahr., over a sand bath, or in the neighbourhood of an oven or fire. In six to twelve hours, if the heat be properly conducted, the spirit will be concentrated, and in a little time longer may be rendered nearly free from water (anhydrous), or of the strength of ninety-seven or ninety-eight per cent. This alcohol will be sufficiently pure for all the common purposes of manufacture, and affords an excellent mode of concentrating spirit for making varnishes, &c. The same bladder will serve more than one hundred times.

3. According to the experiments of Fabbroni, the free alcohol may be separated from fermented liquors by subcarbonate of potash, while the combined alcohol will remain undisturbed.

To bottle Ale.

Follow the same plan as for porter.

Thirteen Experimental Receipts on Dyeing and Calico Printing

I.

Pour a little solution of indigo in sulphuric acid into a glass of water, and add about an equal quantity of solution of carbonate of potash. If a piece of white cloth be dipped in this mixture, it will come out a blue. If a piece of yellow cloth be dipped in, it will become a green, or a red will be converted to a purple. A slip of blue litmus paper immersed in it will immediately become red.

II.

If a little fustic, quercitron bark, or other dye, be boiled in water, the colouring matter will be extracted, and a coloured solution formed. On adding a small quantity of dissolved alum to this decoction, the alumina, or base of the salt, will attract the colouring matter, forming an insoluble compound, which in a short time will subside, and may easily be separated.

III.

Boil a little cochineal in water, with a grain or two of cream of tartar, (supertartrate of potash,) and a dull kind of crimson solution will be formed. By the addition of a few drops of nitro-muriate of tin, the colouring matter will be precipitated of a beautiful scarlet. This, and some of the former instances, will give a tolerably correct idea of the general process of dyeing woollen cloths.

IV.

If a few strips of dyed linen cloth, of different colours, be dipped into a phial of oxymuriatic acid, the colours will be quickly discharged; for there are few colours that can resist the energetic effect of this acid. This experiment may be considered as a complete example of the process of bleaching coloured goods.

V.

Having found a piece of blue linen cloth, that will bleach in oxygenised muriatic acid, dip the tip of the finger in a solution of muriate of tin, and press it while wet with the solution, upon a strip of this cloth. After an interval of a few minutes immerse the cloth in a phial of liquid oxymuriatic acid, and when it has remained in it the usual time, it will be found that the spot which was previously wet with muriate of tin, has preserved its original colour, while the rest of the cloth has become white.

VI.

Dip a piece of white calico in a strong solution of acetate of iron; dry it by the fire, and lay it aside for three or four days. After this, wash it well in hot water, and then dye it black by boiling it for ten minutes in a strong decoction of Brazil wood. If the cloth be now dried, any figures printed upon it with a colourless solution of muriate of tin, will appear o a beautiful scarlet, although the ground will remain a permanent black.

VII.

Dissolve 4 drachms of sulphate of iron in one pint of cold water, then add about six drachms of lime in powder, and 2 drachms of finely pulverised indigo, stirring the mixture occasionally for 12 or 14 hours. If a piece of white calico be immersed in this solution for a few minutes, it will be dyed green; and by exposure to the atmosphere only for a few seconds, this will be converted to a permanent blue.

VIII.

If a piece of calico be immersed in a solution of sulphate of iron, and when dry washed in a weak solution of carbonate of potash, a permanent colour will be produced, viz: the buff of the calico-printers.

IX.

Boil equal parts of arnotto and common potash in water till the whole are dissolved. This will produce the pale reddish-buff so much in use, and sold under the name of nankeen-dye.

X.

If muriate of tin, newly made, be added to a solution of indigo in sulphuric acid, the oxygen of the indigo will be absorbed, and the solution instantly converted to a green. It is on the same principle that muriate of tin is employed in cleansing discoloured leather furniture; as it absorbs the oxygen, and the leather is restored to its natural colour.

XI.

Take a piece of very dark olive-coloured linen that has been dyed with iron and quercitron bark, or weld, and spot it in several places with a colourless solution of muriate of tin. Wherever the cloth has been touched with this solution, the original colour will be discharged, and spots of a bright yellow will appear in its stead.

XII.

Dip a piece of white calico in a cold solution of sulphate of iron, and suffer it to become entirely dry. Then imprint any figures upon it with a strong solution of colourless citric acid, and allow this also to dry. If the piece be then well washed in pure warm water, and afterwards boiled in a decoction of logwood, the ground will be dyed either a slate or black colour, according to the strength of the metallic solution, while the printed figures will remain beautifully white. This experiment is designed to show the *effect of acids* in *discharging vegetable colours.*

XIII.

If lemon-juice be dropped upon any kind of buff colour, the dye will be instantly discharged. The application of this acid by means of the black, is another method by which calico-printing give the *white spots* or *figures* to *piece-goods.* The crystallized is generally used for this purpose.

These thirteen experiments will give some idea of the nature of calico-printing.

Lead Colour.

Whiting, 1 cwt.; road dust, 1 cwt.; blue black, 9 pounds; ground white lead, 35 pounds; lime-water, 10 gallons; Factitious linseed oil to grind in.

Lead Dust.

Lead, charcoal. Melt and mix, then cool, pound, and wash away the charcoal.

Leaden Tree.

Superacetate of lead, ½ an ounce. Put it into a clean bottle, nearly filled with water, and add nitric acid 10 drops; adjust a rod of zinc, one inch long and a quarter of an inch square, and by means of a thread, suspend it to the cork; arrange it so that the zinc may be just in the middle of the bottle; set it aside where it will not be disturbed, and metallic vegetation will commence.

Lead in Grains.

Lead, melt it, and pour it in a small stream from a height into cold water.

Ointment of the White Oxide of Lead.

Simple ointment, 5 pounds; ceruss, 1 pound. Mix. Cooling.

Acetate of Lead Paper.

Acetate of lead, 1 part; water, 16 parts. Dissolve, and dip the paper into the liquor, and dry it.

Subacetate of Lead Paper.

The same as acetate of lead paper, only using the subacetate instead of the acetate.

Plaster of the Oxide of Lead.

1. Sweet oil, 28 pounds; red lead, 16 pounds; black resin, 3 pounds. Mix, with heat.
2. Red lead, 5 pounds; sweet oil, 8 pounds. Mix, with heat.

Venetian White Lead.

Sulphate of barytes, white lead (pure), equal parts. Mix.

To Dye Leather.

Blue.—Steep it in an indigo vat.

Red.—Steep it in alum water, then pass it through a decoction of Brazil wood (warm).

Purple.—Steep the skins in alum water, then in the decoction of log wood (warm).

To Gild or Silver Leather.

Finely-powdered resin, and dust it over the surface of the leather, then lay on the leaf, and apply (hot) the letters or impression you wish to transfer; lastly, dust off the loose metal with a cloth. The cloths used for this purpose become, in time, very valuable, and are often sold to the refiners for twenty to thirty shillings.

Lavender Lozenges.

Powdered sugar, 400 parts; essence of oil of lavender, 3 parts; drop lake (ground in gum), 1 part. Mix with mucilage. Be careful not to injure the colour by using dirty vessels.

Whooping Cough.

A tea-spoonful of castor oil to a table-spoonful of molasses: a tea-spoonful of the mixture to be given whenever the cough is troublesome. It will afford relief at once, and in a few days it effects a cure. The same remedy relieves the croup, however violent the attack.

Accarie's Purified Opium.

Opium, 2 parts; charcoal, 3 parts; water, 10 parts. Digest for three days, then strain and clarify with the white of eggs; evaporate to the consistence of an extract.

Acetate of Ammonia (Mindererus Spirit.)

Muriate of ammonia, 279 parts; acetate of lead, 1000 parts Make a saturated solution of each. Mix while hot and filter.

Acetate of Lead (Sugar of Lead.)

Strong vinegar, and add finely-powdered litharge, until the acid is saturated

Acetate of Morphia.

Morphia, 6 drachms; acetate acid, 3 drachms (fluid); distilled water, 4 ounces (fluid). Dissolve, then evaporate with a gentle heat and crystallize. Dose, one-eighth to one grain.

Mixture of Acetate of Morphia.

Acetate of morphia, 15 grains; acetate acid, 3 drops; spirit of wine, 1 drachm; water, 7 drachms. Mix. Anodyne—dose, five to twenty drops.

Extemporaneous Acetate of Zinc.

Sulphate of zinc, 9 parts; acetate of lead, 12 parts; distilled water, about 60 parts. Mix and filter; the liquid will be a solution of acetate of zinc.

To make a Mercurial Letter Gauge.

In a small upright glass tube, on a stand, is a quantity of mercury, into which is plunged a graduated ivory column, marked ½ ounce, 1 ounce, 1½ ounce, 2 ounce, &c., with a convenient table on the top, to receive the letter to be weighed. According to its weight, the column descends, and the mercury rises, indicating in a moment the exact weight of the letter.

New Miner's Lamp.

Upon the principle of Davy's, but is enclosed in a triangular lantern, with three bull's-eye glasses. The object is to get rid of the danger arising from the use of Davy's, which, should it fall or upset, lets the flame through the wires, and causes an explosion. In this lamp such danger is obviated, as there is gauze on the air-holes of the lantern; and it has this excellent property, that whenever there is danger, this light goes out.

To prevent Murrain in Cattle.

Take equal parts of salt and slaked lime; mix, and give two table spoonsful twice a week during the prevalence of the disease.

To Stain White Marble.

Apply with a brush a strong alcohol tincture made from the root *alkanet*

To colour Oils a beautiful Red.

Take the root *alkanet*, in powder, mix it with the oil and apply heat The same root is employed to colour ointments, pomades, and cheeses.

To make Almond Oil.

Take bitter almonds, and with a hydraulic press squeeze out the oil, either in the cold, or aided by hot iron plates.

Preserving Eggs.

One bushel of quick-lime, 32 ounces of salt, 8 ounces of cream of tartar. Mix the whole together with as much water as will reduce the composition to such a consistency that an egg, when put into it, will swim.

To wash Black Worsted or Woollen Hose.

If new, soak all night, then wash in hot suds with beef's gall, a tablespoonful to half a pail of water. Rinse till no colour comes out. Then stretch on stocking-frames, or iron them when damp on the wrong side.

Naples Yellow.

1. Take 12 ounces of ceruse, 2 ounces of the sulphuret of antimony, ½ an ounce of calcined alum, 1 ounce of sal ammoniac. Pulverize these ingredients, and having mixed them thoroughly, put them into a capsule or crucible of earth, and place over it a covering of the same substance. Expose it at first to a gentle heat, which must be gradually increased till the capsule is moderately red. The oxidation arising from this process requires, at least, three hours' exposure to heat before it is completed. The result of this calcination is Naples yellow, which is ground in water on a porphyry slab with an ivory spatula, as iron would alter the colour. The paste is then dried and preserved for use. It is a yellow oxide of lead and antimony.

There is no necessity of adhering so strictly to the doses as to prevent their being varied. If a golden colour be required in the yellow, the proportions of the sulphuret of antimony and muriate of ammonia must be increased. In like manner, if you wish it to be more fusible, increase the quantities of sulphuret of antimony and calcined sulphuret of alumine.

2. I. Take 1 pound of antimony, 1½ pound of lead, 1 ounce of alum, and 1 ounce of common salt.

II. Take 1½ ounce of pure ceruse, 2 ounces of diaphoretic antimony ½ an ounce of calcined alum, and 1 ounce of pure sal ammoniac.

The ingredients are to be well mixed together, and calcined in a moderate heat for three hours in a covered crucible, till it becomes barely red-hot, when the mass will become of a beautiful yellow colour. With a larger portion of calx of antimony and sal ammoniac, the yellow verges towards gold colour.

Glass may be tinged yellow with the above preparation.

Nankin Dye.

1. Annatto, potash, equal parts; water sufficient. Boil until dissolved.

2. Spanish annatto, 12 parts; alum and potash, each, 1 part; water, sufficient quantity. Unite by boiling.

Napoleon's Pectoral Pills.

Ipecacuanha, powdered, 1 drachm; squills and gum ammoniac, powdered, each, 4 scruples. Mucilage to mix. Divide into 48 pills, and take two night and morning.

To raise Nap on Cloth.

Soak the cloth in water for half an hour, then lay it on a table and raise the nap with a teazle, or hatter's card, filled with flock; let it dry, then use a hard brush.

Narcissus Pomade.

Lard, 56 parts, beef suet, 28 parts. Melt with a gentle heat and strain, then treat as for jasmin pomade, with the difference of the flowers.

Anodyne Necklace.

Of the roots of the hyoscyamus and clusters of hops and make them into a necklace. Cloves and pimento corns may also be added.

Worn by children when teething, and to procure sleep in fever.

Nectar.

1. Red ratifa, 45 gallons; oil of cassia, ¼ ounce; oil of caraway, ¼ ounce; orange wine, 15 gallons. Mix well, then add sugar, 20 pounds; dissolved in water, 1 gallon.

2. Lump sugar, 1 pound; cold water, 1 pint; Madeira, 1 bottle. Grate in nutmeg and lemon-peel.

A little hock or other wine may be added to taste.

Strong Nitrated Ointment of Mercury.

Quicksilver, 1 ounce; nitric acid, 2 ounces. Dissolve, then add while warm, olive oil, 8 ounces; lard, 4 ounces. Mix.

Newmarket Oil.

Linseed oil, 2 pounds; oil of turpentine, 2 pounds; oil of St. John's wort, 2 pounds; oil of vitriol, 1 ounce. Mix.

To prevent the Night-mare.

Avoid heavy suppers, and take either of the following doses on going to bed:

1. Bicarbonate of soda, 1 drachm; tincture of cardamus (comp.), 3 drachms. Mix.

2. Sal volatile, 20 drops; tincture of ginger, 2 drachms. Mix.

3. Magnesia, 20 grains; rhubarb, 15 grains; carbonate of soda, 10 grains. Mix.

Nine Oils or Mixed Oils.

Seal oil, 3 gallons; oil of turpentine, 1 gallon; water of ammonia, 1 pound; oil of amber, 1 pound; Barbadoes tar, 6 pounds; oil of vitriol, 4 ounces; spirits of camphor, 2 pounds. Mix.

A Cement for stopping the Fissures of Iron Vessels.

Take two ounces of muriate of ammonia, one ounce of flowers of sulphur, and sixteen ounces of cast-iron filings or turnings; mix them well in a mortar, and keep the powder dry. When the cement is wanted, take one part of this and twenty parts of clean iron filings or borings, grind them together in a mortar, mix them with water to a proper consistence and apply them between the joints.

This answers for flanges of pipes, &c. about steam engines.

To dissolve Copal in Alcohol.

Copal, which is called gum copal, but which is not, strictly, either a gum or a resin, is the hardest and least changeable of all substances adapted to form varnishes, by their dissolution in spirit, or essential, or fat oils. It, therefore, forms the most valuable varnishes; though we shall give several receipts where it is not employed, which form cheaper varnishes, sufficiently good for many purposes, adding only the general rule, that no varnish must be expected to be harder than the substance from which it is made.

To dissolve copal in alcohol, dissolve half an ounce of camphor in a pint of alcohol; put it into a circulating glass, and add four ounces of copal in small pieces; set it in a sand-heat, so regulated that the bubbles may be counted as they rise from the bottom, and continue the same heat till the solution is completed.

The process abovementioned will dissolve more copal than the menstruum will retain when cold. The most economical method will therefore be, to set the vessel which contains the solution by for a few days, and, when it is perfectly settled, pour off the clear varnish, and leave the residue for future operation.

The solution of copal thus obtained is very bright. It is an excellent varnish for pictures, and would, doubtless, be an improvement in japanning, where the stoves used for drying the varnished articles would drive off the camphor, and leave the copal clear and colourless in the work.

New Acid for Dyeing.

Take of the root of the *aloe,* and by the action of *nitric* acid a beautiful red colour is produced, which will be found very useful to dyers.

To Purify Lamp Oil.

Take *chloride of lime,* 1 lb.; water, 12 lbs. Triturate the chloride of lime in a large mortar, gradually adding the water so as to form a smooth and soap paste, and then add the remainder of the water, which will give the whole the consistence of cream. Now mix this thoroughly with the oil by frequent and careful stirring, in the proportion of 1 quart of the paste for 100 lbs. of oil, or a little more, if the oil be very putrid. Let it remain a few hours, when add 1 lb. of sulphuric acid, previously diluted with 20 or 30 parts of water, and boil, with a gentle heat, constantly stirring during the process, until the oil drops clear from the end of a piece to be dipped into it. After the boiling has been finished, allow the oil to settle for a few hours; then draw it off from the acidulated water. The boiler should be lined with lead, and the mortar for the trituration of the chloride of lime should neither be iron nor copper.

Cure for Milk Sickness.

Take of pulv. rhei, ʒi.; magnes. cal. ℥ss. Mix. A table-spoonful to be given in mucilage every two hours, till purging is produced. If vomited up, a new dose must be immediately administered.

Carbonate or Sesqui-Carbonate of Ammonia.

Dry chalk, 3 parts; sal ammoniac, 2 parts. Sublime.

Ointment of Ammonia.

Ammonia (S. C.), 1 ounce; simple ointment, 8 ounces. Mix. Used as a dressing for ulcers.

Ammoniac Plaster.

Gum ammoniac, 1 pound; distilled vinegar, $1\frac{1}{2}$ pound. Evaporate to a proper consistence.

Ammoniac Plaster, with Mercury.

Mercury, 1 pound; balsam of sulphur, 1 ounce. Kill the silver, then add gum ammoniac, 5 pounds. Unite with heat.

Fluid for Anatomical Preparations.

I.

Water saturated with sulphurous acid, to which add a little creosote.

II.

Chloride of tin, 2 parts; muriatic acid, 1 part; water, 40 parts. Dissolve and filter.

III.

Bichloride of mercury, 3 parts; muriatic acid, 1 part; water, 65 parts. Dissolve and filter.

English Anchovies.

Sprats, 1 bushel; salt, 7 pounds; saltpetre, 3 pounds; prunella, $\frac{1}{4}$ pound; cochineal to colour slightly. Pound in a mortar, then put into a stone pan or empty anchovy barrel, first a layer of sprats, then one of the composition, then a layer of sprats, and so on, until it is filled. Press down tight, and keep them for six months.

Essence of Anchovies.

Anchovies, 14 pounds. Pulp and press them through a sieve, then boil the residuum with salt, $1\frac{1}{2}$ pound; water, 20 pounds. Strain, add flour, $1\frac{1}{2}$ pounds; and the pulp of the fish, boil once more, pass it through the sieve, and add bole to colour, and cayenne, until seasoned to palate.

Anchovy Powder.

I.

Anchovies; wheat flour, equal parts. Beat them to a paste, and expose them in small pieces to dry; then reduce them to fine powder, and pass it through a sieve.

II.

English anchovies or sprats; wheat flour, equal parts. Proceed as before.

Candied Angelica.

Boil the angelica for a quarter of an hour in water, then take it out, dry it, and boil it in thick syrup; drain and dry.

To detect the False Angustura Bark.

Macerate two drachms of the bark in three ounces of water, then add the following tests, and observe the appearances:

	IF TRUE.	IF FALSE.
Chloride of barium.	No precipitate.	Turbidness.
Bichloride of mercury.	.. .. ..	Dirty white precipitate
Perchloride of iron.	Reddish brown do.	Dirty green.
With the decoction.		
Chloride of barium.	Nothing.	Turbidness.
Nitrate of silver.	Yellow precipitate.	None.
Sulphuric acid.	" "	"
Perchloride of iron.	Greyish "	Green without precipitation.
Phosphate of soda.	Nothing.	In a short time a deep brown coloration.

Animal Charcoal.

Bones (cleaned from the integuments, &c.), coarsely powder them, and calcine them in close vessels.

Care must be taken not to raise the heat too high; the proper temperature can only be known by practice.

Purified Animal Charcoal.

Animal charcoal (powdered), 4 parts; hydrochloric acid, 3 parts; water, 3 parts. Mix and digest, with occasional agitation for two or three days in a gentle heat; filter and wash the charcoal well with pure water, then dry it.

To preserve Animal Food without Salting.

Take meat, and cut it into slices of from four to eight ounces each, then immerse them for five minutes in a vessel of boiling water, and dry them on network, at a regular temperature of from 120° to 125° Fahr. Next evaporate the soup formed by washing the meat, to the consistence of a thick varnish, adding a little spice to flavour it; into this fluid immerse the perfectly dry pieces of flesh, and again expose them to the proper drying temperature. Repeat the operation of dipping and drying a second, and even a third time.

For use, the meat must be cooked in the usual way by boiling, &c.

In this manner, meat may be preserved without salt, for fifteen to twenty months.

Anisated Balsam of Sulphur, used in Cutaneous Diseases.

1. Balsam of sulphur, 24 parts; turpentine, 24 parts; oil of aniseed, [illegible] parts. Mix with heat.

2. Flowers of sulphur, 1 ounce; seal oil, 2 pounds. Dissolve with heat then add oil of aniseed, 6 drachms.

Animal Substances,

And objects of natural history, may be preserved in a solution of bichlo ride of mercury, or the solution may be washed over them.

Aniseed Cordial.

Aniseed (bruised), 16 pounds (or more) ; proof spirits, 50 gallons ; water, 60 gallons. Draw over 100 gallons, and sweeten to taste.

Should it be foul, filter it, previously putting a little magnesia into the bag.

Oil of (Factitious) Aniseed.

Oil of aniseed, 10 parts ; rape oil, 15 parts ; spermaceti, 1 part. Mix with heat in a close vessel.

Aniseed Water.

Aniseed, 30 pounds ; water, 20 gallons. Distil off fifteen or sixteen gallons.

Should it turn milky redistil it, or filter it through magnesia.

Anisette de Bourdeaux.

Sugar, 12 ounces ; water, 5 pints ; proof spirit, 3 pints ; oil of aniseed, 15 drops.

Rub the oil with a little of the lump-sugar and spirit before adding it to the mixture.

Anti-Attrition.

Lard, 80 pounds ; black lead, 25 pounds ; spirit of turpentine, 5 pounds soap, 4 pounds. Mix. For machinery.

Anti-Attrition, (Patent.)

Lard, 4 parts ; plumbago, 1 part. Mix.

Anti-ferment, for Cider, Beer, Wine, &c.

Sulphite of lime, 1 part ; powdered mustard-seed, 2 parts. Mix. This is infallible if properly used.

Antimonial Powder.

Powdered antimony ; hartshorn shavings, equal parts. Roast in an iron pot until they become a grey powder, then put it into a crucible with a small hole in the cover, and keep it red-hot for two hours. Lastly, cool and powder.

Antimony Lozenges.

Sulphuret of antimony, 1 ounce ; white sugar, 8 ounces ; starch, 6 ounces. Mucilage to mix.

Anti-putrefactive Fluid.

Alcohol, 2 pounds ; water, 2 pounds ; ammonia, 1 ounce. Mix and dissolve.

Aperient Pills.

Compound extract of colocynth, 2 grains ; extract of rhubarb, 3 grains , aloes (pill), 1 grain. Mix and divide into two pills for a dose

Pure Concentrated Acetic Acid.

1. Fused acetate of potash, 10 pounds; strongest sulphuric acid, 5 pounds. Distil slowly from a glass retort into a glass refrigerator. Redistil from a little acetate of lead, to deprive it of a small quantity of sulphurous acid that contaminates it; the product will then be very pure.

2. Acetate of lead (dried), 12 pounds; strong sulphuric acid, 3 pounds. Mix and treat as before. This affords a weaker acid than No. 1.

3. Sulphate of iron (gently calcined), 4 pounds; acetate of lead 10 pounds. Powder, mix, and carefully distil from a porcelain retort as before. This is a good and economical process.

4. Acetate of copper, any quantity. Dry it in a water bath, then distil in a sand heat. This gives gives an acid slightly contaminated with fragrant pyroacetic spirit.

5. Elegant method of making pure acetic acid. (From the German.) Take a long glass case, and arrange shelves in it, a few inches apart, one above another, on which place small flat dishes of earthenware or wood; then fill these dishes with alcohol, and suspend over each dish a portion of the black powder of platina; then hang strips of porous paper in the case, with their bottom edges immersed in the spirit, to promote evaporation. Set the apparatus in a light place, at a temperature of from 68° to 86° Fahr., for which purpose the sunshine will be found convenient. In a short time the formation of vinegar will commence, and the condensed acid vapours will be seen trickling down the sides of the glass, and collecting at the bottom. We shall find that during this process, produced by the mutual action of the platina and the vapour of alcohol, there will be an increase of temperature, which will continue till all the oxygen contained in the air enclosed in the case is consumed, when the acetification will stop; the case must be then opened for a short time, to admit of a fresh supply of air, before the operation will recommence.

With a case of twelve cubic feet content, and with seven or eight ounces of platina powder, we can produce one pound and one-ninth of absolute acetic acid from one pound of absolute alcohol, and if we reckon the product at the commercial strength of vinegar, the increase will of course be very great.

From 25 pounds of platina powder, and 300 pounds of alcohol, we may produce daily about 350 pounds of pure acid.

It is proper to state that the platina powder does not *waste*, and that the most *inferior* spirit may be employed.

The revenue laws of Great Britain unfortunately forbid the adoption of this *beautiful* process, but there is no statute that prevents any individual using it on the small scale for private consumption. In Germany, however, vinegar is manufactured on this plan, and from the low price of crude alcohol, it must prove very profitable. It will no doubt be shortly introduced into the United States of America, where alcohol may be purchased for less than a dollar a gallon, as well as in other parts where spirit is equally cheap.

Crystallized Acetic Acid.

Acetate of soda dried and melted by a gentle heat, 44 parts; oil of vitriol, 20 parts. Mix and distil. Dry the crystals on bibulous paper.

To Clean Brittania Ware.

Brittania ware should be first rubbed with a woollen cloth and sweet oil; then washed in water and suds, and rubbed with soft leatner and whiting. Thus treated, it will retain its beauty to the last.

Nineteen Experimental Receipts on Temperature.

I.

Take a small phial about half full of cold water; grasp it gently in the left hand, and from another phial pour a little sulphuric acid very gradually into the water. A strong sensation of heat will immediately be perceived. This, by the continued addition of the acid, may be increased to many degrees beyond that of boiling water.

II.

Take a small phial in one hand, containing some pulverized muriate of ammonia; pour a little water upon it, and shake the mixture. In this instance a sensation of cold will immediately be felt.

III.

If the student be in possession of an air-pump, the following experiment may be easily performed:—Let him fix a small tin cup of ether within a large watch-glass containing a little water, and place both under the receiver of the air-pump. The exhaustion of the receiver will cause one of the fluids to boil, and the other to freeze at the same instant.

IV.

Place a phial of water, enclosing a thermometer, in a frigorific mixture, and by avoiding agitation cool it some degrees below the freezing point. If it be now agitated, it immediately becomes solid, and its temperature instantly rises to 32°, an instance of a change of form occasioning an extrication of caloric.

V.

Fill a small glass matrass, or flask, holding about half a pint, with any kind of coloured water, having previously put in a few tea-spoonfuls of ether: then invert the flask in a shallow vessel of water, and by degrees pour boiling water upon its bulb. By the sudden accession of heat the ether will be changed into vapour, which will force out the coloured water and fill the whole of the vessel. This experiment will afford an example of a liquid being converted into an elastic vapour by caloric.

VI.

For want of a proper glass vessel, a table-spoonful of ether may be put into a moistened bladder, and the neck of the bladder closely tied. If hot water be then poured upon it, the ether will expand and the bladder become inflated.

VII.

Take a glass tube with a bulb in form of a common thermometer; fill it with cold water, and suspend it by a string. If the bulb be frequently and continually moistened with pure sulphuric ether the water will presently be frozen, even in summer.

VIII.

Dissolve five drachms of muriate of ammonia, and five drachms of nitre, both finely powdered, in two ounces of water. A thermometer immersed in the solution will show that the temperature is reduced below 32°. If a thermometer tube, filled with water, be now suspended within it, the water will soon be as effectually frozen as in the last experiment.

IX.

If a small thermometer be placed in a glass vessel containing about an ounce of a solution of soda, on adding a sufficient quantity of muriatic acid to saturate the soda, the mercury in the thermometer will expand; affording an instance of heat being produced by the formation of a salt.

X.

Let the last experiment be repeated, with the carbonate of soda instead of pure soda; the mercury will now sink in the thermometer. Here, though the same kind of salt is formed, cold is produced.

XI.

Fill a thermometer tube with tepid water, and immerse it in a glass vessel of water of the same temperature, containing a mercurial thermometer. If the whole be now placed in a bed of snow, or in a frigorific mixture, the water in the tube will suffer a progressive diminution of volume, until it arrives at about 40°; it will then begin to expand gradually until it becomes solid. This shows how ice is enabled to swim on the surface of water.

XII.

Another example on this subject may be shown. Fill a thermometer tube with cold water, at about 32°, and immerse it in a vessel of warm water. In this case, the water in the tube will contract in volume till it arrives at about 42°, when it will appear for a time nearly stationary. If the heat be now continued, the effect will be reversed, for the water in the tube will expand as its temperature is increased. This is a curious instance of a chemical anomaly.

XIII.

Charge a small glass retort with strong muriatic acid, and insert its beak into a tubulated receiver containing a little water; then into this receiver insert two small thermometers, the one immersed in the water, the other suspended above it. By applying the heat of a lamp to the retort, muriatic acid gas will be disengaged in abundance; and if the thermometers be examined, that which is suspended in the gas will be found to have risen only a few degrees, while that which was immersed in the cold water has acquired a boiling heat.

XIV.

Dip the bulb of a thermometer in melted rosin so as to coat the glass with it, and suffer it to cool completely. If the flame of a taper be now applied to the bulb, so as to melt the rosin, the mercury in the thermometer will not rise at the approach of the taper, but will actually be seen to contract as the rosin becomes liquid.

XV.

Take a glass of cold water, pour a little sulphuric ether upon its surface, and inflame it by a slip of lighted paper. The ether will burn for a considerable time, and produce a large volume of flame, but when it is extinguished the water will be found not to have increased in temperature The design of this experiment is to show that water is a bad conductor of caloric, and that when we wish to heat water, the heat ought not to be applied at its surface.

XVI.

Put into a wine-glass about a scruple of the oxidized manganese and nitrate of potash, and an equal quantity of the same compound into another glass. On one pour hot, and on the other cold water. The hot solution will exhibit a beautiful green colour; the cold one a deep purple.

XVII.

If a small portion of the same compound be put into several glasses, and water at different temperatures be poured upon each, the contents of each glass will exhibit a different shade of colour. This experiment affords another instance of metals producing various colours, according to their different modes of treatment.

XVIII.

If a flat bar of iron be hammered briskly on an anvil, its temperature will soon be so increased, that a piece of phosphorus laid upon it would instantly be inflamed. This experiment is designed to show that caloric may be evolved merely by percussion; and that, when evolved, it is as active and energetic as though it had never been latent.

XIX.

In two or three wine-glasses, each containing some distilled water, diffuse a little newly prepared white prussiate of iron, and exclude the action of the air, by covering the contents of each with a thin layer of oil. If these colourless liquids be now exposed to different degrees of cold, it will be perceived that whenever the water in either of them freezes, the white precipitate will become blue.

Simple Ointment.

Take 4 ounces beeswax; ½ a pint of sweet oil, or hog's lard. Mix by heat. To keep the parts soft and from exposure to cold.

Family Basilicum Ointment.

Take 1 ounce of beeswax, 1 ounce of resin, and 1½ ounces hog's lard. Melt all together. Healing and exciting. Used for dressing sores.

Abernethy's Pills for Indigestion.

Calomel, 1 scruple; sulphuret of antimony, 1 scruple; gum guaiacum 2 scruples. Castile soap, to form twenty pills.

Dover's Powder.

Ipecacuanha, in powder, 1 drachm; opium, in powder, 1 drachm; saltpetre, in powder, 1 ounce. The above ingredients should be reduced to a very fine powder. Dose for an adult from 10 to 20 grains.

5

To ascertain the quantity of Alcohol in Wine, Beer, &c.

1. Liquor to be tried, 100 parts; solution of lead, as below, 12 parts. Agitate together and filter, then add fused potash (powdered) as long as it is dissolved; the alcohol will then be seen floating on the top of the mixture in a well-marked stratum; estimate the quantity by means of a graduated tube.

2. A good way to determine the quantity of alcohol contained in a given sample of wine, is to separate it from the non-volatile constituents by distillation. A very neat apparatus for experiments of this nature has been contrived by M. Gay-Lussac; but any species of small still or retort may be employed for the purpose. You take 300 parts of the liquor to be tried, measured in a glass tube. The operation is equally adapted for wines, beer, gin, and all kinds of spirituous liquors. Having inserted the liquor into the still, you carefully and slowly distil over 100 parts, or one third of the liquor in the still, making use of a graduated tube as the recipient, and stopping the operation when the distilled liquor reaches the hundredth degree. You then ascertain the alcoholic strength of the distilled liquor by means of the hydrometer, and, dividing the result by three, you have at once the per centage of alcohol of the liquor submitted to examination. If, for example, the hundred parts of distilled liquor contain thirty parts of alcohol, the wine submitted to distillation contains ten per cent. of alcohol. But if, from want of attention, you distil over more than one hundred parts of the liquor, it will not do to divide the alcoholic strength of the product by three, to obtain the per centage of alcohol of the liquor submitted to distillation: you must employ, as the divisor, the number which expresses the relation of the volume of the distilled product to the bulk of the wine. If, for example, you have one hundred and six parts of distilled liquor, containing (as ascertained by the hydrometer) thirty-three parts of alcohol, you divide three hundred by one hundred and six, which gives 2.83, and then divide 33 by 2.83, which gives 11.66. The last number expresses the per centage of alcohol of the liquor submitted to examination.

Solution of Subacetate of Lead.

Take litharge, powdered, 15 parts; acetate of lead, 12 parts; water, 200 parts. Boil for twenty minutes, or until reduced to one half. Keep it in well-corked phials.

Ale, on the Scotch Plan.

Employ the very best pale malt and hops, and mash but once, with one third of the quantity of the brewing; draw off the wort, then divide the remaining quantity of water into six to ten parts, and sprinkle the malt therewith; set the tap, and when all is drained off, repeat the process till the whole quantity of water is consumed. Boil with four pounds of hops to the quarter of malt, and ferment at 50° Fahr. with less than one per cent, of yeast. Rouse up twice a day. The sprinkling waters are thrown into a flat wooden vessel with a bottom full of small holes, placed over the mashing tub, so that the water descends equally on the malt, similar to a shower bath. There are also from three to four small cocks placed round the bottom, to draw off the wort, so that the water is made to percolate through the whole of the materials. This brewing is never attempted during the summer months.

Alkaline Absorbent.

Take limewater, 4 ounces; liquor of potash, 1 ounce. For dyspepsia and heartburn, one tea-spoonful in a basin of broth or gruel. This is an excellent antacid, but very nauseous.

Almond Bloom.

1. Take Brazil dust, 1 ounce; cochineal, ¼ ounce; water (hot), ½ gallon. Steep for two or three days, then strain, and add isinglass, [illegible] drachm; gum Arabic, 2 drachms; spirit, 2 ounces. Essences to perfume.

2. Take Brazil dust, 3 ounces; isinglass, 2 ounces; cochineal, 1 ounce; alum, 4 ounces; borax, 1 ounce; water, 10 pints. Boil until reduced to a gallon, and strain.

Almond Cake.

Take almonds, blanched and bruised, 1 pound; 10 eggs, well beaten: sugar, 1 pound; flour, ¾ pound. Mix.

Almond Jelly.

Take almond emulsion, hartshorn jelly, equal parts. Add a little orange flower water and a few drops of essence of lemons.

Almond Milk.

Take sweet almonds, 1 ounce; bitter almonds, 3; white sugar, 1½ pound; clear water, 2 pints. Flavour with orange-flower water. Blanch the almonds by steeping them in hot water for a little time, then beat them up in a mortar with the sugar, and add the water gradually; lastly, strain and add the flavouring.

Grey Almond Paste.

Take bitter almonds; winnow, grind, and form them into four or five pound loaves; put these into the press and extract the oil with a gradually increasing pressure for two days, then take out the cakes, grind and sift them, and pack and perfume the powder to taste.

Liquid Almond Paste.

1. Take bitter almonds, blanched, 4 parts; sweet almonds, blanched, 4 parts; oil of almonds, 1 part; juice of lemon, 6 parts; spirit, 1 part; rose-water, 2 parts. Reduce the almonds to the state of milk, then add the other ingredients, and strain.

2. Take blanched almonds, 8 pounds; rose-water, 1 gallon (or less). Reduce to a thick paste, then add honey, 2 pounds. Strain by pressing it through a gauze sieve.

Sweet white Almond Paste.

Take Jordan almonds; steep them in hot water until their skins are loose, then blanch them, and treat them as for Grey Paste.

Celebrated Honey Almond Paste.

Take honey, 1 pound; white bitter paste, 1 pound; expressed oil of bitter almonds, 2 pounds; yolks of eggs, 5. Heat the honey, strain, then add the bitter paste, knead well together, and lastly, add the eggs and oil in alternate portions.

Bitter white Almond Paste.

Take bitter almonds, and follow the same process as for Sweet White.

Sweet Almond Lozenges.

Take white sugar, 3 pounds; starch, 1 pound; blanched almonds, 2 pounds. Beat into a thick paste, then roll it into a cake and cut it into lozenges. A little essence of orange or lemon may be added.

Almond Soap.

Take oil of almonds, 7 pounds; soda, $1\frac{1}{4}$ pounds; water, sufficient quantity. The soda must be rendered caustic, before adding it to the oil, and heat must then be applied. An easy way of preparing the soda, is to treat it in solution, with powdered quicklime.

Bitter Almond Soap.

Take fine hard white soap, 100 pounds; essence of bitter almonds, $1\frac{1}{8}$ per cent. Treat them as for Cinnamon Soap.

Engraving in Alto-Relievo.

In the common operation of engraving, the desired effect is produced by making incisions upon the copper-plate with a steel instrument of an angular shape, which incisions are filled with printing-ink, and transferred to the paper by means of a roller, which is passed over its surface. There is another mode of producing these lines or incisions, by means of diluted nitrous acid, in which the impression is taken in the same way. Another method of engraving is done upon a principle exactly the reverse, for instead of the subject being cut into the copper, it is the interstice between the lines which is removed by diluted aquafortis, and the lines are left as the surface, from which the impression is taken by means of a common type-printing press, instead of a copper-plate press.

This is effected by drawing with common turpentine varnish, covered with lampblack, whatever is required upon the plate; and when the varnish is thoroughly dry, the acid is poured upon it, and the interstice of course removed by its action upon the uncovered part of the copper. If the subject is very full of dark shadows, this operation will be performed with little risk of accident, and with the removal of very little of the interstice between the lines; but if the distance between the lines is great, the risk and difficulty is very much increased, and it will be requisite to cut away the parts which surround the lines with a graver, in order to prevent the dabber with the printing-ink from reaching the bottom, and thus producing a blurred impression. It is obvious, therefore, that the more the plate is covered with work, the less risk there will be in the preparation of it with the acid, after the subject is drawn, and the less trouble will there be in removing the interstice, if any, from those places where there is little shading.

Alumina.

Take a solution of alum, filter, then add a sufficient quantity of solution of ammonia to precipitate the whole of the alumina.

Amber Beer.

Take half pale and half amber malt.

Alum White.

Take alum, 2 parts ; honey, 1 part. Mix and calcine them until of a clear white, then well wash and dry the powder. This forms an excellent white, both in oil and water.

Amalgam for the Cushions of Electrical Machines.

Take zinc, 2 parts ; tin, 1 part ; mercury, 5 parts. Mix. Rub th cushions with a mixture of tallow and beeswax, before applying the amalgam.

Amalgam for Varnishing Plaster Figures, &c.

Take tin, mercury, and bismuth, equal parts ; fuse and cool, then make the amalgam into a varnish with white of egg.

Factitious Oil of Amber.

Take oil of amber, Barbadoes tar, equal parts. Mix.

Essence of Ambergris.

1. Take ambergris, 2 ounces ; bladder musk, 1 ounce ; spirit of ambrette, 3 quarts ; alcohol, 1 quart. Digest for fifty or sixty days, in a temperature of from 100° to 130° Fahr.

2. Take ambergris, 1 drachm ; alcohol, 4 ounces. Mix.

Pale Amber Varnish.

1. Take pale amber, 6 parts : fuse, and then add hot boiled oil (pale), 20 parts ; boil until stringy, cool, and add spirits of turpentine, 35 parts. Mix well together.

2. Take amber, 1 pound ; melt, and then add linseed oil, half a gallon ; and when thoroughly united, spirits of turpentine, 3 pints.

Spirit of Ambrette.

Take ambrette, 23 pounds ; alcohol, 6 gallons ; distilled water, 3 gallons. Draw over twenty-five quarts.

Honey Wine.

Take honey, 20 pounds ; cider, 12 gallons. Ferment, then add rum, ½ gallon ; brandy, ½ gallon ; red or white tartar (dissolved), 6 ounces ; bitter almonds and cloves, each ¼ ounce.

Factitious Amethyst.

1. Take strass, 5000 parts ; oxide of manganese, 37 parts ; oxide of cobalt, 25 parts ; purple of Cassius, 1 part. Fuse for twenty-six hours, and cool slowly.

2. Take paste or strass, 10,000 parts ; oxide of manganese, 25 parts ; oxide of cobalt, 1 part.

Carbonate of Ammonia.

Take sal ammoniac, 1 part ; chalk, 2 parts. Mix in fine powder, and sublime.

Zaffre.

Take roasted cobalt, 1 part ; powdered quartz, 3 parts. Mix and fuse.

Essence of Neroli.

Orange flowers, and pursue the same plan as for Essence of Roses.

Iodide of Lead.

Acetate of lead, 9 ounces; iodide of potassium, 7 ounces; distilled water, 8 pints. Dissolve the acetate in two-thirds of the water, and the iodide in the remaining one-third; mix, and wash and preserve the precipitate.

Used in the composition of an ointment.

Iodide of Mercury.

Mercury, 8 parts; Iodine, 5 parts. Rub them together in a mortar, adding gradually a little alcohol until the union is complete. Dry with a gentle heat, and keep it in a well-stopped bottle, in the dark.

Ointment of Iodide of Mercury.

Lard 3 ounces; Iodide of mercury, 45 grains. Mix.

For venereal ulcers, &c.

Compound Solution of Iodide of Potassium.

Iodide of potassium, 2 scruples; iodine, 1 scruple; distilled water, 2 quarts. Dissolve and filter. Dose, three to seven drops, where iodine is indicated.

Ointment of Iodide of Sulphur.

Ioduret of sulphur, 25 grains; lard, 1 ounce. Mix.

Solution of Iodine.

Iodine, 1 grain; distilled water, 16 ounces. Dissolve.

Tincture of Iodine.

Iodine, 1 part; spirits of wine, 8 parts. Dose, ten to twenty drops.

Ioduret of Sulphur.

Iodine, 4 parts; flowers of sulphur, 1 part. Mix, put them into a bottle and apply a gentle heat.

Keep it in well-corked bottles.

Jonquille Perfume.

Oil of sassafras, 1 part; oil of orange, 1 part; oil of caraway, 2 parts, oil of lavender, 3 parts; essence of lemon, 8 parts; essence of bergamot, 8 parts. Mix.

Perfumer's Oil of Jonquille.

Follow the same plan as for the Oil of Jasmin, which see.

Jonquille Pomade.

Beef suet, 5 parts; lard, 12 parts. Mix, with a gentle heat, and strain then treat it as for Jasmin Pomade, with the difference of the flowers.

To Extract Iron Moulds.

Rub the spot with a little powdered oxalic acid, or salts of lemon and warm water, let it remain a few minutes and well rinse in clean water

Ipecacuanha Lozenges.

Ipecacuanha, 2 ounces; sugar, 5 pounds. Mucilage to mix.

Persulphate of Iron Paper.

The same as the Protosulphate of Iron Paper, with the substitution of the *per* for the *proto* salt.

Protosulphate of Iron Paper.

Protosulphate of iron, 1 part; water, 20 parts. Dissolve; dip the paper into the fluid and dry.

Iron Solder.

Soft brass powder; borax sufficient.

Isinglass Jelly.

Isinglass jelly, ½ pound; water, 1 gallon. Boil until of sufficient consistence, then add, milk, 3 pints; white sugar, 7 ounces.

Isinglass Size.

Isinglass, 1 part; water, 100 parts. Boil until dissolved and of a proper thickness.

Isle of White Sauce.

Soy, Port wine, brandy or spirit, and mushroom ketchup, of each equal parts. Mix, and let them stand until fine.

Issue Peas.

1. Yellow wax, 1 pound; turmeric, ½ pound; orris powder, ¼ pound. Spirits of turpentine to mix. Form into peas.

2. Yellow wax, 1 pound; orris powder, 4 ounces; vermilion, 8 ounces. Venice turpentine to mix.

Raspberry Syrup.

To every quart of fruit add a pound of sugar, and let it stand over night. In the morning boil and skim it for half an hour; then strain it through a flannel bag and pour into bottles, which must be carefully corked and sealed. To each bottle add, if you please, a trifle of brandy, if the weather is so warm as to endanger its keeping.

Raspberry Jam.

Take 1 pound loaf-sugar to every pound of fruit; bruise them together in your preserving-pan with a silver spoon, and let them simmer gently for an hour. When cold, put them into glass jars, and lay over them a bit of paper saturated with brandy—then tie them up so as carefully to exclude the air.

Premium Cheese.

For a cheese of 20 pounds, a piece of rennet about two inches square is soaked about twelve hours in one pint of water. As rennets differ much in quality, enough should be used to coagulate the milk *sufficiently* in about forty minutes. No salt is put *into* the cheese, nor any outside during the first six or eight hours it is being prepared; but a thin coat of fine Liverpool salt is kept on the outside during the remainder of the time it remains in press. The cheeses are pressed forty-eight hours under a weight of seven or eight cwt. Nothing more is required but to turn the cheeses once a day on the shelves

Caustic Issue Peas.

Yellow wax, 18 ounces; verdigris, 6 ounces; Spanish flies, 3 ounces; orris powder, 4 ounces; white helebore, 4 ounces. Mix

Premium Cheese.

The milk strained in large tubs over night; the cream stirred in milk, and in morning strained in same tub; milk heated to natural heat; add colour and rennet; curd broke fine and whey off, and broke fine in hoop with fast bottom, and put in strainer; pressed twelve hours; then taken from hoop, and salt rubbed on the surface; then put in hoop, without strainer, and pressed forty-eight hours; then put on tables, and salt rubbed on surface, and remain in salt six days for cheese weighing 30 pounds. The hoops to have holes in the bottom; the crushings are saved, and set and churned, to grease the cheese. The above method is for making one cheese per day.

Tincture of Roses.

Take leaves of the common rose (*centifolies*), place them, without pressing them, in a bottle, pour good spirits upon them, close the bottle, and let it stand until it is required for use. This tincture will keep for years, and yield a perfume little inferior to otto of roses. A few drops of it will suffice to impregnate the atmosphere of a room with a delicious odour. Common vinegar is greatly improved by a very small quantity being added to it.

Aromatic Beer.

Take 20 drops of the oil of spruce, 20 do. wintergreen, 20 do. sassafras. Pour 2 quarts of boiling water upon the oils, then add 8 quarts of cold water, 1½ pint of molasses, and ½ a pint of yeast. Let it stand two hours and then bottle it.

To Boil a Ham.

Put your ham into the pot at noon the day before you want it for the table, and keep the water hot until that time, then let it boil 15 minutes.

For Roasting Venison.

A large haunch will require three hours. After it is on the spit, rub it all over with butter, baste with flour and a little salt, butter a sheet of white paper, and lay over the fat part, fastening it on with strings or skewers. keep it well basted, and five minutes before sending it to the table take off the paper, dust flour over it, and baste it with butter till the fat is handsomely browned and covered with a good froth.

Rennet, or Wine Custards.

Very simple, and prepared in five minutes. Cut a bit of rennet about four inches square into strips, which put into a bottle filled with wine. It will be fit for use in two or three weeks. To make your custard, first *warm* and *sweeten* the milk, then stir into it a teaspoonful or tablespoonful of the rennet wine, according to its strength, and pour immediately into a pudding-dish, or cups, as you prefer; put away in a cool place for an hour, and grate nutmeg on them. The whey, of which you can make enough, by the addition of extra wine when you prepare it, is a very nourishing drink for invalids.

Sausages, quite rich enough for an Epicure.

Take 30 pounds of chopped meat, 8 ounces of fine salt, 2½ ounces of pepper, 2 teacups of sage, and 1½ cups of sweet marjoram, passed through a fine sieve. For the latter, thyme and summer savory can be substituted if preferred.

Tomato Catsup.

To a gallon skinned tomatos add 4 tablespoonsful salt, 4 do. black pepper, half a spoonful alspice, 8 red peppers, and 3 spoonsful mustard. All these ingredients must be ground fine, and simmered slowly in sharp vinegar for three or four hours. As much vinegar is to be used as to leave half a gallon of liquor when the process is over. Strain through a wire sieve and bottle, and seal from the air. This may be used in two weeks, but improves by age, and will keep several years.

Cold Water.

Cure for persons who have drunk imprudently of cold water or any cold liquid when too much heated. Doses of *liquid laudanum* proportioned to the violence of the attack. From a teaspoonful to near a tablespoonful has been given before relief has been obtained.

A mild Puke.

For a grown person dissolve 20 grains of ipecacuanha in six spoonsful of warm water; give a spoonful every ten minutes until it operates.

An active Puke.

For an adult, dissolve 20 grains of sulphate of zinc (white vitriol) in a cup of warm water. Generally used in very urgent cases, such as when the person has swallowed poison.

Antimonial Wine.

Dissolve 40 grains of tartar emetic in 2 ounces of water; when dissolved, add half a pint of Teneriffe wine. Let it stand three hours and it is made.

Tartar Emetic.

For an adult, warm water, 6 spoonsful; tartar emetic, 6 grains. Mix, and when dissolved, give one tablespoonful every ten minutes until it operates.

An Active Purge.

Calomel, (for an adult,) 25 grains, to be followed next day with a small dose of castor oil.

A Favourite Purge.

For a grown person, calomel, 15 grains; jalap, 15 grains. Mix in some syrup.

Salts, Senna, and Manna.—A purgative.

Take half an ounce of salts, half do. senna, half do. manna, and put them into a pint of hot water, covering the vessel. For an adult give one teacupful every half hour until it operates.

Lee's Antibilious Pills.—A purgative.

Take 5 grains of calomel, 10 do. jalap, 2 do. gambogc, and half do tartar emetic. Make into four pills. The above is for one dose.

To Preserve Apples, &c.

1. Take apples, and pack them in clean, dry, chopped straw, so that they do not touch each other.

2. Dip each apple separately into melted wax, then pack as above.

To Preserve Apples, Pears, &c.

Take apples or pears, and peel them, then cut them into eighths, observing to extract the core; dry in a kiln until quite hard.

In this way fruit is kept in the United States for two or three years.

For use, wash the fruit in water, then pour boiling water on it, let it stand for a few minutes and use it as fresh fruit. The water forms an excellent substitute for fresh juice.

Apple Wine.

Finest cider, 60 gallons; brown sugar, ½ cwt.; bitter almonds, ¼ ounce. Mix the cider and sugar and ferment, then rack the mixture, and put into the cask the almonds, with sixteen or eighteen cloves, and three or four pieces of bruised ginger. When fine, bottle it, and keep it in a cool place.

The addition of a small piece of lump-sugar to each bottle will make the cork fly out, as from champaigne; but do not add this, unless you have a very cold cellar to keep it in.

Arbor Dianæ.

Nitrate of silver, 2 parts; water, 70 parts. Dissolve and filter; put the clear into a convenient bottle, and then add mercury, 2 parts. Set it aside; metallic vegetation will immediately commence.

Lump Archil.

Ground archil, 4 parts; pearlash, 2 parts; lime powder (old), 1 part. Make into a paste with urine, and cut into shapes.

Argentum Musivum.

Bismuth, 2 pounds; tin, 2 pounds. Melt, then add quicksilver, 1 pound.

Aromatic Plaster.

Thuris, 6 ounces; yellow wax, 1 ounce: powdered cassia, 1 ounce; oil of pimento, 1 drachm; essence of lemon, 1 drachm. Mix. For indigestion, dyspepsia, &c.

Cheap Aromatic Vinegar.

Common vinegar, and saturate the acid with chalk, dry the precipitated powder, and pour on it sulphuric acid.

Substitute for Arrow-Root.

Finest potato-starch, ¾ cwt.; lump-sugar, 8 pounds; finely ground rice, 21 pounds. Mix and sift through lawn. Yields 1 cwt. of excellent arrow-root.

Asiatic Dentifrice.

Armenian bole, 3 parts; prepared chalk, 2 parts; ochre, 1 part; pumice stone, one part. Reduce to fine powder and sift through lawn. Scent with musk.

Armenian Cement.

1. "The jewellers of Turkey, who are mostly Armenians, (we are informed by that most respectable and intelligent traveller, Mr. Eton, formerly a consul in that country, and author of a Survey of the Turkish Empire), have a singular method of ornamenting watch-cases, &c., with diamonds and other precious stones, by simply glueing or cementing them on. The stone is set in silver or gold, and the lower part of the metal made flat, or to correspond with the part to which it is to be fixed; it is then warmed gently, and has the glue applied, which is so very strong, that the parts thus cemented never separate: this glue, which will strongly unite bits of glass, and even polished steel, and may of course be applied to a vast variety of useful purposes, is thus made: Dissolve five or six bits of gum mastich, each the size of a large pea, in as much spirits of wine as will suffice to render it liquid, and, in another vessel, dissolve as much isinglass, previously a little softened in water, (though none of the water must be used), in French brandy or good rum, as will make a two ounce phial of very strong glue, adding two small bits of gum galbanum or ammoniacum, which must be rubbed or ground till they are dissolved. Then mix the whole with a sufficient heat. Keep the glue in a phial closely stopped, and when it is to be used, set the phial in boiling water. Mr. Eton observes, that some persons have sold a composition under the name of Armenian cement, in England; but this composition is badly made: it is much too thin, and the quantity of mastich is much too small."

2. Thick isinglass glue, 1 part; thick mastic varnish, 1 part. Melt the glue, mix, and keep it in a closely corked phial. For use, put the phial in hot water.

Factitious Archil.

Rotten onions, 12 parts; pearlash, 12 parts. Steep four days in a sufficient quantity of urine, then add sugar of lead, 3 parts. Shake frequently for four days longer.

This receipt is taken on the authority of a country correspondent; it is doubtful, however, whether it will always produce the required result.

Imitation of Arrack.

Flowers of Benjamin, 1 ounce; rum, 3 gallons; silent spirit, 4 gallons. Mix.

Liquid Asphaltum.

Asphaltum, 4 parts; Scio turpentine, 6 parts. Melt, then add spirits of turpentine, 7 parts.

Asafœtida Plaster.

Diachylon, 2 pounds; asafœtida, 2 pounds; galbanum, 1 pound; yellow wax, 1 pound. Mix. For hysterics, flatulence, &c., applied to the navel.

Astringent Pills.

1. Extract of Peruvian bark, 1 drachm; gum kino, 1 drachm; alum, ½ drachm, nutmeg, 1 scruple; syrup to mix. Divide into thirty-six pills. Dose, one or two, three times a day.

2. Alum, 1 drachm; catechu, 2 drachms; opium, 12 grains. Mix and divide into sixty pills. Dose three, twice a day.

Astringent Ointment.

1. Lard, 1 pound; yellow resin, 1 pound; spirits of turpentine, 1 pound, alum, 8 ounces. Mix.

2. Simple ointment, 4 ounces; oil of turpentine, 2 ounces; acetate of lead, 3 drachms. Mix.

Yellow Arsenic.

Arsenic, 80 pounds; sulphur, 10 pounds. Mix and sublime.

Astringent Pills, for obstinate Gleet or Leucorrhœa, &c.

Gum kino, 1 part; Canadian turpentine, 4 parts; powder of tormentill to mix. Divide into five-grain pills. Dose, two to six, night and morning

Aurum Musivum, or Bisulphuret of Tin.

1. Tin filings, sulphur, sal ammoniac, equal quantities. Mix and sublime. If the fire is raised too high, the product will only be a grey sulphuret.

2. Tin, 12 parts; mercury, 3 parts; sulphur, 7 parts; sal ammoniac, 3 parts. Mix and expose them in a matrass to a gentle heat, in a sand bath, then gradually and cautiously raise the heat a little, and calcine for two or three hours.

Autographic Ink for Lithographers.

White soap, 25 parts; white wax, 25 parts; mutton suet, 6 parts; lampblack, 6 parts; shell lac, 10 parts; mastic, 10 parts. Mix with heat, and proceed as for lithographic ink.

Beautiful Azure.

Mercury, 4 parts; sulphur and ammonia, 1 part each. Grind them together, and expose them to a low heat, then increase the fire until an azure flame arises; cover up and cool.

Fine Azure from Copper.

Soda, 5 parts; flint powder, 7 parts; copper filings, 1 part. Fuse together for two hours.

Dr. Bailey's Itch Ointment.

Sweet oil, 1 pound; suet, 1 pound; root alkanet, 2 ounces. Melt and macerate until sufficiently coloured, then add powdered nitre, 3 ounces; powdered alum, 3 ounces; powdered sulphate of zinc, 3 ounces; powdered vermilion, to colour; oil of aniseed, to perfume; oil of spike, to perfume, oil of origanum, to perfume.

Balsamic Vinegar, for Sick Chambers, &c.

Rue, sage, rosemary, lavender, cassia and cloves, of each, 1 ounce; camphor (powdered), 2 ounces; strong vinegar, ½ gallon. Steep for one week.

Balls for removing Grease and Paint Spots from Cloth, &c.

Fuller's earth, 30 parts; French chalk, 1 part; yellow soap, 20 parts; pearlash, 15 parts. Make into a paste with spirits of turpentine, and give it a slight colour with a little yellow ochre, then cut it into cakes. This form, omitting the French chalk, is that which is sold about the streets

Dr. Bailey's Prescription for Indigestion.

Rose water, 1 pint; sulphate of magnesia, 6 drachms; tincture of cascarilla, 1 ounce. Mix. Dose, 3 table-spoonfuls twice a day.

Baker's Stuff.

Alum, 1 part; salt, 3 parts. Mix and sift.

Factitious Balm of Gilead.

Benzoin, 1 pound; yellow rosin, 14 pound. Melt, and add oil of lemon, 4 ounces; oil of rosemary, 4 ounces; oil of caraway, 4 ounces; spirit to reduce it to a proper consistence.

Balm of Molucca, (Aromatic.)

Proof spirit, 1 gallon; white sugar, 4 pounds; river water, 6 pounds, powdered cloves, ½ ounce; powdered mace, ⅛ ounce; burnt sugar to colour. Macerate for ten days in a close vessel.

Balm Wine.

Same as sage wine, with the substitution of balm for sage.

Factitious Balsam of Peru.

Balsam of Tolu, 3 pounds; gum benzoin, 6 pounds; alcohol, 1 gallon. Mix. Used in perfumery.

Soluble Balsam.

Capaiva, 2 parts; æther, 5 parts; tincture of myrrh, 1 part. Dissolve with heat, in a close vessel.

Barberry Marmalade.

Pulp of barberries; sugar to sweeten. Boil to one-half.

Barclay's Antibilious Pills.

Extract of colocynth, 2 drachms; extract of jalap, 1 drachm; almond soap, 1½ drachms; guaiacum, 3 drachms; tartarized antimony, 8 grains; oil of juniper, 4 drops; oil of caraway, 4 drops; oil of rosemary, 4 drops Form into a mass with syrup of buckthorn, and divide into pills.

Essential Salt of Bark.

Bark (bruised), 1 part; cold water, 10 parts. Digest for two days, then strain and evaporate with a gentle heat.

Extract of Bark.

Bark, 1 pound; water, 1 gallon. Boil, strain while hot, and gradually evaporate. When this article is dried in a water-bath fit for powdering it is then called hard extract of bath.

To Preserve Barks.

Barks may be conveniently preserved, by placing them in coarse brown paper bags, and hanging them up, in some airy and dry situation, until al extraneous moisture has evaporated.

Barnstaple Ale.

Similar to the other kinds of pale ale.

Paregoric.

Take ½ a drachm of opium, or 1 ounce of laudanum, to a pint of spirit of any kind. Add thereto ½ a drachm of flowers of benzoin, oil of anise ½ a drachm, camphor, 1 scruple. Dose for adults 1 to 2 drachms; children from 2 to 4 years, 15 to 20 drops.

Bell Metal.

1. Copper, 25 parts; tin, 5 parts. Mix.
2. Copper, 79 parts; tin, 26 parts. Mix.
3. Copper, 78 parts; tin, 22 parts. Mix.

Common Bell Metal.

Copper, 100 parts; tin 50 parts. Mix.

Parisian Bell Metal.

Copper, 72 parts; tin, 26½ parts; iron, 1½ parts. Used for the bells of small ornamental clocks.

Bengal Flames.

Nitre, 7 parts; sulphur, 2 parts; antimony, 1 part. Mix, press the composition into earthen porringers, and place a quick match on the surface, or a little rocket powder.

Factitious Beryl.

Oxide of cobalt, 1 part; glass of antimony, 16 parts; strass, 2310 parts. Fuse carefully for twenty-five to thirty hours, then cool slowly.

Bichloride of Mercury.

Persulphate of mercury, chloride of sodium, equal parts. Sublime in a stone-ware cucurbit.

Bicarbonate of Potass.

Oil of tartar, saw-dust, each a sufficient quantity. Make into a dough, and heat the mixture in a covered crucible until red-hot, then cool, wash out the salt, and evaporate with a gentle heat.

Bicyanide of Mercury.

Percyanide of iron, 4 ounces; binoxide of mercury, 5 ounces; distilled water, 1 quart. Boil together, then evaporate and crystallize.

Bilberry Wine.

Fruit, cider, and water, each 20 gallons; raw sugar, 60 pounds. Boil and ferment, then add, red tartar, dissolved, ½ pound; spirit, 2 or 3 gallons; ginger (bruised), lavender, and rosemary leaves, of each 4 ounces.

Remedy for Biliary Calculi.

Sulphuric ether, 3 parts; oil of turpentine, 2 parts. Mix. Dose, half a drachm night and morning, in any warm liquid.

Birch Wine.

Birch water, 1 hogshead; malaga raisins (stalks and all), 50 pounds sugar, 100 pounds. Boil and ferment, then rack it, and let it stand for six months.

Biniodide of Mercury.

Mercury, 4 parts; iodine, 5 parts. Mix as for the iodide of mercury.

Solution of Biniodide of Mercury.

Alcohol, 3 ounces; biniodide of mercury, 2 scruples. Dissolve. Dose, 8 to 20 drops in distilled water.

Birdlime.

The middle bark of the holly, any quantity; boil it for seven or eight hours in water, or until it is soft and tender, then drain the water off, and place it in pits under ground, surrounded with stones; let it remain to ferment, and water it if required until it passes into a mucilaginous state. Then pound it well and wash it in several waters, next leave it for four or five days to ferment and purify itself.

Birdlime Varnish for Balloons.

Birdlime, 4 parts; boiled oil, 4 parts. Boil until the birdlime ceases to cackle, then add boiled oil, 6 parts; litharge, 1 part. Boil again till it becomes stringy, then remove it from the fire and add turpentine 6 parts. Apply this varnish lukewarm.

Biscuit Jelly.

White biscuit, 1 pound; white sugar, 3 pounds; water, 2 gallons. Boil to one-half, strain and evaporate to a proper consistence, then add wine, 1 pint; cinnamon, ½ ounce.

Bistre.

Wood soot. Grind it with a little water, then mix it with a large quantity of water, wash it well, collect it and dry it on porous stone.

Lotion for Bites and Stings.

1. Distilled water, 5 parts; laudanum, 1 part. Mix.
2. Distilled water, 15 parts; water of ammonia, 2 parts. Mix.
3. Chloride of lime, 1 part; warm water, 11 parts. Put them into a bottle, cork it close and agitate them well until cold, then pour off the clear.

Bitter Almond Water.

Bitter almonds, bruised, 7 pounds; water, 12 gallons. Draw off 10 gallons.

Bitter Balls.

Powdered gentian, 2 parts; extract of gentian, 1 part; treacle to mix. These are used by brewers for the purpose of imparting a bitter to beer.

Brewer's Bittern.

1. Quassia, 2 parts; cocculus indicus, 1 part; Italian juice, 1 part; water, 25 parts. Boil until reduced to 20 parts, then add copperas, 1 part. Boil to a syrup.
2. Extract of quassia, extract of cocculus indicus, extract of liquorice, sulphate of iron, equal parts. This preparation is used for the same purpose as the last, and also to give an appearance of strength to weak liquor.

Essence of Bitter Almonds.

Essential oil of almonds, 1 pound; alcohol, 7 pounds. Mix.

Black Ball for Leather.

Beeswax, 2 pounds; tallow, ¼ pound; gum arabic, ¼ pound; lamp black, ¼ pound. Melt the tallow and wax, then cool a little and stir in the black and gum, previously made into a thick mucilage.

Blackberry Wine.

Ripe berries, bruised, 20 gallons; pour on them water, hot, 22 gallons. Let them stand three days, then add sugar, 40 pounds. Ferment, rack, and add ginger, bruised, 2 ounces; catechu powder, 2 ounces; red tartar 8 ounces; cloves ½ ounce; spirit, 2 gallons.

Black Cake that will keep a Year.

Sugar, 1 pound; butter, 1 pound; flour, 1 pound; ten eggs; brandy, ¼ pint; raisins, 2 pounds; currants, 2 pounds. Mace, nutmegs, and cloves to flavour. Bake it well.

Black Currant Wine.

Cold soft water, 20 gallons; fruit, 20 gallons; sugar, 60 pounds; ferment, then add red tartar, dissolved, 8 ounces; cloves, ½ ounce; dried orange-peel, ½ ounce; ginger, ½ ounce.

Black Draught.

Senna, small, 2 ounces; ginger, 2 drachms; cassia, 2 drachms; water, 21 ounces; tincture of senna, 2 ounces; Epsom salts, ½ pound. Mix and digest. Dose for an adult, one ounce and a half to two ounces.

Black Drop.

1. Opium, sliced, 16 parts; verjuice, 100 parts; nutmegs, 3 parts; saffron, 1 part; sugar, 8 parts; yeast, 1 part. Boil the first four to a proper consistence, then add the sugar and yeast; let it stand in a warm situation for fifty or sixty days, then decant for use.

2. Opium, sliced, 1 pound; distilled vinegar, 4 pounds. Infuse with occasional agitation for one month, then filter.

Black Dye for Cotton.

Acetate of iron as a mordant; and dye in a bath of madder and logwood.

Black Japan for Leather.

Boiled oil, 1 gallon; burnt umber, 5 ounces; asphaltum, 5 ounces; lampblack, 1 pound. Thin with spirits of turpentine.

Black Japan.

1. Boiled oil, 1 gallon; umber, 8 ounces; asphaltum, 3 ounces, oil of turpentine, as much as will reduce it to the thinness required.

2. Asphaltum, 50 pounds; fuse, then add dark animé, 8 pounds; dark amber, 10 pounds; when melted, put in boiled drying oil, 15 gallons; litharge, 1 pound. Boil until perfectly mixed and stringy, then cool and thin with turpentine.

Black for Miniature Painters.

Take camphor, and set it on the fire, and collect the soot by means of a saucer or paper-funnel inverted over it.

Perfectly Black Hard Glass.

Plain paste, 600 parts; zaffre, 3 parts; manganese, 3 parts; iron, 3 parts.

Black Enamel.

Clay, 2 parts; protoxide of iron, 1 part. Mix.

Blacking Balls for Leather.

Ivory black, 1 pound; lampblack, 1 pound; common gum, ¼ pound; brown sugar, 6 ounces; isinglass or glue, ¼ ounce; water, 1 quart. Mix

Black Liquid.

Ivory black, 2 pounds; treacle, 2 pounds; sweet oil, 1 pound; rub together until well mixed, then add oil of vitriol, ¾ pound. Mix well and dilute with beer bottoms.

Paste Blacking.

Oil of vitriol, 2 parts; sweet oil, 1 part; treacle, 3 parts, ivory black, 4 parts. Mix.

Black Ink Powders.

Sulphate of iron, 2 parts; galls, 5 parts; gum, 1 part. Reduce to a powder and divide into one-ounce papers, each of which will make half a pint of ink.

Blacklead Pencils.

The easiest way of producing, not only blacklead, but all sorts of pencils, is by the following process, which at once combines simplicity, cheapness, and the finest quality.

Take white or pipe-clay: put it into a tub of clean water, to soak for 12 hours, then agitate the whole, until it resembles milk, let it rest two or three minutes and pour off the supernatant milky liquor into a second vessel, allow it to settle, pour off the clear and dry the residue on a filter. Then add blacklead, any quantity. Powder it and calcine it at a white heat in a loosely covered crucible, cool and carefully repulverize, then add prepared clay, prepared plumbago, equal parts. Water to mix. Make them into a paste and put it into oiled moulds of the size required, dry very gradually, and apply sufficient heat to give the required degree of hardness; lastly, the pieces should be taken carefully from the moulds and placed in the groves of the cedar. The more clay and heat employed, the harder the crayon; less clay and heat of course produces a contrary effect. The shade of black may also be varied in the same way. Each mould must be made of four pieces of wood nicely fitted together.

Wash to fix Blacklead Pencil Drawings.

1. Isinglass, 1 part; water, 50 parts. Dissolve with heat and filter.

2. Take skimmed milk, and strain. For use, pour the liquid on a surface sufficiently large, and take the drawing by the corners, lay it flat on the wash, then carefully remove it. and place it on a slanting surface to drain and dry. This will also answer for chalk drawings.

To economize Grain. (Singular.)

In July, 1842, Mr. Palmer put one grain of wheat in a common garden pot. In August, he divided it into four plants, which in three weeks were again divided into twelve; which in September were divided into thirty-two; which in November were again divided into fifty, and set in open ground. July 1843, twelve failed, but the remaining thirty-eight were healthy. They were cut down August 19, and counted 1,972 stems, with an average of 50 grains to the stem, affording a yield of 98,600 !

Cure for Bronchitis.

Croton oil, it is said, will entirely remove this complaint. For instance. A minister of the presbyterian church, resident in Greene county, who has been laid aside from his pastoral office by the bronchitis, for three years past, has entirely recovered his voice by the application of croton oil to the surface of the throat, against the organ affected, sent him three weeks ago by Dr. White of Hudson. One drop, daily rubbed over the surface, produced a singular but powerful eruption of the skin, which, as it progressed, restored his voice to its full tone and vigour, so as to enable him to commence public speaking, anew.

Gardening in Ceylon.

I often practise taking off large branches from some kinds of trees, so as to form new ones, according to the Eastern plan, by causing water continually to drop upon matting bound round part of a branch, into which a sufficient incision has been made, and where, in a short time, a good root is formed. The branch is then entirely sawed off, and being planted in the place intended for it, we have at once a handsome tree of the same kind. producing the same fruit or blossoms as that from which it was taken.

To Fatten Pigs very Fat.

Feed them on boiled rice.

Precipitation of Alum by adding Alkaline Salts.

Separate from the concentrated clear liquor, the alum in the state of powder or small crystals, by addition of the proper alkaline matter, and leave the mingled foreign salts, such as the sulphate of iron or magnesia, in solution, instead of trying to abstract these salts by a previous crystallization.

To Wash the Alum Powder.

This crystalline pulverulent matter has a brownish colour, from the admixture of the ferruginous liquors, but is freed by washing it with *very cold* clear water, which dissolves not more than one sixteenth of its weight of alum. A second washing will render the alum nearly pure. The less water is used, and the more effectually it is drained off, the more complete is the process.

Crystallization of Alum.

The washed alum is put into a leaden pan, with just enough water to dissolve it at a boiling heat; fire is applied, and the solution is promoted by stirring. When it is dissolved in a saturated state, it is run off into the crystallizing vessels which are called *rocking* casks.

To kill Borers in Trees.

Stop up their holes with hard soap. It is a simple and a very good remedy.

Fruit Trees.

All kinds of fruit trees put out a great many sprouts from the limbs and roots, called suckers. Take these, cut the butt end into a wedge; take the root of any wood the same size, split it and run the sucker into that split, and they will unite, and the root will support the shoot, till new roots can put out. Let it stand till it shall attain the size desired, and then transplant it.

To destroy Thistles, Fern, and Coltsfoot.

Run over your fields once or twice about the first of June, with a heavy cast-iron roller.

Cure for what is called a Run-round on the Finger.

The first symptom of the disease is a heat, from swelling and pain, and a redness at the top of the nail. To cure—first open with a pin; then, with the point of a penknife, scratch the whole surface of the nail, both lengthwise and across. This alone, it is said, checks and cures the complaint.

Zest for Gravies.

Take powdered thyme, sage, cayenne pepper, pimento, black pepper coriander seeds, and mace, in fine powder, equal parts. Well mix.

Bleeding at the Nose.

To cure it, apply to the neck behind and on each side, a cloth dipped in cold water: or, put the legs and arms in cold water: or, wash the temples, nose and neck, with vinegar: or, snuff up vinegar and water.

To make Amadou.

This is prepared from a species of agaric, the *boletus igniarius*, a kind of mushroom, which grows on the trunks of old trees, such as the oak, ash, beech, &c. It must be gathered in the months of August and September. Cut off the outer bark of this substance with a sharp knife, separating carefully the spongy substance of a yellow brown colour, which lies within it, from the ligneous matter below. This substance must then be cut into thin slices, and beat with a mallet to soften it, until it can be easily pulled asunder between the fingers. In this state the *boletus* is a valuable substance for stopping *oozing hemorrhages*, and some other surgical purposes. To convert it into tinder, boil it in a strong solution of *nitre*; drying it, beating it anew, and putting it a second time into the solution. Sometimes, in order to render it very inflammable, it is imbued with gunpowder, whence the distinction of black and brown *Amadou.*

To Fatten Poultry quick.

Boil rice in sweet milk, and feed them with it.

To Raise Bread without Yeast.

Mix in your flour, of pearlash or subcarbonate of soda, 2 parts; tartaric acid, 1 part; both finely powdered. Make up your bread with warm water, adding but a little at a time, and bake soon.

To prevent Swelling from a Bruise.

Immediately apply a cloth, five or six fold, dipped in cold water, and new dipped when it grows warm.

A Burn or Scald.

If it be but skin deep, immediately plunge the part in cold water; keep it in an hour, if not well before. Perhaps longer.

A Deep Burn or Scald.

Apply the inner rind of elder well mixed with fresh butter. When this is bound on with a rag, plunge the part into cold water. This will suspend the pain till the medicine heals. Or, mix lime-water and sweet oil to the thickness of cream, and apply it with a feather several times a day. This is a most effectual application.

Chilblains.

Bathe the feet often in cold water, and when this is done, apply a turnip poultice.

Children.

To prevent the rickets, tenderness, and weakness, dip them in cold water every morning, at least till they are eight or nine months old. No roller should ever be put round their bodies, nor any stays used. Instead of them, when they are put into short petticoats, put a waistcoat under their frocks. It is best to wean a child when seven months old, if it be disposed to rickets. It should lie in the cradle at least a year. No child should touch any spirituous or fermented liquor. Their drink should be water. Tea, they should never taste till ten or twelve years old. Milk, milk-porridge, and water-gruel, are the proper breakfast for children.

Chin-cough or Whooping-cough.

Rub the feet thoroughly with hog's lard, before the fire, on going to bed, and keep the child warm therein. Or, rub the back, at lying down, with old rum: it seldom fails. Or, give a spoonful of juice of penny-royal, mixed with brown sugar candy, twice a day. Or, half a pint of milk, warm from the cow, with the quantity of a nutmeg of conserve of roses dissolved in it, every morning. In desperate cases, change of air will have a good effect.

Cholera Morbus, i. e. *Flux and Vomiting of Bile.*

Boil a chicken an hour in two gallons of water, and drink of this till the vomiting ceases. Or, decoction of rice, or barley, or toasted oaten bread. If the pain is very severe, steep the belly with flannels dipped in spirits and water. The third day after the cure, take ten or fifteen grains of rhu barb.

Chaps in Women's Nipples.

Apply balsam of sugar. Or, apply butter of wax, which speedily heals them.

To prevent Chapped Hands.

Wash them with flour of mustard, or in bran and water boiled together

To Cure—Wash them with soft soap, mixed with red sand. Or, wash them in sugar and water.

A Cold.

Drink a pint of cold water, lying down in bed. Or, a spoonful of molasses in half a pint of water. Or, to one spoonful of oatmeal and one spoonful of honey, add a piece of butter the bigness of a nutmeg: pour on gradually near a pint of boiling water: drink this lying down in bed.

The Colic, in the Fit.

Drink of camomile tea. Or, take from thirty to forty grains of yellow peel of oranges, dried and powdered, in a glass of water. Or, take from five to six drops of oil of aniseed on a lump of sugar. Or, apply outwardly a bag of hot oats. Or, steep the legs in hot water a quarter of an hour. Or, take as much Daffy's elixir as will presently purge. This relieves the most violent colic in an hour or two.

Daffy's Elixir is made thus:—Senna, 2 ounces; jalap, 1 ounce; coriander seed, half an ounce; Geneva, or proof spirit, 3 pints. Let them digest seven days, strain, and add loaf-sugar, 4 ounces.

To prevent the Dry Colic.

Drink ginger tea.

Colic in Children.

Give a scruple of powdered aniseed in their meat, or small doses of magnesia; or a drachm of anisated tincture of rhubarb every three hours till it operates.

Bilious Colic.

Drink warm lemonade, or give a spoonful of castor oil.

An Habitual Colic.

Wear a thin soft flannel on the part.

A Dry or Convulsive Asthma.

It is said that the juice of radishes is good in this complaint. A small dose of castor oil, taken occasionally, will be found beneficial; or new milk drunk morning and evening. Other remedies are recommended, such as garlic, saffron, ipecacuanha.

To Cure Asthma.

Take a pint of cold water every morning, washing the head therein immediately after, and using the cold bath once a fortnight. Or, cut an ounce of stick liquorice into slices. Steep this in a quart of water twenty-four hours, and use it, when you are worse than usual, as common drink. I have known this give much ease. Or, half a pint of tar-water twice a day. Or, live a fortnight on boiled carrots only. It seldom fails. Or, take from ten to twenty drops of elixir of vitriol, in a glass of water, three or four times a day. Or, into a quart of boiling water, put a tea-spoonful of balsamic ether, receive the steam into the lungs, through a fumigator, twice a day.

Corns.

Never cut your corns: it is dangerous. To remove them when they become hard, soak them in warm water, and then with a small pumice stone, rasp down the corn. Try it, and you will never use a knife afterwards.

Magnesia,

If you have not French chalk, will effectually remove grease spots from silk, on rubbing it in well, and after standing awhile, apply a piece of soft brown paper to the wrong side, on which press a warm iron gently, and what grease is not absorbed by the paper can be removed by washing the spot carefully with cold water.

Cook's Pills.—A purgative.

Take equal parts of calomel, rhubarb, and aloes, and with a little honey form into pills of a common size. Dose, from three to four.

To dye Grey or Red Hair Black.

Take slaked lime, 1 pound; litharge, 4 ounces; chalk, 4 ounces; ceruse, (white lead,) 2 ounces. Mix into a thick paste with warm water immediately on going to bed. Comb the hair well on to the top of the head, then apply the paste, while warm, completely embedding the hair; then, with a cotton cloth sufficiently large to cover the head, dipped into warm water and wrung out, the head is to be enveloped, while the cloth is warm; then tie over all a large silk handkerchief, or a piece of oiled silk. The object of thus enveloping the head is to keep the paste warm, and at the same time from drying. In two hours the hair will turn brown, and by morning it will be a good black. The powder can easily be removed by a brush. As soon as the hair is cleansed, apply some olive oil, to give the hair a fine appearance. This is the best receipt known; it will not stain the skin, and the only disagreeable result that can arise, is to those who have a very tender skin, which will become a little inflamed. If it is desirable to have the hair of a brown colour, the paste may be removed in two hours, in the manner above mentioned, or by moistening the paste and using a fine-tooth comb.

Forty-two Experimental Receipts on Combustion and Detonation.

1. Spread a piece of tin foil, such as is used for coating electrical jars, upon a piece of thick paper; spread some powdered crystals of nitrate of copper upon it, and sprinkle it with water. Fold it up quickly, and wrap it round carefully with the paper, more effectually to exclude the atmospheric air. Place it then upon a tile, and in a short time combustion will commence, and the tin will inflame.

2. Take 3 parts of nitre, 2 of potash, and one of sulphur; all of these should be thoroughly dry; then mix them by rubbing them together in a warm mortar: the resulting compound is called fulminating powder. If a little of this powder be placed upon a fire-shovel over a hot fire, it gradually blackens, and at last melts. At that instant it explodes with a violent report. *Note.* This mixture is not dangerous, like the metallic fulminating powders, none of which should be intrusted in the hands of young people.

3. If a few pounds of a mixture of iron filings and sulphur be made into paste with water, and buried in the ground for a few hours, the water will be decomposed with so much rapidity, that combustion and flame will be the consequence.

4. Put a little fresh calcined magnesia in a tea-cup upon the hearth, and suddenly pour over it as much concentrated sulphuric acid as will cover the

magnesia. In an instant sparks will be thrown out, and the mixture wil be completely ignited.

5. Make a little charcoal perfectly dry, pulverize it very fine, and put it into a warm tea-cup. If some strong nitrous acid be now poured upon it, combustion and inflammation will immediately ensue.

6. If strong nitrous acid be poured upon a small quantity of a mixture of oxymuriate of potash and phosphorus, flashes of fire will be emitted at intervals for a considerable time.

7. Put a bit of phosphorus into a small phial, then fill it one-third with boiling olive oil, and cork it close. Whenever the stopper is taken out in the night, light will be evolved sufficient to show the hour upon a watch.

8. Burn a piece of iron wire in a deflagrating jar of oxygen gas, and suffer it to burn till it goes out of itself. If a lighted wax taper be now let down into the gas, this will burn in it for some time, and then become extinguished. If ignited sulphur be now introduced, this will also burn for a limited time. Lastly, introduce a morsel of phosphorus, and combustion will also follow in like manner. These experiments show the relative combustibility of different substances.

9. When antimony is heated to whiteness in a crucible, and in this state agitated, in contact with the air, it inflames with a sort of explosion, and presents while burning a very singular kind of white flame, forming what have been formerly called argentine flowers.

10. When antimony is well fused upon charcoal, and if, at the moment when its surface is not covered with any particle of oxide, we throw it suddenly on the ground, the globules into which it divides in its fall burn with a very lively flame, throwing out on all sides brilliant sparks, different from that of any other metal.

11. Mix five or six grains of sulphuret of antimony with half its weight of oxy-muriate of potash, and then, if a sudden stroke be given to the mixture, upon a steel anvil, it fulminates with a loud report, emitting, according to Fourcroy, a flame as brilliant and rapid as lightning.

12. Into a tea-cup, placed upon a hearth, and containing about a table-spoonful of oil of turpentine, pour about half the quantity of strong nitrous acid, previously mixed with a few drops of sulphuric acid. The moment the acids come in contact with the turpentine, heat and flame will be produced. In performing this experiment, it is advisable to mix the acids in a phial, to tie the phial to the end of a stick, and, at arm's length, to pour its contents into the oil, as the sudden combustion sometimes occasions a part of the liquids to be thrown out of the vessel.

13. Pour a little pure water into a small glass tumbler, and put one or two small pieces of phosphuret of lime into it. In a short time flashes of fire will dart from the surface of the water, and terminate in ringlets of smoke, which will ascend in regular succession.

14. Into an eight-ounce retort pour 4 ounces of pure water, add a little solution of pure potash, and give it a boiling heat with a lamp. When it boils, drop a small piece of phosphorus into it, and immerse the beak of the retort in a vessel of water. Bubbles of phosphuretted hydrogen gas will issue from the retort, rise through the water, and take fire the moment they come in contact with atmospheric air, somewhat similar to the appearance mentioned in Experiment No. 13.

15. Put 30 grains of phosphorus into a Florence flask, with 3 or 4 ounces of water. Place the vessel over a lamp, and give it a boiling heat. Balls of fire will soon be seen to issue from the water, after the manner of an artificial fire-work, attended with the most beautiful coruscations. An experiment to show the extreme inflammability of phosphorus.

16. Fix a small piece of solid phosphorus in a quill, and write with it upon paper. If the paper be now carried into a dark room, the writing will be beautifully luminous.

17. Pour a little phosphuretted ether upon a lump of sugar, and drop it into a glass of water, a little warm. The surface of the water will soon become luminous, and if it be moved by blowing gently with the mouth, beautiful and brilliant undulations of its surface will be produced, exhibiting the appearance of a liquid combustion.

18. If any part of the body be rubbed with liquid phosphorus, or phosphuretted ether, that part, in a dark room, will appear as though it were on fire, without producing any dangerous effect, or sensation of heat.

19. Take 2 grains of oxymuriate or chlorate of potash, and 1 grain of flowers of sulphur; rub them together in a mortar, and a smart detonating noise will be produced. Continue to rub the mixture hard, and the reports will be frequently repeated, accompanied with vivid flashes of light. If the same mixture be wrapped in paper, laid on an anvil, and struck with a hammer, the report will be as loud as what is usually produced by a pistol.

20. Take 2 grains of the oxymuriate or chlorate of potash, and 1 grain of phosphorus. Treat this mixture as in the last experiment, and very violent detonations will be produced. It is advisable never to exceed the quantity of phosphorus that is prescribed here, and in other similar experiments.

21. Take a similar quantity of oxymuriate of potash, with 3 or 4 grains of flower of sulphur, and mix the ingredients very well on paper. If a little of this mixture be taken up on the point of a knife and dropped into a wine-glass containing some sulphuric acid, a beautiful column of flame will be perceived, the moment the powder comes in contact with the acid.

22. Put a little oxymuriate of potash and a bit of phosphorus into an ale-glass, pour some cold water upon them cautiously, so as not to displace the salt. Now take a small glass tube, and plunge it into some sulphuric acid: then place the thumb upon the upper orifice, and in this state withdraw the tube, which must be instantly immersed in the glass, so that, on removing the thumb, the acid may be immediately conveyed upon the ingredients. This experiment is an example of a very singular phenomenon, combustion under water.

23. Proceed in all respects as in the last experiment, and add a morsel of phosphuret of lime. Here, besides the former appearance, we shall have combustion also on the surface of the water.

24. Prepare a mixture of equal parts of lump-sugar and oxymuriate of potash; put a small quantity of this mixture upon a plate or a tile; then dip a piece of sewing-thread into a phial of sulphuric acid, so as to convey the smallest quantity of the acid: with this touch the powder, and an immediate burst of flame will be the consequence.

25. Mix, without much friction, 10 grains of oxymuriate of potash with

1 grain of phosphorus, and drop the mixture into concentrated sulphuric acid. This is an instance of detonation and flame being produced by the mixture of a powder with a *cold* liquid.

26. Add a few grains of oxymuriate of potash to a teaspoonful or two of alcohol, drop one or two drops of sulphuric acid upon the mixture, and the whole will burst into flame, forming a very beautiful appearance.

27. A mixture of oxymuriate of potash and arsenic furnishes a detonating compound, which takes fire with the utmost rapidity. The salt and metal, first separately powdered, may be mixed by the gentlest possible triture, or rather by stirring them together on paper with the point of a knife. If two long trains be laid on a table, the one of gunpowder and the other of this mixture, and they be in contact with each other at one end, so that they may be fired at once, the arsenical mixture burns with the rapidity of lightning, while the other burns with comparative slowness.

28. Into an ale-glass of water put a few pieces of zinc, and a small bit of phosphorus; then drop a little sulphuric acid upon the mixture by means of a glass tube, as described in Experiment 22, and phosphuretted hydrogen will presently be disengaged, which will inflame on rising to the surface of the water.

29. Take a small piece of phosphuret of lime a little moistened by the air, and let a single drop of concentrated muriatic acid fall upon it. In this case phosphuretted hydrogen will also be evolved, accompanied by small balls of fire darting from the mixture, and the most intolerable fetid smell that can be conceived.

30. If 20 grains of phosphorus, cut very small, and mixed with 40 grains of finely granulated zinc, be put into 4 drachms of water, and 2 drachms of concentrated sulphuric acid be added thereto, bubbles of inflamed phosphuretted hydrogen gas will quickly cover the whole surface of the fluid in succession, forming a real aqueous fountain of fire.

31. If any light substance, capable of conducting heat, be placed upon the surface of boiling water, and a bit of phosphorus be laid upon it, the heat of the water will be sufficient to set the phosphorus on fire.

32. If 1 grain of dry nitrate of bismuth be previously mixed with 1 of phosphorus, and then rubbed together in a metallic mortar, a loud detona tion will be produced.

33. Drop a piece of phosphorus about the size of a pea into a tumbler of hot water, and from a bladder, furnished with a stop-cock, force a stream of oxygen gas directly upon it. This will afford the most brilliant combustion under water that can be imagined.

34. Put a little alcohol in a tea-cup, set it on fire, and invert a large bell-glass over it. In a short time an aqueous vapour will be seen to condense upon the inside of the bell, which, by means of a dry sponge, may be collected, and its quantity ascertained. This may be adduced as an example of the formation of water by combustion.

35. Take the metallic substance formed in the 36th experiment, called potassium, make it very hot, and confine it in a small glass vessel of oxygen gas. Here a rapid combustion, with a brilliant white flame will be produced, and the metallic globules will be converted into a white and solid mass, which will be found to be regenerated pure potash.

36. Take a small piece of pure potash, gently breathe on its surface, and place it on an insulated plate connected with the negative side of a powerful galvanic battery in a state of intense activity. Then bring a metallic wire from the positive side of the battery in contact with the upper surface of the alkali, and soon a very vivid action will be observed. Small globules, having a high metallic lustre, and of the appearance of quicksilver, will be seen, some of which will burn with explosion and a bright flame as soon as they are formed. Thus potash may be decomposed, and its metallic base rendered visible in a separate state.

37. Place a small piece of potassium within a dry wine-glass, and in order to acquire an idea of its specific gravity, pour a little alcohol, ether, or naphtha upon it; when, quitting the bottom of the glass, it will immediately rise to the surface of the liquid, it being, notwithstanding its metallic appearance, the lightest fluid body known.

38. If a little potassium be dropped into a jar of oxymuriatic gas, it burns spontaneously, and emits a bright red light. In this experiment a white salt is formed, being a true muriate of potash.

39. If a globule of potassium be thrown upon water, it decomposes it with great violence: an instantaneous explosion is produced with brilliant flame, and a solution of pure potash is the result.

40. If a similar globule be placed upon ice, it will spontaneously burn with a bright flame, and perforate a deep hole in the ice, which will contain a solution of potash.

41. Take a piece of moistened turmeric paper and drop a globule of potassium upon it. At the moment that it comes into contact with the water it burns and moves rapidly upon the paper, as if in search of moisture, leaving behind it a deep reddish-brown trace.

42. When a globule of sodium is thrown into *hot* water, the decomposition of the water is so violent that small particles of the metal are thrown out of the water, and actually burn with scintillations and flame in passing through the atmosphere.

Sheep Husbandry.

1. If the production of wool is the object, take the Merino and Saxon, and, if possible, procure Rambouillet and Paular rams to cross on the first, as they are the largest and most superior class of animals we know, they being originally derived from the same source, viz: the Merinos of Spain.

2. If delicate mutton is wanted, with a medium fibre of wool, take South Downs.

3. If larger mutton, with somewhat coarser quality of wool than the last, though much longer and more of it, is desired, procure Cotswold, Leicester, Bakewell, Lincoln, or New Oxford.

4. Many of those who have crossed the South Downs with the Leicester and the other long-woolled sheep, prefer these, for the reasons stated in No. 2.

5. Others greatly prefer a cross of the Leicester with the Merino, half and half, and then breeding those grades together. Their reasons in favour of this cross are these:—1st, It gives a large sheep, with plenty of mutton. 2d. A large fleece of wool, and of sufficient fineness for all purposes of do

mestic manufacture,,and gets rid of the troublesome length of the pure Leicester. 3. The animal is in good shape, good constitution, thrifty, hardy, and comes to maturity one year sooner than the Merino, has nothing of his rugged appearance, and has little or no gum in his wool.

Twelve Experimental Receipts on the Earths.

1. Pour a little lime-water into a wineglass and put some solution of oxalate of ammonia, equally transparent, into another glass. If the two clear liquors be poured together, a white precipitate of oxalate of lime will immediately become visible.

2. Pour a little lime-water into a phial, and throw some carbonic acid into it. The carbonic acid will seize the lime, and precipitate it in the state of carbonate of lime.

3. Take the phial made use of in the last experimen, vith its contents, and convey an additional portion of carbonic acid into it. The carbonate of lime will now be re-dissolved, and the liquor rendered transparent.

4. Take the transparent liquid produced in the last experiment, and give it heat. The earth will now be precipitated in the state of carbonate of lime, as before.

5. Pour some lime-water into a wine-glass, and a little solution of carbonate of potash into another glass. When these two transparent fluids are thrown together, an abundant precipitate of carbonate of lime will be the consequence.

6. Proceed as in the last experiment, but instead of carbonate of potash, pour a solution of Epsom salt into one of the glasses. When these transparent fluids are poured together, a mixed precipitate of carbonate of magnesia and sulphate of lime will be produced.

7. For another experiment, take in the same manner, separately, lime-water and a solution of alum. The union of these solutions will produce a mixed precipitate of alumina and sulphate of lime.

8. If a strong solution of caustic potash and a saturated solution of Epsom salt be mixed, the union of these transparent fluids will produce also an abundant precipitate. But this will consist of magnesia and sulphate of potash.

9. To a glass of water suspected to contain carbonic acid, add a small quantity of any of the other acids. If carbonic acid be present, it will become visible by a sparkling appearance on the sides of the glass and surface of the fluid.

10. Prepare two glasses of pure water, and into one of them drop a single drop of sulphuric acid, and mix it with the water. Pour a little muriate of barytes into the other glass, and no change will be perceived; pour some of the same solution into the first glass, containing the sulphuric acid, and a white precipitate of sulphate of barytes will be produced.

11. Prepare two glasses of water as before, conduct the experiment in the same way as the last, but instead of muriate of barytes, use nitrate of lead. In this case sulphate of lead will be precipitated.

12. Fill a glass tumbler half full of lime-water; then breathe into it frequently, at the same time stirring it with a piece of glass. The fluid, which was before perfectly transparent, will presently become quite white, and if suffered to remain at rest, real chalk will be deposited.

Black Lozenges.

Liquorice, 2 parts; lump-sugar, 5 parts; powdered gum tragacanth, 2 parts. Make into a smooth paste, sufficiently thick to bear cutting into lozenges.

To restore the Black Leather of Old Furniture.

Eggs, yolk and white well beaten, 6 parts; treacle, 1 part; isinglass, 1 part; water, 5 parts. Dissolve the isinglass in the water, then add it to the other articles. Mix well. Colour with lampblack. This also forms a good varnish for dress shoes.

Black Oil.

Oil of turpentine, ½ gallon; oil of vitriol, 12 ounces. Mix cautiously, then add rape oil, 1 gallon.

Common Black Paint.

Ivory or lampblack, 1 cwt.; road dust, 2 cwt.; lime-water, 15 gallons; oil to grind (factitious linseed).

Black Pectoral Lozenges.

Liquorice, 1 pound; white sugar, 2 pounds; powdered ipecacuanha, 2 ounces. Mix with mucilage.

Black Reviver.

1. Galls, bruised, 1 pound; logwood, 1 pound; water, 1¼ gallon. Boil until reduced to one gallon, then add green copperas, 4 ounces. Dissolve and strain, when cold add ox gall, 8 ounces. Mix and bottle for use.

2. Galls, 2 ounces; logwood, 2 ounces; sumach, 2 ounces; water, 3 pints. Boil to two pints, strain and add sulphate of iron, 1 ounce. Dissolve and add prepared ox gall, 1½ ounces. Shake until mixed. Keep it closely corked.

3. Logwood, 4 parts; galls, 1 part; soft water, 12 parts; sulphate of the protoxide of iron, 1 part. Boil the first three for one hour, then cool, decant the clear liquid, add the iron, and cork immediately.

Black Sealing Wax.

1. Shell lac, 2 parts; yellow resin, 3 parts; ivory black, 2 parts. Powder fine and mix by melting carefully.

2. Yellow resin, 15 pounds; lard, 1 pound; beeswax, 1 pound; lampblack, 3 pounds. Mix with heat.

To Clean Black Silks.

To bullock's gall, add boiling water sufficient to make it warm, and with a clean sponge rub the silk well on both sides; squeeze it well out, and proceed again in like manner. Rinse it in spring water, and change the water till perfectly clean, dry it in the air, and pin it out on a table; but first dip the sponge in glue-water, and rub it on the wrong side; then dry it before a fire.

To Dye Woollens Black.

Take the cloth previously dyed blue and boil it for two hours in a bath of gall-nuts, then pass it for two hours through a hot bath of logwood and copperas.

Black Soap.

Take common soft soap; ivory black or chimney soot to colour.

Black Sprinkle for Leather Book-Covers, &c.

Green copperas, 1 part; soft water, hot, 6 parts. Dissolve.

Black Stain for Glass.

1. Black scales of iron, 29 parts; white crystal glass, 4 parts; antimony, 2 parts; manganese, 1 part; vinegar to mix.

2. Glass of antimony, 1 part; oxide of copper, 2 parts; crystal glass, 3 parts. Mix.

Black Varnish.

Take any varnish, of the class you wish, 16 parts; lampblack, 2 parts. Grind the black in a small quantity of the varnish, then mix it with the remainder.

To Clean Black Veils.

Pass them through a warm liquor of bullock's gall and water; rinse in cold water; then take a small piece of glue, pour boiling water on it, and pass the veil through it; clap it, and frame to dry.

Black Wash.

Calomel, 120 grains; lime-water, 1 pint. Mix. Used as a wash for syphilitic ulcers, &c.

Bleeding of a Wound.

1. Make two or three tight ligatures towards the lower part of each joint; slacken them gradually.

2. Apply tops of nettles, bruised.

3. Strew on it the ashes of a linen rag, dipped in sharp vinegar and burnt.

4. Take ripe puff-balls, break them warily, and save the powder. Strew this on the wound and bind it on. This will stop the bleeding of an amputated limb.

Spitting of Blood.

1. Take two spoonfuls of the juice of nettles every morning, and a large cup of the decoction of nettles at night, for a week.

2. Take three spoonfuls of sage-juice in a little honey. This presently stops either spitting or vomiting blood.

3. Take twenty grains of alum in water every two hours.

Vomiting of Blood.

1. Take two spoonfuls of nettle juice. This also dissolves blood coagulated in the stomach.

2. Take as much saltpetre as will lie upon half a crown, dissolved in a glass of cold water, two or three times a day.

To Dissolve Coagulated Blood.

1. Bind on the part for some hours a paste made of black soap and crumbs of white bread.

2. Take grated root of burdock spread upon a rag: renew this twice a day.

Biles.

1. Apply a little Venice turpentine.
2. An equal quantity of soap and brown sugar, well mixed.
3. A plaster of honey and wheat flour, or figs.
4. Or a little saffron in a white bread poultice. It is proper to purge also.

Hard Breasts.

Apply turnips roasted till soft, then mashed and mixed with a little oil of roses. Change this twice a day, keeping the breast very warm with flannel.

Sore Breasts and Swelled.

Boil a handful of camomile, and as much mallows in milk and water Foment with it between two flannels, as hot as can be borne, every twelve hours. It also dissolves any knot or swelling in any part where there is no inflammation.

A Bruise.

1. Immediately apply molasses spread on brown paper.
2. Apply a plaster of chopped parsley mixed with butter.

Pain in the Stomach from bad Digestion.

1. Take fasting, or in the fit, half a pint of camomile tea. Do this five or six mornings.
2. Take from twenty to forty drops of elixir of vitriol in sage tea twice or thrice a day.
3. Take two or three tea-spoonfuls of stomachic-tincture, in a glass of water, three times a day. The tincture is made thus: gentian-root, sliced, 1 ounce; orange-peel, dried, ½ ounce; proof brandy, 1 pint. In three or four days it is fit for use. This is useful in all disorders that arise from a relaxed stomach.

Choleric Hot Pains in the Stomach.

Take a pint of the decoction of ground ivy, with a tea-spoonful of the powder of it, five or six mornings.

Pain in the Stomach, with Coldness and Wind.

Swallow five or six grains of white pepper for six or seven mornings.

Stone, to ease or cure.

1. Boil half a pound of parsnips in a quart of water. Drink a glass of this morning and evening, and use no other drink all the day. It usually cures in six weeks.
2. Take morning and evening a tea-spoonful of onions, calcined in a fire-shovel into white ashes, in white wine. An ounce will often dissolve the stone.
3. Take a tea-spoonful of violet-seed, powdered, morning and evening It both wastes the stone, and brings it away.

Stone in the Kidneys.

Boil an ounce of common thistle-root, and four drachms of liquorice in a pint of water. Drink half of it every morning.

Blisters

On the feet, occasioned by walking, are cured by drawing a needle-fu of worsted through them ; clip it off at both ends, and leave it till the skin peels off.

In a raging Fit.

1. Beat onions to a pulp and apply them, as a poultice, to the back, or to the groin. It gives speedy ease in the most racking pain.

2. Apply heated parsley.

The Stranguary.

1. Sit over the steam of warm water.

2. Drink largely of a decoction of turnips, sweetened with clarified honey.

3. Drink of warm lemonade.

4. Dissolve half an ounce of saltpetre in a quart of water ; drink a glass of it every hour. Dangerous.

Sunburn, Smarting.

Wash the face with sage tea.

Indolent Swellings,

Are often cured by warm steams.

Soft and Flabby Swellings.

1. Pump cold water on them daily.

2. Use constant frictions, or proper bandages.

A White Swelling on the Joints.

1. Pump on the part half an hour every morning. This cures also pains in the joints. It seldom fails.

2. A stream of cold water one day, and warm the next, and so on by turns. Use these remedies at first, if possible. It is likewise proper to intermix gentle purges to prevent a relapse.

3 Boiled nettles applied to the part.

To dissolve White or Hard Swellings.

1. Take white roses, elder flowers, leaves of fox-glove, and of St. John's-wort a handful of each ; mix them with hog's lard, and make an ointment.

2. Hold them morning and evening, in the steam of vinegar, poured on red-hot flints.

To Fasten the Teeth.

Put powdered alum, the quantity of a nutmeg, in a quart of spring water for twenty-four hours. Then strain the water and gargle with it.

To Clean the Teeth.

Rub them with the ashes of burnt bread.

To prevent the Tooth-Ache.

Wash the mouth with cold water every morning, and rinse it after every meal.

Barley Sugar.

"Take a quantity of clarified sugar in that state, that on dipping the finger into the pan the sugar which adheres to it will break with a slight noise; this is called *crack*. When the sugar is near this, put in two or three drops of lemon-juice, or a little vinegar, to prevent its graining. When it has come to the *crack* take it off instantly, and dip the pan into cold water to prevent its burning; let it stand a little, and then pour it on a marble which must be previously rubbed with oil. Cut the sugar into small pieces, when it will be ready for use. One drop of citron will flavour a considerable quantity."

Barley Water.

1. Pearl barley, 4 ounces; water, 6 pints. Boil to four pints and strain.

2. Barley (pearl), 4 ounces; water, 6 pints. Boil to four pints, then add figs, 4 ounces; stoned raisins, 2 ounces. Boil for ten minutes and strain.

A Simple Barometer.

Take a common phial, and cut off the rim and part of the neck, by means of a piece of cord passed round it, and moved rapidly to and fro, in a sawing direction; the one end being held in the left hand and the other fastened to any convenient object, while the right hand holds and moves the phial; when heated, dip it suddenly into cold water, and the part will crack off; or separate it with a file. Then nearly fill the phial with clean water, place your finger on the mouth and invert it; withdraw your finger and suspend it in this position with a piece of twine. In dry weather the under surface of the water will be level with the neck of the bottle, or even concave; in damp weather, on the contrary, a drop will appear at the mouth and continue until it falls, and is then followed by another in the same way.

Black Basilicon.

1. Yellow wax, 14 pounds; yellow resin, 28 pounds; black resin, 28 pounds; rape oil, 44 pounds. Mix with heat.

2. Yellow wax, 23 pounds; yellow resin, 23 pounds; black resin, 23 pounds; rape oil, 40 pounds. Melt and partly cool, then stir in water, 1 gallon.

Yellow Basilicon.

1. Yellow wax, 10 pounds; yellow resin, 65 pounds; rape oil, 28 pounds. Melt and well mix, then add water, 2 gallons. Well stir in. If too thick, thin with rape oil.

2. Yellow resin, 27 pounds: yellow wax, 27 pounds; Burgundy pitch, 27 pounds; rape oil, 28 pounds; spirits of turpentine, 5 pounds. Melt the first four articles together, then cool a little and stir in the turpentine.

Bates' Anodyne Balsam.

Laudanum, 1 part; opodeldoc, 2 parts. Mix.

Blue Sprinkle for Bookbinders.

Strong sulphuric acid, 8 ounces; Spanish indigo, powdered, 2 ounces. Mix in a bottle that will hold a quart, and place it in a water-bath to promote solution. For use, dilute a little to the required colour in a teacup.

Barry's Resinous Extract of Bark.

Bark (bruised), 1 pound ; alcohol, 7 pounds. Macerate in a close vessc for one week, then decant the tincture and distil until it is of the consistence of a thin extract, then remove the rosin on its surface, and evaporate to the proper consistence.

Blue Sealing-Wax.

Shell lac, 2 parts; smalts, 1 part; yellow resin, 2 parts. Powder and mix carefully with heat.

Blue Verditer.

1. Dissolve copper (cold) in nitric acid (aqua fortis), and produce a precipitation of it by means of quick-lime, employed in such doses that it will be absorbed by the acid, in order that the precipitate may be pure copper; that is, without any mixture. When the liquor has been decanted, wash the precipitate, and spread it out on a piece of linen cloth to drain. If a portion of this precipitate, which is green, be placed on a grinding-stone, and if a little quicklime in powder be added, the green colour will be immediately changed into a beautiful blue. The proportion of the lime added is from seven to ten parts in a hundred. When the whole matter acquires the consistence of paste, desiccation soon takes place.

Blue verditer is proper for distemper, and for varnish ; but it is not fit for oil-painting, as the oil renders it very dark. If used, it ought to be brightened with a great deal of white.

2. Into 100 pounds of whiting pour the copper-water, and stir them together every day for some hours, till the water grows pale; then pour that away, set it by for other use, and pour on more of the green water, and so till the verditer be made; which, being taken out, is laid on large pieces of chalk in the sun, till it be dry and fit for market.

3. Fully saturate the liquor which is used in parting with silver, which is precipitated by adding very pure copper. This nitrous solution of copper must be properly diluted with very pure water,—distilled is the best, and the copper precipitated on chalk properly prepared. The colour and chalk must be well mixed together and properly dried.

4. To a solution of nitrate of copper add lime or lime-water, as long as any green precipitate falls down. Filter the solution and dry the precipitate, which must be ground and kept quite free from dust: the green colour will, by this time, be converted into a beautiful blue.

Body Varnish.

African copal, 1 part. Fuse, then add pale oil, 2 parts. Boil very gently until quite stringy, cool a little, and add spirits of turpentine, 4 parts. Mix well.

Quick Drying Body Varnish.

Copal (pale), 16 parts; pale oil, 32 parts; dried sugar of lead, 1 part; spirits of turpentine, 55 parts. Boil until stringy and strain, then gum animé, 16 parts; pale oil, 32 parts ; spirits of turpentine, 55 parts; white copperas, dried and powdered, 1 part. Boil and strain as before, then mix the two quantities together.

Twenty-six Experimental Receipts on the Gases.

1. Put about an ounce of marble grossly pulverized into an eight-ounce phial, with about an equal quantity of water Pour upon it a little sulphuric acid, and carbonic acid gas will be evolved.

2. Put some iron wire into a phial with about three or four ounces of water; pour a little sulphuric acid upon the contents, and hydrogen gas will be evolved.

3. Pour water into a small glass retort, so as to occupy about one-third of its capacity, lute its beak into the end of a gun-barrel, the middle of which must be kept hot in a furnace, or by a chafing-dish; then if a lamp be applied to the retort so as to cause the water to boil, the steam will pass through the red-hot iron tube, and the water in this case also will be decomposed; for, as the oxygen combines with the iron, the hydrogen gas will be liberated, and may be collected in the usual way.

4. Put some sulphuret of iron into a phial, pour a little diluted sulphuric acid over it, and attach a bladder, prepared as directed for Experiment No. 1, to the phial. Sulphuretted hydrogen, a gas extremely fetid and disagreeable, will immediately be evolved: though the ingredients here employed were destitute of smell.

5. Put an ounce or two of the black oxide of manganese into a small glass retort, pour a little concentrated sulphuric acid upon it, and apply the heat of a lamp. Oxygen gas will be disengaged in abundance.

6. If the leaves of a plant, fresh gathered, be placed in the sun, very pure oxygen gas may be collected.

7. Into a small glass retort put a mixture of two parts of quicklime, and one of muriate of ammonia, both in powder. Apply the heat of a lamp, and ammoniacal gas will come over.

8. Pour a little sulphuric acid upon a small quantity of quicksilver in a glass retort, apply heat, and sulphurous acid gas may be collected.

9. Take some copper-wire or a few shreds of copper, and pour over them a little diluted nitrous acid, in the proportion of about three parts of water to one of acid. The gas evolved in this case is nitrous gas.

10. Upon an ounce or two of nitrate of potash in a glass retort pour some sulphuric acid; give it heat by means of a lamp, and collect nitric acid gas.

11. Treat muriate of soda in the same manner with sulphuric acid, and muriatic acid in the gaseous form will rise from the retort.

12. Convey some muriatic acid gas into a glass jar containing a portion of the gas produced in Experiment 7. From the mixture of these two invisible gases a solid substance will be produced, viz: the common sal ammoniac; this may be perceived to deposit itself upon the sides of the vessel in a neat crystallized form.

13. Convey some carbonic acid gas into a glass jar containing a portion of ammoniacal gas. The instant the two gases come into contact, a great absorption will take place, and solid carbonate of ammonia will be formed on the inner surface of the jar.

14. Whenever uncombined muriatic, or any volatile acid is suspected to be present in any chemical mixture, it may be detected by ammonia. A single drop of ammonia on a feather, or small slip of paper, held over the mixture, will immediately render the vapour visible.

15. Ammonia in solution may in like manner be detected by a single drop of muriatic, or acetic acid, which will produce very evident white fumes. This is merely the reverse of the former experiment.

16. Procure a bladder furnished with a stop-cock, fill it with hydrogen gas, and then adapt a tobacco-pipe to it. By dipping the bowl of the pipe into a lather of soap, and pressing the bladder, soap-bubbles will be formed, filled with hydrogen gas. These bubbles will rise into the atmosphere, as they are formed, and convey a good idea of the principle upon which air-balloons are inflated.

17. Procure a bladder similar to that described in the last experiment, and charge it with a mixture of oxygen and hydrogen gases. With this apparatus blow up soap-bubbles as before, and touch them with a lighted match. The bubbles as they rise will explode with a smart noise.

18. Fill a bladder with hydrogen gas; apply a lighted match to the end of the tobacco-pipe, and press the bladder gently. A pencil of flame, extremely beautiful, will be seen issuing from the pipe, till the whole of the hydrogen gas is consumed.

19. Place some small phials on the shelf of the pneumatic tub filled with water, and inverted as usual for receiving gases. Now fill these with mixed oxygen and hydrogen gases from the bladder. A lighted match will cause any one of them to explode with violence. When the phials are used, it will be prudent to fold them round with a handkerchief, to prevent any injury being received from the glass in case of bursting; but if small bladders be employed in place of the phials, this precaution will be unnecessary.

20. Procure a glass jar, such as is generally used for deflagrating the gases, and fill it with oxymuriatic acid gas. If nickel, arsenic, or bismuth in powder, be thrown into this gas, and the temperature of the atmosphere be not lower than 70°, the metal will inflame, and continue to burn with the most brilliant combustion.

21. Put a small piece of phosphorus into a crucible, cover it closely with carbonate of lime or pulverized common chalk, so as to fill the crucible. Let another crucible be inverted upon it, and both subjected to the fire. When the whole has become perfectly red-hot, remove them from the fire; and when cold, the carbonic acid of the chalk will have been decomposed, and the black charcoal, the basis of the acid, may be easily perceived amongst the materials.

22. Place a lighted wax taper within a narrow glass jar, then take a jar or phial of carbonic acid gas, and cautiously pour it into the jar containing the taper. This being an invisible gas, the operator will appear to invert merely an empty vessel, though the taper will be as effectually and instantaneously extinguished as if water itself had been used.

23. Let sulphuric acid be poured into a saucer upon some acetate of potash. Into another saucer put a mixture of about two parts of quick-lime, and one of sal ammoniac, both in powder, adding to these a very small quantity of boiling water. Both saucers while separate will yield invisible gases: but the moment they are brought close together, the operator will be enveloped in very visible vapours. Muriate of soda, in this experiment, may be substituted for acetate of potash

24. It is an interesting experiment to place a glow-worm within a jar of oxygen gas, in a dark room. The insect will shine with much greater brilliancy than it does in atmospheric air, and appear more alert. As the luminous appearance depends on the will of the animal, this experiment probably affords an instance of the stimulus which this gas communicates to the animal system.

25. Paste a slip of litmus paper within a glass jar, near the bottom, then fill the jar with water, and invert it on the shelf of a pneumatic trough. If as much nitrous gas, previously well washed, be passed into the jar as will displace the water below the level of the paper, the colour of the litmus paper will still remain unaltered; but on passing up atmospheric air it will immediately be reddened; showing the formation of an acid, by the mixture of two gases.

26. Take a few grains of citric acid, and twice as much dry carbonate of potash, or of soda, both in powder; mix them, and put them into a dry glass. No chemical change will take place in either of these salts; but the moment water is poured upon them, an effervescence and extrication of gas will ensue, affording an instance of the necessity of water to promote some chemical decompositions.

Boiled or Drying Oil.

1. Linseed oil, 16 pints; litharge, finely powdered, 3 pounds. Mix and digest at a boiling heat for two hours.

2. Linseed oil, 20 parts; finely powdered litharge, 4 parts. Keep them together for one month in a warm place, occasionally shaking the bottle, then draw off the clear.

3. Linseed oil, 2 gallons; water, 2 gallons; finely powdered white vitriol, 1 pound. Boil until reduced to two gallons.

Bologna Phial.

The Bologna, or philosophical phial, is a small vessel of glass which has been suddenly cooled, open at the upper end, and rounded at the bottom. It is made so thick at the bottom, that it will bear a smart blow against a hard body without breaking; but if a little pebble, or piece of flint, is let fall into it, it immediately cracks, and the bottom falls into pieces; but, unless the pebble or flint is large and angular enough to scratch the surface of the glass, it will not break.

Bon-Bons.

Provide leaden moulds, which must be of various shapes, and be oiled with oil of sweet almonds. Take a quantity of brown-sugar syrup in the proportion to their size, in that state called a blow, which may be known by dipping the skimmer into the sugar, shaking it, and blowing through the holes, when parts of light may be seen; add a drop of any esteemed essence. If the bon-bons are preferred white, when the sugar has cooled a little, stir it round the pan till it grains, and shines on the surface; then pour it into a funnel and fill the little moulds, when it will take a proper form and harden; as soon as it is cold take it from the moulds; dry it two or three days, and put it upon paper. If the bon-bons are required to be coloured, add the colour just as the sugar is ready to be taken off the fire

To Clean Boots.

To make boots look well, always use boot-trees, and brush your blacking off while damp. On no account lay on too much blacking, so as to make the leather wet, and do not let it dry before polishing.

To render Boots Waterproof.

Boiled oil, 16 parts; turpentine (spt.), 2 parts; bee's-wax, 1 part; resin, 1 part; turpentine (Venice), 2 parts. Melt, and use hot.

Boquet de la Reine.

Essence of bergamot, 8 parts; English oil of lavender, 3 parts; oil of cloves, and aromatic vinegar, together, 1 part; alcohol, 20 parts; essence of musk, 1 part. Mix, and agitate occasionally for a week.

Engraver's Border-Wax.

Bee's-wax, 1 part; pitch, 2 parts; tallow, 1 part. Mix.

Botany Bay Cement, for China.

Yellow gum, 16 parts; fine brick-dust, 17 parts. Mix.

Common Bottle Cement.

Resin, pitch, ivory-black, equal parts. Used to secure the corks.

Bottle Glass.

Sand, 100 parts; kelp, 40 parts; glauber salts, 5 parts; wood ashes, 200 parts. Melt.

Art of Bottling Wine.

Procure clean bottles, good velvet corks, wine fine and brilliant; then proceed to bottling, and be careful to drive the corks in tight; lastly, stow the wine away, laying every bottle on its side, and do not spare the saw-dust. It is better to compress the corks by means of a cooper's bottling machine before you place them in the bottles.

To Ripen Bottled Malt Liquors.

Yeast, 1 part; sugar, 4 parts; water, 5 parts. Mix, and put a spoonful into each bottle before corking. This will make malt liquors brisk in twelve to twenty hours in warm weather.

Instantaneous Light Bottles.

Take a suitable bottle, and one-third fill it with asbestos or powdered glass, then pour in a sufficient quantity of concentrated sulphuric acid to fill up the pores of the powder or asbestos, without running about. To be used with an instantaneous light match. The tip of the match on touching the acid will immediately inflame.

Black Bottle Wax.

Common resin, 20 pounds; tallow, 5 pounds; lamp-black, 4 pounds. Mix, with heat.

Red Bottle Wax.

Common resin, 15 pounds; tallow, 4 pounds; red lead, 5 pounds. Mix, with heat. Any colour may be employed.

Balsamic Ether.

Put 4 ounces of spirits of wine, and 3 ounces of balsam of tolu, into a phial with 1 ounce of ether. Keep it well corked. But it will not keep above a week.

To make Elixir of Vitriol.

Drop gradually 4 ounces of strong oil of vitriol into a pint of spirits of wine, or brandy; let it stand three days, and add to it, ginger sliced, half an ounce, and Jamaica pepper, whole, 1 ounce. In three days more it is fit for use.

To prevent Abortion.

Women of a weak or relaxed habit, should use solid food, avoiding great quantities of tea, and other weak and watery liquors. They should go soon to bed and rise early; and take frequent exercise, but avoid fatigue.

If of a full habit, they ought to use a spare diet, and chiefly of the vegetable kind, avoiding strong liquors, and every thing that may tend to heat the body or increase the quantity of blood.

In the first case, take daily half a pint of the decoction of lignum vitæ; boiling an ounce of it in a quart of water five minutes. In the latter case, give half a drachm of powdered nitre, in a cup of water-gruel, every five or six hours. In both cases, she should sleep on a hard mattress, and be kept cool and quiet. The bowels should be kept regular by a pill of white walnut extract, or bitter root.

To Remove Freckles.

Take tincture of benzoin, 1 pint; tincture of tolu, ½ pint; oil of rosemary ¼ ounce. Mix. One tea-spoonful of the tincture to be put in half a gill of water, and with a towel dipped in this rub well the face, night and morning

A Liquid to clean Clothes from Grease.

This is the best receipt known for the extraction of grease. Take one peck of lime; add thereto as much water as will dissolve the lime and leave about two gallons of clear water after it has been well stirred and settled. Let it stand about two hours, and then pour off the clear liquid into another vessel. Now add to it three ounces of pearlash for every gallon of the liquid, stir it well, and, when settled, bottle it for use. This liquor is to be diluted with water, to suit the strength or delicacy of the colour of the cloth. It is applied with a piece of coarse sponge, rubbing out the grease, and applying clear water afterwards.

Baldness.

Take water, 1 pint; pearlash, ½ ounce; onion juice, 1 gill. Mix, and cork in a bottle. Rub the head hard with a rough linen towel dipped in the mixture.

Remedy for Chapped Hands.

Take one ounce of bitter almonds; peel them and mash them into a paste with oil of sweet almonds and the yolk of an egg, adding a little tincture of benzoin, so as to form a thick cream. Now add a few drops of oil of caraway. It is to be rubbed on the hands at night, and a soft kid glove is to be worn during the treatment.

Dr. Bateman's Itch Ointment.

Take sulphur, 2 ounces; powdered pearlash, 1 ounce; lard, 4 ounces; melt, then stir in rose-water, 1 ounce; vermilion, 2 drachms; bergamot, 1 drachm.

Bath Metal.

1. Take brass, 32 parts; spelter, 9 parts. Mix.
2. Take brass, 35 parts; zinc, 9 parts. Mix.

Bath Pipe.

Take powdered white sugar, 16 parts; Italian juice, dissolved in a little water, 2 parts; powdered gum Arabic, 1 part. Make them into a stiff mass with warm water, and roll it into the usual form.

Temperature of Baths. (Thompson.)

The hot bath, (balneum calidum,) from 90 to 100 degrees. The tepid bath, (balneum tepidum,) from 62 to 96 degrees. The vapour bath, (balneum vaporis,) from 100 to 130 degrees.

Bartley's Green Senna Powder.

Pick out the yellowest senna leaves you can find, and add a little powdered indigo, or charcoal, to produce the desired colour.

Bartley's Liquor Opii Sedativus.

Take opium, 2 parts; distilled vinegar, 1 part; water sufficient to reduce it to the proper strength. Digest for one month, then add to every pint, alcohol 2 drachms, and filter.

Brown Mixture.

Take extract of liquorice, 3 drachms; dissolve it in 5 ounces of boiling water, by rubbing it in a mortar, and adding the water gradually. Then add powdered gum arabic, 2 drachms. Let the mixture cool, and add antimonial wine, 2 drachms; acetic tincture of opium, 1 drachm. This is is a valuable expectorant. The same quantity of laudanum, or three times the quantity of paregoric elixir, may be substituted for the acetic tincture of opium, if this be not at hand. Dose, for an adult, a tablespoonful every two or three hours.

Baynton's Adhesive Plaster.

Take simple diachylon, 4 pounds; yellow resin, 3 ounces. Mix with heat.

Oil of Bays, for Horses, &c.

Take bay leaves, 2 pounds; bay berries, 1 pound; cabbage leaves, 1 pound; lard, 5 pounds. Boil and strain.

To ascertain the Quality of Beef.

If young, the flesh will have a fine smooth, open grain, of a good red colour, and feel tender. The fat should be white; if yellow, or deep yellow, the animal has (generally) been fed on oil cake, and the flesh will be flabby. *Cow beef* has whiter fat, lean duller red, and closer grain. *Bull beef*, grain still closer, fat hard and skinny, lean deeper red, and a stronger scent. Heifer beef, finely red.

Cheap Beer.

Take water, 15 gallons; hops, ¼ pound. Boil half the water with the hops, then add it to the other half in the tun, and well mix it with one gallon of molasses and a little yeast. Ferment.

To ascertain beforehand the Colour and Age required for Beer, &c.

This depends on the temperature at which the malt has been made. and on its colour, as under:

Malt made at 119 degrees produces a white,—at 124 deg. a cream colour,—at 129 deg. a light yellow,—at 134 deg. an amber colour.

These, when properly brewed, become spontaneously fine, even as far as 138 degrees. When brewed for amber, by repeated fermentations, they become pellucid.—At 138 deg. a high amber.—At 143 deg. a pale brown.

By precipitation, these grow bright in a short time.—At 148 deg. a brown.—At 152 deg. a high brown.

With precipitation these require eight or ten months to be bright.—At 157 deg. a brown, inclining to black.—At 162 deg. a brown speckled with black.

With precipitation, these may be fined, but will never become bright.—At 167 deg. a blackish brown, speckled with black.. At 171 deg. a colour of burnt coffee.—At 176, a black.

These with difficulty can be brewed without setting the goods, and will by no means become bright, not even with the strongest acid menstruum.

Good Table Beer.

Take malt, 8 bushels; hops, 7 pounds; treacle, 25 pounds. Brew for ten barrels.

Beer Heading.

Take alum and sulphate of iron, equal quantities. Mix.

Cauliflower Beer Heading.

Take sulphate of iron, alum, common salt; equal parts. Mix.

Required Time to keep Beer.

This must depend on the heat employed to dry the malt. Malt made at 119° Fahr. may be drawn in 14 to 21 days; at 124°, 30 to 40 days; at 129, 80 to 90 days; at 134, 4 to 5 months; at 140, 6 to 7 months; at 145, 8 to 9 months; at 150, 10 to 11 months; at 155, 12 to 15 months; at 158, 15 to 18 months; at 162, 20 to 24 months. It is not however to be supposed that many public brewers allow their liquor such a length of time to ripen; artificial means are generally resorted to.

To bottle Beer

Follow the same plan as for porter.

To improve the Flavour of Beer, &c.

Put an ounce of ginger, bruised, and half an ounce of cloves, with a dozen coarse biscuits, and a few scalded hops, to every hogshead

Bell's Bougies.

Take litharge plaster, 1 pound; yellow wax, 6 ounces; olive oil 9 ounces. Mix with heat, and roll into cylinders of the sizes required

To colour Candied Sugar.

1. *Red.*—Boil an ounce of cochineal in half a pint of water for five minutes, add an ounce of cream of tartar, half an ounce of pounded alum, and boil them on a slow fire ten minutes; if it shows the colour clear on white paper, it is sufficient. Add two ounces of sugar, and bottle it for use.

2. *Blue.*—Put a little warm water on a plate, and rub indigo in it till the colour has come to the tint required.

3. *Yellow.*—Rub with some water a little gamboge on a plate; or infuse the heart of a yellow lily flower with milk-warm water.

4. *Green.*—Boil the leaves of spinach about a minute in a little water, and when strained bottle the liquor for use. In colouring refined sugars, taste and fancy must guide the workman.

To Candy Sugar.

To prepare Sugar for Candying.—The first process is *clarifying*, which is done thus: Break the white of an egg into a preserving pan; put to it four quarts of water, and beat it with a whisk to a froth. Then put in twelve pounds of sugar, mix all together, and set it over the fire. When it boils, put in a little cold water, and proceed as often as necessary, till the scum rises thick on the top. Then remove it from the fire, and when it is settled, take off the scum, and pass it through a straining bag. If the sugar should not appear very fine, boil it again before straining it.

To Candy Sugar.—After having completed the above first process, put what quantity is wanted over the fire, and boil it until it is smooth enough. This is known by dipping the skimmer into the sugar, and touching it between the fore-finger and thumb; and immediately on opening them a small thread will be observed drawn between, which will crystallize and break, and remain in a drop on the thumb, which will be a sign of its gaining some degree of smoothness. Boil it again, and it will draw into a larger string; it is now called *bloom sugar*, and must be boiled longer than in the former process. To try its forwardness, dip again the skimmer, shaking off the sugar into the pan; then blow with the mouth strongly through the holes, and if certain bladders go through, it has acquired the second degree. To prove if the liquid has arrived at the state called *feathered sugar*, redip the skimmer, and shake it over the pan, then give it a sudden flirt behind, and the sugar will fly off like feathers.

It now arrives to the state called *crackled sugar;* to obtain which the mass must be boiled longer than in the preceding degree; then dip a stick in it, and put it directly into a pan of cold water, draw off the sugar which hangs to the stick in the water, and if it turns hard and snaps, it has acquired the proper degree of crystallization: if otherwise, boil it again until it acquires that brittleness.

The last stage of refining this article is called *carmel sugar;* to obtain which it must be boiled longer than in any of the preceding methods; prove it by dipping a stick first into the sugar, and then into cold water, and the moment it touches the latter, it will, if matured, snap like glass. Be careful that the fire is not too fierce, as by flaming up against the sides of the pan, it will burn and discolour the sugar.

To prepare Bladders.

Soak them for twenty-four hours in water, to which a little chloride of lime or potass has been added, then remove the extraneous membranes well wash them in clean water and dry them.

Lemon Blancmange.

Isinglass, 1 part; water, 16 parts; lemon-juice, 2 parts; Lisbon wine, 8 parts. Sugar to sweeten, and a little grated lemon-peel to flavour. Clarify with an egg.

Mrs. Hoffman's Blancmange.

Isinglass, ¼ pound; rose-water, ½ pint; milk, 2 quarts; milk of almonds, ½ pint. Boil, and when milk-warm, pour into the moulds.

Bleached Sponge.

Hydrochloric acid, 1 part; water, 35 parts. Mix, and soak the sponge in it for a week, frequently squeezing it, then soak it in clear water for a week, repeatedly changing the water. Lastly, sulphurous acid, 1 part; water, 20 parts. Mix, and soak the sponge until sufficiently white, then repeat the operation of rinsing and squeezing in clear water, and perfume with rose, orange, or lavender.

Blistering Ointment for Cattle.

1. Yellow resin, 14 pounds; spirits of turpentine, 3 pounds; tallow, 2 pounds; lard, 20 pounds; powdered Spanish flies, 10 pounds; euphorbium, 1 pound; vinegar, 1 gallon. Mix.

2. Tallow, 16 pounds; oil of origanum, 4 pounds; powdered flies, 1 pound; powdered euphorbium, 1 pound. Mix.

3. Lard, 7 pounds; oil of turpentine, 1 pound; tar, 1 pound; powdered flies, 17 ounces. Mix.

4. Lard, 5 pounds; resin, 5 pounds; spirits of turpentine, 5 pounds; powdered flies, 2 pounds; oil of origanum, ½ pound. Mix.

Blistering Plaster.

1. Burgundy pitch, 12 pounds; turpentine, 4 pounds; Spanish flies, 6 pounds; wax, 1 pound; suet, 1 pound. Mix.

2. Yellow resin, 8 parts; yellow wax, 4 parts; suet, 3 parts; powdered Spanish flies, 7 parts; simple plaster, 10 parts; vinegar, 4 parts. Mix.

Compound Blistering Plaster.

Venice turpentine, 18 pounds; Burgundy pitch, 12 pounds; Spanish flies, 12 pounds; yellow wax, 4 pounds; verdigris, 1 pound; mustard, 3 ounces; black pepper, 3 ounces. Melt, and then stir in the flies.

Lotion for Blows, Bruises, and Sprains in Horses.

Laudanum, 1 part; oil of origanum, 2 parts; water of ammonia, 4 parts; oil of turpentine, 4 parts; camphor, 4 parts; spirits of wine, 32 parts. Put them into a bottle and shake them until mixed.

Blue Enamel.

Fine paste (not metallic), 10 parts; nitre, 3 parts. Oxide of cobalt to colour.

Blue Fire.

Nitre, 2 parts; sulphur, 3 parts; zinc, 3 parts; meal gunpowder, 4 parts. Mix.

Blue Fire for Lances, Rockets, &c.

Fine zinc filings, 1 part; antimony, 2 parts; nitre, 4 parts. Mix

Blue Flame.

Gunpowder, 1 part; King's yellow, 1 part; sulphur vivum, 2 parts; crude antimony, powdered, 4 parts; nitrate of potash, 14 parts. Mix and sift through lawn.

Blue Glass.

Plain paste, 300 parts; zaffre, 3 parts; manganese, 1 part. If the glass should be of too deep a blue, use less zaffre and manganese; if too purple, omit the manganese altogether.

Blue Marble for Books, &c.

Colour the edges with King's yellow, and when dry tie the book between boards. Throw on blue spots in the gum trough, wave them with the iron pin, and apply the edges thereon.

Blue Ointment.

Quicksilver, 3 pounds; Venice turpentine, 4 ounces. Kill the silver by rubbing in a mortar, then add lard, 12 pounds.

Common Blue Ointment.

For a very cheap article it is usual to omit half or more of the quicksilver, and bring up the colour with blue black.

Mild Blue Ointment.

Quicksilver, 1 pound; Venice turpentine, 2 ounces. Kill the silver then add lard, 5 pounds.

Strong Blue Ointment.

Quicksilver, 1 pound; milk of sulphur, 4 drachms; lard, 2 pounds Mix. The effect of the sulphur in killing the silver is almost immediate; that of the turpentine a little slower. The sulphur has a tendency to blacken the ointment if exposed to damp; the turpentine, if used in *any quantity*, may also be detected by its smell.

Blue Paint.

Blue black, ¼ cwt.; whiting, 1 cwt.; road dust, 2 cwt.; blue, ½ cwt.; lime-water, 12 gallons. Factitious linseed oil to grind.

Brazil Wood Paper.

Dip the paper into a decoction of Brazil wood.

Alkalized Brazil-Wood Paper.

Take red Brazil-wood paper, and brush it over with a weak alkaline solution.

Bread (for one Sack of Flour.)

Flour, 5 bushels; alum, ½ pound; salt, 4 pounds; yeast, ½ gallon; water sufficient. Mix.

Bread on Mrs. Cobbett's Plan.

Suppose the quantity be a bushel of flour. Put this flour into a trough that people may have for the purpose, or, it may be in a clean smooth tub of any shape, if not too deep, and sufficiently large. Make a pretty deep hole in the middle of this heap of flour. Take (for a bushel) a pint of good yeast, mix it and stir it well up in a pint of soft water milk-warm. Pour this into the hole in the heap of flour. Then take a spoon and work it round the outside of this body of moisture, so as to bring into it by degrees flour enough to make it form a thin batter, which must be stirred about well for a minute or two. Then take a handful of flour and scatter it thinly over the head of this batter, so as to hide it. Then cover the whole over with a cloth to keep it warm; and this covering, as well as the situation of the trough, as to distance from the fire, must depend on the nature of the place and state of the weather, as to heat and cold. When the batter has risen enough to make cracks in the flour, begin to form the whole mass into dough, thus: begin round the hole containing the batter, working the flour into the batter, and pouring in as it is wanted to make the flour mix with the batter, soft water, milk-warm, or milk. Before beginning this, scatter the salt over the heap, at the rate of half a pound to a bushel of flour. When the whole is sufficiently moist, knead it well. This is a grand part of the business; for, unless the dough be well worked, there will be little round lumps of flour in the loaves; and besides, the original batter, which is to give fermentation to the whole, will not be duly mixed. It must be rolled over, pressed out, folded up, and pressed out again, until it be completely mixed, and formed into a stiff and tough dough.

When the dough is made, it is to be formed into a lump in the middle of the trough, and, with a little dry flour thinly scattered over it, covered over again to be kept warm and to ferment; and in this state, if all be done rightly, it will not have to remain more than about fifteen or twenty minutes. The oven should be hot by the time that the dough has remained in the lump about twenty minutes. When both are ready, take out the fire and wipe the oven clean, and at nearly the same moment, take the dough out upon the lid of the baking trough, or some proper place, cut it up into pieces and make it up into loaves, kneading it again in these separate parcels, shaking a little flour over the board to prevent the dough adhering to it. The loaves should be put into the oven as quickly as possible after they are formed; when in, the oven lid or door should be fastened up very closely; and, if all be properly managed, loaves, of about the size of quartern loaves, will be sufficiently baked in about two hours. But they usually take down the lid, and look at the bread, in order to see how it is going on.

Bread from Iceland Moss.

This vegetable may be used alone, or with flour in the making of bread Boil 7 pounds of lichen meal in 100 pints of water; and afterwards mix the same with 69 pounds of flour, and when baked the product will be 160 (?) pounds of good household bread. Whereas, without this addition, the flour would not produce more than 79 pounds of bread. To prepare it, use 1 pound of lichen meal in the form of paste, to about 8¾ pounds (?) of flour

Extemporaneous Bread.

1. Flour. Water highly charged with carbonic acid gas, a sufficient quantity to make a dough, and bake immediately. The whole of this process should be carried on in as cold a place as possible, and the articles employed should be also cold.

2. Flour, 14 pounds; ammonia, 2 ounces; bicarbonate of soda, 2 ounces; water to mix. Reduce to a dough rather thinner than for yeast, then cut into loaves and bake.

3. Add a little bicarbonate of ammonia to the water, then add the flour and make the dough of the usual consistence. This bread is ready for the oven as soon as made into loaves.

Bread for Horses. (Silesian Method.)

Oat or rye meal, 3 parts; mashed potatoes, 2 parts; a little salt and yeast to ferment. Mix and bake. Give 4 four-pound rations daily. It is stated that this method effects a great saving over the common plan of feeding horses.

Good Bread.

Flour, 1 sack; salt, 4 pounds; water, sufficient quantity; yeast, 4 pints. Dissolve the salt in 3 gallons of the water (warm), then add a little of the flour and the whole of the yeast; keep it in a warm place until it rises, then add more flour and warm water, and after three or four hours the remainder of the flour and sufficient water to bring the dough to a proper consistence. When the whole mass of dough is in a proper state, it is to be cut into loaves and baked.

The bakers employ alum in making their bread, as it not only makes the dough more retentive of moisture, but improves the colour of the bread. The proportion is usually 8 to 14 ounces of alum per sack, or even more. By this process a sack of flour will produce from 345 to 350 pounds of *well*-baked bread, or if less baked, from 370 to 385 pounds.

Drop Cakes.

One quart of milk, a large tea-spoonful of sal-eratus, dissolved in a cup of cream; to which stir in flour very smoothly until a thick batter. Then dip your spoon in milk and with it place your batter at short distances in a buttered pan. Very delicate, made entirely of cream, either with or without eggs.

Buckwheat Cakes

Are less tough and not as liable to sour, when mixed with salt-rising instead of hop yeast.

Soft Gingerbread, very Nice.

Four tea-cups of flour, two cups of molasses, half a cup of butter, two cups of butter-milk, a cup of thick cream, three eggs, a table-spoonful of ginger, and the same of sal-eratus. Mix them all together, with the exception of the butter-milk, in which the sal-eratus must be dissolved, and then added to the rest. It must not stand long before being sent to bake.

Butter

Is improved by working the second time after the lapse of twenty-four hours, when the salt is dissolved, and the watery particles can be entirely removed.

Caoutchouc or Elastic Gum Bougies.

Strips of cloth twisted up, pieces of whipcord, or pieces of catgut. Coat them, until of a sufficient size, with a solution of caoutchouc in naphtha or ether.

White Bougies.

Yellow wax, 1 pound; spermaceti, 1 ounce; acetate of lead, 5 drachms. Mix, with heat, and spread upon slips of cloth, then roll them up, the spread side outwards.

Bowle's Herb Tea.

Wood betony, wood sage, ground pine, each equal parts. For gout, headache, and nervous disorders.

Boyle's Fuming Liquor.

Slaked lime, 6 parts; sal ammoniac, 4 parts; flowers of sulphur, 2 parts. Mix and distil.

Bougies.

Pieces of catgut of different sizes, coat them with mercurial plaster, and roll them smooth on a marble slab. Or, pieces of old linen, roll them up, and proceed as before.

British Brandy.

.. Silent spirit (pf.) 98 gallons; red tartar, 5 pounds; acetic ether, 3 pounds; wine vinegar, 3 gallons; bruised French plums, 7 pounds; bitter almonds, bruised, 1 ounce; water sufficient. Dissolve the tartar in the water, then add the other ingredients, and draw over 120 gallons; lastly, add burnt-sugar colouring as required.

2. Clean spirit, 100 gallons; nitric ether, 2 pounds; cassia buds (ground), ½ pound; bitter almond meal, ½ pound; orris root (sliced), 6 ounces; powdered cloves, 1 ounce; capsicum, 1 ounce; good vinegar, 2 gallons; brandy colouring, 1 quart. Mix well in an empty cognac cask, and let them macerate for a fortnight, occasionally stirring. The proportion of the ingredients may be varied by the skilful brewer, as much depends on their respective strengths.

3. Clean spirit, 100 gallons; strong vinegar, 3 gallons; bitter almonds (ground), ¼ pound; cassia buds (ground), ½ pound; orris root (ground), 7 ounces; Guinea pepper (ground), 6 ounces; powdered cloves, 1 ounce; tincture of catechu, 4 pints; nitric ether, 2 pints; brandy colouring, 1 quart. Put them on the lees into a fresh emptied cognac cask, and macerate as before. Instead of tincture of catechu you may use half a pound of the powder mixed with hot water to a paste.

4. Good plain malt spirit (17 up), 100 gallons; finely-powdered catechu, 12 ounces; tincture of vanella, 2 ounces; burnt-sugar colouring, 1 quart or more. Mix well.

British Cognac Brandy.

Clean spirit (17 up), 100 gallons; high-flavoured cognac, 10 gallons; oil of cassia, 1½ ounce; oil of bitter almonds (essential), ½ ounce; powdered catechu, 10 ounces; cream of tartar (dissolved), 16 ounces; Beaufoy's concentrated acetic acid, 3 pounds; colouring (sugar), 1 quart or more Put the whole into a fresh emptied brandy piece, and let them remain a week, together with occasional agitation, then let them stand to settle.

Brandy Shrub.

1 Sugar (good), 1½ cwt. or more; spirit (silent proof), 20 gallons; British brandy 10 gallons; bitter almonds, 1½ ounce: orris powder, 3 ounces; powdered cassia, 2 ounces; essence of orange, 1 ounce; lemons, sliced, 1 dozen; water, 25 gallons; tartaric acid (in solution) to produce the necessary acidity. Put the whole into a proper sized cask and rummage every day for one week, then add water to make up 103 gallons, and one quart of colouring and two dozen eggs.

2. Tartaric acid (powdered), 8 pounds; lump-sugar, 240 pounds or less. Dissolve in water, 35 gallons. Put it into a cask, then add spirit, or brandy, 35 gallons or less; brandy colouring, 1 pint; oranges (sliced), 2 dozen; bitter almonds (bruised), ½ ounce; cassia (bruised), ½ ounce cloves (bruised), ½ ounce. Rummage repeatedly for a week, keeping the cask in the interim well bunged, then add twenty eggs, (yellows, whites and shells), beaten to a froth. Well mix and bung close.

Bran Beer.

Good bran, 1 bushel; water (to produce), 18 gallons; hops, ¼ pound Mash with hot water, and ferment in the usual way. This beer will cost about three-pence per gallon; two or three pounds of sugar, or four or five of treacle, improve it.

Brandy Bitters.

Bruised gentian, 8 ounces; orange-peel, 5 ounces; cardamoms, 3 ounces; cassia, 1 ounce; cochineal, ¼ ounce; spirit, 1 gallon. Digest for one week, then decant the clear, and pour on the dregs, water, 5 pints. Digest for one week longer, decant, and mix the two tinctures together.

Boot-Top Liquid.

Oxalic acid, 1 part; white vitriol, 1 part; water, 30 parts. Dissolve and apply with a sponge to the leather previously washed with water, then wash the composition off with water, and dry. This liquid is poisonous

Brass.

Copper, 3 parts. Melt, then add zinc, 1 part.

Button-Maker's Fine Brass.

Brass, 8 parts; zinc, 5 parts. Mix.

Button Maker's Common Brass.

Button brass, 6 parts; tin, 1 part; lead, 1 part. Melt.

Bright Brass Colour.

Brass reduced to fine powder.

Red Brass Colour.

Copper filings, 3 parts; bole, 2 parts. Mix.

Fine Brass.

Copper, 2 parts; zinc, 1 part. Mix.

Brass for Wire.

Copper, 34 parts; calamine, 56 parts. Mix.

To Polish Brass Inlaid Work.

File the brass very clean with a smooth file; then take some tripoli powdered very fine, and mix it with the linseed oil. Dip in this a rubber of hat, with which polish the work until the desired effect is obtained.

If the work is ebony, or black rose-wood, take some elder-coal powdered very fine, and apply it dry after you have done with the tripoli, and it will produce a superior polish.

The French mode of ornamenting with brass differs widely from ours, theirs being chiefly water-gilt (*or moulu*), excepting the flutes of columns, &c., which are polished very high with rotten stone, and finished with elder-coal.

To Brass, Plates of Copper.

The plates previously sufficiently heated, and expose them to the fumes of zinc.

To Clean Brass.

1. Finely powdered sal ammoniac; water to moisten.

2. Roche alum, 1 part; water, 16 parts. Mix. The articles to be cleaned must be made warm, then rubbed with either of the above mixtures, and finished with fine tripoli. This process will give them the brilliancy of gold.

To Brass, Vessels of Copper.

Argol, 1 part; amalgam of zinc, 1 part; muriatic acid, 2 parts; water to fill the vessel. Boil.

Brazil Wood Lake.

1. Brazil (ground), 1 pound; water, 5 quarts. Boil for half an hour, then add solution of tin, 1 ounce; alum, 1 ounce. Boil again, strain and add a solution of pearlash (strained), as long as it occasions a precipitate.

2. A beautiful lake may be prepared from Brazil wood, by boiling three pounds of it for an hour in a solution of three pounds of common salt in three gallons of water, and filtering the hot fluid through paper; add to this a solution of five pounds of alum in three gallons of water. Dissolve three pounds of the best pearlashes in a gallon and a half of water, and purify it by filtering; put this gradually to the other, till the whole of the colour appear to be precipitated, and the fluid be left clear and colourless. But if any appearance of purple be seen, add a fresh quantity of the solution of alum by degrees, till a scarlet hue be produced. Then pursue the directions given in the first process with regard to the sediment. If half a pound of seed lac be added to the solution of pearlashes, and dissolved in it before its purification by the filter, and two pounds of the wood and a proportional quantity of common salt and water be used in the coloured solution, a lake will be produced that will stand well in oil or water, but it is not so transparent in oil as without the seed lac. The lake with Brazil wood may be also made by adding half an ounce of annatto to each pound of the wood; but the annatto must be dissolved in the solution of pearl ashes.

After the operation, the dryers of plaster, or the bricks, which have extracted the moisture from the precipitate, are exposed to the sun, that they may be fitted for another operation.

Pale Brass Lacker.

Alcohol, 4 gallons; cape aloes (small), 6 ounces; pale shellac, 32 ounces; gamboge, 2 ounces. Dissolve.

Eleven Receipts on Sympathetic Inks.

1. Write upon paper with a diluted solution of muriate of copper, when dry it will not be visible, but on being warmed before the fire the writing will become of a beautiful yellow.

2. Write with a solution of muriate of cobalt, and the writing, while dry, will not be perceptible; but if held towards the fire, it will then gradually become visible; and if the muriate of cobalt be made in the usual way, the letters will appear of an elegant green colour.

3. Write with acetate of cobalt, or with a muriate of cobalt, previously purified from the iron which it generally contains. When the writing is become dry, these letters will also be invisible. Warm the paper a little, and the writing will be restored to a beautiful blue.

4. Draw a landscape with Indian ink, and paint the foliage of the vegetables with muriate of cobalt, some of the flowers with acetate of cobalt, and others with muriate of copper. While this picture is cold it will appear to be merely an outline of a landscape, or winter scene; but when gently warmed, the trees and flowers will be displayed in their natural colours, which they will preserve only while they continue warm. This may be often repeated.

5. Write with dilute nitrate of silver, which when dry will be entirely invisible; hold the paper over a vessel containing sulphate of ammonia, and the writing will appear very distinct. The letters will shine with the metallic brilliancy of silver.

6. Write with a solution of nitrate or acetate of lead. When the writing is dry it will be invisible. Then having prepared a glass decanter with a little sulphuret of iron strewed over the bottom of it, pour a little very dilute sulphuric acid upon the sulphuret, so as not to wet the mouth of the decanter, and suspend the writing, by means of the glass stopper, within the decanter. By an attention to the paper the writing will become visible by degrees, as the gas rises from the bottom of the vessel.

7. Write with a weak solution of sulphate of iron, let it dry, and it will be invisible. By dipping a feather in tincture of galls and drawing the wet feather over the letters, the writing will be restored and appear black.

8. Write with a similar solution, and when dry wash the letters in the same way with prussiate of potash, and they will be restored of a beautiful blue.

9. Write with a solution of sulphate of copper, wash as before with prussiate of potash, and the writing will be revived of a reddish-brown colour.

10. Write on paper with a solution of nitrate of bismuth; when this is dry the writing will be invisible; but if the paper be exposed to sulphuretted hydrogen gas, the words will be distinctly legible.

11. A letter written with a diluted solution of bismuth, becomes, when dry, illegible: but a feather dipped in a solution of sulphuret of potash, will instantly blacken the oxide, and revive the writing.

How to prepare Vegetable Oysters.

Boil salsify, or vegetable oysters till the skin will come off easily. When you have taken it off neatly, cut the roots in bits as long as an oyster; put into a deep vegetable dish a layer of crumbs of bread or crackers, a little salt and pepper and nutmeg, and a covering of butter as thin as you can cut it; then a layer of oysters, till your dish is filled, having crumbs at top. Fill the dish with water, and brown them handsomely. They can remain two hours in the oven without injury, or be eaten in half an hour.

Indian-Meal Cakes.

To three pints of Indian-meal, a piece of butter as large as an egg, and a tea-spoonful of salt. Put two tea-cupfuls of boiling water, stir it in, then add three eggs, and milk to make it to the consistency of batter. Half a tea-spoonful of sal-eratus.

To prepare a Round of Fresh Beef for Boiling.

Put the beef in a dish of sufficient size, and add water enough to cover the lower part of the meat. Then put a quantity of salt on the top. In a few hours it becomes well seasoned, and when thoroughly boiled, makes a most palatable dish.

To purify the Breath.

Gum catechu, 2 ounces; white sugar, 4 ounces; orris powder, 1 ounce. Make into a paste with mucilage, and add a drop or two of neroli.

Brewer's Flour of Corianders.

Coriander-seeds 4 parts; quassia, 3 parts; aloes and nux vomica each 1 part. Grind well together. This is used to adulterate beer, but from containing nux vomica, is a very dangerous preparation.

To fit up a small Brewhouse.

1. Procure a copper, in size, according to the quantity you intend to brew, with a gauge-stick to ascertain the number of ullage gallons. 2. A mash tub or tun. 3. Three or four shallow coolers. 4. One or two wooden bowls. 5. A thermometer. 6. A few sweet empty casks. 7. A large funnel or tunner. 8. A hand-pump. 9. Two or three wooden buckets. The copper and mash tun must each hold about two-thirds the quantity you intend to brew.

Oil of Bricks.

Sweet oil, 5 parts; brick-dust, 1 part. Distil.

Brine for Salting Meat, &c.

Soft water, 1 gallon; dry salt, 4 pounds. Dissolve in the water, previously heated, then strain.

Brittania Metal.

1. Tin, 82 parts; lead, 18 parts; brass, 5 parts; antimony, 5 parts. Mix.

2. Brass, 1 part; antimony, 4 parts; tin, 20 parts. Mix.

3. Plate brass, tin, bismuth, and antimony, of each equal parts. Add this mixture to melted tin until it acquires the proper colour and hardness.

Breeches Balls.

Pipe-clay, whiting, yellow ochre, ox gall to mix, equal parts. Mix. Any other colour may be used instead of ochre, or it may be entirely omitted.

Bronze.

1. Copper, 83 parts; zinc, 11 parts; tin, 4 parts; lead, 2 parts. Mix.
2. Copper, 14 parts; melt, and add zinc, 6 parts; tin, 4 parts.

Ancient Bronze.

Copper, 100 parts; lead and tin, each 7 parts. Mix.

To give an Antique Appearance to Bronze Figures

Salt of sorrel, 1 part; sal ammoniac, 4 parts; white vinegar 224 parts. Dissolve, and apply with a camel-hair pencil, just sufficient to damp the bronze, previously warmed. Repeat the operation if required.

Keller's Bronze.

Copper, 91 parts; tin, 2 parts; zinc, 6 parts; lead, 1 part. Mix.

Alloy for Bronze Ornaments.

Copper, 82 parts; zinc, 18 parts; tin, 3 parts; lead, 3 parts.

Bronze Powder.

Bichloride of mercury, 1 part; borax and nitre, each 8 parts; tutty, 16 parts; verdigris, 32 parts; oil to make into a paste. Melt.

Beautiful Red Bronze Powder.

Sulphate of copper, 100 parts; carbonate of soda, 60 parts. Apply heat until they unite into a mass, then cool, powder, and add copper filings, 15 parts. Well mix, and keep them at a white heat for twenty minutes, then cool, powder, and wash and dry.

Bronzing Fluid for Guns, &c.

Nitric acid, sp. gr. 1.2, nitric ether, alcohol, muriate of iron, each 1 part. Mix, then add sulphate of copper, 2 parts; dissolved in water, 10 parts.

Broomley's Remedy to cure the Fit of Drunkenness.

Aromatic water of ammonia, 2 drachms; distilled water, 2 ounces. Mix.

Brown Colour for Marbling or Sprinkling Books.

1. Logwood chips, 1 part; annatto, 1 part; boil in water, 6 parts. If too light, add a piece of copperas about the size of a pea.

2. Umber, any quantity. Grind it on a slab with ox gall and a little lampblack. Dilute with ale.

Browning.

Lump-sugar (powdered), 32 parts; salad oil, 8 parts. Heat in an iron vessel until quite brown, then add Port wine, 32 parts; Cape wine, 64 parts; elder wine, 32 parts; shalots, 6 parts; mixed spice, 4 parts; black pepper, 4 parts; mace, 1 part; salt, 8 parts; lemon-juice, 16 parts; catsup, 32 parts. Boil, then let it settle and decant the clear liquid for use. This gives a fine colour and flavour to gravies.

Brown Hard Spirit Varnish.

Gum sandarach, 1¼ pounds; shell lac, 1¼ pounds; alcohol (65 op.), 1 gallon. Dissolve in a close vessel, then add turpentine varnish, 20 ounces. Mix well.

Brown Paint.

Venetian red, or Spanish brown, 1 cwt.; road dust, 3 cwt.; common soot, 28 pounds; lime-water, 15 gallons. Factitious linseed oil to grind.

Brown Stout.

Burnt-malt colouring and treacle, and add it to porter.

Brown Tincture.

Alcohol (weak), and pour it on some burnt bread and a little bruised rhatany root. Let it stand until coloured.

Brucine.

Bark of brucea antidysenterica, 1 part; ether, 2 parts. Digest and strain, then steep the residue in alcohol for some time, filter and evaporate to dryness; dissolve the remainder in distilled water, and add a little solution of acetate of lead; filter, and add liquid sulphuretted hydrogen; filter a third time, and add a little magnesia, filter again, and wash the sediment very cautiously with cold water, and dry; then digest in alcohol, filter and gradually distil off the spirit. This preparation may be purified still further, by neutralizing it with oxalic acid, crystallizing, and exposing it to the action of alcohol and ether, then dissolving it in water, and neutralizing the acid with magnesia; next filter, digest the residue in alcohol; filter again, and evaporate.

Brunswick Black for Grates.

1. Asphaltum, 5 pounds; melt, and add boiled oil, 2 pounds; spirits of turpentine, 1 gallon. Mix.

2. Litharge, 7 pounds; asphaltum, 45 pounds; melt, then add boiled oil, 7 gallons. Boil until the mixture strings well, and on cooling a little becomes quite hard, then take it from the fire and add spirits of turpentine, 25 gallons, or enough to thin it sufficiently.

Cheap Brunswick Black.

Black pitch, 28 pounds; black resin, 28 pounds; melt, and add black tar, 28 pounds; mix well, and further add boiled oil, 12 gallons; ground litharge, 12 pounds. Boil until stringy, and lastly thin it down with spirits of turpentine.

Burnt Almonds.

Take some fine Valencia or Jordan Almonds, and sift all the dust from them; put a pint of clarified syrup into the pan for each pound of almonds, and place it with the almonds on the fire; boil to the ball, then take it off, and stir the mixture well, that the sugar may grain and become almost a powder, whilst each almond has a coating. Sift the loose sugar from them with a coarse sieve, and separate those which adhere. When cold, boil to the feather more clarified syrup, put in the almonds, give them two or three boils, take them from the fire, stir them until the sugar grains, sift and separare them. A third coat may be given them in the same manner.

Burnt Almonds—Red.

These are made in the same manner as the last, using prepared cochineal to colour the syrup whilst it is boiling.

Bole Ammoniac.

There is also the French and German bole. These earths are of a pale red, and possess alexipharmic qualities; they are frequently used in confectionary for painting and gilding.

Brown Stain for Glass.

White glass, 2 parts; manganese, 1 part. Mix.

British Oil, or Oil of Petre.

Oil of turpentine, 1 gallon; Barbadoes tar, 5 pounds. Mix.

Brown Sprinkle for Leather Book Covers, &c.

Pearlash or potash, 1 part; soft water, 4 parts. Dissolve and strain.

Buckthorn Paper.

Dip the paper into buckthorn juice and dry.

To Clean Buff Cloth.

Take pipe-clay, and mix it with water until as thick as cream, spread this over the cloth, and when dry use a hard brush.

To remove Bugs, &c.

1. Corrosive sublimate, 1 ounce; muriatic acid, 2 ounces; water, 4 ounces; dissolve, then add turpentine, 1 pint; decoction of tobacco, 1 pint. Mix. For the decoction of tobacco boil two ounces of tobacco in a pint of water. The mixture must be applied with a paint-brush. This wash is a *deadly poison!*

2. The most certain way to destroy bugs, is to put the bedstead into a close room and set fire to the following composition, placed in an iron pot upon the hearth, having previously closed up the chimney, then shut the door; let them remain a day. Sulphur, 10 parts; saltpetre, powdered, 1 part. Mix. Be sure to open the door of the room five or six hours before you venture to go into it a second time.

To hasten the Blowing of Bulbous-Rooted Flowers.

Nitrate of potash, 12 ounces; common salt, 4 ounces; pearlash, 3 ounces; sugar, 5 ounces; rain-water, 1 quart. Dissolve, and put a spoonful of this liquid into the flower-glass, then fill it with soft water. Change the wate every nine days.

Burton Ale.

Pale malt, 1 quarter; E. K. hops, 8 pounds; grains of paradise, ¼ pound. Water sufficient to produce 1¾ barrels. 180° Fahr. first mash; second mash, 190° Fahr.; tun at 58°.

To clarify Butter.

Take butter, melt it in a warm bath, then let it settle, pour off the clear, and cool as quickly as possible. Butter prepared in this way will keep a long time good.

Butter of Wax.

Wax, 1 part; sweet oil, 2 parts. Mix, with heat.

Brown Salt.

Browning, 1 part; weak spirit, 1 part; table-salt sufficient quantity to mix. Evaporate to dryness, and rub through a sieve.

To Cure Butter.

1. Lump-sugar, 5 parts; saltpetre, 8 parts; common salt, 32 parts. Powder fine and sift, then use one ounce of this mixture to every pound of butter; pack in wood or vitrified jars, not glazed pans. This will keep butter for two or three years.

2. Common salt, 2 parts; sugar, 1 part; saltpetre, 1 part. Mix in fine powder and use one ounce of this composition to every pound of butter. Butter prepared with this mixture will keep three years.

To remove the Turnip Flavour from Butter.

Nitre, 1 part; water, 20 parts. Dissolve, and put a little into the milk, warm from the cow.

Bottled Buxton Water.

Tartrate of soda, 35 grains; bicarbonate of soda, 20 grains; sulphate iron, 1½ grains. Put them into a soda-water bottle, fill it with clean water and fit the cork ready: then add sulphuric acid seven or eight drops, and cork and wire immediately.

Cabinetmaker's Varnish.

Pale shell lac, 700 parts; mastic, 65 parts; strongest alcohol, 1000 parts. Dissolve. Dilute with alcohol.

Callot's Soft Etching Varnish.

Linseed oil, 8 parts; benzoin, 1 part; white wax, 1 part. Melt, and keep it heated until reduced to two-thirds.

Calomel, or Protochloride of Mercury.

1. Bichloride of mercury, 4 parts; quicksilver, 3 parts. Triturate them together in a marble mortar until the metallic globules perfectly disappear, then collect the powder and sublime; next powder fine, and well wash the sublimate with clean water.

2. Quicksilver, 9 parts; nitric acid (sp. 1.2), 8 parts; digest, then make a solution with common salt, 8 parts; water, 250 parts. Dissolve, and mix the two solutions at nearly the boiling point, collect the precipitate and carefully wash it in water.

3. *Process adopted at Apothecaries' Hall.*—Mercury, 100 parts; strong sulphuric acid, 140 parts. Boil in a cast-iron pot until a dry persulphate is obtained, then triturate of the above salt, 124 parts; with mercury, 81 parts: until the globules disappear and a protosulphate is formed, then add common salt, 68 parts. Well mix and sublime in a stone-ware cucurbit. The product varies from 190 to 200 parts.

Camphor Cerate.

Suct, 2 ounces; lard, 3 ounces; camphor, 1 ounce. Mix.

Calves' Feet Jelly.

Take eight calves' feet and boil them until the water becomes a good jelly, then add sugar, 1 pound; Port wine, 2 pints; white of two eggs and shells. Boil for five minutes, and clarify.

Cambrian and Westphalian Essence.

Barbadoes tar, 1 part; liquid burnt sugar, 2 parts; common salt, 4 parts; water, 100 parts; spirit of wine, 1 part. Mix, and let it stand for a week. Two or three table-spoonfuls mixed with the salt will be found quite sufficient for a common-sized ham.

Cameleon Mineral.

Pure potass, black oxide of manganese. Fuse together in a crucible. When this compound is dissolved in water, it changes from green to red, whence its name.

Oil of Camphor.

Camphor (cut small), 1 ounce; sweet oil, 1 pound. Pour the oil (hot) on the camphor in a well-corked vessel, and shake it until dissolved.

To render permanent Chalk or Pencil Drawings.

Lay the drawing on its face and give the back two or three thin coats of the following (No. 1.) mixture; let it dry, and turn it with the chalk upwards, and give that side one or two coats also; lastly, if you choose, give it one or two coats of No. 2.

1. Isinglass or gum arabic, 5 parts; water, 12 parts. Mix.
2. Canada balsam, 4 parts; turpentine, 5 parts. Mix.

Chalybeate Pills for Leucorrhœa, &c.

1. Sulphate of iron, 1 scruple; balsam of copaivi and liquorice powder to mix. Divide into forty pills. Dose– three or four, three times a day.

2. Sulphate of zinc, 40 grains; extract of camomile, 60 grains; extract of gentian, 120 grains; syrup to mix. Divide into fifty pills. Dose—two, twice a day.

Chalybeate Water.

Water, 2 gallons; iron filings, 1 pound. Put them into a proper vesse. and force into it six or seven atmospheres of carbonic-acid gas; let it stand in a cool place for one day, occasionally shaking, then let it settle; pour off the clear, and bottle immediately.

2. Protosulphate of iron, 3 grains; bicarbonate of potass, 61 grains. Put them into a wine-bottle, filled with water, and cork it immediately, then agitate it well.

Gaseous Chalybeate Water Powder.

Bicarbonate of soda, 98 parts; tartaric acid, 116 parts; sulphate of iron, 3 parts; sugar (white), 280 parts. Mix in the state of coarse powder, and keep dry. This is the quantity for one bottle (quart).

To Crystallize Tin.

Mix one spoonful of muriatic acid, one of nitric acid, eight of water. Warm block tin over the fire, and rub it with a cloth dipped in the mixture. Ornament with coloured varnish.

Pure Carburetted Hydrogen.

Take alcohol, 1 part; sulphuric acid, 4 parts. Mix in a glass retort, and apply heat.

Factitious Beeswax.

Take yellow resin, 70 pounds; suet, 35 pounds; powdered turmeric, 5 pounds (or less); potato flour, 9 pounds. Mix, and form into cakes as seon as it begins to cool. Rub over each cake when cold with some flour. A little ivory black prevents too bright a colour.

Camp Vinegar.

Take sliced garlic, 4 ounces; soy, 2 ounces; walnut catsup, 2 ounces; cayenne pepper, 1 ounce; black pepper, 1 ounce; chopped anchovies, 15; vinegar, 1 gallon; cochineal, 1 drachm. Infuse for one month, and strain.

Capillaire.

1. Take white sugar, 1 cwt.; water, 8 gallons. Boil to a proper state, then clarify with eggs, and when cold flavour with orange-flower water, or rose-water.

2. Take loaf-sugar, 1 cwt.; water, 12 gallons; white of 12 eggs. Put them into a cold copper, and dissolve, then apply heat and skim it until quite clear; filter, if necessary, and add orange-flower water, or essence of neroli, to flavour. A spoonful or two added to water or grog gives it a very pleasant flavour.

Caraway Brandy.

Take caraway seeds, bruised, 7 pounds; proof spirit, 80 gallons; sugar 42 pounds, dissolved in 20 gallons of water. Mix and steep for a month

Caraway Cordial.

Take oil of caraway, 3 ounces; oil of cassia, 1 drachm; oil of lemon, 15 drops; oil of orange, 15 drops; proof spirit, 25 gallons, or less. Mix well, then add sugar, 70 pounds; dissolved in water, 15 gallons. Mix and fine with eggs.

Factitious Oil of Caraway.

Take oil of caraway, 1 part; castor oil, 2 parts. Mix.

Caraway Water.

Take caraways, 28 pounds; water, 30 gallons. Distil off 27 gallons.

Carmine.

Take cochineal, 1 pound; carbonate of potass, 3½ drachms; water, 7 gallons. Simmer for a little time, then remove the copper from the fire, and scatter powdered alum, 8 drachms, over the surface; let it stand fifteen minutes, until clear, then decant and put the solution into a clean copper, heat it, and add isinglass, 3½ drachms, previously dissolved in 2 quarts of water and strained. Then bring it to a boil, and when a coagulum is formed, take it from the fire and stir it with a clean spatula; let it rest for twenty minutes, and the carmine will be found at the bottom of the liquid Decant, and drain the carmine upon a piece of fine linen.

The remaining solution will make fine carminated lake.

Liquid Carmine.

Take carmine, 2 parts; ammonia, 3 parts; water, 20 parts. Dissolve.

German Carmine.

Take cochineal, 1 pound; water, 7 gallons. Boil for five minutes, then add alum, 1 ounce. Boil for five minutes more, filter and set aside the decoction in glass or porcelain vessels for three days, then decant the liquor and dry the carmine in the shade. The remaining liquor will still deposit colour of an inferior quality, by standing.

To improve Common Carmine.

Take carmine, one part; water of ammonia to dissolve. Digest in the sun until the ammonia is saturated with the colouring part of the carmine, then precipitate the colour with alcohol and acetic acid. Wash the precipitate carefully with alcohol and dry it.

Carminated Lake.

Take cochineal, 5 ounces; water, 1½ gallon. Boil for one hour, then add alum in quantity according to the intended quality; dissolve, strain, and add a solution of carbonate of potass, until it ceases to produce a precipitate.

Cannon Metal.

Take tin, 10 parts; copper, 90 parts. Melt.

Pale Carriage Varnish.

Take copal, 32 parts; pale oil, 80 parts; fuse and boil until stringy, then add dried white copperas, 1 part; litharge, 1 part. Boil again, then cool a little, and mix in spirits of turpentine, 150 parts. Strain.

While making the above—Take gum animé, 32 parts; pale oil, 80 parts; dried sugar of lead, 1 part; litharge, 1 part; spirits of turpentine, 170 parts. Pursue the same treatment as before, and mix the two varnishes while hot.

Second Quality Carriage Varnish.

Take gum animé, 32 parts; oil, 100 parts; spirits of turpentine 150 parts: litharge, 1 part; dried sugar of lead, 1 part; dried copperas, 1 part. Proceed as before.

To keep Empty Casks sweet.

Bung them close as soon as emptied.

To sweeten Musty or Stinking Casks.

1. First wash them with sulphuric acid, and then with clear water; afterwards wash them well out with water.
2. For large casks, unhead them and whitewash them with quicklime.
3. Or match them with sulphur mixed with a little nitrate of potash, and afterwards wash them well with water.
4. Char the inside of the staves.

Observe in every case to *scald* or *well wash* the casks out before use.

Cassia Pommade.

Take finely powdered cassia, 4 parts; beef suet, 5 parts; lard, 12 parts Mix and treat as for Rose Pommade, which see.

Cassia Water.

Take cassia, ½ cwt. (or less); water, 62 gallons. Distil off 55 gallons Sold for cinnamon water.

Scented Cassolettes.

Take oil of Sanders wood, 30 drops; tragacanth, 1 ounce; essence of roses, 1 ounce; benzoin, 2 ounces; rose powder, 4 pounds; black amber, 7 pounds. Reduce them to fine powder, then make into a paste with water.

Castile Soap.

Made like almond soap, only using olive oil. It is mottled by adding a solution of sulphate of iron while in a liquid state.

Cast Engravings.

Take the engraved plate you intend to copy, and arrange a support of suitable materials round it, then pour on it the following alloy in a state of perfect fusion: tin, 1 part; lead, 64 parts; antimony, 12 parts. These "cast plates" may be worked off on a common printing-press, and offer a ready mode of procuring cheap copies of the works of our celebrated artists.

Common Castor Oil.

Take pale vegetable oil, 1 gallon; castor oil, 2 gallons. Mix.

Catechu Lozenges.

Take finely-powdered catechu, 4 ounces; finely-powdered sugar, 1 pound; mucilage to mix. Add oil of cassia, 20 drops.

Portugal Catechu Lozenges.

The same as for the plain lozenges, only varying the perfume.

Catechu Ointment.

Take catechu powder, 4 ounces; alum, 1 ounce; simple ointment, 14 ounces. Mix the catechu and alum with a little warm water to the proper consistence, then add the ointment. An excellent pile ointment; it is also suitable to dress ulcers with in warm climates.

Caoutchouc Catheters.

1. Take a piece of catgut, coat it with wax, and dip it into an etherial solution of caoutchouc, until sufficiently covered, then dry it in a warm room or stove, and afterwards boil it in water to melt out the wax and catgut.

2. Take a polished wire of the proper size, and wrap round it (spirally) a thin ribbon of caoutchouc, previously boiled in water, or steeped for a few minutes in ether. Over this, wind a damp piece of tape, also in a spiral direction and as tight as possible, and lastly go over it with a piece of common packthread. When dry, dip the whole into boiling water, and withdraw the wire.

Cayenne Pepper.

Take dried capsicums, salt, equal parts; rose pink and bole to colour Grind, and sift the powder through a sieve of proper fineness.

Common Cayenne Pepper.

Take good cayenne, common salt, chipped logwood, equal parts. Proceed as before.

Crystallized Soluble Cayenne Pepper.

Take powdered cayenne, 1 pound; red sanders wood, 4 ounces; alcohol, 3 pounds. Macerate with heat in a close vessel for a week, then strain and add common salt, 4 pounds. Evaporate in a vessel suitable for saving the alcohol; then take the dry powder and rub it through a coarse sieve. This pepper is wholly soluble. The same alcohol will do for future operations.

English Cayenne Pepper.

Take chillies, salt, colour, equal parts. Mix, grind, and pass the powder through a sieve.

Liquid Cayenne Pepper.

Take powdered cayenne, 2 parts; spirit of wine, 10 parts; water, 10 parts; red sanders wood, 1 part. Digest in a close vessel, at a moderate heat, for four days, then strain off the clear.

Prepared Cayenne Pepper.

Take the residue from manufacturing Soluble Cayenne, 5 parts; good cayenne pepper, 1 part. Mix.

Cayenne Wine.

Take cayenne pepper, 6 ounces; white wine, 1 gallon. Macerate for a week, and strain.

Cream of Cedrat.

Take lump-sugar, 14 pounds; hot water, 3 gallons. Dissolve, then add spirit of cedrat, 2 pounds; spirit of citron, 1 pound; alcohol, 2 pounds. Mix well and filter.

Water of Cedrat.

Take loaf-sugar, 5 pounds; water, 7 quarts; spirit of cedrat, 2 quarts; spirit of citron, 1 quart. Mix together in a close vessel, and let them stand for one week; then filter.

Catsup for Sea Stores.

Take beer, 1 gallon; vinegar, 3 quarts; anchovies (washed) 1½ pounds; shallots, 1½ pounds; mace, cloves, black pepper, each, ½ ounce; ginger powder, 1 ounce; mushroom flaps, rubbed to pieces, 2 quarts. Boil until reduced to ten pints, then strain, cool, and bottle. To be used with a little butter.

Iron Cement.

Take iron borings, 98 parts; sal ammoniac, 2 parts; water to make them into a paste for use.

A Good Cement.

1. Take shell lac, 1 part; alcohol barely enough to dissolve.
2 Take shell lac, 1 part; borax, 1 part; water to dissolve. Apply heat

Cheap Cement.

Take brimstone, resin, equal parts. Mix with heat.

Fourteen Miscellaneous Experiments.

1 Take a slip of blue litmus paper, dip it into acetous acid, and it will immediately become red. This is a test so delicate, that, according to Bergman, it will detect the presence of sulphuric acid, even if the water contain only one part of acid to thirty-five thousand parts of water. Litmus paper which has been thus changed by immersion in acids, is, when dried, a good test for the alkalies; for, if it be dipped in a fluid containing the smallest portion of alkali, the red will disappear, and the paper be restored to its original blue colour.

2. Take a slip of turmeric paper, and dip it into any alkaline solution; this will change the yellow to a deep brown. In many cases turmeric is preferable to litmus paper for detecting alkali in solution, as it suffers no change from carbonate of lime, which is often found in mineral waters. This paper will detect the presence of soda, though it should amount to no more than $\frac{1}{2200}$dth part of the water. The paper thus changed by an alkali, would, if dried, be still useful as a test for acids, as these restore its original yellow.

3. Into a large glass jar, inverted upon a flat brick tile, and containing near its top a branch of fresh rosemary, or any other such shrub, moistened with water, introduce a flat thick piece of heated iron, on which place some gum benzoin in gross powder. The benzoic acid, in consequence of the heat, will be separated, and ascend in white fumes, which will at length condense, and form a most beautiful appearance upon the leaves of the vegetable. This will serve as an example of sublimation.

4. Introduce a little carbonate of ammonia into a Florence flask, and place that part of the flask which contains the salt on the surface of a bason of boiling water: the heat will soon cause the carbonate of ammonia to rise undecomposed, and attach itself to the upper part of the vessel, affording another example of simple sublimation.

5. Mix a little acetate of lead with an equal portion of sulphate of zinc, both in fine powder; stir them together with a piece of glass or wood, and no chemical change will be perceptible: but if they be rubbed together in a mortar, the two solids will operate upon each other; an intimate union will take place, and a fluid will be produced. If alum or glauber salt be used instead of sulphate of zinc, the experiment will be equally successful.

6. Pour a little water into a phial containing about an ounce of olive oil. Shake the phial, and if the contents be observed we shall find that no union has taken place. But if some solution of caustic potash be added, and the phial be then shaken, an intimate combination of the materials will be formed by the disposing affinity of the alkali, and a perfect soap produced.

7. Put a little common sulphur with one-eighth of its weight of nitre, into an iron dish, place it under a jar of oxygen gas, and set fire to it, and sulphuric acid will be formed. This is an example of the formation of an acid by combustion.

8. Take the acid formed in the last experiment, concentrate it by boiling, mix it with a little powdered charcoal, and submit the mixture in a Florence flask to the heat of an Argand's lamp. By this process sulphur will be regenerated, and will sublime into the neck of the flask. An example of the decomposition of an acid.

9. Melt sulphur in a small iron ladle, and carry it into a dark room in the state of fusion. If an ounce or two of copper filings be now thrown in, light will be evolved.

10. Fuse a small quantity of nitre in a crucible, and, when in complete fusion, throw pulverized coal into it by small quantities at a time. The carbonaceous matter will decompose the nitre, and the bituminous part will burn away without acting upon it. This experiment will exhibit a mode of analyzing coal; for every 100 grains of nitre that are decomposed in this way, denote ten grains of carbon.

11. If hot water be poured into a glass jar of cold water, it will remain on the surface; but if cold water be poured upon hot water, it will sink to the bottom of the vessel. This experiment may be rendered more obvious by colouring that portion of the water which is poured in. The design of this experiment is to show the change of the specific gravity of the same body, merely by the agency of caloric.

12. Into a glass of water containing a small portion of common salt, drop some of a clear solution of nitrate of silver, and an insoluble precipitate of muriate of silver will be produced. This experiment is designed to give the pupil some idea of the method of analyzing mineral waters. Every 100 grains of this precipitate, when dried, indicate 42 grains of common salt.

13. Into a glass of Aix-la-Chapelle water, or water holding a small portion of potash, drop a little of the solution of nitro-muriate of platina, and an immediate yellow precipitate will be produced. This affords another instance of the nature of the means usually employed to detect whatever substances may be dissolved in mineral waters.

14. Into distilled water drop a little spirituous solution of soap, and no chemical effect will be perceived; but if some of the same solution be added to hard water, a milkiness will immediately be produced, more or less, according to the degree of its impurity. This is a good method of ascertaining the purity of spring water.

Low or Fever Diet

Panada; gruel; milk, thickened with arrow-root; plain bread-pudding; arrow-root· salep, and tapioca jellies; rice-milk; chicken or veal-tea.

Drink for Invalids.

1. Barley-water, acidulated with lemon-juice; milk and water; lemon or orange-whey; thin gruel; bohea, balm, or mint tea.

2. Fresh small-beer; porter; port or claret wine with water; weak brandy and water.

3. Brisk cider and perry; sherry, port, or claret-wine; rum or brandy diluted with water.

Restorative or Convalescent Diet.

Rice or bread-pudding; hartshorn; isinglass, or calves'-feet jelly; oysters and shell-fish; flounder and soles; veal, fowl, rabbit, and lamb.

Generous or Full Diet.

Rice or bread-pudding; broth or gravy-soup; oysters and shell-fish, veal, fowl, lamb, mutton, beef, pork, &c., jelly of hartshorn, calves'-feet, or isinglass; meat-soups with vegetables.

Brass or Hard Solder.

Brass, 2 parts; zinc, 1 part. A little tin is occasionally added.

Paste for Cleaning Brass.

Starch, 1 part; powdered rotten-stone, 12 parts; sweet oil, 2 parts oxalic acid, 2 parts. Water to mix.

Collyrium.

1. Sulphate of zinc, 15 grains; rose-water, 2 ounces. Mix.
2. Goulard-water, 1 drachm; rose-water, ½ pint; laudanum, 60 drops. Mix.
3. Goulard-water, 1 drachm; rose-water, 1 pint. Mix.

To Clean Coloured Silks.

Put some white soap into boiling water, and heat it until dissolved in a strong lather. At a hand-heat put in the article. If strong, it may be rubbed as in washing; rinse it quickly in warm water, and add oil of vitriol, sufficient to give another water a sourish taste, if for bright yellows, crimsons, maroons, and scarlets; but for oranges, fawns, browns, or other shades, use no acid. For bright scarlet, use a solution of tin. Gently squeeze and then roll it in a coarse sheet, and wring it. Hang it in a warm room to dry, and finish it by calendering or mangling.

For pinks, rose colours, and thin shades, &c., instead of oil of vitriol, or solution of tin, prefer lemon-juice, or white tartar, or vinegar.

For blues, purples, and their shades, add a small quantity of American pearlash; it will restore the colours. Wash the articles like a linen garment, but, instead of wringing, gently squeeze and sheet them, and when dry, finish them with fine gum-water, or dissolved isinglass, to which add some pearlash, rubbed on the wrong side; then pin them out.

Blues of all shades are dyed with archil, and afterwards dipped in a vat; twice cleaning with pearlash, restores the colour. For olive-greens, a small quantity of verdigris dissolved in water, or a solution of copper, mixed with the water, will revive the colour again.

Colourless Soft Sealing-Wax.

Bees'-wax, 11 parts; turpentine, 3 parts; olive-oil, 1 part; shell lac, 5 parts. Mix with heat. Any colour may be given to this wax, by mixing it with a sufficient quantity of any of the usual pigments employed in painting, previously reduced to fine powder.

Essence of Coltsfoot.

Balsam of tolu, 1 part; compound tincture of benzoin, 1 part; rectified spirits, 4 parts. Mix.

Copal Varnish.

Copal, 30 parts; drying oil, 25 parts; spirits of turpentine, 50 parts. Put the copal into a vessel capable of holding 200 parts, and fuse it as quickly as possible, then add the oil previously heated to nearly the boiling point; well mix, next cool a little, add the spirits of turpentine, again well mix and cover up until the temperature has fallen to 140° Fahr., then strain.

Compound Colours, in Dyeing,

Are produced by mixing together two simple ones; or, which is the same thing, by dyeing cloth first of the simple colour, and then by another. These colours vary to infinity, according to the proportions of the ingredients employed. From blue, red, and yellow, red-olives and greenish-greys are made.

From blue, red, and brown, olives are made from the lightest to the darkest shades; and by giving a greater shade of red, the slated and lavender-greys are made.

From blue, red, and black, greys of all shades are made, such as sage, pigeon, slate, and lead-greys. The king's or prince's colour is duller than usual; this mixture produces a variety of hues or colours almost to infinity.

From yellow, blue, and brown, are made the goose-dung and olives of all kinds.

From brown, blue, and black, are produced brown-olives, and their shades.

From the red, yellow, and brown, are derived the orange, gold colour, feuille-mort, or faded leaf, dead carnations, cinnamon, fawn, and tobacco, by using two or three of the colours as required.

From yellow, red, and black, browns of every shade are made.

From blue and yellow, greens of all shades.

From red and blue, purples of all kinds are formed.

Plain Confectionary Drops.

Double-refined sugar, pound and sift it through a hair-sieve, not too fine; and then sift it through a gauze-sieve, to take out all the fine dust, which would destroy the beauty of the drop. Put the sugar into a clean pan, and moisten it with any favourite aromatic; if rose-water, pour it in slowly, stirring it with a paddle, which the sugar will fall from, as soon as it is moist enough, without sticking. Colour it with a small quantity of liquid carmine, or any other colour, ground fine. Take a small pan with a lip, fill it three parts with paste, place it on a small stove, the half hole being of the size of the pan, and stir the sugar with a little ivory or bone handle, until it becomes liquid. When it almost boils, take it from the fire and continue to stir it; if it be too moist take a little of the powdered sugar, and add a spoonful to the paste, and stir it till it is of such a consistence as to run without too much extension. Have a tin plate, very clean and smooth; take the little pan in the left hand, and hold in the right a bit of iron, copper, or silver wire, four inches long, to take off the drop from the lip of the pan, and let it fall regularly on the tin plate; two hours afterwards take off the drops with the blade of a knife.

To dissolve Copal in Spirit.

Take the copal and expose it in a vessel formed like a colander to the front of a fire, and receive the drops of melted gum in a basin of cold water, then well dry them in a temperature of about 95° Fahr. By treating copal in this way, it acquires the property of dissolving in alcohol

Solution of Conitine.

Unripe grape-juice, 8 ounces; pure conitine, 20 grains. Dissolve.

Cement for Floors.

Earthen floors are commonly made of loam, and sometimes, especially to make malt on, of lime and brook sand, and gun dust or anvil dust from the forge. The manner of making earthen floors for plain country habitations, is as follows :—Take two thirds of lime and one of coal-ashes well sifted with a small quantity of loam clay, mix the whole together, and temper it well with water, making it up into a heap; let it lie a week or ten days, and then temper it over again. After this, heap it up for three or four days, and repeat the tempering very high, till it becomes smooth, yielding, tough, and gluey. The ground being then levelled, lay the floor therewith about two and a half or three inches thick, making it smooth with a trowel; the hotter the season is the better; and when it is thoroughly dried it will make the best floor for houses, especially for malt-houses. If any one would have their floors look better, let them take lime of rag-stones, well tempered with whites of eggs, covering the floor about half an inch thick with it, before the under flooring is too dry. If this be well done, and thoroughly dried, it will look, when rubbed with a little oil, as transparent as metal or glass. In elegant houses, floors of this nature are made of stucco, or of plaster of Paris beaten and sifted, and mixed with other ingredients.

Parisian Cement.

Take gum arabic, 1 ounce; water, 2 ounces; starch to thicken.

Plumber's Cement.

Take resin, 1 part; brickdust, 2 parts. Mix with heat.

Stone Cement.

Take river sand, 20 parts; litharge, 2 parts; quicklime, 1 part; linseed oil to mix.

Simple Cerate.

1. Sweet oil, 4 pounds; suet, 4 pounds; white wax, 3 pounds; spermaceti, 1 pound. Melt and add water, 2 pounds, and stir the whole until cold.

2, Take white wax, 1 pound; sweet oil, 2 pounds; water, 12 ounces. Melt and stir until cold.

Chalk Lozenges.

1. Take powdered white sugar, 8 parts; prepared chalk, 1 part; mucilage sufficient to mix. Form the mass into lozenges of the usual size.

2. Take prepared chalk, 1 pound; starch, 2 pounds; white sugar, 4 pounds; mucilage to mix. Add a few drops of essence of cinnamon, nutmeg, or ginger.

Chalk Mixture.

1. Take prepared chalk, 4 drachms; white sugar, 4 drachms; powdered gum, 4 drachms; water, 1 pint. Mix gradually until reduced to a milk. Used as an antacid in diarrhœa.

2. Take creta, p. p. 3 ounces; loaf sugar, 1 ounce; powdered gum, 1 ounce; tinct. catechu, 1 ounce; laudanum, 2 drachms; water, 6 ounces Mix. Dose: one table-spoonful every two hours.

Cephalic Plaster.

Take Burgundy pitch, 32 parts; labdanum, 16 parts; yellow resin, 4 parts; yellow wax, 4 parts; oil, 1 part. Mix with heat.

Cephalic Snuff.

1. Take asarabacca leaves, marjoram, light Scotch snuff, equal parts. Grind them, and sift the resulting powder.

2. Take powdered asarum, 1 pound; powdered Scotch snuff (dry), 1½ pounds; simple powder, 2 pounds; hellebore, 4 ounces. Mix and sift.

Gum of Violets.

Violet flowers one pound, picked gum two pounds, sugar four ounces in syrup. Pour three pints of water at the boiling point on the flowers in an earthen jar; stop it perfectly close, and keep it in a warm place for ten or twelve hours; strain the infusion by expression into a flat pan or dish, place it on an inclination, and let it rest for an hour that the fæces may subside; pour off the clear gently from the bottom on settling, and add to it six grains of turnsole bruised, and six grains of carmine, as this clear infusion is not sufficiently coloured to give it the beautiful tint of the violet. Mix in the powdered gum and sugar, stir it over a moderate fire until dissolved, pass it through a sieve, and finish in the bain-marie, as jujubes.

The gum of violets, like most gum compounds, when dry, may be crystallized.

Detergent Ointment.

Take yellow resin, 1 pound; yellow wax, 1 pound; lard, 1 pound; suet, 1 pound; powdered verdigris, 4 ounces; powdered black pepper, 4 ounces; euphorbium, 2 ounces. Mix, with heat.

De Velvo's Syrup.

Take angelica, dockwort, liquorice, and dulcamara, of each equal parts; boil them in sixteen times their weight of water, then add sugar to make a syrup.

Compound Diachylon.

Take gum ammoniac, 1 pound; turpentine, 4 ounces. Melt, then add yellow wax, 2 pounds; yellow resin, 2 pounds; linseed oil, 1 pound; fenugreek seeds, 2 ounces. Mix, with heat.

Yellow Diachylon.

Take simple diachylon, 16 parts; galbanum (reduced), 3 parts; turpentine, 1 part; thuris, 1 part. Mix, with heat.

White Diachylon.

Take litharge, 10 parts; water, 5 parts; sweet oil, 16 parts. Mix, with heat.

Diamond Cement.

Take isinglass, soak it in water until it becomes soft, then dissolve it in proof-spirit, and add a little resin varnish. Used for joining china, glass, &c., and, under the name of "Armenian cement," for joining and fixing precious stones.

Draught for Diarrhœa.

Take tincture of opium, 30 drops; prepared chalk, 2 drachms; powdered gum, 4 drachms; tincture of catechu, 2 drachms; rose-water, 2 ounces. Mix, and take a table-spoonful three or four times a day.

A Natural Dentifrice.

The juice of the strawberry.

Diet Tables.

LOW DIET.

Breakfast and Tea.—Warm new milk and water; weak black tea, its astringent properties corrected by a due addition of milk. Gruel, toast of brown or household bread, at least one day old, and without butter. Rusks sopped in the above fluids.

Dinner.—Gruel, new milk and arrow-root, sago, or tapioca; chicken and veal broths; roast apples; light bread puddings. Pastry of every description must be avoided. (By *pastry*, is meant custards, trifles, tartlets, sponge-cakes, puffs, buns, cheese-cakes, and other abominations. The same interdiction applies equally to all other stages in a course of dietetics.)

Supper.—Gruel, arrow-root.

Occasional Drinks.—Filtered or spring water; toast-water made with toasted bread or browned biscuit; barley-water; whey; lemonade of subdued acidity Sweet oranges may be freely taken, if the sense of thirst be oppressive Great regularity must be observed in taking these meals.

MIDDLE DIET.

Breakfast and Tea.—Same as in low diet, with the addition of mixed tea. Dry toast, rusks, captain's biscuits.

Luncheon (if required).—A cup of isinglass, arrow-root, sago, tapioca, with biscuit, or two or three bars of toasted (stale) bread; or these with oranges.

Dinner.—In addition to "low diet," boiled chickens; calves' and sheep's feet stewed; mutton broth; beef tea; boiled soles, whiting, turbot, &c.; lamb; potatoes, asparagus, light bread or rice pudding, roast apples. After the repast, may be taken one glass of port, old sherry, or Madeira wine, diluted with at least twice its quantity of water.

Supper.—A cup of gruel, sago, tapioca, or arrow-root.

FULL DIET.

Breakfast and Tea.—Same as in "middle diet;" in addition to which may be taken coffee or chocolate. Stale or toasted bread, but very sparingly buttered.

Luncheon.—A biscuit and a glass of table ale or porter.

Dinner.—The "middle diet" bill of fare may be augmented by boiled lamb, chickens, mutton-chop, rump-steaks, roast or boiled fresh meats, light bread puddings, fruit pies (avoiding the pastry), baked or boiled rice or tapioca puddings. At this meal table-beer or porter may be taken as common drink, and after it, one or even two glasses of port, old sherry, or Madeira, carefully noting the symptoms produced by their effect.

Supper.—Same as in "middle diet."

An additional glass of wine at dinner, or luncheon, will convert this "full" into "generous" diet.

Milk, Farinaceous, Vegetable and Fruit Diet.

The articles of food within this range are milk, eggs lightly boiled, gruel, sago, arrow-root, tapioca, isinglass, wheaten and barley bread, rice, potatoes, carrots, parsnips, turnips, artichokes, peas, cauliflowers, cabbage, spinach, water-cress, celery. Fruit may be regarded rather as a luxury than as nutriment; however when taken in moderation it is wholesome; when to excess, poisonous. Stone fruit, as nectarines, apricots, peaches, plums and cherries, are the least digestible, and should never be taken but when ripe; apples and pears are not so apt to run into the acetous fermentation as stone fruit, but, unless ripe and well masticated, had better be eaten cooked. Oranges, gooseberries (avoiding the skins), grapes without the husks and seeds, currants, ripe strawberries and raspberries, follow consecutively in the order in which they are here enumerated, the first being most easy of digestion. Notwithstanding such an ample store of materials, the selection must of course depend upon season, appetite, and the known effects of each upon individual constitutions.

Digestive Ointment, for Cattle.

1. Tallow, 9 pounds; red precipitate, 1 pound; lard, 2 pounds. Mix.

2. Tallow, 3 pounds; resin, 3 pounds; spirits of turpentine, 3 pounds; powdered verdigris, 1 pound. Mix.

Paste resembling the Diamond.

Take white sand, 1800 parts; red lead, 1200 parts; pearlash, 900 parts, nitre, 600 parts; arsenic, 100 parts; manganese 1 part. To render this paste still harder, use less lead, and if it should incline to yellow, add a little more manganese.

Dill Water.

Take seeds, 28 pounds, or less; water, 16 gallons. Distil off fourteen or fifteen gallons.

To Estimate Distance.

Observe how many seconds elapse between a flash of lightning and the thunder, and multiply them by 1142, the number of feet sound travels in a second, the product will be the distance in feet. The same process may be applied to the flash and report of a gun, or any other sound, provided we can ascertain the time at which it is produced, and the interval that elapses before it reaches the ear.

Illustration. Saw a flash of lightning five seconds before I heard the thunder: required the distance.

$$\frac{5 \times 1142}{3 \times 1760} = 1\tfrac{43}{528} \text{ mile distant.}$$

In the absence of a watch, the pulsations at the wrist may be counted as seconds, by deducting one from every seven or eight.

To recover Spoiled Distilled Waters.

To every pint add borax, 1 grain, alum, 1 grain.

To prevent Distilled Waters turning Sour.

To every gallon add one ounce of finely-powdered calcined magnesia, and shake them well together, then allow the mixture to settle.

Flexible Asphaltic Roofing.

To supersede the use of slates, tiles, zinc, thatch, &c., in the covering and lining of farm-buildings, sheds, cottages, and other erections. It is durable, light, and economical: its weight is only 60 pounds to a square of 100 feet, so that the walls and timbers to support it require to be but half the usual substance; it is also a non-conductor of heat, is impervious to damp, and will bear a heat of 220° without injury.

Chambers's Remedy for Drunkenness.

Tartar emetic, 8 grains; rose-water, 4 ounces. Mix. Put a table-spoonful into the whole quantity of liquor drunk each day by the patient, and let him take it as usual. Be careful not to exceed a table-spoonful or half an ounce.

Oil of Camomile.

Flowers, 4 pounds; rape oil, 1 gallon. Beat them together and macerate for a few days, then express the oil.

British Champagne.

1. Loaf sugar, 56 pounds; brown sugar (pale), 48 pounds; water (warm), 45 gallons; white tartar, 4 ounces. Mix, and at a proper temperature add yeast, 1 quart; afterwards add sweet cider, 5 gallons; bitter almonds (bruised), 6 or 7 in number; pale spirit, 1 gallon; orris powder, ½ ounce.

2. Take three gallons of water and nine pounds of raw sugar; boil the water and sugar half an hour, skim it clean, and then pour the boiling liquor upon one gallon of currants, picked from the stalks but not bruised; and when cold, work it for two days with half a pint of ale yeast: afterwards pour it through a flannel bag, and put it into a clean cask, with half a pint of isinglass finings. When it has done working, bung it, and let it stand a month; then bottle it, putting into every bottle a very small lump of loaf-sugar. This is an excellent wine, and has a beautiful colour. This must be kept in sand.

3. Gooseberries (hardly ripe and bruised), 20 gallons; water, 20 gallons. Mix and stir well for two days, then strain, squeezing the mixture well, and return the liquor two or three times; then add to every gallon of the liquor 2 to 3½ pounds of lump-sugar, and allow it to ferment; after some days, take off the scum and add half a pint of alcohol to every gallon, and afterwards one pint of finings, then bung up close.

4. Mashed ripe white gooseberries, 20 gallons; soft water, milk-warm, 20 gallons; lump-sugar, 20 pounds. Mix and ferment without yeast, and when only a slight hissing noise is head, rack it into a clean cask, and add proof spirit, 1½ or 2 gallons; dried orange-peel, bruised, ¼ ounce; dried lemon-peel, bruised, ¼ ounce; dried orris root, bruised, ½ ounce; white tartar, 1 ounce. Place it in a cellar where the temperature is low, and in a fortnight taste it, if not sweet enough add more lump-sugar with half a pint or a pint of finings, then bung close.

5. Cold water, 9 gallons; white gooseberries, 10 gallons; ferment, then add white sugar, 12 pounds; raisins, 3 pounds; white tartar, dissolved, 2 ounces; dried orange-peel, ½ ounce; dried lemon-peel, ¼ ounce; orris root, bruised, ½ ounce; spirit of wine (pf.), 1 gallon; a handful of sweet briar blossoms.

Pink Champagne.

Cochineal 1½ ounces. Bruise it, and put it into a hogshead of white champagne

Catechu Lozenges.

Sugar four pounds, catechu twelve ounces. Make into paste with dissolved gum.

Catechu à l'Ambergris.

To the paste for catechu lozenges add sixteen grains of Ambergris.

Catechu with Musk.

The same as for catechu, adding sixteen grains of musk.

Catechu with Orange-Flowers.

As before, adding twelve drops of essence of neroli.

Catechu with Violets.

As before, adding Florence orris-root in powder, three drachms. These are all used to fasten the teeth, and disguise an offensive breath.

Cheap Beer.

Fill a boiler with the green shells of peas, pour on water till it rises half an inch above the shells, and simmer for three hours. Strain off the liquor, and add a strong decoction of the wood sage, or the hop, so as to render it pleasantly bitter; then ferment in the usual manner. The word sage is the best substitute for hops, and being free from any anodyne property, is entitled to a preference. By boiling a fresh quantity of shells in the decoction before it becomes cold, it may be so thoroughly impregnated with saccharine matter, as to afford a liquor, when fermented, as strong as ale.

Cheap Cement.

Quick-lime, 1 part; white of egg, 2 parts. Mix, and apply at once.

Chelsea Pensioner's Remedy for Gout and Rheumatism.

1. Gum guaiacum, 1 ounce; rhubarb (powder), 2 drachms; flowers of sulphur, 2 ounces; cream of tartar, 1 ounce; ginger powder, 1 ounce. Make them into an electuary with treacle. Dose—two tea-spoonfuls night and morning.

2. Powdered guaiacum, 1 part; powdered rhubarb, 2 parts; cream of tartar, 8 parts; flowers of sulphur, 16 parts; nutmeg, 2 parts; honey, 130 parts. Dose for rheumatism, &c., two large spoonfuls night and morning.

Cheltenham Salts.

Glauber salts, common salts, Epsom salts, equal parts, powder. Dose—half an ounce to one ounce.

Bottled Cheltenham Water.

Take soda-water bottles and nearly fill them with clear water, then add Rochelle salt, 1 drachm; bicarbonate of soda, 25 grains; chloride of sodium, 5 grains; sulphuric acid, 7 drops. Cork and wire them immediately.

Effervescing Cheltenham Salts.

Tartaric acid, dried, 25 parts; tartrate of iron, 1 part; seidlitz salt, 120 parts. Mix. Dose—a full tea-spoonful in a glass of water.

Chemic Blue.

Indigo, 1 part; oil of vitriol, 9 parts. Dissolve.

Cherry Brandy.

1. Treacle, 125 pounds; spirit (45 up.), 95 gallons; bruised bitter almonds, 12 ounces (more or less, to taste); cloves, ½ to 1 ounce; cassia, ½ to 1 ounce. Put the ingredients into a large cask, well mix and let them lie a month, occasionally stirring.

2. Cherries, bruised, 25 gallons; sugar, 30 pounds; cloves, cassia, each ½ ounce; spirit (35 up.), 60 gallons; bitter almonds, bruised, 3 ounces. Dissolve the sugar in a little water, and then put the whole into a cask and macerate for three months, occasionally stirring.

Perfumed Cherry juice Paper.

Dip the paper into the prepared juice and dry.

Cherry Wine.

Water, 10 gallons; fruit, bruised, 10 gallons; sugar, 22 pounds; cherry-stones, bruised, 2 pounds; honey, 5 pounds. Boil and ferment, then add spirit, 1 gallon; red tartar, 6 ounces; cardamoms, bruised, 1 ounce.

Chevalier Ruspini's Tooth Powder.

Cuttle-fish bone, 16 parts; cream of tartar, 4 parts; prepared chalk, 4 parts; roach alum, 2 parts; orris powder, 3 parts; oil of rhodium, 10 drops; oil of lavender, 10 drops. Reduce them to a fine powder and sift through gauze.

Factitious Chia Turpentine.

1. Yellow resin, 56 pounds; spirits of turpentine, 2 gallons; Canada balsam, 10 pounds; rape oil, 8 pounds; lard, 8 pounds. Melt, then cool a little and stir in water, 15 pounds.

2. Yellow resin, 84 pounds; spirits of turpentine, 4 gallons; rape oil, 1 gallon; water, 2 gallons. Melt the first three together, then cool a little and stir in the water.

To clean China.

Use a little fuller's earth and soda, or pearlash with your water.

To make an Aquatic Life Hat.

The upper part of the crown of the hat is made air-tight and waterproof, so that in the event of the wearer falling into the water, it will save him by its buoyancy from being drowned, if he only holds it in his hand. It is to be fastened by a small riband to the button-hole of the wearer's coat, in aquatic expeditions, &c. In order to render the hat still more efficacious, and enable it to save more lives than one, the lining is formed so as to be capable of being pulled out and inflated by the breath, and then closed at the extremity; in which state it will save several persons in the water.

English Iron-Stone China.

Flint-glass, 1 part; China clay, 20 parts; Cornish stone, 30 parts. Mix

Excellent China Ink.

Finest lamp-black, 75 parts; thick mucilage, 15 parts; strong ink, pale new, 50 parts; ox gall, 12 parts. Grind them well together, and if too soft evaporate a little of the water by a gentle heat; if too thick add more ink.

Chinese Depilatory.

Fresh-burnt lime, 16 ounces; pearlash, 2 ounces; sulphuret of potash, 2 ounces. Reduce them to fine powder in a mortar, then put it into closely-corked phials. For use, the part must be first soaked in warm water, then a little of the powder made into a paste must be immediately applied should it irritate the skin, wash it off with hot water or vinegar.

Chinese Edge for Books.

1. Colour the edge with light liquid blue and dry; then take a sponge charged with vermilion, and dab on spots according to fancy: next throw on rice, and finish the edge with dark liquid blue.

2. Colour light blue on different parts of the edge with a sponge; do the same where there are vacancies with yellow and Brazil red; dry and dab on a little vermilion in spots; then throw on rice and finish with a bold sprinkle of dark blue. Burnish.

Chinese Fire.

When the bore of the cases is less than three-quarter inch, take gunpowder, 16 parts; nitre, 8 parts; charcoal, 3 parts; sulphur, 3 parts; powdered cast-iron borings, 10 parts. Mix.

When more than three-quarter inch bore, take gunpowder, 16 parts; nitre, 12 parts; charcoal, 3 parts, sulphur, 3 parts; coarse borings, 12 parts. Mix.

Chinese Marble for Leather Book-Covers, &c.

Colour the cover of the book dark brown, and when dry, put it into the cutting-press with the boards perfectly flat; mix whiting and water of a thick consistence and throw it on, in spots or streaks, some large and some small, which must remain till dry. Spot or sprinkle the cover with liquid blue, and lastly, throw on large spots of liquid red. The colours must be dry before washing off the whiting.

Chinese Paste.

Bullock's blood, 9 parts; quick-lime, 1 part. Beat to a paste. For use, beat it to a proper consistence with water.

Chinese Paste for Stars, &c.

Camphor, 1 part; linseed oil, 1 part; nitre, 4 parts; meal powder, 1½ parts; sulphur, 16 parts. Spirit to mix.

Chinese Purging Cups.

These cups are made of red sulphuret of arsenic. Wine left in them all night becomes purgative by the morning, and is taken as such. A dangerous and uncertain medicine.

Ching's Worm Lozenges.

The yellow.—Powdered saffron, 1 ounce; protochloride of mercury, 12 ounces; sugar, ¼ cwt. Mucilage to mix. Divide the mass into 5760 lozenges. Dose—one to six going to bed.

The Brown.—Protochloride of mercury, 7 ounces; jalap, 3½ pounds. sugar, 9 pounds. Mucilage to mix. Divide into 6720 lozenges. Dose—one to six early the following morning.

Chlorate Matches.

Vermilion, 2 parts; gum, 5 parts; sugar, 8 parts; flowers of sulphur, 10 parts; chlorate of potash, 30 parts. Water to make a paste. Reduce each separately to fine powder, using the utmost caution, then make the whole into a paste with water, and dip the tips of the matches into it. For use, dip the match into strong sulphuric acid.

Chocolate and Cocoa for Icing.

Chocolate, 2 ounces; cream for icing, 2 pints; yolks of 4 eggs. Mix well ready for icing.

Chocolate Drops.

Powdered chocolate, 1 ounce; sugar, 1 pound. Mix and follow the plan for confectionary drops. Cocoa may be used instead of chocolate.

Potato Yeast

Is made of mealy potatoes boiled thoroughly soft; they are then skinned, and mashed as smooth as possible, when as much hot water shauld be put on them as will make a mash of the consistency of good beer yeast. Add to every pound of potatoes two ounces of treacle, and when just warm stir in for every pound of potatoes two large spoonsful of yeast. Keep it warm till it has done fermenting, and in twenty-four hours it will be fit for use. A pound of potatoes will make nearly a quart of yeast, and it is said to be equally as good as brewers' yeast.

Another kind of yeast is made as follows:—Take half a pound of fine flour, the same quantity of coarse brown sugar, and a quarter of a peck of bruised malt; boil these over the fire for a quarter of an hour, in half a gallon of water, then strain the liquor through a sieve into an upright jug, and when cooled to 80 deg. of heat, add one pint of the artificial Seltzer water, or, if procurable, Seltzer water itself, or water impregnated with fixed air—the mixture will soon begin to ferment. It should then be set before the fire, and when ebullition ceases, the yeast will sink to the bottom. Pour off the clear liquor, and the yeast will be fit for use.

The *Patent Yeast*, used extensively by London bakers, is made by taking half a pound of hops and two pailsful of water; mix and boil till it is reduced to one pailful; strain the decoction into the seasoning tub, and when sufficiently cool add half a peck of malt. In the meantime, put the hops, strained off, again into two pailsful of water, and boil till reduced to one, as before; then strain the liquor, while hot, into the seasoning tub. Again repeat the same process of boiling, and strain off as before. When the liquor has cooled to about blood-heat, strain off the malt, and add to the liquor two quarts of yeast from the previous making;—brewers' yeast will not answer the purpose. This yeast occupies, in making, about eight hours.

Cooling Fever Drink.

Vinegar, 1 pound; honey, 2 pounds; water, 6 pounds. Mix.

Soluble Copaiba.

Balsam of copaiba, 1 part; caustic potash, 2 parts. Dissolve with heat. This is suitable both for pills or aqueous solution.

Factitious Balsam of Copaiba.

1. Castor oil (pale), 3 gallons; balsam of copaiba, 2 gallons; yellow resin, 6 pounds; turpentine, 1 pound. Digest with heat in a close vessel until perfectly mixed.

2. Castor oil, 1 gallon; yellow resin, 4 pounds; Canada balsam, 7 pounds; spirits of turpentine, 1 pound. Mix and dissolve with a gentle heat, then add oil of juniper, 1 drachm; oil of savine, 1 drachm.

Black Copal Varnish.

Take lamp-black or ivory black in fine powder, and mix it with the varnish.

Blue Copal Varnish.

Indigo, Prussian blue, blue verditer, or ultra marine. All these substances must be powdered fine. Proceed as before.

Fine Pale Copal Varnish.

Pale African copal, 1 part. Fuse, then add hot pale oil, 2 parts. Boil until the mixture is stringy, then cool a little and add pale turpentine (spt.), 3 parts. Mix well.

Flaxen Grey Copal Varnish.

Ceruse, which forms the ground of the paste, mixed with a small quantity of Cologne earth, as much English red, or carminated lake, and a particle of Prussian blue, and colour the varnish therewith.

Green Copal Varnish.

Verdigris, crystallized verdigris, compound green, (a mixture of yellow and blue). The first two require a mixture of white in proper proportions, from a fourth to two-thirds, according to the tint intended to be given. The white used for this purpose is ceruse, or the white oxide of lead, or Spanish white. Proceed as before.

Improved Copal Varnish.

Caoutchoucine (white and scentless), strongest alcohol, equal parts; copal in the proportion of two pounds to a gallon. Digest in a close vessel, without heat, for one week.

Pearl Grey Copal Varnish.

White and black; white and blue; for example, ceruse and lamp-black; ceruse and indigo: mix them with the varnish, according to the tint required.

Purple Copal Varnish.

Prussian blue and vermilion, or any other blue and red, then proceed as before.

Red Copal Varnish.

1. Vermilion, red oxide of lead (minium), red ochre, or Prussian red &c., and proceed as before.

2. Dragon's blood, brick red, or Venetian red, &c., and proceed as before.

Violet Copal Varnish.

Vermilion, blue, white, in proportions as required to colour the varnish

White Copal Varnish.

Copal, 16 parts. Melt, and add linseed oil (hot), 8 parts; spirits of turpentine, 15 parts; finest white lead to colour.

Yellow Copal Varnish.

Yellow oxide of lead, or Naples and Montpellier, both reduced to impalpable powder. These yellows are hurt by the contact of iron and steel; in mixing them up, therefore, a horn spatula with a glass mortar and pestle must be employed. Or, gum guttæ, yellow ochre, or Dutch pink, according to the nature and tone of the colour to be imitated, and proceed as before.

Bean-shot Copper.

Take copper, melt it, and pour it in a small stream into boiling water.

Feather-shot Copper.

Take copper, melt it, and pour it in a small stream into cold water.

Copying Ink.

Add one ounce of moist sugar to every pint of common ink.

Copying Paper.

Lay open your quire of paper, (clean white, of large size), take the brush and cover it with the following varnish, then hang it up on the line; take another sheet and repeat the operation, until you have finished your quantity. If not clear enough, give each sheet another coat when dry:—Canada balsam, turpentine, equal parts. Mix.

Artificial Coral.

Yellow resin, 4 parts; vermilion, 1 part. Melt. This gives a very pretty effect to glass, twigs, cinders, stones, &c., dipped into it. It is also useful for a cement for ladies' fancy work, such as grottoes, &c.

Coral Tooth Powder.

Bole, 1 pound; prepared chalk, 2 pounds; cassia, 3 ounces. Mix and powder fine, then sift through gauze.

Real Coral Tooth Powder.

Coral (red), 1 ounce; chalk, 2 ounces; bole, 1½ ounce; cassia, 4 drachms. Powder fine, and sift through gauze.

To represent Cordage in Fireworks.

Antimony, 1 part; juniper resin, 1 part; nitre, 2 parts; sulphur, 12 parts. Mix, and imbue soft ropes with the composition.

To Distil Cordials or Compound Spirits.

The perfection of this grand branch of distillery depends upon the observation of the following general rules, which are easy to be observed and practised: 1. The artist must always be careful to use a well-cleansed spirit, or one freed from its own essential oil. For as a compound cordial is nothing more than a spirit impregnated with the essential oil of the ingredients, it is necessary that the spirit should have deposited its own. 2. Let the time of previous digestion be proportioned to the tenacity of the ingredients, or the ponderosity of their oil. 3. Let the strength of the fire be proportioned to the ponderosity of the oil intended to be raised with the spirit. 4. Let a due proportion of the finest parts of the essential oil be united with the spirit; the grosser and less fragrant parts of the oil not giving the spirit so agreeable a flavour, and at the same time rendering it thick and unsightly. This may in a great measure be effected by leaving out the feints, and making up to proof with fine soft water in their stead.

A careful observation of these four rules will render this extensive part of distillation far more perfect than it is at present. Nor will there be any occasion for the use of burnt alum, white of eggs, isinglass, &c., to fine down the cordial waters, for they will presently be fine, sweet and pleasant.

It must be observed, however, that most cordials may be made without distillation, though not of such fine quality.

Coriander Cordial.

Coriander seeds (bruised), 7 pounds; proof spirit, 30 gallons; orange-peel (dried), 5 ounces, cloves and caraways, 1 ounce. Macerate for a week, then add sugar, 85 pounds; dissolved in water, 40 gallons. Mix and fine.

Paste resembling the Red Cornelian.

Plain paste, 1000 parts; glass of antimony, 500 parts; calcined vitriol, 63 parts or less; manganese, 4 parts. Melt together.

Paste resembling the White Cornelian.

Plain paste, 1000 parts; yellow ochre, 8 parts; calcined bones, 31 parts. As before.

Cornette's Purified Opium.

Extract of opium, and dissolve it in three times its weight of water, then strain and evaporate.

Corn Plaster.

1. Bees'-wax, 1 pound; resin, 4 ounces; Venice turpentine, 8 ounces ulphate of copper, 8 ounces; arsenic, 1 ounce. Mix with heat.

2. Yellow wax, 1 pound; Burgundy pitch, 6 ounces; turpentine, 4 unces; powdered verdigris, 2 ounces. Mix, with heat, then spread the composition on linen or leather, and polish the surface. Cut it into small pieces.

Sir H. Davy's Corn Solvent.

Potash, 2 parts; salt sorrel, 1 part. Mix in fine powder. Lay a small quantity on the corn for four or five successive nights, binding it on with rags

Corn Solvent.

Pearlash (dried), 1 part; water, 2 parts. Mix. Apply with a rag.

Simple and Elegant Cosmetic.

Take half a pound of soft soap, melt over a slow fire with a gill of sweet oil, add two or three table-spoonfuls of fine sand, and stir the mixture together until cool. The shelly sea-sand, sifted from the shells, has been found better than that which has no shells.

This simple cosmetic has, for several years past, been used by many ladies who are remarkable for the delicate softness and whiteness of their hands, which they, in a great measure, attribute to the use of it; though they add, that they have found common soap, used in the ordinary way, with the addition of the abovementioned sand at the moment of washing, to answer the same purpose.

The cheapness of the above cosmetic forms a strong recommendation of it.

To allay the Itching produced by Cowhage.

Wash the part with a solution of sulphate of iron, or warm oil.

Cough Mixture.

1. Almond milk, 96 parts; syrup of tolu, 16 parts; sal volatile, 1 part; ipecacuanha wine, 2 parts. Mix, and take two table-spoonfuls three times a day.

2. Paregoric, 2 parts; syrup of tolu, 1 part; ipecacuanha wine, 1 part; almond milk, 12 parts. Mix, and take a table-spoonful three or four times a day.

3. Paregoric, 1 ounce; syrup of squills, 2 ounces; antimonial wine, 4 drachms; water, 6 ounces. Mix. Dose, two tea-spoonfuls every half hour, until the cough abates.

Court Plaster.

1. Balsam of benzoin, 1 part; alcohol, 12 parts. Mix, then isinglass, 2 parts; water barely to dissolve. Strain the two solutions separately, then mix them. For use, place the bottle in warm water, and give the silk, previously strained, ten or twelve coats with a brush; when dry, give it a coat of the following; Chia turpentine, 1 part; tincture of benzoin, 2 parts. Mix.

2. Thick mucilage, 8 ounces; thick syrup, 1 ounce; tincture of benzoin, 1 ounce. Mix. Apply as before.

3. Isinglass, 4 ounces; water, 3 ounces. Dissolve, then add tincture of benzoin, 1 ounce. Apply warm.

4. Isinglass, 1 ounce; gum arabic, 4 ounces; water, 6 ounces. Dissolve, then add balsam of Peru, 2 drachms. Apply warm.

5. Isinglass, 1 ounce; water, 4 ounces. Dissolve, and add alcohol, 8 ounces; tincture of benzoin, 2 ounces. Give the silk, previously strained, four or five coats with this varnish; and, when thoroughly dry, two coats of the following to finish: Chia turpentine, 4 ounces; tincture of benzoin 6 ounces. Mix.

6. Spread either of the compositions on goldbeater's skin instead of silk.

Cough Lozenges.

Laudanum, 1 ounce; balsam of tolu, 1½ ounce; liquorice, 3½ ounces, ipecacuanha powder, 2 ounces; oil of aniseed, ½ ounce; starch, 1 pound; sugar, 3 pounds; mucilage to mix.

Cough Pills.

Compound squill pill, 16 parts; opium, 2 parts; tartar emetic, 1 part. Mix, and divide into three-grain pills, and take one twice a day.

Cowslip Mead.

Mead wine, 3 parts; cowslip wine, 2 parts; lemon wine, 1 part. Mix and fine.

Cowslip Perfume.

Oil of lavender, 1 part; oil of caraway, 2 parts; essence of lemon, 4 parts; essence of bergamot, 8 parts. Mix.

Cowslip Red Wine.

Cowslip white wine, 30 gallons; red beet sliced, 3 pounds; red tartar, 9 ounces; cloves and cassia, each, ½ ounce. Let them stand together for fourteen days, then rummage well, and add one pint of filings.

Cowslip White Wine.

Water, 18 gallons; Malaga raisins, 36 pounds; cowslip flowers, 16 pounds. Boil gently, then ferment and add white tartar, 3 ounces; spirit, 3 quarts or a gallon.

To Choose Crabs.

The heaviest are the best, and those of the middle size sweetest; the joints of the legs should be stiff, eyes lively, and the body possess a very agreeable smell.

Crayons.

1. Shell lac, 6 parts; spirit, 4 parts; turpentine, 2 parts; colour, 12 parts; pale clay, 12 parts. Mix.

2. Pipe-clay, colour as required, water to mix. Form into a stiff paste and roll it into crayons.

To Fix Crayon Colours.

Paste your paper on canvass, in a frame, in the usual way, then brush over the back two or three times with the following mixture, and when the last coat is dry give the face of the picture one or two coats in the same way. This will make it resemble an oil painting. Spirits of turpentine, 10 parts; boiled oil, 6 parts. Mix.

Species for Crayons.

Pipe-clay, alabaster, equal quantities. Mix with water. Any colour may be added as required.

Cream Balls.

White hard soap, 6 pounds; starch, 1 pound. Form into balls with water and roll them in powdered starch.

A Substitute for Cream.

Take two or three eggs, break them into a basin and beat them well then add half a pint of good milk (hot), and beat them again until quite smooth. If milk cannot be procured, water may be used instead.

Cream for Ices.

White sugar, 2½ ounces; yolks of two eggs; new milk (warm), 1 pint Rub together, strain and keep for use.

Cream for the Hair.

Lard, 2 parts; oil of almonds, 1 part. Melt and scent with jessamine or bergamot.

Cream of Roses.

Oil of almonds, 1 pound; rosewater, 1 pint; white wax and spermaceti, each, 1 ounce. Mix in a pipkin with a little heat, then add essence of neroli, 20 drops; ottar of roses, 15 drops. Put it into pots and tie it over with skin or oiled leather.

Crême de Macarons.

Sugar, 7 pounds; proof spirit, 8 pounds; water, 10 pounds; white sugar, 8 pounds; blanched bitter almonds (bruised), ½ ounce; powdered cloves, 50 grains; powdered cinnamon, 50 grains; powdered mace, 50 grains. Tinge to a violet with tincture of turnsole and cochineal. Macerate for ten days and filter.

Crême de Noyeau de Martinique.

Sugar, 100 pounds; spirit, 15 gallons; orange flower water, ½ gallon; bitter almonds (bruised), 3 pounds; essence of lemon, 1 ounce; water, 25 gallons. Macerate the almonds and essence in the spirit for fourteen days, then add the sugar, previously dissolved in the water; let them stand together for one month, then strain.

Crême des Barbades.

Two dozen lemons, sliced; six large citrons, sliced; fresh balm leaves, ½ pound or less; loaf-sugar, 30 pounds; proof spirit, 3 gallons; water, 4 gallons. Put the fruit into the spirit and macerate for four days, then pour the water on the balm leaves, steep for half an hour and strain the liquor on the sugar; lastly, add the spirit.

Crême d'Orange.

Six dozen of oranges (sliced), orange flower water, 1 gallon; spirit, 4 gallons; saffron, ½ ounce. Macerate for fourteen days, then add sugar, 40 pounds; dissolved in water, 10 gallons.

To remove Crickets.

Put a little chloride of lime and powdered tobacco in their holes.

Crimson Flame.

Take alcohol, any quantity, and dissolve a little of one of the salts of strontia in it.

Croton Pills for Costiveness.

Castile soap, 1 drachm; croton oil, 20 drops; pil. rhei, ½ drachm. Mix and divide into 30 pills. Dose, one pill; if this should prove insufficient, two may be taken the next time.

Croton Soap.

Croton oil, 2 parts; water of caustic potass, 1 part. Rub together in a mortar. Purgative. Dose, one to three grains.

Crown Glass.

Arsenic, 1 part; borax, 2 parts; nitre, 30 parts; pearlash, 60 parts; white sand, 100 parts; broken glass, 300 parts; lime, 60 parts. Mix.

Crystal Glass.

Manganese, 1 part; nitre, 60 parts; pearlashes, 125 parts; red lead, 150 parts; fine white sand, 375 parts. Mix.

Crystal Powder.

Take quartz, heat it red-hot, and throw it into cold water, then dry and pound it in an agate mortar.

Crystal Varnish.

Pure Canada balsam, pale spirits of turpentine, equal parts. Put them into a close strong vessel, and apply a gentle hand-heat, with agitation, then allow the vessel to rest for two or three days and pour off the clear.

To Pickle Cucumbers.

Trim and wash them in salt and water, drain, and put them into the bottles, add a little mace, cloves, capsicum and mustard-seed, then cover them with white vinegar nearly boiling hot; cork immediately.

To Preserve Cucumbers, &c.

Trim, wash, and dry them, then serve them as fruit, which see.

Culinary Pepper.

Cassia, 1 pound; pimento, 1 pound; ginger, 1 pound; nutmegs, 1 pound; common salt, 6 pounds; cloves, ¼ ounce; mace, ¼ ounce; cayenne, ¼ ounce. Grind and sift.

Cumin Plaster.

Burgundy pitch, 32 parts; cumin seeds, 2 parts; caraway, 2 parts; berries of the bay tree, 2 parts; sweet oil, 1 part; water, 1 part. Mix Discutient.

Cumin Water.

Cumin seeds, 7 pounds; water, 12 gallons. Distil off nine or ten gallons.

Rob of Currants.

Take the juice, and evaporate it slowly to a proper consistence. Some persons add sugar.

Currant Vinegar.

This is made in the same way as that from gooseberries, only pick off the currants from the stalks.

Curaçoa.

1. Cinnamon, 2 ounces; brandy or spirit, 3 quarts; white sugar, 2½ pounds; Seville oranges, 2 dozen. Digest for three weeks.

2. Proof spirit, 10 pounds; water, 5 pounds; sugar, 4 pounds; peels of six Seville oranges; powdered cassia, 2 scruples; powdered mace 2 scruples; ground Brazil, 1 ounce; burnt sugar to complete the tint. Macerate for ten days and strain.

3. Five gallons of highly rectified spirits, four pounds of fresh orange-peel, one drachm of the oil of bitter almonds, one drachm of the oil of cassia (first killed in spirits of wine), two ounces of pulverized Brazil wood, and two quarts of syrup; let them be well stirred up every day for a fortnight, then add one gallon of water, and colour it with caramel; let it stand to brighten; and if not quite bright, pass it through a filtering-bag.

Currant Wine (French Method).

Water, 30 gallons; honey, 2 gallons; red currants (bruised), 10 pounds; sugar, 15 pounds; red tartar, 2 ounces. Mix, and allow it to ferment, then rack it into a clean cask. If it does not appear disposed to ferment, add a little yeast.

Currie Powder.

1 Coriander seeds, 20 parts; black pepper, 3 parts; cayenne, 1 part; turmeric, 6 parts; cumin seeds, 6 parts. Reduce to powder and well mix.

2. Corianders, 7 pounds; turmeric, 7 pounds; black pepper, 2 pounds; mustard, 2 pounds; ginger, 2 pounds; cardamons, 1 pound; cayenne, 9 ounces; cassia, 9 ounces; cumin seeds, 9 ounces. Mix.

Cyanide of Silver.

Nitrate of silver, 18 drachms; dilute hydrocyanic acid, 1 pint; distilled water, 1 pint. Dissolve the nitrate in the water, then add the acid; wash the precipitate and dry.

British Cyprus Wine.

Soft water, 50 gallons; elder juice, 50 gallons; raw sugar, 120 pounds; cloves (bruised), ½ ounce; ginger, 1 ounce. Boil and ferment, then rack it into a cask with three gallons of spirit, three pounds of raisins (bruised), and one quart of finings. Observe not to crack the stones in the berries in squeezing out the juice.

Daffy's Elixir.

1. Small senna (waste), 3 parts; bruised jalap, 1 part; bruised rhubarb, 1 part; coriander seed, 1 part; ginger, 1 part; treacle, 12 parts; proof spirit (common), 96 parts. Digest with moderate heat.

2. Waste senna, ¼ cwt.; common rhubarb, ¼ cwt.; common jalap, 14 pounds; caraways, 14 pounds; aniseed, 14 pounds; treacle, ¾ cwt.; red sanders, 7 pounds; spirit from tincture bottoms, 140 gallons. Reduce the rhubarb, &c., to coarse powder and digest for twenty-one days.

Currie Vinegar.

Currie powder, 5 ounces; vinegar, 1 gallon. Infuse for a week and strain.

Currie Wine.

Currie powder, 5 ounces; white wine, 1 gallon. Digest for one week and strain.

Dalby's Carminative.

1. Magnesia, 2 drachms; oil of peppermint, 3 drops; oil of nutmeg, 7 drops; oil of aniseed, 9 drops; tincture of castor, 1½ drachm; tincture of assafœtida, 45 drops; tincture of opium, 18 drops; tincture of (ess.) pennyroyal, 50 drops; tincture of cardamons (comp.), 95 drops; peppermint water, 7 ounces. Mix.

2. Laudanum, 2 drachms; oil of peppermint, 1 drachm; oil of caraway, 2 drachms; proof-spirit, 6 ounces; carbonate of magnesia, 12 ounces· syrup of poppies, 36 ounces; fetid spirit of ammonia, 3 ounces; distilled water, 5 pints. Mix.

3. Magnesia, 40 grains; oil of peppermint, 1 drop; oil of nutmeg, 2 drops; oil of aniseed, 3 drops; tincture of castor, 30 drops; tincture of assafœtida, 15 drops; tincture of opium, 5 drops; spirits of pennyroyal, 15 drops; compound tincture of cardamons, 30 drops; peppermint water, 2 ounces. Mix.

To preserve Walls from Dampness.

When the walls are about two feet high, use for one row of stones or bricks, a mixture of tar, pitch, and fine sand, in the same way as mortar. The composition must be previously melted to a proper consistence.

Damson Wine.

Water, 12 gallons; damsons (bruised), 8 gallons; raw sugar, 30 pounds. Ferment, then add red tartar (dissolved), 6 ounces; cloves (bruised), ¾ ounce. Let it stand until fine, then bottle it.

Dandelion Coffee.

Good colonial coffee, 3 parts; hard extract of dandelion, 1 part; chicory, 1 part. Reduce them to coarse powder, and mix and grind them together.

Dawson's Lozenges.

Powdered lump-sugar, 26 parts; powdered gum arabic, 2 parts; Italian juice, 1 part; starch, 3 parts. Mix, with warm water, and form into lozenges.

The Delight of the Mandarins.

Proof-spirit, 1 gallon; water, 1 gallon; lump-sugar, 6 pounds; anisum chinæ, ½ ounce; ambrette, ½ ounce; safflower, ¼ ounce. Mix, and let them remain together for one week, occasionally shaking the mixture, then filter or decant the clear.

Darby's Oil.

Oil of amber, 1 part; balsam of sulphur, 1 part; Barbadoes tar, 1 part. Mix, with heat.

Huxham's Tincture of Bark.

Peruvian bark, 1 pound; orange-peel, ¾ pound; snake-root, 2 ounces, saffron, 6 drachms; cochineal, 2 drachms; alcohol, 6 pints; water, 5 pints. Macerate for fifteen days.

Delphine.

Make a paste with blanched staveacre seeds and water, add more water and boil, strain and add calcined magnesia, boil for a few minutes, strain and wash the sediment with water; then digest it in alcohol, decant the tincture and distil off the spirit. The white pulverulent residue is the Delphine.

Hydrated Peroxyde of Iron, (an antidote for Arsenic.)

Sulphate of iron, 1000 parts; sulphuric acid (sp. g. 1.847), 200 parts; water, 4000 parts; nitric acid, q. s. Dissolve the sulphate in the water, add the sulphuric acid and heat the mixture to ebullition; then add the nitric acid, until all effervescence has ceased, and red fumes are no longer produced on the addition of more acid; let it cool, and add twenty or thirty times its weight of water; then precipitate the iron by adding ammonia in excess; wash the gelatinous precipitate until the water ceases to render barytes water turbid; dry and preserve it in the gelatinous state.

Tincture of Hydriodate of Potash.

Hydriodate of potash, 6 grains; distilled water, 6 drachms; proof-spirit, 2 drachms. Dose, forty drops, two or three times a day.

Hydrochlorate of Morphia.

Opium (cut small), 1 pound; crystallized chloride of lead, 2 ounces; animal charcoal, 4 ounces; hydrochloric acid and ammonia, a sufficient quantity. Macerate the opium in three pints of distilled water for twelve hours, then pound it and macerate with agitation for twelve hours more, hen strain, and pour one pint of fresh water on the remainder, and repeat the operation with a second and third pint, or until the water becomes tasteless. Mix the several liquors and evaporate to the consistence of a syrup, then add three pints of distilled water, and filter; to this add gradually the chloride of lead, previously dissolved in two quarts of boiling water, until it produces no further precipitation. Pour off the liquor and wash the residue in distilled water; mix the liquids together, evaporate and crystallize. Wipe the crystals with a cloth, then dissolve them in a pint of warm distilled water, with two ounces of the charcoal, filter, evaporate with a gentle heat, and set it aside to crystallize. Precipitate the remainder of the morphia left in the liquor with the ammonia, wash the precipitate, then add sufficient hydrochloric acid to saturate. Digest with the remainder of the charcoal, and proceed as before.

Hydrogen Gas.

Iron or zinc filings, 1 ounce; water, 5 pints; oil of vitriol, 2 ounces. Mix, and collect the gas.

Vegetable Hygrometer.

The dried calyx of the prickly carline thistle; in dry weather it expands itself horizontally; in wet weather it will remain closed.

Jackson's Itch Ointment.

Lard, sulphur vivum, palm oil, white hellebore, equal parts. Mix.

James's Powder.

Powdered antimony, 1 part; hartshorn shavings, 2 parts. Mix, and roast them in an iron pot until they become a greyish powder, then put it into a crucible with a small hole in the lid, and keep it in a red heat for two hours; lastly, cool and powder.

Japan Colouring, for Leather Book-Covers, &c.

After the book is covered and dry, colour the cover with potash-water mixed with a little paste, give it two good coats of Brazil wash, and glaire it. Put the book between wands, allowing the boards to slope a little Dash on copperas-water, then with a sponge full of red liquid, press out on the back and on different parts, large drops, which will run down each board and make a fine shaded red. When the cover is dry, wash it over two or three times with Brazil wash, to give it a brighter colour.

Japanese Cement, or Rice Glue.

Rice flour, water, sufficient quantity. Mix together cold, then bring the mixture to a boil, stirring it all the time. Observe to boil it in a vessel that will not colour it.

Transparent Liquid Japan for Metal.

Copal varnish, 35 parts; camphor, 1 part; boiled oil, 2 parts. Mix.

Japanner's Copal Varnish.

Copal (picked), 5 pounds; linseed oil, 20 ounces. Melt and digest until dissolved, then withdraw it from the fire and add oil of turpentine, 6 pounds. Well mix.

Japanner's Gold Size.

Gum ammoniac, 1 pound; boiled oil, 8 ounces; spirits of turpentine, 12 ounces. Melt the gum, then add the oil, and lastly the spirits of turpentine.

Oil of Jasmin.

Take an iron plate, on this place a cotton cloth imbued with olive oil, then a layer of flowers, then a cloth, and lastly an iron plate; repeat the series as convenient, and change the flowers for fresh ones until a proper scent is imparted; then apply pressure, collect the oil in glass bottles, and let it rest until fine; lastly, pour off the clear.

Jasmin Pommade. (French Method.)

Take a frame formed of four pieces of wood, two inches deep and one foot square, with a groove arranged to support a piece of glass, which is to form a moveable bottom, on this spread a layer of the following pommade Beef suet, 1 part; lard, 3 parts. Into this stick fresh jasmin flowers, in different parts every day, or every other day, for one, two, or three months, or until the pommade is sufficiently scented. In this way, in some of the large manufactories in France, are treated from 2000 to 5000 frames, which are piled on each other to a convenient height, by which method the perfume is prevented escaping, or what flies off is absorbed by the surrounding frames.

Ice Cream.

Any preserved fruit, 5 pounds; cream, 1 gallon; juice of six lemons, sugar to sweeten. Pass the whole through a sieve, then put it into the freezing pot, and work it until frozen.

Portable Ice House.

Two casks, one six or seven inches longer and wider than the other, into the largest put charcoal powder, about three or four inches deep, then place the smaller cask on this, and fill up the vacancy between the two with charcoal powder, and drive it down tight; arrange a double cover and fill it in the same way; then bore a hole one inch in diameter through the bottoms of the two casks, and insert a wooden pipe to let the water run out; lastly, put it in the coldest place possible.

To Improve the Flavour of Iceland Moss.

Soak the moss in water for a few hours.

To Procure Ice.

Nearly fill a gallon stone bottle with hot spring water (leaving room for about a pint), and put in two ounces of refined nitre; the bottle must then be stopped very close, and let down into a deep well. After three or four hours it will be completely frozen; but the bottle must be broken to procure the ice. If the bottle is moved up and down, so as to be sometimes in and sometimes out of the water, the consequent evaporation will hasten the process.

Incombustible Cloth.

1. Sal ammonia, 1 part; water, 4 parts. Dissolve and impregnate the cloth with the solution.

2. Alum, 1 part; water, 7 parts. Dissolve. As above.

Composition for Jet Fires.

Gunpowder, 16 parts; charcoal, 3 parts. Or, if larger than three-quarters of an inch bore, gunpowder, 16 parts; steel filings, 4 parts. Mix.

Jews' Lozenges.

Cassia in fine powder, 3 parts; myrrh, 2 parts; saffron, 2 parts; calamus aromaticus, 8 parts; sugar, 100 parts; honey to mix.

Imperial, or Ginger Pop.

1. Cream of tartar, 1 pound; ginger, 1½ ounce; white sugar, 7 pounds; essence of lemon, 1 drachm; water, 6 gallons; yeast, ½ pint. Mix. Tie the corks down.

2. Cream of tartar, 1½ ounce; sliced ginger, 1 ounce; white sugar, 12 ounces; oranges sliced, 3 in number; boiling water, 1 gallon. Digest until cold, then pour off the clear and add a little yeast; lastly, bottle it.

Impermeable Varnish.

Boiled oil, 100 parts; finely powdered litharge, 6 parts; genuine bees'-wax, 5 parts. Boil until sufficiently thick and stringy, then pour off the clear

Paste resembling the Chrysolite.

Plain paste, without the saltpetre, 200 parts; calcined iron, 1 part.

Cider.

After the apples are gathered from the trees, they are ground into what is called *pommage*, either by means of a common pressing stone, with a circular trough, or by a cider mill, which is either driven by the hand or by horse-power. When the pulp is thus reduced to a great degree of fineness, it is conveyed to the cider-press, where it is formed by pressure into a kind of cake, which is called the *cheese.*

This is effected by placing clear sweet straw, or hair cloths, between the layers of pommage, till there is a pile of ten or twelve layers. This pile is then subjected to different degrees of pressure in succession, till all the *must* or *juice* is squeezed from the pommage. This juice, after being strained in a coarse hair-sieve, is then put either into open vats or close casks, and the pressed pulp is either thrown away, or made to yield a weak liquor called washings.

After the liquor has undergone the proper fermentation in these close vessels, which may be best effected in a temperature of from forty to sixty degrees of Fahrenheit, and which may be known by its appearing tolerably clear, and having a vinous sharpness upon the tongue, any farther fermentation must be stopped by racking off the pure part into open vessels, exposed for a day or two in a cool situation. After this the liquor must again be put into casks and kept in a cool place during winter. The proper time for racking may always be known by the brightness of the liquor, the discharge of the fixed air, and the appearance of a thick crust formed of fragments of the reduced pulp. The liquor should always be racked off anew, as often as a hissing noise is heard, or as it extinguishes a candle held to the bung-hole.

When a favourable vinous fermentation has been obtained, nothing more is required than to fill up the vessels every two or three weeks, to supply the waste by fermentation. By the beginning of March the liquor will be bright and pure, and fit for final racking, which should be done in fair weather. When the bottles are filled, they should be set by uncorked till morning, when the corks must be driven in tightly, secured by wire or twine and melted rosin, or any similar substance.

Devonshire Cider.—Prefer the bitter-sweet apples, mixed with mild sour, in the proportion of one-third. Gather them when ripe, and lay them in heaps in the orchard. Then take them to the crushing-engine, made of iron-rollers at top and stone beneath; after passing through which, they are received into large tubs or cives, and are then called pommage. They are afterwards laid on the vat in alternate layers of the pommage and clean straw, called reeds. They are then pressed, the juice running through a hair sieve. After the cider is pressed out, it is put into hogsheads, where it remains for two or three days previously to fermenting. To stop the fermentation, it is drawn off into a clean vessel, but if the fermentation be very strong, two or three cans of cider are put into a clean vessel, and a match of brimstone burnt in it: it is then agitated, by which the fermentation of that quantity is completely stopped. The vessel is then nearly filled, the fermentation of the whole is checked, and the cider becomes fine:

but if, on the first operation, the fermentation is not checked, it is repeated till it is so, and continued from time to time till the cider is in a quiet state for drinking.

Some persons, instead of deadening a small quantity with a match, as above directed, put from one to two pints of an article called *stum* (bought of the wine coopers) into each hogshead : but the system of racking as often as the fermentation appears is generally preferred by the cider manufacturers of Devonshire.

About six sacks, or twenty-four bushels of apples, are used for a hogshead of sixty-three gallons. During the process, if the weather is warm, it will be necessary to carry it on in the shade, in the open air, and by every means keep it as cool as possible.

In nine months it will be in condition for bottling or drinking; if it continues thick, use some isinglass finings, and if at any time it ferments and threatens acidity, the cure is to rack it and leave the head and sediment.

Scotch method.—The apples are reduced to mucilage, by beating them in a stone trough (one of those used at pumps for watering horses) with pieces of ashpoles, used in the manner that potatoes are mashed. The press consists of a strong box, three feet square and twenty inches deep, perforated on each side with small auger or gimblet holes. It is placed on a frame of wood, projecting three inches beyond the base of the box. A groove is cut in this projection one inch and a half wide, and one inch deep, to convey the juice when pressed out of the box into a receiving pail. This operation is performed in the following manner. The box is filled alternately with strata of fresh straw and mashed fruit, in the proportion of one inch of straw to two inches of mucilage : these are piled up a foot higher than the top of the box ; and care is taken in packing the box itself, to keep the fruit and straw about one inch from the sides of the box which allows the juice to escape freely. A considerable quantity of the liquor will run off without any pressure. This must be applied gradually at first, and increased regularly towards the conclusion. A box of the above dimensions will require about two tons weight to render the residuum completely free from juice. [The residuum is excellent food for pigs, and peculiarly acceptable to them.]

The necessary pressure is obtained very easily, and in a powerful manner, by the compound lever pressing upon a lid or sink made of wood about two inches thick, and rendered sufficiently strong by two cross-bars. It is made to fit the opening of the box exactly ; and as the levers force the lid down, they are occasionally slacked or taken off, and blocks of wood are placed on the top of the lid, to permit the lever to act, even after the lid has entered the box itself. Additional blocks are repeated, until the whole juice is extracted. The pressure may be increased more or less, by adding or diminishing the weight suspended at the extremity of the lever.

The liquor thus obtained is allowed to stand undisturbed twelve hours, in open vessels, to deposit sediment. The pure juice is then put into clean casks, and placed in a proper situation to ferment, the temperature being from fifty-five to sixty degrees.

Cinnamon Drops.

For confectionary drops, and flavour with oil of cassia.

Champagne Cider.

Good cider, pale, 1 hogshead; spirit, 3 gallons; honey or sugar, 20 pounds. Mix, and let them rest for a fortnight, then fine with skimmed milk, ½ gallon. This will be very pale; and a similar article, when bottled in champagne bottles, and silvered and labelled, has been often sold to the ignorant for champagne. It opens very brisk if managed properly.

Cheap-made Cider.

Cider, good, 1 hogshead; water, 1 hogshead; treacle, 50 pounds; alum, dissolved, ½ pound. Match with brimstone.

General Rules for making Cider.

1. Always choose perfectly ripe and sound fruit.

2. Pick the apples by hand. (An active boy with the bag slung over his shoulder, will soon clear a tree. Apples that have lain any time on the soil, contract an earthy taste, which will always be found in the cider.)

3. After sweating, and before being ground, wipe them dry, and if any are found bruised or rotten, put them in a heap by themselves, for an inferior cider to make vinegar.

4. Always use hair cloths, instead of straw, to place between the layers of pommage. The straw, when heated, gives a disagreeable taste to the cider.

5. As the cider runs from the press, let it pass through a hair-sieve into a large open vessel, that will hold as much juice as can be expressed in one day. In a day, or sometimes less, the pumice will rise to the top, and in a short time grow very thick: when little white bubbles break through it, draw off the liquor by a spigot, placed about three inches from the bottom, so that the lees may be left quietly behind.

6. The cider must be drawn off into very clean, sweet casks, and closely watched. The moment the white bubbles before mentioned are perceived rising at the bung-hole, rack it again. When the fermentation is completely at an end, fill up the cask with cider, in all respects like that already contained in it, and bung it up tight; previous to which a tumbler of sweet oil may be poured into the bung-hole.

Cider Red Wine.

Cider, 16 gallons; honey, 27 pounds; tartar, red, 8 ounces; raw sugar, 3 pounds; sliced red-beet, 6 pounds. Boil, ferment, then add cassia, ½ ounce, ginger, ½ ounce; spirit, 5 quarts.

To improve Cider.

Cider, 1 hogshead; rum, weak flavoured, 2 gallons; alum, dissolved, 1 pound; honey, or coarse sugar, 15 pounds; sugar colouring sufficient; bitter almonds, ½ pound; cloves, ½ pound. Mix, and after three or four days fine it down with isinglass. For champagne cider omit the colouring, and fine it with two quarts of milk: this will render it very pale.

Cider White Wine.

Cider, 100 gallons; honey, 80 pounds; sugar, 20 pounds. Mix and ferment, then add spirit, 6 gallons; white tartar, 1½ pounds; bitter almonds, bruised, 1 ounce.

Cider Vinegar.

The poorest sort of cider will serve for vinegar, in managing which proceed thus: First draw off the cider into a cask that has had vinegar in it before; then put some of the apples that have been pressed into it, set the whole in the sun, and in a week or nine days it may be drawn off into another cask. This is a good table vinegar.

Cinchonine.

Peruvian bark, alcohol sufficient quantity. Boil in a close vessel until all the bitterness is extracted, then distil off the spirit; dissolve the residue in boiling water rendered acidulous with hydrochloric acid, add calcined magnesia, and boil until the liquor becomes clear; cool, filter, and wash the precipitate with cold water, dry and expose it to the action of boiling alcohol until all the bitterness is extracted; pour off the spirit, evaporate a little, and allow it to cool: the cinchonine will be produced in crystals. It may be purified by solution in any weak acid, and precipitation by adding an alkali.

Cinnamon Cordial.

Oil of cassia, 1 ounce; essence of lemon, 30 drops (or more); spirit, 15 gallons; sugar, 50 pounds; water, 10 gallons. Mix the spirit with the oil and essence, then add the sugar dissolved in the water, and filter.

Cinnamon Lozenges.

Finely-powdered cinnamon, ½ pound; finely-powdered sugar, 4 pounds finely-powdered starch, 1 pound. Mix with mucilage.

Cinnamon Lozenges. (Second Quality.)

Lump-sugar, 7 pounds; starch, 2 pounds; gum powder, 1 pound; oil of cassia to flavour. Mix with water, in which a little cochineal has been steeped, to impart a faint colour.

Cinnamon Soap. (First Quality.)

Palm oil soap, 2 parts; good tallow soap, 3 parts. Reduce to shavings, then liquefy by adding a little water, and placing the mixture in a water-bath until perfectly united; next cool to about 135° Fahr., and add finely-powdered yellow ochre to colour, and a sufficiency of the following perfume: Essence of cinnamon, 7 parts; essence of bergamot, 2 parts; essence of sassafras, 1 part. Well mix the whole together and mould.

Cinnamon Soap. (Second Quality.)

New white hard soap, palm soap, equal parts. Perfume with oil of cassia, and colour as before.

Cinnamon Water.

Cinnamon, 11 pounds; water, 17 gallons. Draw off 15 gallons. Cassia water is usually sold for this article.

Lozenges of Citrate of Iron.

Powdered gum acacia, 20 parts; fine sugar, 640 parts; essence of lemon, [illegible] part; citric acid, 40 parts; citrate of iron, 40 parts. Water to mix. Divide into ten-grain lozenges, five or six to be taken every day for gout.

Donovan's Mercurial Ointment.

1, Take genuine strong mercurial ointment and heat it in a water bath for one hour, let it cool, then remove the grey upper stratum. The mercury in the heavy residuum may be recovered by heat, or used in making blue ointment.

2. Protoxide of mercury, 1 pound; lard (purified), 16 pounds; suet, 4 pounds. Mix, and keep them in a heat of 325° Fahr. for two hours, constantly stirring them. The lard and suet must be perfectly pure, as the presence of salt would decompose a part of the oxide, and produce a portion of protochloride of mercury or calomel. This preparation is more powerful than the strong mercurial ointment.

To prevent the creaking of Doors.

1. Apply a little soap to the hinges.

Take lard, soap, black lead, equal parts. As before.

Dorchester Ale.

Pale malt, 1 quarter; amber malt, 2 quarters; hops, 19 pounds. Mash for the first liquor at 170° Fahr.; second liquor, 180° Fahr.; boil for thirty minutes. Use water sufficient to produce two barrels per quarter.

Factitious Dragon's Blood.

1. Red sanders, 7 parts; yellow resin, 9 parts; castor oil, 2 parts; benzoic acid, 3 parts; oxalate of lime, 1 part; phosphate of lime, 2 parts. Mix, with heat.

2. Yellow resin, 24 pounds, sperm oil, 3 pounds; red sanders, powdered, 5 pounds; Venetian red, 3 pounds. Mix, with heat, and form to sample.

Dram-drinker's Bitters.

Cloves, 1 part; bruised cascarilla, 2 parts; proof-spirit, 5 parts; water boiling, 30 parts. Steep the cloves and bark in the water for two hours, strain and add the spirit. Dose; a wine-glassful four times a day.

To gild or silver Drawings, &c.

Lay on the colours with a little size or gum; when dry, breathe on the design, and apply the leaf.

Dressing Ointment for Canker in Horses.

Tar, 1 pound; tallow, 1 pound; powdered verdigris, 4 ounces. Mix.

Dressing Ointment for Cattle.

Tar, 1 pound; resin, 1 pound; spirits of turpentine, 1 pound; tallow, 3 pounds; oil of vitriol, 5 ounces: sulphate of copper, 5 ounces; alum, 5 ounces. Mix very cautiously.

Remedy for Strains in Horses.

Take whiskey, half a pint; camphor, 1 ounce; sharp vinegar, 1 pint. Mix. Used for bathing.

Another for the same.

Take opodeldoc, warm it, and rub the strained part twice or thrice a day.

Druggist's Colours.

Yellow.—Take iron filings, hydrochloric acid to dissolve. Dilute with water.

Red.—Solution of sal ammoniac, cochineal to colour.

Blue.—1. Sulphate of copper, 1 part; alum, 1 part; water, 16 parts; oil of vitriol, q. s.

2. Indigo, 1 part; oil of vitriol, 3 parts. Dissolve, then dilute with water.

3. Ferrocyanide of iron, 1 part; hydrochloric acid, 2 parts. Dissolve, then dilute with water.

Green.—1. Verdigris, dilute sulphuric acid to dissolve. Dilute with water.

2. Verdigris, 1 part; acetic acid, 3 parts. Dissolve, and dilute with water.

Purple.—1. Sugar of lead, 1 ounce; cochineal, 25 grains. Dissolve.

2. Infusion of logwood, water of ammonia, q. s.

3. Logwood, alum, water, q. s. Make a decoction, and add a little spirit

To cure the Fit of Drunkenness.

Take half an ounce of mindererus spirit in a cupful of water. Repeat the dose every fifteen minutes.

Kyan's Patent Preventive of Dry Rot.

A solution of corrosive sublimate in water.

To choose Ducks.

Buy those which have supple feet, and are hard and thick on the breast.

Dutch Drops.

Balsam of sulphur, oil of turpentine, equal parts. Mix.

Remedy for the Staggers.

Bleed freely. Then make a drench out of the following ingredients:—Sassafras tea, 3 half pints; plantain juice, half a pint: assafœtida, half an ounce; saltpetre, one tea-spoonful. Mix. Drench thrice a week.

Another for the same.

Give a mash twice a week, composed of one gallon of bran, one table-spoonful of sulphur, one tea-spoonful of saltpetre, one quart of boiling sassafras tea, and an eighth of an ounce of assafœtida. Do not let the horse have any cold drink for half a day afterwards.

Remedy for the Mange.

Take flowers of sulphur and hog's lard, equal parts. Mix, and anoint twice a day. Bleed, and give two or three mashes, (composed of bran sulphur, saltpetre and sassafras,) within a week afterwards.

Hide-bound.

Bleed, and give a mash (at night) composed of one gallon of bran scalded with sassafras tea, one table-spoonful of flowers of sulphur, and one tea-spoonful of saltpetre. No cold water to be given for six hours afterwards.

To afford Assistance to a Person in Danger of Drowning.

If the spectator is unable to swim, and can make the sufferer hear, he ought to direct him to keep his hands and arms under water, until assistance comes; in the mean time, throw towards him a rope, a pole, or any thing that may help to bring him ashore, or on board; he will eagerly seize whatever is placed within his reach: thus he may, perhaps, be rescued from his perilous situation.

But this desirable object appears attainable by the proper use of a man's hat and pocket-handkerchief, which, being all the apparatus necessary, is to be used thus: spread the handkerchief on the ground, or deck, and place a hat, with the brim downwards, on the middle of it; then tie the handkerchief round the hat, like a bundle, keeping the knots as near the centre of the crown as possible. Now, by seizing the knots in one hand, and keeping the opening of the hat upwards, a person, without knowing how to swim, may fearlessly plunge into the water, with whatever may be necessary to save the life of a fellow-creature.

The best manner in which an expert swimmer can lay hold of a person he wishes to save from sinking, is to grasp his arm firmly between the shoulder and the elbow: this will prevent him from clasping the swimmer in his arms, and thus forcing him under water, and, perhaps, causing him to sink with him.

Dutch Currant Wine.

Warm water, 9 gallons; red currants, 8 gallons; raw sugar, 12 pounds (or more). Ferment, then add red tartar (dissolved), 2 ounces; bitter almonds, ½ ounce; cloves, ½ ounce; bruised ginger, 1 ounce. Bung close.

Dutch White Lead.

Sulphate of barytes, 28 pounds; pure white lead, 84 pounds. Mix.

Dupuytren's Eye Salve.

Red oxide of mercury, 6 grains; sulphate of zinc, 10 grains; lard, 1 ounce. Mix.

Dupuytren's Pomatum.

Prepared suet, 2 parts; lard, 1 part; oil of almonds, 1 part. Mix over a gentle fire, and perfume to taste.

Dyer's Spirit.

Aquafortis, 10 parts; sal ammoniac, 5 parts; tin, 2 parts. Dissolve.

Paste resembling Eagle Marine.

1. Plain paste, 10 pounds; smalts, 12 pounds.
2. Plain paste, 10 pounds; sulphuret of copper, 4 ounces; zaffre, 1 scruple.

Earthenware Varnish.

Flint glass, soda, equal parts. Mix.

East India Pomatum.

Take suet, 7 pounds; lard, 7 pounds: beeswax, 1 pound. Melt, then add essence of lemon, 4 ounces; gum benzoin, 3 ounces; musk, 2 scruples; oil of cloves, 25 drops; oil of rhodium, 25 drops. Mix well

Eau de Bouquet.

Scented honey water, 1 pint; eau sans pareille, 1½ pint; essence de jasmin, 8 ounces; oil of cloves, ¾ ounce; spirit of violets, 4 ounces; calamus aromaticus, 4 ounces; lavender, 4 ounces; essence of neroli, 6 drachms; essence of musk and ambergris, 1 drachm; spirit, 3 pints. Mix

Eau de Barbades.

Orange-peel (fresh), 1 ounce; lemon-peel, 4 ounces; cloves (coarsely powdered), ½ drachm; corianders (coarsely powdered), 1 drachm. Macerate in proof-spirit, ½ gallon; water, ½ gallon. Distil, then add powdered lump-sugar, 1 pound.

Eau de Cologne.

1. Essence of bergamot, 1 ounce; essence of lemon, 1 ounce; essence of rosemary, 1 ounce; essence of Portugal, 1 ounce; neroli, ½ ounce; alcohol, 9 or 10 gallons. Mix well in a close vessel.

2. Essence of bergamot, 6 ounces; essence of neroli, 3 drachms; essence of cedrat, 4 drachms; essence of lemon, 6 drachms; oil of rosemary, 2 drachms; eau de melisse des carmes 5 drachms; spirit, (25 op.), 4 gallons. Mix, and distil or filter.

Excellent Eau de Cologne.

Take the whole of the articles named in the form for Farina's Cologne, and macerate for ten days, with occasional agitation, then well mix with it calcined magnesia, 2 pounds; rummage together for one hour, then bung down and let it stand a week. Draw it off without disturbing the bottom, and filter the thick residue. All perfumed spirits are better distilled, and it is found that even the addition of essences, &c. to the distilled spirit, as in Farina's Cologne, does not produce so fine an article as if the whole were at once mixed, subjected to agitation for six or eight hours in a close vessel, and then distilled.

Farina's Eau de Cologne.

Spirit, 70 gallons; sage, 6 drachms; thyme, 6 drachms; balm mint, 12 ounces; spear mint, 12 ounces; calamus aromaticus, ½ ounce; angelica root, ¼ ounce; petals of roses, 4 ounces; violets, 4 ounces; lavender flowers, 2 ounces; orange flowers, ½ ounce; wormwood, 1 ounce; nutmegs, ½ ounce; cloves, ½ ounce; cassia, ½ ounce; mace, ½ ounce; sliced lemons, 2; sliced oranges, 2. Macerate for twenty-four hours, then draw over fifty gallons, then add essence of lemon, 1½ ounces; essence of cedrat, 1½ ounces; essence of balm mint, 1½ ounces; essence of lavender, 1½ ounces: seeds of anthos, ½ ounce; neroli, ½ ounce; essence of jasmin, 1 ounce; essence of bergamot, 12 ounces. Agitate for twelve days, then allow them to rest for a week, and draw off the clear. If not fine, filter through magnesia.

Very fine Eau de Cologne.

Alcohol, 1 gallon; neroli, 50 drops; essence of cedrat, 50 drops; essence of orange, 50 drops; essence of lemon, 50 drops; essence of bergamot, 50 drops; essence of rosemary, 50 drops; lesser cardamons, 2 drachms Distil, or macerate and filter.

Seventy-nine Experimental Receipts with the Metals.

1. Prepare two glasses of rain-water, and into one of them drop a single drop of sulphuric acid. Pour a little nitrate of silver into the other glass, and no change will be perceptible. Pour some of the same solution into the first glass, and a white precipitate of sulphate of silver will appear.

2. Prepare two glasses, as in the last experiment, and into one of them put a drop or two of muriatic acid. Proceed as before, and a precipitate of muriate of silver will be produced.

3. Take two glasses, as in Experiment 1, and into one of them put a drop of sulphuric acid, and a drop or two of muriatic acid : proceed as before with the nitrate of silver, and a mixed precipitate will be produced, consisting of muriate of silver and sulphate of silver.

4. Take the glass containing the mixed precipitate of the last experiment, and give it, by means of a lamp, the heat of boiling water. The sulphate of silver, if there be a sufficiency of boiling water, will now be re-dissolved, and the muriate of silver will remain separate at the bottom of the vessel. This experiment exhibits a method of separating these metallic salts whenever they occur in a state of mixture.

5. Mix one ounce of litharge of lead with one drachm of pulverized muriate of ammonia, and submit the mixture to a red heat in a clean tobacco-pipe. The increase of temperature will separate the ammonia in the form of gas, and the muriatic acid will combine with the lead. When the compound is well melted, pour it into a metallic cup, and you will have a true muriate of lead of a bright yellow colour, the brilliancy of which may be much heightened by grinding it as usual with oil. In this state it forms the colour called patent yellow.

6. Take one ounce of red lead, and half a drachm of charcoal, in powder, incorporate them well in a mortar, and then fill the bowl of a tobacco-pipe with the mixture. Submit it to an intense heat in a common fire, and when melted, pour it upon a slab. The result will be metallic lead completely revived.

7. Take a little red lead, expose it to an intense heat in a crucible, and pour it out when melted. The result will be metallic glass, and will furnish an example of the vitrification of metals.

8. Drop upon a clean plate of copper a small quantity of solution of nitrate of silver ; in a short time a metallic vegetation will be perceptible branching out in very elegant and pleasing forms, furnishing an example of metallic revivification.

9. Dissolve an ounce of acetate of lead in about a quart or more of water, and filter the solution. If this be put into a glass decanter, and a piece of zinc suspended in it by means of a brass wire, a decomposition of the salt will immediately commence, the lead will be set at liberty, and will attach itself to the remaining zinc, forming a metallic tree.

10. Procure a phial with a glass stopper accurately ground into it; introduce some copper wire, then entirely fill it with liquid ammonia, and stop the phial so as to exclude all atmospheric air. If left in this state, no solution of the copper will be effected. But if the bottle be afterwards left open for some time, and then stopped, the metal will dissolve and the solution will be colourless. Let the stopper be now taken out, and the fluid

will become blue, beginning at the surface, and spreading gradually through the whole. If this blue solution has not been too long exposed to the air, and fresh copper filings be put in, again stopping the bottle, the fluid will once more be deprived of its colour, which it will recover only by the re-admission of air. These effects may thus be repeatedly produced.

11. Pour concentrated nitric acid upon pieces of iron, and very little action will be seen : but if a few drops of water be added, a most violent effervescence will immediately commence ; the acid will be decomposed with rapidity, clouds of red nitrous gas will be evolved in abundance, and a perfect solution of the metal effected.

12. Take any solution of iron, a chalybeate water for instance, and add a small quantity of succinate of ammonia ; in a little time a precipitate will be visible, being succinate of iron. By this test the quantity of iron in any solution may be accurately ascertained.

13. In like manner add sulphuretted hydrogen to a solution of lead, and a deep brown precipitate will be occasioned. This is an effectual mode of detecting this and some other pernicious metals.

14. Dissolve some quicksilver in nitrous acid, and drop a little of the solution upon a bright piece of copper. If it be then gently rubbed with a bit of cloth, the mercury will precipitate itself upon the copper, which will be completely silvered. This experiment is illustrative of the precipitation of one metal by another.

15. Take a phial with a solution of sulphate of zinc, and another containing a little liquid ammonia, both transparent fluids. By mixing them, a curious phenomena may be perceived :—the zinc will be immediately precipitated in a white mass, and if then shaken, will be almost as instantly re-dissolved.

16. If a colourless solution of galls be added to a solution of bismuth in nitric acid equally colourless, a brown precipitate will be produced. This is a distinguishing characteristic of this metal.

17. If a colourless solution of arsenic in caustic potash be poured into a colourless solution of copper, a green precipitate will be produced, forming an arseniate of copper similar to an ore found in the Cornish mines. These metals may be thus reciprocally detected.

18. Alloy a piece of silver with a portion of lead, place the alloy upon a piece of charcoal, attach a blow-pipe to a gasometer charged with oxygen gas, light the charcoal first with a bit of paper, and keep up the heat by pressing upon the machine. When the metals get into complete fusion, the lead will begin to burn, and very soon will be all dissipated in a white smoke, leaving the silver in a state of purity. This experiment is designed to show the fixity of the noble metals.

19. If oxide of cobalt be dissolved in ammonia, a red solution will be produced, different in colour from that of all other metallic oxides.

20. If nickel be dissolved in nitric acid, a beautiful green solution will be formed. The oxide of this metal is used to give a delicate grass green to porcelain.

21. When colourless prussiate of potash is added to a solution of titanium, this metal will be precipitated also of a green colour.

22. Add a little colourless solution of galls to a clear solution of antimony in nitro-muriatic acid, and the metal will be precipitated of a pale yellow colour.

23. If a solution of tungstate of potash be poured into a solution of the green sulphate of iron, a yellow precipitate will fall down. By this experiment the distinguishing characteristic of this metal is exhibited.

24. If a solution of the green sulphate of iron be dropped into a nitro muriate of gold, the last metal will be immediately precipitated. In this state it is often employed in gilding china.

25. If flowers, or any other figures, be drawn upon a riband or silk with a solution of nitrate of silver, and the silk, moistened with water, be then exposed to the action of hydrogen gas, the silver will be revived, and the figures, firmly fixed upon the silk, will become visible, and shine with metallic brightness.

26. By proceeding in the same manner, and using a solution of gold in nitro-muriatic acid, silks may be permanently gilt at a most trifling expense, and will exhibit an appearance the most beautiful that can be conceived.

27. To a similar solution of gold add about a fourth part of ether ; shake them together, and wait till the fluids separate ; the upper stratum, or ethereal gold, is then to be carefully poured off into another vessel. If any polished steel instrument or utensil be dipped into this solution, and instantly plunged into water, the surface will have acquired a coat of pure gold, being a very elegant and economical mode of preserving polished steel from rust.

28. If nitro-muriate of platina be mixed with a fourth part of its bulk of ether, and the mixture suffered to settle, the ethereal solution of platina may be decanted as in the preceding experiment. Polished brass, and some other metals immersed in this solution, will be covered with a coat of platina. This process may be applied to many useful purposes.

29. Prepare a very dilute and colourless solution of platina by dropping a small quantity of the nitro-muriate of that metal into a glass of water. If a single drop of the solution of muriate of tin be added to this, a bright red precipitate will be instantly produced. A more delicate test than this of any metal cannot be conceived.

30. If a morsel of the dried crystals of nitrate of silver (not the lunar caustic) be laid on a piece of burning charcoal, the metallic salt will immediately deflagrate, throw out the most beautiful scintillations that can be imagined, and the surface of the charcoal will be richly coated with metallic silver.

31. To a colourless solution of nitrate of mercury add an equally colourless solution of sub-borate of soda. This will produce a double decomposition, and form a bright yellow precipitate of borate of mercury, giving an instance of difference of colour in metals, by their union with different acids.

32. Into a diluted solution of sulphate of copper, pour a little liquid caustic ammonia. This will precipitate the copper of a bluish-white. During its examination, however, the precipitate will be re-dissolved, and a beautiful blue liquid, called aqua celestis, will be the result.

33. Dissolve a few crystals of nitro-muriate of gold in about eignt times their weight of pure water ; place a thin slip of charcoal in the solution,

and heat the whole by means of a sand-bath. When the solution has acquired nearly a boiling heat, the gold will precipitate itself on the charcoal, in its metallic splendour, forming a singular and beautiful appearance. This experiment is designed to show that metals become insoluble the moment they impart their oxygen to foreign bodies.

34. Proceed as in the last experiment, and submit the vessel with its contents to the rays of the sun. Here the metal will be reduced, and the charcoal as effectually gilt as before. This is illustrative of the deoxidizing power of the sun's rays.

35. Drop a little leaf gold into nitro-muriatic acid, and it will instantly disappear. This experiment is designed to show the great solubility of the metals, when submitted to a proper menstruum.

36. Pour a little purified nitric acid into one wineglass, and muriatic acid into another, and drop a little leaf gold into each. Here neither of these corrosive acids will act at all upon the metal, the gold will remain untouched. Now pour the whole contents of the two glasses together, and the metal will disappear, and be as effectually dissolved as in the last experiment.

37. If a little metallic arsenic in powder be mixed with a few zinc filings, and then treated with diluted sulphuric acid, arsenuretted hydrogen gas may be collected, which burns with a peculiar kind of lambent flame.

38. If a portion of this gas, issuing from a very small tube, be set on fire, and then immersed in a large glass receiver of oxygen gas, and the stream of arsenuretted hydrogen kept up by the pressure of the bladder, a blue flame of uncommon splendour will be produced.

39. Take an amalgam of lead and mercury, and another amalgam of bismuth, let these two solid amalgams be mixed by triture, and they will instantly become fluid.

40. If a little pure white calomel be rubbed in a glass mortar with a little colourless solution of caustic ammonia, the whole will become intensely black.

41. A little of the solution of the sulphate of manganese being exposed in a glass phial to the light of the sun, its rose colour will entirely fade. This is another experiment to show the deoxidizing power of the sun's rays. If the phial be removed into a dark room, the original colour of the solution will be restored.

42. Dissolve about a drachm of pulverized sulphate of copper in a little boiling water, and an equal quantity of powdered muriate of ammonia in a separate vessel, in hot water. By mixing the contents of the two glasses, a quadruple salt will be formed, which gives a yellow colour to the solution while hot, and becomes green when cold.

43. Mix 3 grains of sulphur with 9 grains of dry nitrate of silver, and lay the mixture in a small heap on an anvil, or on any piece of solid metal. If the mixture be now struck smartly with a *cold* hammer, the sulphur will inflame, but no detonation will ensue. This is an instance of a metallic salt being decomposed, and a combustible substance inflamed by percussion.

44. If the experiment be repeated, and the mass be struck with a *hot* hammer, the mixture detonates, and the silver is reduced.

45. Pour a solution of nitrate of silver into a glass vessel, and immerse a few slips of copper in it. In a short time a portion of the copper will be dissolved, and all the silver precipitated in a metallic form. If the solution, which now contains copper, be decanted into another glass, and pieces of iron added to it, this metal will then be dissolved, and the copper precipitated, yielding a striking example of peculiar affinities.

46. Melt a portion of grain tin, and pour it into a metallic cup. Allow it to cool till it is congealed to some depth, then pierce the solid crust, and carefully pour out that portion which is still liquid. If what remains in the vessel be suffered to cool entirely, it will present rhomboidal crystals of considerable size, formed by the assemblage of a great number of small needles longitudinally united.

47. Treat silver in the same way; and we shall procure a metallic mass crystallized in quadrangular or octohedral prisms.

The two experiments immediately preceding will succeed better if the metal be poured into a vessel with an orifice in the bottom, which must be stopped with a proper plug, and this removed as soon as the upper crust hardens; the liquid metal will then run out, and that which is congealed will exhibit a regular crystallization.

48. Form an amalgam with four parts of silver-leaf and two of mercury, and dissolve this amalgam in diluted nitric acid. Then add water to the solution, equal to thirty times the weight of the metals employed, and put the whole aside for use. If an ounce of this solution be at any time poured into a phial, and a small piece of soft amalgam of silver dropped in, filaments of reduced silver will shoot from it, and extend upwards, in the form of a shrub. The appearance of arborescence is called the tree of Diana.

49. If two parts of sulphate of copper, and three of carbonate of ammonia, (the one a blue, the other a white salt,) be rubbed together in a glass mortar till the carbonic acid be expelled, the mass will become soft and humid, and, when dried, forms a crystalline powder of a most beautiful deep violet colour. This compound was formerly called cuprum ammoniacum.

50. If a little colourless and recently prepared muriate of tin be poured into a rich green solution of muriate of copper, the copper will be deprived of a portion of its oxygen, and a white muriate of copper precipitated.

51. Into the phial containing the white muriate of the last experiment, pour a little muriatic acid. The precipitate will quickly be dissolved, and the solution will be colourless.

52. Procure some solution of sulphate of iron at the minimum of oxidizement, by digesting iron filings with the common sulphate. Into this, when filtered, drop a little of the solution of prussiate of potash, and a white prussiate of iron will be precipitated.

53. If a very little colourless nitric acid be added to a solution of sulphate of iron prepared as in the last experiment, the addition of the prussiate of potash will produce not the white, but the blue prussiate of iron.

54. Pour some pure nitric acid on the black oxide of manganese, and no solution will be effected. But if a little sugar be added, the sugar will abstract a part of the oxygen from the nitric acid, and then the acid will be enabled to dissolve the metal.

55. Expose an ounce of nitric acid for an hour, in an open phial, to the direct rays of the sun, and pour another ounce of the same acid, that has not been so exposed, into another phial. If a little of the black oxide of manganese be now put into each, the oxide in the first phial will be dissolved, while that in the other will not be affected by the acid.

56. If a piece of bright silver be dipped in a solution of sulphate of copper, it will come out unchanged : but if the blade of a clean penknife, or any piece of polished iron, be dipped in the same solution, the iron will instantly put on the appearance of copper.

57. Take the piece of silver employed in the last experiment, hold it in contact with the iron, and then, in this situation, dip them into the same solution, and both will be covered with copper.

58. Dissolve some oxide of nickle in caustic ammonia, which will produce a solution of a rich blue colour. By exposure to the air this gradually changes to a purple, and lastly to a violet. The addition of an acid, however, converts the whole to green.

59. Take the green solution of the last experiment, and pour caustic ammonia upon it. The original blue colour will now be reproduced.

60. Prepare a colourless solution of tartrate of potash and antimony (the common emetic tartar), and pour into it a little liquid sulphuretted hydrogen. This will combine with the metallic oxide, and form an orange-coloured precipitate.

61. Melt together equal parts of copper and antimony, the one a yellow, the other a white metal, and the alloy that results from this mixture will take the colour of the violet.

62. If the grey sulphuretted oxide of antimony be fused in a crucible, we procure a beautiful transparent glass, which is called the glass of antimony. This takes the colour of the hyacinth.

63. Dissolve dry nitrate of silver in pure water ; add a little oil of turpentine, shake the mixture and cork it close. Submit the phial with its contents to the heat of boiling water for an hour, when the metal will be revived, and the inside of the phial, where the oil reposed on the aqueous solution, will be beautifully silvered, the revived metal forming a metallic ring, extending quite round the phial.

64. Immerse a slip of white silk in a solution of nitro-muriate of gold in distilled water, and dry it in the air. Silk thus prepared will not be altered by hydrogen gas : but if another piece of silk be dipped in the solution, and exposed while *wet* to the same current of hydrogen gas, instant signs of metallic reduction will appear ; the colour will change from yellow to green, and a brilliant film of reduced gold will soon glitter on its surface.

65. If a piece of silk be immersed in a solution of nitrate of silver, and dried in a dark place, and then submitted to hydrogen gas, the silver will not be reduced ; but if exposed while *wet* to a stream of the same gas, the surface will quickly be coated with reduced silver ; various colours, such as blue, purple, red, orange, and yellow, will accompany the reduction and the threads of the silk will look like silver wire.

During these experiments the silk should be constantly kept wet with distilled water.

66. Dissolve some crystals of muriate of tin in distilled water, then dip a piece of white silk in the solution, and dry it in the air. If this be now immersed in hydrogen gas, no change will be observed; but if it be exposed while *wet* to the same current of gas, the reduction will soon commence, attended with a great variety of beautiful colours, as red, yellow, orange, green, and blue, variously intermixed.

67. Prepare a strong solution of phosphorus in sulphuric ether, and dip piece of white silk in the solution; then, when the ether has evaporated, and the phosphorus begins to fume, apply a solution of nitro-muriate of gold, made by dissolving the crystals of that salt in distilled water; the silk will in an instant be covered with a splendid coat of metallic gold.

68. Proceed as in the last experiment, and instead of the solution of gold, apply, with a camel's-hair pencil, a solution of nitrate of silver. Here the silver will instantly be restored to its metallic brilliancy, and frequently be attended by spangles of a beautiful blue.

69. If a bit of white silk be immersed in an ethereal solution of gold, and dried, the application of phosphorized ether will only impart a brown colour to the silk; but if, as soon as the phosphorus begins to fume, it be placed on the palm of the hand, and breathed on for a considerable time, the brown will be succeeded by a purple tinge, and the metallic lustre of the gold will soon begin to appear.

70. An aqueous solution of nitro-muriateof gold was poured into a china cup containing some phosphorized ether; instantly the gold began to assume its metallic splendour, attended with a variety of colours, as purple, blue, and red, the beauty of which cannot be described, but which depends on the different degrees of the reduction.

71. With a needle pass a thread through a small bit of phosphorus, previously freed from moisture by immersing it in alcohol. If this be suspended in an aqueous solution of nitro-muriate of gold, in a few minutes the phosphorus will become covered with pure gold.

72. If a piece of white silk be dipped in an aqueous solution of nitro-muriate of gold, and exposed while wet to sulphurous acid gas, the whole piece will in a few seconds be covered with a coat of reduced gold, which remains permanent.

73. If a piece of white silk be immersed in an aqueous solution of nitrate of silver, thoroughly dried in the dark, and then exposed to sulphurous acid vapours, it will suffer no change; nor, if it be wetted with alcohol and then replaced in the vapour, will any sign of reduction appear; but if it be wetted with pure water, and then exposed to the vapour, metallic silver will immediately be seen on its surface.

A glass funnel is a convenient apparatus for the foregoing experiments. The silk may be suspended by a thread passed through it, and made fast to the funnel with a cork. The funnel is then to be placed on a table, and by moving it a little over the edge of the table, a lighted match may be readily introduced, and when the glass is full of vapour, the match may be withdrawn. The vapour is confined by sliding the funnel back upon the table; and thus the phenomena of the experiment may be easily observed.

74. Dip a piece of white calico in an aqueous solution of acetate of lead, and then drop a little solution of sulphuret of potash upon it. If this be

now placed in the palm of the hand, the lead will be observed gradually to revive, and will soon be reduced to its metallic state.

75. Dissolve some sulphuret of potash in alcohol, and immerse a slip of white silk in the solution. If a drop of an aqueous solution of sulphate of manganese be now applied, films of metallic manganese, bright as silver, will instantly appear.

76. If a bit of silk be immersed in diluted acetate of lead, and exposed while *wet* to a stream of sulphuretted hydrogen gas, a brown tinge will instantly diffuse itself, like a passing shadow, over the whole surface of the silk, accompanied with a bright coat of reduced lead, resembling silver.

77. If a piece of silk be immersed in an aqueous solution of muriate of tin, and exposed while *wet* to a stream of the same gas, reduced tin of great brightness will immediately cover the surface, and in a little time this will be accompanied by various colours, such as blue, orange, and purple.

78. A piece of silk, treated in the same way, but dipped in an aqueous solution of muriate of arsenic, will be covered with resplendent metallic arsenic, attended with a citron-yellow colour.

79. Prepare two glasses of very dilute nitrate of copper; into one drop a little liquid ammonia, and into the other some diluted arseniate of potash. The addition of these two colourless solutions will produce very different effects, for the one glass will have an abundant precipitate, of a brilliant sapphire-blue, and the other a precipitate of a beautiful grass-green.

Remedy for Surfeit in a Horse.

First bleed from the neck; then give a mash of bran, say one gallon, mixed well with hot sassafras tea, in which a teaspoonful of saltpetre and a tablespoonful of sulphur has been added. To be given three times a week. Never give the horse to drink for half a-day after having been fed with this mash. As a drink, give sassafras tea, with a little saltpetre, say one fourth of an ounce to the quart. As an ointment, equal parts of sulphur and hog's lard.

Sweet Potatoes.

Make a bed of long manure, from eight to twelve inches thick, surrounding it with a rough frame of boards. Put three or four inches of mould over the manure; split the potatoes and lay them thick on the mould, and cover with four inches of mould. As soon as the sprouts begin to come above the ground, draw them, laying one hand on the potato to keep it in its place. The sprouts must be drawn as they come up, as long as the planting season remains. They are to be set out in the hills after a rain, two sprouts in a hill, or in rows fourteen inches apart. By commencing early, a bushel of seed potatoes will plant an acre. This plan is decidedly preferable to planting the potato itself. When nights are cold, boards must be laid across the bed. In making the bed, the manure may be omitted by those who do not like the trouble, but the sprouts will come forward much later. The bed, in dry weather, must be frequently watered.

Sore Tongue in Horses.

Take 1 part sugar of lead, 1 part bole ammoniac, and 2 parts burnt alum, the whole to be added to 3 quarts of good vinegar. With this wash out the mouth twice a-day.

Fruit Trees.

Be careful in planting to give the trees a fair chance for life and health by digging the holes in which they are set wide and large, so that they may be surrounded by loose earth, that can be easily penetrated by the tender fibres of the roots which are to convey nourishment for their sustenance and growth. A tree properly planted will grow as much in five years as one carelessly and badly set in will in ten; and often the chance of survivorship is dependent on slight circumstances. An excellent plan for preventing young fruit trees from becoming hide-bound and mossy, and for promoting their health and growth, is to take a bucket of soft soap, and to apply it with a brush to the stem or trunk, from top to bottom; this cleanses the bark and destroys the worms or the eggs of insects; and the soap, becoming dissolved by rains, descends to the roots, and causes the tree to grow vigorously.

Gold in Powder.

1. Gold (grain), 1 part; mercury, 6 parts. Heat the mercury to nearly the boiling point, and triturate it with the gold, then distil off the mercury or dissolve it out with nitric acid; wash the residue well in water, and heat it to redness.

2. Gold, 1 part; nitro-muriatic acid, q. s. Dissolve and precipitate the gold with a solution of sulphate of iron, 4 parts. Wash the precipitate and heat it to redness.

Powder to Clean Gold Lace.

Roche alum (burnt and finely powdered), 5 parts; levigated chalk, 1 part. Mix. Apply with a dry brush.

Gold Lacker.

Ground turmeric, 1 pound; ground gamboge, 1½ ounce; ground gum sandarach, 3 pounds; ground bleached lac, 1 pound; alcohol, 2 gallons; turpentine varnish, 3 pints. Put the whole into a suitable vessel, cork close, and agitate until dissolved.

Gold Lustre for Stone-ware.

Gold, 6 parts; aqua regia, 36 parts. Dissolve, then add, tin, 1 part. Next add, balsam of sulphur, 3 parts; oil of turpentine, 1 part. Mix gradually in a mortar, and rub it until the mixture becomes hard, then add, oil of turpentine, 4 parts. It is then ready to be applied to a ground prepared for the purpose.

Gold or Yellow Paste.

Take plain paste (made without the saltpetre), 100 parts; oxide of iron 1 part. Fuse.

Big Head in Horses.

Take arsenic (white), 6 grains, in fine powder. This is to be wrapped in a small piece of fine paper. Now make an incision in the skin over the hard tumour, insert the paper containing the arsenic, give the incision one stitch and tie. Bleed, and let the horse run alone in good pasture; if in the winter, let him be stabled. In a few days the arsenic will begin to operate, and the head will swell until the arsenic is taken up by the humours. It will take from one to three months to effect a cure.

Ointment of Sodo-chloride of Gold.

Sodo-chloride of gold, 2 grains; lard, 1 ounce. Mix with great care, to render the distribution of the salt perfectly equal throughout the whole of the lard. An excellent application to venereal ulcers.

Gold Shells.

Take gold leaf, grind it in gum-water, and spread it over the inside of the shell.

Gold Size.

Yellow ochre, 1 part; copal varnish, 2 parts; linseed oil, 3 parts; turpentine, 4 parts; boiled oil, 5 parts. Mix. The ochre must be in the state of the finest powder, and ground with a little of the oil before mixing.

Gold Solder.

Pure gold, 6 parts; pure silver, 1 part; pure copper, 2 parts. Melt together.

Gold Sprinkle for Books.

Put into a marble mortar half an ounce of pure honey and one book of gold leaf, rub them well together until they are very fine, add half a pint of clear water, and mix them well together: when the water clears, pour it off, and put in more, till the honey is all extracted, and nothing remains but the gold. Mix one grain of corrosive sublimate in a teaspoonful of spirits of wine, and when dissolved, put the same, together with a little gum-water, to the gold, and bottle it close for use. The edges of the book may be sprinkled or coloured very dark, with green, blue, or purple, and lastly, with the gold liquid, in small or large spots, very regular, shaking the bottle before using. Burnish the edges when dry, and cover them with paper to prevent the dust falling thereon. This sprinkle will have a most beautiful appearance on extra work: ladies may use it for ornamenting their fancy-work, by putting it on with a pen or camel's-hair brush, and when dry burnish it with a dog's tooth.

Fistula in Horses.

Make a strong decoction of any of the following herbs by boiling, to wit: wormwood, camomile, mullen, or life-everlasting. Apply hot, with woollen cloths. When the tumour is ripe, lance, and then wash it with warm weak soap-suds. Then apply an ointment made as follows:—verdigris, ½ an ounce; ointment of yellow rosin, 4 ounces; copperas, ½ an ounce; oil of turpentine, 1 ounce. Mix, and apply occasionally until healthy matter appears, then discontinue the ointment, and heal up by washing the fistula with warm weak soap-suds.

Essence of Ginger.

The best Jamaica or China ginger two ounces, proof spirit one pint. Powder the ginger, mix it with the spirit, stop close, and let it steep for twelve or fourteen days. This is the same as is sold for (Oxley's concentrated essence of Jamaica ginger."

Sap Green.

This is prepared from the fruit of the buckthorn, and is purgative. It is used by confectioners for colouring.

Gold Varnish.

1. Turmeric, 1 drachm ; gamboge, 1 drachm ; oil of turpentine, 2 pints shell lac, 5 ounces ; sandarach, 5 ounces ; dragon's-blood, 7 drachms ; thin mastic varnish, 8 ounces. Digest, with occasional agitation, for fourteen days in a warm place, then set it aside to fine, and pour off the clear.

2. Dutch leaf, 1 part ; gamboge, 4 parts ; gum-dragon, 4 parts ; proof spirit, 18 parts. Macerate for 12 hours, then grind on a stone slab.

Gooseberry Vinegar.

Bruise the gooseberries, when ripe, and to every quart put three quarts of water; stir them well together, and let the whole stand for twenty-four hours, then strain it through a canvass bag. To every gallon of liquor add one pound of brown sugar, and stir them well together before they are put into the cask. Proceed in all other respects as before. This vinegar possesses a pleasant taste and smell; but raspberry vinegar, which may be made on the same plan, is far superior in these respects. The raspberries are not required to be of the best sort, still they should be ripe and well-flavoured.

Mode of Increasing the Potato Crop.

An English writer says, by carefully removing the buds as they appear on the potato vines, the crop of large ones is very much augmented. The theory is plausible, and worthy a fair trial.

Soak your Seed Corn in a Solution of Saltpetre.

It destroys the worm, is not relished by crows or squirrels, and yields much more abundantly than when planted without.

Peach Worm.

It is said that a mixture of one ounce of saltpetre and seven ounces of salt, applied on the surface of the ground, in contact and around the trunk of a peach tree seven years old and upwards, will destroy the worm, prevent the *yellows*, and add much to the product and quality of the fruit.—Also, sow the orchard with the same mixture, at the rate of two bushels to the acre.

Gooseberry Wine.

Gooseberries, 1 cwt.; water, 15 gallons; sugar, 30 pounds. Mix and ferment.

Gooseberry Wine (French method).

Half ripe gooseberry juice, 30 gallons; sugar, 45 pounds; cream of tartar, 2 ounces. Mix, and let it ferment of itself.

Goulard's Extract.

Powdered litharge, 1 part; distilled vinegar, 4 parts. Dissolve.

Goulard's Ointment.

Goulard's extract, 3 pounds; yellow wax, 7 pounds; rape oil, 8 pounds. Mix.

To Preserve Grain from Vermin.

Sprinkle garlic about the place it is stored in, or plant the wood-work with coal tar.

Fistula in Horses.

When the fistula makes its first appearance, place a seton in each shoulder, just below the inflamed parts, and keep them running for two or three weeks. This will often remove the disease without any further attention.

Gowland's Lotion.

1. Blanched sweet almonds, 4 parts; distilled water, 32 parts; bichloride of mercury, 1 part; alcohol, 2 parts; ottar of roses, 2 drops. Rub the almonds to a milk with the water; strain through gauze; then add the other ingredients. This is a most useful lotion for removing eruptions from the skin.

2. Bitter almonds, 1 ounce; jordan, 1 ounce; white sugar, 1 ounce; clear water, 1 quart. Reduce to an emulsion, then add, bichlorate of mercury, 45 grains, dissolved in a little warm water; spirits of wine, 4 drachms; hydrochloric acid, 1 drachm. Mix well and strain.

To Correct Damaged Grain.

Put it for fifteen minutes into a warm oven and turn it frequently.

To Preserve all kinds of Grain.

Kiln-dry it.

To prevent the dropping off of Grapes.

Make a circular incision in the wood, cutting away a ring of bark, about the breadth of the twelfth of an inch. The wood acquires greater size about the incision, and the operation accelerates the maturity of the wood, and that of the fruit likewise. The incision should not be made too deep, and further than the bark, or it will spoil both the wood and the fruit.

Grape Wine.

Vine cuttings, 1 cwt.; water, 20 gallons. Infuse for some time, then add sugar, ½ cwt. Ferment with a little yeast.

Grape Red Wine.

Grapes (any colour), 30 pounds; water, 6 gallons; sugar, 10 pounds. Ferment, then add red beet (sliced), 2 pounds; red tartar (powdered), 3 ounces; gum catechu, 3 ounces; cloves (bruised), ¼ ounce; spirit, 1 quart, or more.

Grape White Wine.

Grape juice (white), 14 gallons; sugar, 12 pounds; water, 3 gallons. Ferment, then add white tartar, 7 ounces; spirit, 3 quarts.

Pills for Gravel.

Castile soap, 8 parts; caustic soda, 4 parts; oil of tartar to mix. Divide into three-grain pills, one to be taken every two hours.

Grease Balls.

White soap, 1 pound; spirits of turpentine, 4 ounces; Fuller's earth, 6 ounces; ox-gall, 5 ounces. Beat to an even mass and form into cakes ½ an inch thick, 1¼ inch wide, and 2½ inches long.

Syrup of Citrate of Iron.

1. Take citrate of iron, dissolved in a little water, 1 part; mix with pure syrup, 120 parts. Each ounce of this syrup contains four grains of citrate of iron.

2. Take simple syrup, 458 parts; citrate of peroxide of iron, 30 parts; spirit of lemon and alcohol, 7 parts.

Candied Citron.

Cut the peels in half, then soak them in water for two hours; change the water, and soak for two hours more; repeat the operation until the water ceases to be bitter; drain them, and put them into saturated (hot) syrup, until they become soft and partly transparent, then take them out and dry them.

Essence of Civette.

Civette, 1 ounce; alcohol, 1 pound. Mix.

British Claret.

1. Cider (rough), 35 gallons; red Cape, 45 gallons; red tartar, dissolved, 1½ pound. Mix well and fine.

2. Spirit, 5 gallons; cider, 50 gallons; red Cape, 35 gallons; good Port, 15 gallons; red tartar, dissolved, 2 pounds. Mix well and fine.

3. Cider, 50 gallons; spirit, 7 gallons; red Cape, 42 gallons; good Port, 5 gallons; red tartar, 2 pounds. Mix well and fine.

4. Red Cape or Port, 50 gallons; cider, 50 gallons; spirit, 10 gallons; red tartar, 2 or 3 pounds. Mix well and fine.

5. Six gallons of water, two gallons of cider, and eight pounds of Malaga raisins, bruised; put them all together, and let them stand closely covered in a warm place for a fortnight, stirring them well every second day: then strain out the liquor into a clean cask, and put to it a quart of barberries, a pint of the juice of raspberries, and a pint of the juice of black cherries. Work it up with a little mustard-seed, and cover the bung with a piece of dough; let it stand at the fireside for four days; then bung it up, and let it remain a week, and bottle it off. When it becomes fine and ripe, it will drink like claret.

6. Rough Port, 50 gallons; cider, 50 gallons; cream of tartar, 3 pounds powdered catechu, ½ pound; spirit, 4 gallons. Mix. Red Cape may be used for Port.

Claret Rags.

Take clean linen rags and colour them with Auvergne archil, juice of red grapes, juice of mulberries, or the lees of red wine, &c. Used to colour confectionary, jellies, cheese, &c.

To fine Claret.

Take white of eggs, beat them to a froth, and then mix them with the wine.

Claret Vine-leaf Wine.

Claret vine-leaves, 3 pecks; water, 18 gallons. Macerate for three days, then add sugar, 50 pounds; red tartar, dissolved, 8 ounces. Ferment, then add spirit, 7 quarts; powdered cochineal, 1 ounce; sassafras chips, ½ pound.

Clark's Sauce.

Port wine, 5 parts; Cape wine, 5 parts; scraped horse-radish, 3 parts; cayenne, 1 part; garlic, 5 parts; cloves, 2 or 3 in number to every pint. Boil for fifteen minutes; and, when cold, strain, or let it stand until fine, and then decant.

To extract Grease from Clothes.

Lay a piece of brown paper doubled over the spot, and apply a hot iron.

To Perfume Clothes.

Cloves, in coarse powder, 1 ounce; cassia, in coarse powder, 1 ounce; lavender flowers, in coarse powder, 1 ounce; lemon-peel, in coarse powder, 1 ounce. Mix, and put them into little bags, and place them where the clothes are kept, or wrap the clothes round them. These bags will also keep off insects.

Clothes' Ball.

Pipe-clay, whiting, fuller's earth, equal parts. Mix.

To dry clean Cloth.

Extract the grease spots with a solution of soap or ox gall, then beat fine damp sand into the cloth, and brush it out again with a stiff brush; then rub two or three drops of olive oil over a hat-brush, and pass it equally over the cloth.

To render Cloth Water-proof.

1. Isinglass, 1 part; water to reduce it to a size. Rub the wrong side of the cloth with this solution (warm), then let it dry and go over it with a soft sponge, charged with a warm, strained solution of galls. Repeat the latter operation two or three times.

2. Soap (soda), 1 part; water, 2 parts. Dissolve, and work the solution into the wrong side of the cloth, dry; then apply a solution of alum, with a soft sponge.

Clove Cordial.

Cloves, bruised, 7 pounds; pimento, 1 pound; proof-spirit, 50 gallons. Macerate for fourteen days, then add sugar, 150 pounds; dissolved in water, 45 gallons. Mix well, and fine down with 12 eggs.

To extinguish Fire. New Invention.

Mr. Wivell has invented a machine, which has, for its merit, been attached to the establishment of the Royal Society for the Protection of Life from Fire. This machine consists of a water-cart and a ladder 29 feet long; the ladder has a folding-joint, which allows of its being placed on the cart in a manageable form; lines and buckets are attached, by which water can be conveyed into the first and second floors. As a proof of the celerity with which the machine may be brought into action, intelligence was taken from Brunswick-square to a supposed station 400 yards distant; the water-cart was brought, the ladder raised, and eight buckets of water handed up to the height on the second floor, in five minutes and a few seconds. At a fire in Middle-row, Holborn, the cart from Bedford-row arrived in three minutes; and the fire-escape stationed against the Foundling Hospital in seven minutes, after the alarm was given.

Clove Drops.

Take oil of cloves, and flavour the confectionary drops with it.

Clove Lozenges.

1. Finely-powdered cloves, 1 ounce; lump-sugar, 2 pounds; starch, 1 pound; powdered gum, ½ pound. Mix with a weak decoction of Brazil.

2. Oil of cloves, 1 drachm; white sugar, 2 pounds; powdered gum, 1 ounce. Mix with Brazil-water as before.

Coffee Drops.

Coffee, 1 ounce; water, 1 pint. Boil for five minutes, then use the liquor to flavour the confectionary drops.

Essence of Coffee.

Coffee, 1 part; water, 5 parts. Keep them at a heat of 209° Fahr., in a close vessel for ten minutes, then strain and evaporate at a low temperature in a vacuum, until reduced to one part.

Coffee for Icing.

Strong coffee, 3 ounces; icing cream, 2 pints; sugar, 1 ounce; yolks of 3 eggs. Mix well and strain, ready for icing.

Iris or Sylvester Coffee.

Take the seeds of the yellow water-flag, and treat them as for genuine coffee. This forms a most excellent substitute for the colonial article.

Coffee Milk.

Milk, 1 pint; coffee, ½ ounce. Boil for five minutes and strain or fine it down, then preserve the clear liquid for use.

Rye Coffee.

Take rye and roast, and grind it, like genuine coffee. This is similar to Hunt's breakfast powder, Dellenius's coffee, British coffee, &c.

Substitutes for Coffee.

1. Bread raspings.
2. Roasted wheat or rye, or Hunt's breakfast powder.
3. Slice and dry the yellow-beet root, then grind it with a little coffee.
4. Peeled acorns roasted with a little fat.
5. Sassafras, nuts or chips.

To improve Coffee.

Coffee, 13 parts; chicory, 3 parts. Grind together.

To make and Fine Coffee.

Put a sufficient quantity of coffee into the pot and pour boiling water on it, stir it and place it on the fire, bring it to a boil, and as soon as four or five bubbles have risen, take it off the fire and pour out a tea-cupful and return it; set it down for one minute, then pour gently over the top one tea-cupful of cold water, let it stand one minute longer, and it will be bright and fine. The cold water (by its greater density) sinks and carries the grounds with it.

Rice Coffee.

Take good rice and roast, and grind it, &c., in the same way as coffee.

To take Impressions from Coins, &c.

Make a thick solution of isinglass in water, and lay it hot on the metal, let it remain for twelve hours, then remove it, breathe on it and apply gold or silver-leaf on the wrong side. Any colour may be given to the isinglass instead of gold or silver, by simple mixture.

Red Colcothar.

1. Sulphate of iron, 1 part; water, 60 parts. Dissolve and add a solution of carbonate of an alkali, until the whole of the oxide of iron is precipitated, then wash, and calcine the precipitate.

2. Green sulphate of iron, 100 parts; common salt, 42 parts. Mix and calcine until all the muriatic acid is driven over, then wash out the remaining sulphate of soda, and recalcine the residue.

Cold Cream.

1. Lard, prepared, 2 pounds; suet, 1 pound. Melt, cool a little, and then stir in bergamot, 2 drachms; essence of lemon, 1 drachm; neroli, 20 drops; rose-water, 4 ounces.

2. Lard, 1 pound; spermaceti, 3 ounces. Melt with a gentle heat, and when cooling stir in orange-flower water, 1 ounce; essence of lavender, 26 drops.

3. Oil of almonds, 5 pounds; white wax, 1 pound; spermaceti, ½ pound. Melt by a gentle heat, then stir in rose-water, 1 pound; ottar of roses, 6 drops.

4. Lard, 10 parts; oil of almonds, 4 parts; suet, 2 parts; spermaceti, 1 part. Melt in a warm bath, and when removed from the fire stir in one part each of rose, cinnamon, and orange-flower waters, with a few drops of oil of lavender or bergamot.

5. Oil of almonds, 1 pound; white lard and suet, each 1 pound; spermaceti and white wax, each 1 ounce. Melt with as little heat as possible, and stir in rose or orange-flower water 4 ounces; essence of bergamot or lavender 35 drops.

Method of preventing Cold Feet at Bed-time.

Draw off your stockings just before undressing, and rub your ancles and feet well with your hand, as hard as you can bear the pressure, for five or ten minutes, and you will never have to complain of cold feet in bed. It is hardly conceivable what a pleasurable glow this diffuses. Frequent washing of the feet, and rubbing them thoroughly dry with a linen cloth or flannel, is very useful.

To prevent the Bad Effects of Drinking Cold Liquors.

Brandy or other spirits, 2 ounces; laudanum, 30 drops. Mix, and drink immediately as the shivering fit comes on, then lie down for an hour or so.

To kill Roaches.

Wafers, made out of red lead, and wheat flour.

Eau de Luce.

Water of ammonia, essential oil of amber, sufficient. Mix.

Eau de Melisse.

1. Dried balm leaves, 1 pound; dried lemon-peel, ½ pound; nutmegs and corianders (bruised), 2 ounces; cloves, cassia, and dried angelica, (bruised,) 1 ounce; spirit, 1 gallon. Mix and distil, or macerate and filter.

2. Spirit of balm, 1 gallon; spirit of lemon-peel, 2 quarts; spirit of nutmegs, 1 quart; spirit of corianders, 1 quart; spirit of rosemary, 1 pint; spirit of marjoram, 1 pint; spirit of thyme, 1 pint; spirit of hyssop, 1 pint: spirit of cassia, 1 pint; spirit of sage, 1 pint; spirit of aniseed, 1 pint; spirit of cloves, 1 pint; spirit of angelica, 1 pint; spirit of wine, 4 pints. Mix and distil, or macerate and filter. This is said to be the original receipt of the barefooted Carmelites, now in possession of the Company of Apothecaries at Paris.

Eau de Mille Fleurs.

Spirit of wine, 5 gallons; orange-flower water, 1 gallon; balsam of Peru, 4 ounces; essence of bergamot, 8 ounces; essence of musk, 8 ounces; essence of cloves, 4 ounces; essence of neroli, 2 ounces; essence of thyme, 1 ounce. Mix.

Eau de Mousseline.

Spirit of wine, 2 quarts; spirit of roses, 2 quarts; spirit of jasmin, 2 quarts; spirit of orange flowers, 2 quarts; spirit of clove gilly-flower, 1 quart; essence of vanilla, 2 ounces; essence of musk, 2 ounces; red sanders wood, ½ ounce; orange-flower water, 1 quart; rose-water, 1 pint. Mix.

Eau de Tain.

Water, 7 gallons; lemon thyme, 5 pounds. Draw over five gallons.

Eau Divine.

Essence of lemon, 1 drachm; bergamot, 1 drachm; spirit, 1 gallon. Macerate for four days, frequently shaking the bottle, then add water, 2 gallons; sugar, 4 pounds; orange-flower water, 1 pint. Mix and filter.

To stain Wood like Ebony.

Take a solution of sulphate of iron, and wash the wood over with it two or three times: let it dry, and apply two or three coats of a strong decoction of logwood; wipe the wood when dry with a sponge and water, and polish with oil.

Economical White House Paint.

Skim milk, 2 quarts; fresh slaked lime, 8 ounces; linseed oil, 6 ounces; white Burgundy pitch, 2 ounces; Spanish white, 3 pounds. The lime to be slaked in water, exposed to the air, mixed in about one fourth of the milk; the oil, in which the pitch is previously dissolved, to be added a little at a time; then the rest of the milk, and afterwards the Spanish white. This quantity is sufficient for twenty-seven square yards, two coats, and the expense not more than ten-pence.

Economical Pearl-grey House Paint.

If a particle of blue be added to the preceding composition, or if this blue be combined with a slight portion of black, a silver or pearl-grey will be obtained.

Edinburgh Ale.

Employ the best pale malt.

1st. Mash two barrels per quarter, at 180°; mash three quarters of an hour, let it stand one hour, and allow half an hour to run off the wort

2d. Mash one barrel per quarter, at 183°; mash three quarters of an hour, let it stand three quarters of an hour, and tap as before.

3d. Mash one barrel per quarter, at 170°; mash half an hour, let it stand half an hour, and tap as before.

The first and second wort may be mixed together, boiling them about an hour or an hour and a quarter, with a quantity of hops proportioned to the time the beer is intended to be kept. The first two may be mixed at the heat of 60° in the gyle tun, and the second should be fermented separately for small-beer. The best hops should also be used, in the proportion of about four pounds for every quarter of malt employed.

Edinburgh Lozenges.

Extract of poppies, 1 part; lump-sugar, 8 parts. Thick mucilage to mix.

Egg Powder Test.

Take white of egg, evaporate it by a gentle heat until hard, then powder.

Oil of Eggs.

1. Raw yolks, 1 part; water, 2 parts. Beat them together, then add alcohol, 1 part, and let it stand until the oil floats on the top, then carefully take it off.

2. Heat the yolks in an iron vessel until the oil begins to exude, then apply pressure. Ten to twelve eggs yield one ounce of oil.

Portable Eggs.

Take fresh laid eggs, any quantity, break them into an evaporating basin, and expose them to a heat of 125° Fahr. in a water-bath, until hard, then pack them in air-tight vessels. For use, take cold water, 3 parts; dried egg, 1 part. Beat them well together.

To obtain Pure Elaine.

Olive oil, 1 part; alcohol, 9 parts. Mix and heat to the boiling point, in a close vessel, then allow it to cool, and place it in a freezing mixture until the whole of the stearine is deposited, then decant the clear and distil off the alcohol in a water-bath, the remainder will be pure elaine. This elaine or pure oil will not freeze in frosty weather, and neither thickens nor corrodes when applied to metals. It is a perfect cure for "lame" chronometers, watches, &c.

Elder flower Water.

Take elder flowers, 1 cwt.; water, 50 gallons. Draw off forty-four gallons.

Egyptian Marble for Leather Book-Covers.

1. *Yellow.* Boil quercitron bark with water and a little powdered alum, over a slow fire, until it is a good strong yellow. Pour the liquid into a broad vessel, sufficiently large to contain the cover when extended. Before the liquid is cool, take the dry cover, and lay the grain side flat on the colour; press it lightly that the whole may receive the liquid: let it soak some time, and then take it from the vessel. The book must be covered in the usual manner, and permitted to dry from the fire. Glaire the book; when dry, place it between the wands; take a sponge and water, and press large spots thereon; dip a quill-top into the vinegar black, with it touch the water on the cover in different parts, which will have a fine effect when managed with care. Let it stand a few minutes, then take off the water with a clean sponge.

2. *Green.* Colour the cover in a large vessel, as mentioned before, with Scott's liquid blue; when done, put it into a vessel of clear water for an hour. Take it out and press out the water, then cover the book. Glaire the cover; when dry, place it between wands, and drop weak potash water from a sponge thereon; dip the quill-top into the strong black, and touch the water with it. This must be repeated till you have a good black. When dry, clear it with a sponge and water.

3. *Red.* Boil Brazil dust in rain-water on a slow fire, with a little powdered alum and a few drops of solution of tin, till a good colour is produced. Dip a piece of calf leather into the liquid, and you may ascertain the colour wanted. If too light, let it boil till it is reduced to one half of the quantity; take it from the fire, add a few more drops of the solution of tin, and pour it into a large vessel. Put the dry cover on the liquid, and let it remain for a quarter of an hour, then press out the water. Colour it over with a sponge and the quercitron bark water, and cover the book. Glaire the cover, place it between wands, dash on water with a brush, also potash-water; and, lastly, finish it with the strong vinegar black, with the quill-top. Observe that too much black is not put on; the intention of the marble is to show the red as transparently as possible.

Alkalized Elderberry Paper.

Take elderberry paper and brush it over with a solution of ammonia.

Elderberry Wine.

Cold soft water, 20 gallons; Malaga raisins, 56 pounds; elderberries, 5 gallons; red tartar (dissolved), 8 ounces. Boil and ferment, then add spirit, 2 gallons; cloves, mace and cassia, each, ½ ounce; ginger, 1½ ounce, dry lemon-peel, 1½ ounce; dry orange-peel, 1½ ounce.

Oil of Elder Flowers.

Elder flowers, 1 part; rape oil, 4 parts. Pour the oil, hot, on the flowers, and macerate for one week, then express the oil.

Elder or Green Ointment.

Lard, 90 pounds; elder leaves, 28 pounds. Boil until the leaves are crisp; strain, and add suet, 20 pounds; water, 1 gallon. Stir until cold If not sufficiently bright coloured, add powdered verdigris as required.

Cheap Elder or Green Ointment.

Lard, 1 cwt.; brown resin, 20 pounds; suet, 50 pounds; verdigris to colour. Melt, then add water, 3 gallons. Stir until cold.

Elder or Green Oil.

Elder leaves, 1 part; rape oil, 3 parts. Boil until of a proper colour, then express the oil.

Factitious Elder or Green Oil.

Rape oil, 1 gallon; powdered verdigris, 1 ounce. Boil until sufficiently coloured.

Ointment of Gum Elemi.

1. Suet, 4 pounds; gum elemi, 2 pounds; turpentine, 1 pound; sweet oil, 6 ounces. Mix, with heat.

2. Elemi, 1 pound; white wax, ½ pound; lard, 4 pounds. Mix.

Elephant's Milk.

Benjamin, ¼ pound; spirit of wine, 2 gallons; balsam of tolu, 1 ounce. Dissolve, then add sugar, 20 pounds, dissolved in 3 gallons of water. Mix well, and strain.

To clean Embroidery and Gold Lace.

For this purpose no alkaline liquors are to be used; for while they clean the gold, they corrode the silk, and change its colour. Soap also alters the shade, and even the species of certain colours. But spirit of wine may be used without any danger of its injuring either colour or quality; and, in many cases, proves as effectual for restoring the lustre of the gold, as the corrosive detergents. But, though spirit of wine is the most innocent material employed for this purpose, it is not in all cases proper. The golden covering may be in some parts worn off; or the base metal, with which it has been alloyed, may be corroded by the air, so as to leave the particles of the gold disunited; while the silver underneath, tarnished to a yellow hue, may continue a tolerable colour to the whole, so it is apparent that the removal of the tarnish would be prejudicial, and make the lace or embroidery less like gold than it was before.

Factitious Emerald.

1. Oxide of chrome, 1 part; green oxide of copper, 20 parts; strass, 2300 parts. Fuse with care for 26 hours, then cool slowly.

2. Strass, 10,000 parts; acetate of copper, 150 parts; protoxide of iron, 3 parts. As before.

3. Strass, 6600 parts; carbonate of copper, 60 parts; glass of antimony, 6 parts. Fuse with care.

4. Strass, 500 parts; glass of antimony, 20 parts; oxide of cobalt, 3 parts. As before.

Emetic Cups.

Cups made of antimony, (regulus,) or an alloy of antimony and tin in equal proportions, (regulus Jovis.) Wine placed in these cups for ten or twelve hours, becomes emetic. A very uncertain and dangerous way of preparing emetic wine.

Indian Rubber Water-proof, for Boots and Shoes.

Spermaceti, 4 parts; Indian rubber (small), 1 part. Melt with a gentle heat, then add tallow or lard, 10 parts; amber or copal varnish, 5 parts. Well mix and apply the composition to the leather with a paint-brush. Cut the rubber into very small pieces, and let it take its time to dissolve, say four or five hours.

Metallic Anatomical Injection.

Bismuth, 5 parts; tin, 2 parts; lead, 3 parts; quicksilver to render it fusible at the required temperature.

Ipecacuanha Lozenges.

Sugar four pounds, ipecacuanha one ounce, apothecaries' weight, dissolved gum sufficient to make a paste. Make 960 lozenges, each containing half a grain of ipecacuanha. An expectorant and stomachic, used in coughs.

Indian Ink.

1. Take finest lamp-black, and make it into a thick paste with thin isinglass; size, then mould it, attach the gold-leaf, and scent with a little essence of musk.

2. Take lamp-black, make it into a thick paste with gum-water, and mould it.

Black Ink.

1. Blue galls (bruised), 28 pounds; water, 20 gallons. Boil for one hour, draw off the clear, and add to the galls water, 15 gallons. Simmer for one hour more, draw off the liquor and mix it with the first; (the two together should be about twenty-eight gallons); put this decoction into a barrel, then add powdered green copperas, 8 pounds; gum Senegal, 10 pounds. Bung close and agitate every day for a week; lastly, let it settle for use.

2. Bruised galls, ½ cwt. Put them into a hogshead and add water, 60 gallons. Agitate occasionally for two or three days, then add gum, 20 pounds. Macerate with agitation for two or three days longer, and add green copperas (powdered), 20 pounds. Bung close, repeat the previous treatment for a week, and let it settle for use. Both this and the preceding receipt produce the most durable black ink that can be made.

3. Galls (bruised), 14 pounds; chipped logwood, 15 pounds; water, 30 gallons; powdered green copperas, 7 pounds; gum, 7 pounds. Put them into a barrel, bung close, and macerate with occasional agitation for one week, then let it settle for use.

4. Logwood chips, ¼ cwt.; copperas, 5 pounds; alum, 2 pounds; gum Senegal, 7 pounds; water to make a barrel. This ink is very limpid, and has a pleasing colour, but is not so durable as either of the preceding.

Exchequer Ink.

Bruised Aleppo galls, 1 cwt.; gum, ¼ cwt.; chipped logwood, ¼ cwt. copperas, ¼ cwt.; water (soft), 120 gallons. Pour the water boiling hot on the galls and logwood, and steep for twenty days, then add the gum, and the next day the copperas; or boil the galls and logwood in the water for one hour, then add the gum, and lastly the copperas. This ink will preserve its colour for centuries.

Indestructible Ink.

1. Powdered copal, 25 parts; oil of lavender, 200 parts; lamp-black, 2 parts; indigo, 1 part. Dissolve.

2. Asphaltum, 1 part; lamp-black, ¼ part. Melt, then add oil prepared for printers' ink, by boiling and burning until sufficiently stringy, 1½ part. Mix together, and add spirits of turpentine, 3 or 4 parts. We would propose this ink, made with less turpentine, so as to be sufficiently thick for stamping, as the most perfect preventive of fraud, as when applied to the surface of an engraving, or letter-press, nothing will remove it that will not also discharge the ink of the stamp. It will stand the action of the alkalies, chlorine, acids, &c., even in a heated state, when they will at once destroy the texture of the paper.

Sympathetic Ink.

1. A dilute solution of nitro-muriate of cobalt. When heated, the writing performed with this ink assumes a fine green colour and disappears again when cooled.

2. An acetic solution of oxide of cobalt, to which add a little nitre. On exposing writing performed with the above to heat, it will assume a fine rose colour, which disappears on cooling.

3. Sal ammoniac, sulphate of copper, equal parts; water sufficient. This assumes a yellow colour when heated, and, like the preceding, disappears when cooled.

To Prevent Mould in Ink.

Alcohol, 1 pint; oil of cloves, ½ ounce. Mix, and add a few drops to the ink.

To Remove Oiliness from Ink.

Add a little ox-gall and vinegar to the ink. This is Carstair's plan.

Indelible Ink, for Marking Linen.

1. The juice of sloes, 1 pint; gum, ½ ounce. This requires no mordant, and is very durable.

2. Nitrate of silver, 1 part; water, 6 parts; gum, 1 part. Dissolve If too thick, dilute with warm soft water.

To Destroy Insects, on Trees, Shrubs, &c.

Tie up some flowers of sulphur in a piece of gauze, and dust the plants with it.

Iodic Acid.

Iodine; water to dissolve. Then pass gaseous chlorine through the solution until it becomes colourless.

To Collect and Preserve Leaves.

Collect leaves just before the opening of the flowers; and if from biennial narcotic plants, they should be of the second year's growth. They should then be scattered over paper trays, and dried in a heat of from 88° to 130° Fahr.; when dry, sift off the dust and dirt. Only the perfect leaves should be preserved.

Pure Crystallized Lemon Acid.

Take lemon-juice, any quantity. Put it into a vessel of china, glass, or wood, and add finely-powdered chalk until the whole of the acid is saturated, noting the exact weight of the dry chalk employed; then collect the precipitate and well wash it with water, and for every ten parts of chalk consumed, add sulphuric acid, 9½ parts; diluted with water, 60 parts. Mix while still warm with the precipitate, and stir well together; let them remain for twelve hours; then decant the clear, wash the white powder with clear water, and mix the two liquors; lastly, strain, evaporate, and crystallize. To purify it, repeat the operation of washing the crystals, dissolving and crystallizing two or three times. Great care must be used in evaporating the solution, for if too much heat should be employed, or the process carried too far, the acid product will be injured.

Lemonade.

White sugar, 1 pound; tartaric acid, ¼ ounce; essence of lemon, 30 drops; water, 3 quarts. Mix.

Effervescing Lemonade.

Tartaric acid, 50 parts, bicarbonate of soda, 30 parts; powdered lump-sugar, 200 parts; essence of lemon to flavour. Mix in fine powder and keep it dry, if for powders; but if for bottling, put it into a soda-water bottle, and fill it up with water; cork down as quick as possible. This may also be made in the same way as soda-water, only adding the extra articles.

Portable Lemonade.

1. Tartaric acid, 1 ounce; white sugar, 5 pounds; essence of lemon, ¼ ounce. Powder, and keep dry for use. A dessert-spoonful will make a tumbler of lemonade.

2. Tartaric acid, 1 part; powdered white sugar, 90 parts; essence of lemon to flavour. Mix, and keep it in a bottle; for use, put one full tea spoonful into a glass of water, and stir it until dissolved.

Portable Ærated Lemonade.

Essence of lemon, 1 part; lump-sugar (powdered), 160 parts; bicarbonate of soda, 15 parts. Mix, and divide into three-drachm papers (white), then tartaric acid, 20 parts, and divide it into the same number of papers (blue).

Lemon Brandy.

Proof-spirit, 70 gallons; essence of lemon, 3 ounces; sugar, 50 pounds, dissolved in water, 20 gallons. Mix, and rummage repeatedly for fourteen days.

Lemon Drops.

1. Sugar, 2 pounds; tartaric acid, ½ ounce; essence of lemon, 20 drops Make a saturated syrup with one half the sugar and acid, then add the other half with the essence, and form into drops.

2. Sugar, 7 pounds; essence of lemon, 1 drachm; sulphuric acid to acidify. Manage as before.

Lemon Cordial.

Essence of lemon, 2 ounces; proof-spirit, 25 gallons. Mix, and agitate well, then add sugar, 50 pounds; dissolved in water, 20 gallons. Mix well, and fine with eggs.

Factitious Lemon-Juice.

Pale or lump-sugar, 1½ pound; tartaric acid, 1 ounce (more or less); water (hot), 1 gallon; essence of lemon, 1 drachm. Mix well together in a close vessel, and frequently shake for one day.

Candied Lemon-Peel.

Take lemon-peels and boil them in syrup, then take them out and dry them.

Essence of Lemon-Peel.

Alcohol, 1 pound; oil of lemons, 6 drachms. Mix.

Lemon-Peel Water.

Lemon-peel (fresh), 1 cwt.; water, 80 gallons. Distil off seventy-five gallons.

Lemon Pickle.

1. Vinegar, 1 gallon; salt, 1 pound; garlic, 1 ounce; horse-radish, 1 ounce; cloves, 3 drachms; mace, 3 drachms; nutmegs, 3 drachms; cayenne, 3 drachms; essence of lemon, 2 drachms. Pour the vinegar (boiling) on the other articles, in a jar, then cork it and macerate for a month.

2. Lemon-juice, 4 gallons; vinegar, 4 gallons; ginger, 16 ounces, allspice, 14 ounces; black pepper, 11 ounces; lemon-peel (grated), 10 ounces; bird pepper, 2 ounces; mace, 2 ounces; nutmeg, 2 ounces. Macerate for one month, then strain.

3. Lemon-juice, vinegar, equal parts. Essence of lemon, salt, and spice, to palate.

Essential Salt of Lemons.

1. Superoxalate of potash, supertartrate of potash, equal quantities. Mix. This composition is poisonous.

2. Cream of tartar, 1 part; oxalic acid, 1 part; salt of sorel, 1 part. Mix in fine powder. Poison.

Lemon Sugar.

Tartaric acid, 4 ounces; white sugar, 7 pounds; essence of lemon, 3 drachms. Mix, and well rub together.

Lemon Wine.

Sugar, 60 pounds; raisins (bruised), 15 pounds; water, 30 gallons. Boil, then add cider, 15 gallons. Ferment, and add spirit, 3 gallons; white tartar, 12 ounces; essence of lemon, 2 ounces; finings, 1 pint. Observe to shake the essence, with a pint of the spirit, until it becomes milky, before adding it to the wine.

Jelly of Alum, or Hydrate of Alumina.

Take a solution of alum, and precipitate the alumina with a solution of ammonia.

To Disinfect Letters, &c.

Expose them to the fumes of chloride of lime, or burning sulphur.

Astringent Injection for Leucorrhœa.

1. Compound solution of alum, 6 drachms; water, 1 quart. Mix, and use it lukewarm.

2. Sugar of lead, 60 grains; water, 1 quart. Mix.

3. Catechu, 1 drachm; myrrh, 1 drachm; lime-water, 12 ounces. Mix and dilute with water.

4. Nitrate of silver, 35 grains; water, 1 quart. Mix.

5. Sulphate of zinc, 40 grains; water, 1 quart. Mix.

To Escape the Effects of Lightning.

1. Avoid standing under trees, to escape from the rain during a thunder storm, but boldly expose yourself to the wet; it will preserve you from the lightning.

2. Avoid standing close to any metallic bodies, as lead pipes or iron railings, &c.

3. When in doors during a thunder-storm, sit or stand as near to the middle of the room as convenient; avoid standing at the window, or sitting near the wall.

To Produce Artificial Lightning.

1. Take the pollen of club-moss (lycopodium), and scatter it rapidly and extensively over the flame of a candle.

2. Finely powdered resin, 5 parts; finely powdered gunpowder, 1 part. Mix, and use it as above.

Light Red.

Take yellow ochre; calcine it until of the required tint.

Light Phial, for seeing the Time by a Watch at Night.

Dry phosphorus, 1 part; olive oil, 6 parts. Put them into a phial, cork it, and place it in warm water for two or three hours. For use, pull out the cork, and sufficient light will be emitted to enable you to see the time by a watch. One bottle will last for years if well corked as soon as used. Ether may be employed instead of olive oil.

Oil of (Factitious) Lilies.

1. Rape oil, 1 gallon; simple syrup, 4 ounces. Well mix.

2. Rape oil, 1 gallon; rasped parsnips, 8 ounces. Steep for a few days. Rape oil is usually sold for this article.

Lime Water.

Quicklime, 1 part; water, 16 parts. Mix, and after a short time well shake the vessel, then let it stand to settle, and decant the clear. This article should be both made and kept in a close vessel.

Limpidum, for adapting Common Ink to Steel Pens.

Lump-sugar, 2 parts; ox-gall to make into a paste. Mix, dry slowly and powder fine.

Factitious Linseed Oil.

Fish or vegetable oil, 100 gallons; acetate of lead, 7 pounds; litharge, 7 pounds; dissolved in vinegar, 2 gallons. Well mix with heat, then add boiled oil, 7 gallons; turpentine, 1 gallon. Again well mix.

To render Linen and Cloth Water-proof.

Boiled oil, 25 parts; bees'-wax, 2 parts; litharge, 2 parts; lamp-black, 2 parts. Mix, and use it at discretion. Any other colour may be used instead of lamp-black.

Lip-Salve à la Rose.

Alkanet root, 1 ounce; olive oil, 12 ounces. Digest with a gentle heat, then add suet, 16 ounces; lard, 8 ounces. Strain, and while cooling, stir in rose-water, 3 ounces; ottar of roses, 3 drops.

Carnation Lip-Salve.

Olive oil, 1 pound; alkanet root, 1 ounce or less. Macerate with heat until the oil is well coloured, then add white wax, 6 ounces; spermaceti, 6 ounces; oil of lavender, 30 drops; essence of bergamot, 1 drachm.

Red Lip-Salve.

1. Olive oil, 1 pound; root alkanet, 2 ounces or less. Macerate with heat until the oil is well coloured, then add spermaceti, 2 ounces; white wax, 8 ounces; suet (prepared), 12 ounces. When nearly cold, stir in orange-flower water, 1 ounce; oil of lavender, ½ drachm.

2. Prepared suet, 1 pound; prepared lard, 1 pound; alkanet root, 2 ounces. Macerate in a gentle heat until sufficiently coloured, then cool a little, and stir in rose-water, 6 ounces; oil of lavender, 10 drops; essence of neroli, 10 drops; essence of lemon, 10 drops; essence of bergamot, 10 drops.

White Lip-Salve.

1. Prepared suet, 1 pound; prepared lard, 1 pound. Melt, and, when cooling, stir in rose-water, 4 ounces; oil of rhodium, 2 drops; oil of cloves, 5 drops. Or other scent, to taste.

2. Olive oil, 1 pound; spermaceti, 1 pound; white wax, 1 pound; prepared lard, 1 pound. Melt, and, while cooling, stir in rose-water, 8 ounces; essence of lemon, 2 drachms; bergamot, 2 drachms.

3. Lard, 1 pound; suet, 1 pound. Melt and strain, then, while cooling, stir in a little perfume.

Liqueur Orgeat.

Take of blanched almonds half a pound, and mash them in a mortar, one drachm of the oil of bitter almonds, half a drachm of the oil of Seville orange-peel, one quart of syrup, and three quarts of clean spirits forty under proof. Kill the oils in spirits of wine, and mix all together.

Linseed Lozenges.

Lump-sugar; mucilage, or decoction of linseed, to mix.

Jeweller's Metal.

Copper, 30 parts; brass, 10 parts; tin, 7 parts. Mix.

Remedy for Botts.

First drench your horse with sweet milk and molasses. Second, in a reasonable time drench him again with a quart of beef brine. Alum water is good: so is saltpetre water. A purge should always be given soon after the drench. A strong solution of salt and water, with a little alum, would perhaps be as good as the brine.

Hooks or Haws.

Never cut the *caruncle* if it can be removed otherwise by bleeding and purging, which will reduce the fever and remove the disease.

Stone or Gravel in the Bladder.

Take gravel root (if it can be had) and make into a tea, and give to drink night and morning until the disease is removed; or make a drench of marsh-mallows, water-melon seed, and asparagus, of each two large handfuls, boil them in three quarts of water down to one quart, adding a tea-spoonful of nitre. It should be strained. The sheath and penis should be well washed and greased, and gently rubbed, in order to excite the bladder.

Remedy for Colic or Gripes in Horses.

After bleeding from the neck, drench with the following mixture. Laudanum, 1 ounce; of mint tea, warm, 1 quart. Mix. After which give an injection made of warm water, salt, meal, hog's lard, and molasses.

Another.

Drench with a solution made as follows. Camphor, ¼ ounce; oil of turpentine, ½ ounce; mint tea, warm, 1 pint. Cover the horse with blankets, and use every means to get him into a sweat.

Remedy for Scratches in Horses.

Wash with strong soap-suds, then with strong copperas-water. Repeat this twice a day until he is cured: for a daily drink give sassafras or spice-wood tea, or a little saltpetre dissolved in his drink. Some recommend the juice of Jamestown weed, or a decoction of red oak bark; others, spirits of turpentine, or blue-stone water, greasing after with hog's lard. Poke-root is also good. But by all means keep the horse's feet clean.

Remedy in Botts and Grubs.

This disease is easily known, by the horse's inclination to lay down, his looking round to his sides, he groans, he whips his tail between his legs, is feverish (to discover feel his ears), and frequently turns up his upper lip. Take copperas, 2 spoonfuls; warm water, 1 pint. Dissolve and drench. Repeat if necessary, or drench with linseed oil, or with equal parts of milk and molasses, always repeating if the animal is not apparently better in half an hour.

Another.

Take fresh meat (raw), and in small pieces force it down the throat, or give the horse in his food two ounces of Æthiop's mineral; in two days give a purge; and to prevent their return give a decoction of bitter herbs.

Strangles.

Feed with light, cooling (green if it can be had) food; mix the food with sassafras tea, in the which a spoonful of powdered sulphur and a tea-spoonful of saltpetre has been added. Assafœtida tied in a rag and placed in the watering bucket, another in like manner placed in the manger, is highly recommended.

Yellow Water.

Gentle exercise, a clean stable, and a little blood taken. For a drench give him, in decoction, one ounce of assafœtida; spirit of camphor, four table-spoonfuls; warm water, one pint. Mix. To be repeated for three or four mornings in succession. Give in six quarts of mashed bran of flour of sulphur, one table-spoonful, of antimony and saltpetre, each twenty grains. The bran is to be mixed with sassafras tea, scalding hot, and this food is to be given three times a week, and never suffer the horse to drink cold water. It ought to be about milk-warm.

To make Hens lay perpetually.

Give your hens half an ounce of fresh meat each, chopped fine, once a day, while the ground is frozen, and they cannot get worms or insects; allow no cocks to run with them, and they will lay perpetually. Try it. They also require plenty of grain, water, gravel, and lime.

Blisters for Horses.

Spanish flies, half an ounce; oil of turpentine, one ounce; hog's lard, one quarter of a pound. Mix.

Another.

Tar, one quarter of a pound; vitriolic acid, two drachms; oil of origanum, half an ounce; hog's lard, two ounces; Spanish flies, two ounces. Good for spavin.

Fomentations, or Poultices.

Bran, two quarts; hot vinegar, one pint; hog's lard, two ounces. Mix.

Another.

Make a poultice of a strong decoction of red oak bark and Indian meal.

Another.

Make a poultice thus: Vinegar, one pint; meal, two quarts; hog's lard. four ounces. Boiling water sufficient to mix.

To put Black Spots on a White Horse.

Lime (quick), powdered, half a pound; litharge, four ounces. Well beat and mix the litharge with the lime. The above to be put into a vessel and a sharp ley is to be poured over it. Boil and skim off the substance which rises on the surface. This is the colouring matter, which must be applied to such parts of the animal as you wish to have dyed black. Red hair may be dyed black with a very similar composition. Thus, boil four ounces of lime with four ounces of litharge, in fresh water; the scum that rises will have the same effect. If the hair be entirely free from grease, one night will be sufficient to stain it black.

Clysters for Animals.

1. Salt, twelve ounces; warm water, one gallon; olive oil, one quarter of a pound. Mix.

2. Warm, thin gruel made of corn-meal.

To preserve Fruit.

1. Pick the fruit from the stems and put it into bottles, which must be quite filled; place the corks loosely in them, and set them upright in a pan of warm water; place them on the fire, and heat the water until it nearly boils; let them stand fifteen minutes, then fill each bottle within an inch of the cork with boiling water; cork tight, and let them cool. Pack them on their sides to keep the corks moist. The fruit is better when not quite ripe; in this case it will keep two or three years.

2. Take the fruit, hardly ripe, and put it into bottles, and fill them with good spirit or brandy. In this way any fruit may be preserved whole.

To preserve Fruit with Sugar.

Clarified syrup boiled to a weak candy height, and pour it hot on the fruit; let it stand for twenty-four hours, then pour off the syrup, and again concentrate it by heat, to the same consistence as before; lastly, pour it on the fruit in wide-mouthed bottles or jars, and bung close. Should the fruit be very succulent, it should be previously soaked in weak alum-water and drained.

To keep Insects off Fruit Trees, &c.

Dip a piece of rag or canvass in coal tar and tie it to the tree.

Remedy for Poisoning from Fungi.

Ether, 2 drachms; tincture of capsicum, 1 drachm. Mix and divide into two doses. First, induce vomiting, and administer some active clyster, then give the above at intervals of half an hour, in a little warm fluid.

Furniture Balls.

Yellow resin, 1 part; yellow wax, 9 parts; add them in a melted state to linseed oil, 7 parts. Previously coloured by heating for some hours over alkanet root, 1 part. Make into balls of a convenient size.

Furniture Cream.

1. Pearlash, 1 ounce; water, 8 ounces; beeswax (genuine), 6 ounces. Mix with heat, and add sufficient water to reduce it to the consistence of cream. For use, add more water, and spread it on the wood with a painter's brush; let it dry, and polish with a hard brush or cloth. If white wax is used, it may be applied to polish plaster casts, statues, and the like.

2. Beeswax, 3 ounces; pearlash, 2 ounces; water, 6 ounces. Melt with heat, and add boiled oil, 4 ounces; oil of turpentine, 5 ounces. Mix.

Furniture Oil.

1. Alkanet root, 1 part; shell lac varnish, 4 parts; linseed oil, 16 parts; turps, 2 parts; wax, 2 parts. Mix, and let them stand together for a week.

2. Beeswax, 3 parts, alkanet, 1 part; turpentine, 3 parts; boiled oil, 12 parts. Mix, with heat.

Furniture Paste.

1. Beeswax, 1 part; oil of turpentine, 1 part; boiled oil, 1 part. Mix with heat. Colour with alkanet.

2. Yellow wax, 16 parts; resin, 1 part; alkanet root, 1 part; turpentine, 6 parts; linseed oil, 6 parts. First steep the alkanet in the oil with heat; and, when well coloured, pour off the clear on the other ingredients and again apply heat until they are all dissolved.

Furniture Varnish.

White wax, 15 ounces; yellow resin, 1 ounce, powdered; spirits of turpentine, 1 quart. Digest until dissolved. Lay it on with a brush or cloth, and well polish with a clean piece of woollen.

To preserve Furs from Moths, &c.

Wrap up a few cloves or peppercorns with them, when you put them away for any length of time, and always keep them in a dry place.

Fusible Alloy.

1. Bismuth, 8 parts; lead, 5 parts; tin, 3 parts. This is fusible at the heat of boiling water.

2. Zinc, lead, and bismuth, equal parts. This may be fused in a bit of writing paper, and will melt even in hot water.

3. Lead, 3 parts; tin, 2 parts; bismuth, 5 parts. Mix. This alloy melts at 197° Fahr. In using this composition to take casts of seals, gems, &c., it should be employed at the lowest possible temperature at which it will keep fluid; for this purpose we may let it become pasty, and then forcibly impress the substances together.

4. Bismuth, 2 parts; tin, 3 parts; lead, 5 parts. Melt. This alloy fuses in boiling water.

To make a Mash.

Bran, 1 gallon; powdered brimstone, 1 ounce; saltpetre, 1 tea-spoonful; sassafras tea (scalding hot), 1 quart. Mix.

Another way.

Sulphur, in powder, 1 tea-spoonful; an equal quantity of saltpetre; oats 1 gallon; boiling water, 1 quart. Mix.

Another Mash.

Bran, 1 gallon; glauber salts, ¼ pound; sulphur, 1 table-spoonful; sassafras tea, boiling hot, 1 quart. Mix. No drink to be given for six hours.

Salt, Lime, and Peat.

Take one bushel of salt and one cask of lime. Slack the lime with the brine made by dissolving the salt in water sufficient to make a stiff paste with the lime, which will not be quite sufficient to dissolve all the salt. Mix all the materials then well together in a heap for ten days, and then be well mixed with three cords of peat; shovel well over for about six weeks, and it will be fit for use. Here, then, are produced three cords of manure, for about the cost of \$2 10 cents per cord:—Salt, 60 cents; lime \$1 20 cents; peat, \$4 50 cents—\$6 30.—3)\$6 30(\$2 10.

Tar

For greasing wagons, we think an absurd article. In the hottest weather it soon gums up and becomes adhesive, and in cold weather is always so. Wherever iron axle-trees are used, black-lead mixed with grease is best—or flour mixed with lard.

To preserve Fruit whole.

Put them into wide-mouthed bottles, fill them up with clarified saturated syrup, put them into water in a copper, and when it boils, cork them tight and keep them in a cold place. A small quantity of spirit added to each bottle will prevent fermentation.

Factitious Galbanum.

Galbanum, 7 pounds; Burgundy pitch, 3 pounds; yellow resin 2 pounds; spirits of turpentine, ¾ pound. Mix.

Factitious Strained Galbanum.

Galbanum, 2 pounds; resin, 2 pounds; Burgundy pitch, 2 pounds; assafœtida, ½ pound; sagepenum, ½ pound; spirits of turpentine, 1 pound; water, 1 pound. Melt the gums, cool a little, and then stir in the turpentine and water.

Galbanam Plaster.

Simple dyachylon, 9 pounds; galbanum, 2 pounds; yelllow wax, 1 pound. Mix.

Prepared Ox Gall.

Take the gall, let it stand for a few days and then pour off the clear.

Factitious Garnet or Ancient Carbuncle.

1. Oxide of manganese, 1 part; purple of cassius, 1 part; glass of antimony, 128 parts; paste or strass, 260 parts. Fuse carefully for thirty hours and cool slowly.

2. Strass or pure white paste, 1000 parts; glass of antimony, 498 parts; manganese, 1⅔ parts; powder of cassius, $1\frac{1}{10}$ parts. As before.

3. Plain paste, 1000 parts; glass of antimony, 500 parts; manganese, 5 parts; purple of cassius, 5 parts.

To choose Geese.

A young goose has a yellow bill, if red it is a sign of age; if fresh, the feet will be pliable, but stale if stiff and dry.

Gentianine.

Take powdered gentian-root, digest it in ether for 48 hours, filter and evaporate to the consistence of an extract, then add alcohol until it no longer becomes coloured; evaporate to dryness, redissolve in weak alcohol, filter and again evaporate; then dissolve in water, filter, and add a little magnesia; boil, filter, digest the sediment in ether and evaporate to dryness. Aromatic bitter. Dose—1½ to 2¼ grains.

German Silver.

Nickel, 1 part; zinc, 1 part; copper, 2 parts. This alloy forms an excellent substitute for silver.

German Paste. (For Birds.)

Oatmeal, 25 parts; sweet almonds, 6 parts; rape oil, 2 parts; sugar, 1 part; caraways, 1 part; a little saffron. Make into a paste and granulate through a sieve.

Fine White German Silver.

Iron, 1 part; nickel, 10 parts; zinc, 10 parts; copper, 20 parts. Mix.

German Silver for Castings, &c.

Lead, 3 parts; nickel, 20 parts; zinc, 20 parts; copper, 60 parts. Mix.

German Silver for Rolling.

Nickel, 5 parts; zinc, 4 parts; copper, 12 parts. Mix.

Genuine German Silver.

Copper, 40½ parts; nickel, 31½ parts; zinc, 25½ parts; iron, 2½ parts —100. Mix.

German White Lead.

Pure white lead, 1 part; sulphate of barytes, 2 parts. Mix.

To Gild Copper, Brass, &c. (Patent.)

Fine gold, 5 parts; nitric acid (sp. g. 1.45), 21 parts; hydrochloric acid (sp. g. 1.15), 17 parts; pure water, 14 parts. Digest with heat in a glass vessel until all the gold is dissolved, and till red or yellow fumes cease to rise. Decant the clear liquid into some convenient vessel, and add water, 500 to 600 parts. Boil for two hours, let it stand to settle and pour off the clear into a suitable vessel. For use, heat the liquid and suspend the articles (previously well cleaned) by means of a hair or fine wire, until sufficiently coated with gold, then well wash them in pure water.

Lice on Cattle.

1. Mercurial ointment rubbed on the animal from the crown of the head to the root of the tail, down the back-bone, will effectually kill lice in a day or two. This, however, is a dangerous remedy to use, unless the animal is kept in the stable, and requires great care to preserve him from the effects of cold and wet.

2. Corrosive sublimate is another effectual remedy. This is to be applied as before prescribed, but, like No. 1, is dangerous.

3. A strong decoction of larkspur is also a sure and safe remedy. This should be applied as recommended for No. 1.

4. Spirits of turpentine is also a sure remedy. It should be applied as No. 1.

5. A decoction of tobacco, applied as No. 1, will destroy the lice.

6. A mixture of Scotch snuff and fish oil, rubbed on the affected parts, will destroy the lice.

7. A mixture of soft soap and Scotch snuff, well rubbed on the parts, will also eradicate them.

As an auxiliary to whatever remedy may be used, the currycomb and brush should be freely applied, after a day or two, in order that the hide and hair of the animal may be kept clean. No animal which is well fed, and daily curried and brushed, will either breed or retain lice; the latter operation, however, few who have much stock can regularly attend to.

Varnish for Gilded Articles.

Gum lac, gamboge, dragon's blood, annotto, each 4 parts; saffron, 1 part. Dissolve each resin separately in eight parts of alcohol, and make separate tincture with the dragon's blood and annotto, also in eight parts of alcohol each, then mix the former together and add a sufficient quantity of the tinctures to give the required shade and colour to the varnish.

Gilder's Wax.

1. Yellow wax, 3 pounds; verdigris, 1 pound; sulphate of zinc, 1 pound; red oxide of iron, 2½ pounds. Powder the last three articles very fine.

2. Yellow wax, 7 pounds; colcothar, 7 pounds; verdigris, 3 pounds; borax, ¼ pound; alum, ¼ pound.

Gin.

Take 100 gallons of clean, rectified spirits; add, after you have killed the oils well, 1½ ounces of the oil of English juniper, ½ ounce of angelica-essence, ½ ounce of the oil of bitter almonds, ½ ounce of the oil of coriander, and ½ ounce of the oil of caraway; put this into the rectified spirit and well rummage it up: this is what the rectifiers call strong gin.

To make this *up*, as it is called by the trade, add 45 pounds of loaf-sugar, dissolved; then rummage the whole well up together with 4 ounces of roche alum. For finings, there may be added two ounces of salts of tartar.

Cordial Gin.

Of the oil of bitter almonds, vitriol, turpentine, and juniper, ½ a drachm each; kill the oils in spirits of wine: 15 gallons of clean, rectified proof-spirits, to which add 1 drachm of coriander seeds, 1 drachm of pulverized orris root, ½ pint of elder-flower water, with 10 pounds of sugar and 5 gallons of water or liquor.

English Gin.

Plain malt spirit, 100 gallons; spirits of turpentine, 1 pint; bay salt, 7 pounds. Mix and distil. The difference in the flavour of gin is produced by varying the proportion of turpentine, and by occasionally adding a small quantity of juniper-berries.

Ginger Beer.

Bruised ginger, 2 ounces; water, 5 gallons. Boil for one hour, then add, when sufficiently cool, lump-sugar, 3½ pounds; cream of tartar, 1½ ounce; essence of lemon, 1 drachm; yeast, ½ pint. Strain, bottle, and wire down the corks.

2. Loaf-sugar, 1 pound; rasped ginger, 1 ounce; cream of tartar, ¼ ounce; boiling water, 1 gallon. Mix and cover them up close for one hour, then add essence of lemon, 15 drops; yeast, 2 or 3 spoonfuls. Strain, bottle, and wire down the corks.

To destroy the Bee Miller.

To a pint of water, sweetened with honey or sugar, add half a gill of vinegar, and set it in an open vessel on the top or by the side of the hive. When the miller comes in the night, he will fly into the mixture and be drowned.

To restore and improve Musty Flour.

Carbonate of magnesia, 3 parts; Flour, 760 parts. Mix, and use the flour in the usual way. This will not only greatly improve bad flour, but the bread will be much lighter, more wholesome, and keep longer, than when alum is used.

To correct Musty Grain.

Take a bushel of grain, and pour on it two bushels of boiling water. Let them stand until cold, then skim off the floating grains and husks, and discard them; drain off the water, and dry the remainder in a kiln. The musty quality rarely penetrates through the husk.

Myrtle-flower Water.

Myrtle flowers, 30 pounds; water, 13 gallons. Draw over ten gallons

Factitious Manna.

Powdered sugar, powdered tragacanth, flour; Aleppo scammony, 2 drachms to every pound of the mixture. Water to mix. A little colour may be added. Dose, two to four drachms.

Manna Vinegar.

Take onions and press out the juice, ferment, and allow it to acetify.

To renovate Old Manuscripts.

Wash them lightly with a solution of ferro-cyanide of potash in clear water.

Map Colours.

YELLOW.

1. Dissolve gamboge in water.
2. Make a decoction of French berries, strain, and add a little gum arabic

RED.

1. Make a decoction of Brazil dust in vinegar, and add a little gum and alum.
2. Make an infusion of cochineal and add a little gum.

BLUE.

A weak mixture of sulphate of indigo and water, to which add a little gum.

GREEN.

1. Dissolve crystals of verdigris in water, and add a little gum.
2. Dissolve sap green in water, and add gum.

Marasquin.

Bitter almonds (bruised), 2 ounces. Macerate for three days in one gallon of spirit, then add four pounds of sugar, dissolved in two quarts of boiling water.

Marasquin de Groseilles.

Ripe gooseberries (bruised), 100 pounds; cherry and gooseberry leaves, each 5 pounds; water sufficient. Bruise and ferment, then distil over 6 gallons, and add sugar, 30 pounds (or less), dissolved in water, 6 pints spirit, 6 pints.

Emetine.

Take genuine ipecacuanha powder, and digest it in ether at a temperature of 60°, then decant and distil. Repeat the process until the ether comes off quite pure, then digest the powder in alcohol, pour it off and digest in fresh alcohol; repeat the process for a third time. Distil to dryness and dissolve the residue in cold water; add a little magnesia to separate the gallic acid, filter, dry, and dissolve again in alcohol; filter, and evaporate to dryness. Emetic; dose, one fourth to one third of a grain.

Election Cake.

Flour, 10 pounds; sugar, 4 pounds; butter, 2 pounds; milk, 1 quart; eggs, 10; yeast and spice. Mix.

Fluxes for Enamel Colours.

1. Flint powder, 1 part; calcined borax, 1 part; flint glass, 3 parts; red lead, 4 parts. Keep them in a state of fusion, in a Hessian crucible, for three hours: then pour into cold water, dry and powder.

2. Glass powder, 11 parts; white arsenic, 1 part; nitre, 1 part. Mix.

White Enamel.

Arsenic, 14 parts; potash, 25 parts; nitre, 12 parts; glass, 13 parts flint, 5 parts; litharge, 3 parts.

Entomologist's Cement.

Equal parts of thick mastic varnish and isinglass size.

Candied Eringo.

Take the eringo, slit and wash it, then candy it, by boiling it in thick syrup for a short time; drain and dry.

Eschalotte Sauce.

Sliced shallots, 1 part; port wine, 5 parts; vinegar, 6 parts; mushroom catsup, 4 parts: add a small bit of lemon thyme. Mix and macerate for fourteen days, then decant the clear.

Esprit de Suave.

Spirit of jasmin, 1 quart; spirit of cassia, 1 quart; spirit of wine, 1 pint; spirit of tuberose, 10 ounces; essence of cloves, 7 scruples; essence of bergamot, 7 scruples; neroli, 15 drops; essence of musk, 1 ounce; rose-water, 16 ounces. Mix well and filter carefully.

Essence de Jasmin.

Take the flowers and steep them in spirit, then distil or filter.

Essence of Orange-Peel.

Spirit, 1 pound; orange-peel, 1 pound. Digest for two days, then add white wine, 6 pints; water, 1½ pints. Digest one day longer, and decant

Essentia Bina.

Take coarse sugar, and roast it until it acquires a proper colour.

Essex Ale.

Brew as for other pale ale.

Essence of Peppermint.

Oil of peppermint, 1 pound; rectified spirit, 2 gallons; green pepper mint to colour. Mix.

Essentia Odorifera.

Musk, 11 grains; balsam of Peru, 11 grains; civet and oil of cloves, 5 grains; oil of rhodium, 2 grains; salt of tartar, 30 grains; alcohol, 2 ounces. Macerate for two or three days, then pour off the clear. This is said to be a beautiful perfume.

Fluid for Etching on Copper.

Verdigris, 4 parts; salt, 4 parts; sal ammoniac, 4 parts; alum, 1 part, water, 16 parts: strong vinegar, 12 parts. Dissolve with heat.

Acid for Etching on Steel.

Pyroligneous acid, 5 parts; alcohol, 1 part; nitric acid, 1 part. Mix the first two, then add the nitric acid.

Ointment for the Mange.

1. Lard, 1 pound; sulphur vivum, 1 pound; spirit of turpentine, 1 pound; oil of tar, 1 pound; suet, 2 pounds. Mix.

2. Sulphur vivum, oil of turpentine, rape oil, tallow, each, 7 pounds. Mix.

Manheim Gold.

Copper, 3 parts; zinc, 1 part. Melt separately, then suddenly mix them, and stir well.

Mottled Wash Balls.

1. Cut white soap previously softened in water into small slices, and rub them in the colour you wish to mottle with, then mix them with similar cuttings of white soap, and form them into balls, observing to be careful to spread the colour as little as possible. Powdered bole, vermilion, or red lead may he used for red; thumb blue for blue, &c. &c.

2. White soap, coloured sufficient. Reduce to a paste with water, and well mix, then evaporate and form into slices; when sufficiently hard, take of these any quantity, and white soap, sliced and softened, a like pro portion, and form into balls.

To prevent Mould in Ink.

Add a few cloves to the ink.

Moutarde Superbe.

Vinegar, 100 parts; shallots, 1 part; thyme, 1 part; lemon-peel, 1 part; cayenne, 1 part. Mix, and make your mustard with the liquor, after it has stood for two or three days, or more.

Mucic Acid.

Take gum arabic, 1 part; digest in nitric acid, 2 parts.

Oil of Mucilages.

Rape oil, 1 gallon; water, 5 pints; linseed, 2 pounds. Boil until the water is evaporated.

Mulberry Wine.

1. Juice of the fruit, 10 gallons; or of mulberries bruised, 15 gallons; water, 15 gallons; sugar, 35 gallons. Boil and ferment, then add spirit, 2 or three gallons; red tartar, 7 ounces; cassia, ½ ounce; bitter almonds, ½ ounce.

2. Ripe mulberries, ripe apples, equal quantities; sugar or honey, one pound to the gallon. Express the juice, put it into a cask, and add the sugar. Ferment with yeast, 1 quart to every hhd.; catechu, ½ pound; red argol, ½ pound.

Multum.

Quassia, liquorice; water to make an extract.

Hard Multum. (Black Extract.)

Coculus Indicus; water to make an extract. Both these articles are employed by fraudulent brewers. Their use subjects the party to a fine of £500, in England.

Dr. Munroe's Cough Medicine.

Paregoric, 1 ounce; sulphuric ether, 4 drachms; tinct. tolu, 2 drachms Dose; one tea-spoonful night and morning.

Muscadel.

Sugar, 1 cwt.; water, 40 gallons. Boil, then let it cool, and add clary flowers, 6 gallons; yeast, 1 quart. Ferment and rack, then add pale spirit, 2 gallons.

Mushroom Catsup.

Mushroom juice, 1 gallon; allspice, 1 ounce; pepper, cloves, ginger, each, ½ ounce; salt, 4 pounds. Boil for one hour, strain, and bottle.

To distinguish Mushrooms from Poisonous Fungi.

1. Sprinkle a little salt on the spongy part or gills of the sample to be tried. If they turn yellow, they are poisonous: if black, they are wholesome. Allow the salt to act, before you decide on the question.

2. False mushrooms have a warty cap, or else fragments of membrane adhering to the upper surface, are heavy, and emerge from a vulva or bag; they grow in tufts or clusters in woods, on the stumps of trees, &c., whereas the true mushrooms grow in pastures.

3. False mushrooms have an astringent, styptic and disagreeable taste;

4. When cut they turn blue;

5. They are moist on the surface, and generally

6. Of a rose or orange colour.

7. The gills of the true mushroom are of a pinky red, changing to a liver colour;

8. The flesh is white;

9. The stem is white, solid, and cylindrical.

To pickle Mushrooms.

Clean them with salt and water, then put them into a saucepan with a little salt, keep them over the fire until the heat draws the liquor from them, then put them to drain, next bottle them, adding a blade of mace, and distilled vinegar sufficient to cover them.

Mushroom Powder.

Take mushrooms, any quantity; onions, cloves, mace and pepper to taste. Cut them into slices and dry them, then reduce to powder and sift.

To stain Musical Instruments.

Crimson.—Boil one pound of ground Brazil-wood in three quarts of water for an hour; strain it, and add half an ounce of cochineal; boil it again for half an hour gently, and it will be fit for use.

Purple.—Boil a pound of chip logwood in three quarts of water for an hour; then add four ounces of alum.

Essence of Musk.

1. Bladder musk (cut small), 5 parts; civet, 1 part; spirit of ambrette, 100 parts; strongest alcohol, 35 parts. Put them into a close vessel, and digest for two months in a heat of from 100 to 150° Fahr.

2. Grain musk, 2 drachms; alcohol, 1 pound. Mix. As before.

Factitious Musk.

Rectified oil of amber, 1 part; nitric acid, 4 parts. Digest until a black matter is deposited, which must be washed and preserved.

Musk Hair Powder.

Starch or farina, 7 pounds; musk, 2 scruples. Mix.

Musk Soap.

Good tallow soap, 30 pounds; palm soap, 26 pounds. Treat as for cinnamon soap, and perfume with the following mixture:—Powdered cloves, 5 ounces; powdered pale roses, 5 ounces; powdered gillyflower, 5 ounces; essence of bergamot, 4 ounces; essence of musk, 3¾ ounces. Colour with brown ochre, 4½ ounces.

Tincture of Musk.

Powdered musk, 1 ounce; civet, 30 grains; ottar of roses, 25 drops; oil of cloves, 10 drops; alcohol, 4 pints. Digest.

M. Soye's Patent Mustard.

Mustard-seed, 1 part; weak wood vinegar, 2 parts. Macerate for a fortnight, then grind the whole into a paste, in a mill, and put it into pots; lastly, thrust a red-hot poker into each of them.

Patent Mustard.

Flour of mustard, 8 pounds; wheaten flour, 2 pounds; bay salt, 2 pounds; cayenne pepper, 3 ounces; water to mix.

Factitious Must.

Sugar, 8 parts; warm water, 24 parts; cream of tartar, ½ part. Dissolve. This is an excellent form for a must, which may be coloured and treated with the usual substances for flavouring wine.

To judge of the Qualities of Mutton.

Choose this meat by the fineness of its grain, good colour, and firm white fat.

Le Mort's Ointment.

Lard, 7 pounds; turpentine, 1 pound; litharge, 1 pound; ceruse, 1 pound; alum, ½ pound; bichloride of mercury, ½ pound; red lead, ¼ pound Mix.

Colours for Liqueurs.

Blue—Sulphate of indigo, nearly saturated with chalk.

Yellow—Infusion of safflowers in water.

Green—Equal parts of each of the above.

Red—Cochineal in small quantities.

Violet—Turnsole.

Fawn colour—White sugar, and heat it until of a proper colour.

Dark red or brandy colour—Burnt sugar or brandy colouring.

Liquid Blister for Horses.

1. Spanish flies, 1 ounce; boiling water, 7 ounces. Macerate for twelve hours, then add bichlorate of mercury, 1 drachm; hydrochloric acid, 3 drachms; spirits of wine, 2 ounces. Mix well together.

2. Spanish flies (powdered), 1 ounce; oil of turpentine, 2 ounces; lin seed oil, 3 ounces. Mix.

3. Blistering plaster, 3 parts; linseed oil, 1 part. Mix together with heat, then add oil of turpentine, 1 part.

Liquid Gas for Spirit or Naphtha Lamps.

Oil of turpentine, 16 parts; alcohol, 1 part or less. Mix. This fluid gives a most brilliant light, quite equal to gas, but requires to be burnt in peculiar shaped lamps, generally known by the name of "naphtha lamps" or "liquid-gas" lamps.

Liquid Gold, for Vellum, &c.

Take gold-leaf and grind it with gum-water; then add a small quantity of bichloride of mercury, and bottle for use.

Liquid Silver, for Vellum, &c.

Take silver-leaf and grind it, with gum-water or glaire of egg.

Honey Water for the Hair.

Honey, 2 parts; sand, 1 part. Mix, and distil in a large retort with a gentle heat.

Hops.

Put from half a pound to a pound of hops to every bushel of malt (according to their strength), for mild liquor; for stale beer, put one to one and a half pound, according to the time you intend to keep it. Before boiling hops, it is better to let them soak fourteen or fifteen hours in cold water.

Substitute for Hops.

1. For every pound of hops required, use two ounces of marsh trefoil; or,

2. Gentian root (bruised, q. s.; or,

3. Quassia, (rasped), q. s.

To Choose Hops.

When rubbed between the fingers or on the palm of the hand, good hops will feel glutinous, have a fragrant smell, and develop a fine yellow dust. The seeds should be ripe, and the leaves full and unbroken, and of a fine brownish-yellow green. Avoid yearlings, unless you can get them in good condition and two-thirds the price of new hops. The best hops for old beer are Farnhams and Countrys; for mild beer, East Kents, Kents and Sussex.

Hoof Ointment.

Tallow, 1 pound, tar, 1 pound; black resin, 1 pound; lard, 2 pounds; spirits of turpentine, 1 pound. Mix.

Horehound Candy.

1. Take horehound, and boil it until the juice is extracted, then add it to a sufficient quantity of sugar, boil and stir until it grows thick, then pour it out into a paper case, lined with fine sugar, and cut it into squares; dry and put it into finely-powdered sugar.

2. Horehound juice, 1 pint; brown sugar, 6 pounds; white sugar, 6 pounds. Mix.

Lotion for Sore Backs in Horses.

Sulphate of copper, 1 part; water, 30 parts. Apply four or five times a day.

Hudson's Cold Cream.

Oil of almonds, 8 ounces; white wax, 1 ounce; spermaceti, 1 ounce. Melt, and when cooling, stir in rose-water, 4 ounces; orange-flower water, 1 ounce.

Huile Antique.

Oil of almonds, 2 pounds; oil of olives, 3 pounds. Mix, and perfume to taste.

Genuine Huile Antique.

Olive oil, 25 ounces; oil of vitriol, ½ ounce. Mix and agitate until the whole is perfectly united, let it stand for fourteen days, and pour off the clear. It will then be ready to take any perfume.

Huile Antique à la Fleur d'Orange.

Huile antique, 1 pound; essence of neroli, 1 drachm. Mix.

Huile Antique à la Rose.

Huile antique, or olive oil, 1 pound; ottar of roses, 35 drops. Mix

Huile Antique à la Tuberose.

Huile antique, 1 pound; essence of tuberose to perfume.

Huile Antique à la Violette.

Olive oil, 1 pound; orris powder, 2 ounces (finest.) Digest in a warm place for two or three days, then strain with expression.

Huile Antique au Jasmin.

Huile antique, 1 pound; essence of jasmin, 30 drops. Mix.

Huile Antique aux Mille Fleurs.

Olive oil, 1 pound; mille fleur perfume, 1½ drachms. Mix.

Huile Antique Rouge à la Rose.

Huile antique, 1 pound; alkanet, 1 drachm. Macerate with heat until sufficiently coloured, then add ottar of roses, 25 drops; oil of rosemary, 7 drops.

Huile Antique Verte.

Olive oil, 1 pound; gum guaiacum, 1 drachm. Macerate with heat for a few hours, then pour off the clear and strain. Scent to tast

Huile de Venus.

Wild carrot flowers, 1 pound; proof-spirit, 4 gallons. Distil or macerate, and add an equal quantity of capillaire. Colour with cochineal.

Hungary Water.

Rosemary flowers (fresh), 1 part; spirit of wine, 2 parts; water sufficient. Distil over two parts.

To Choose Lobsters.

Press your fingers on the eyes, and if fresh, the claws will have a strong motion; the heaviest are the best.

Locatel Balsam.

Sweet oil, 30 pounds; Venice turpentine, 15 pounds; red sanders (ground), 1 pound; powdered cassia, ¾ pound. Mix. Pectoral.

Lord Stamford's Oils.

Rectified spirit, 2 pounds; oil of turpentine, 2 pounds; oil of origanum, 6 ounces; oil of camomile, 1 gallon; camphor, 3 ounces. Mix.

Lycopodium.

If some of the pollen be strewed upon the surface of a vessel containing water, a person may plunge the hand to the bottom without wetting it.

Lupinine.

Take the lupinus terminis, boil it in alcohol of the specific gravity of 936, filter and evaporate to dryness. Dissolve the residuum in water, and add a little animal charcoal, filter, evaporate, and crystallize. Evaporate the remaining syrup to dryness, heat it with boiling alcohol, and again evaporate to dryness; the solid yellow residue is the lupinine. Given in intermittent fevers.

Macaroni Cordial.

This favourite French liqueur is very little known abroad. Put into half a pint of spirits of wine half an ounce of the oil of bitter almonds; shake it up two or three times a day for three days; infuse the above for ten days, with one ounce of Spanish angelica root, in three gallons of brandy, one drachm of the essence of lemon, three quarts of clarified sugar, two quarts of mille-fleur-water and five quarts of soft water, then filter the whole through a bag

Macaroni.

Take wheat of the finest quality, reduce it to a coarse powder, or flour, by means of a pair of light mill-stones, set a little farther apart than usual, then make it into a dough with water, and form as for vermicelli.

Lovage.

Lovage root (fresh), 1 pound; valerian, ¼ pound; celery, ¼ pound; sweet fennel, ¼ pound; caraway seeds, 1 ounce; cassia, 1 ounce; proof-spirit, 12 gallons. Macerate for a week, then add loaf-sugar, 20 pounds; dissolved in water, 10 gallons. Mix and fine.

Macassar Oil.

Olive oil, 1 pound; oil of origanum, 1 drachm; oil of rosemary, 1 scruple. Mix.

Factitious Oil of Mace.

Oil of mace, 1 pound; palm oil, 2 pound; beef suet, 2 pound. Beat to a paste.

Macquer's Acid Soap.

Castile soap, 2 pounds; water sufficient to render it soft; oil of vitriol, 1 ounce. Add the acid gradually, and keep rubbing them in a mortar, until the whole becomes of an equal consistence. Detergent.

Madder Lake.

Ground madder, 1 pound; water, 8 pounds. Boil for fifteen minutes, then add alum, 2 ounces. Dissolve and strain, then precipitate the colour, with a strained solution of pearlash, added gradually; lastly, collect and well wash the powder. The lake thrown down on the first addition of the potash is of the finest quality, and each successive portion decreases in value.

London Madeira.

1. London sherry, 100 gallons; Cape Madeira, 25 gallons; green citrons (bruised), 1 dozen; spirit, 2 gallons. Let them stand a month, then fine
2. Vidonia, 60 gallons; Madeira, 30 gallons. Rack into a fresh emptied Madeira cask (lees and all).

British Madeira.

Pale malt, 1 bushel; boiling water, 12 gallons. Mash and strain, then add white sugar, 4 pounds; yeast, 1 pound. Ferment, next add raisin o Cape wine, 3 quarts; brandy, 3 quarts; sherry, 2 quarts; port, 2 quarts. Bung down. The malt may be again mashed for table-beer.

To Fine Madeira.

Wine finings, 1 quart; skimmed milk, 1 quart. Whisk them to a froth and mix them with the wine, then keep it in a warm place.

Magelp.

1. Mastic varnish, 1 part; drying oil, 2 parts. Mix.
2. Mastic varnish, 1 part; drying oil, 1 part. Mix.
3. Mastic varnish, drying oil, turpentine, equal parts. Mix.
4. Mastic varnish, 2 parts; boiled oil, 2 parts; turpentine, 1 part. Mix

Calcined Magnesia.

Subcarbonate of magnesia. Calcine it at a red heat for two hours.

Henry's Magnesia.

Epsom salts, 1 part; water, 50 parts. Dissolve, then precipitate with a solution of subcarbonate of potash; wash the powder first with clean water, and lastly with rose-water.

Liquid Carbonated Magnesia.

Magnesia, 1 ounce; water, 2 gallons. Mix, and force carbonic acid gas through it, in the same way as in making soda water.

Magnesia Lozenges.

1. Magnesia (carbonate), 1 pound; starch, 2 pounds; white sugar, 5 pounds. Mix with mucilage. Add a little essence of lemon or orange or rose, to perfume.

2. Best white sugar (powdered), 2000 parts; smalts, 1 part; heavy magnesia, 125 parts; Howard's precipitated chalk, 125 parts; oil of nutmeg to flavour. Mix with mucilage.

Magnesian Aperient.

Calcined magnesia, 3 parts; bicarbonate of soda, 3 parts; tartaric acid (dried), 4 parts. Mix.

Prepared Carbonate of Magnesia.

Epsom salts, 12 parts; dissolve in water, 50 parts. Then add pearlash, 10 parts; dissolved in water, 30 parts. Mix the two solutions, allow the precipitate to settle, then pour off the fluid portion, and wash the powder with two or three waters; lastly, dry it.

Mahogany Stain for Wood.

1. Linseed oil, 2 pounds; alkanet, 3 ounces. Heat them together and macerate for six hours, then add resin, 2 ounces; bees'-wax, 2 ounces. Boiled oil may be advantageously used instead of the linseed oil.

2. Brazil-wood (ground); water sufficient; add a little alum and potash. Boil.

3. Logwood, 1 part; water, 8 parts. Make a decoction and apply it to the wood; when dry, give it two or three coats of the following varnish: Dragon's-blood, 1 part; spirits of wine, 20 parts. Mix.

To take Stains out of Mahogany.

Spirits of salts, 6 parts; salt of lemons, 1 part. Mix, then drop a little on the stains, and rub them until they disappear.

Mahogany Varnish.

Dark gum anime, 32 parts; dark oil, 100 parts; litharge, 1 part; sugar of lead, 1 part. Boil until stringy, then add, when cooled a little, spirits of turpentine, 175 parts. Mix, and strain.

Mallow-Flower Paper.

Stain the paper with an infusion of mallow-flowers, then dry it.

English Malmsey.

Parsnip (sliced), 100 pounds; water, 33 gallons. Boil, and squeeze off the liquor on loaf-sugar, 70 pounds. Ferment, then add spirit, 2 gallons; white tartar, ½ pound; finings, 1 pint.

Weak Nitrated Ointment of Mercury.

Quicksilver, 1 ounce; nitric acid, 2 ounces. Dissolve, then add sweet oil, 1½ pound; lard, ¾ pound. Mix well. Used in eruptions of the skin.

Nitrated or Oxygenized Lard.

Lard, 1 pound; nitric acid, 7 drachms. Melt the lard, and when nearly cold add the acid, and keep stirring them with a spatula or rod until quite cold. Use a glass or Wedgwood vessel. Stimulant.

Pills of Nitrate of Silver.

Nitrate of silver, 1 part; extract of gentian, 2 parts; rhubarb pill, 5 parts. Divide into two-grain pills. One to be taken night and morning. Tonic.

Nitre Drops.

Nitre, 3 ounces; sugar, 1 pound; water to mix. Add a few drops of essence of lemon, or oil of cassia.

Nitre Lozenges.

1. Nitrate of potash (pure), 4 parts; white sugar, 26 parts. Powder fine, and mix with mucilage. For sore throat, &c.

2. Nitre, 4 ounces; sugar, 16 ounces; essence of lemon, 20 ounces. Mix with mucilage.

Norfolk Fluid.

Yellow resin, 6 ounces; yellow wax, 12 ounces; boiled oil, 3 pints; neat's-foot oil, 2 pints. Melt, then add oil of turpentine, 1 part. For leather.

Noyeau.

Bitter almonds (bruised), 4 ounces; cassia, and cloves (bruised), each ¼ ounce; essence of orange-peel, 1 drachm; essence of lemon, 1 drachm; spirit, 20 gallons. Macerate, then add sugar, 30 pounds; dissolved in water, 5 gallons.

Nutmeg Lozenges.

White sugar, 5 pounds; starch, 2 pounds; oil of nutmeg, 6 drachms. Mix with mucilage.

Nutmeg Water.

Nutmegs (bruised), 1 pound; water, 20 gallons. Draw over seventeen or eighteen gallons.

To save Oats in feeding Horses.

Bruise or crush your oats in a mill, or otherwise as convenient, and your horse will become fatter on half his usual allowance of these oats than he was before on double the quantity unprepared. If you cannot bruise the oats, pour hot water on them and let them soak for a few hours.

Marbled Sealing Wax.

Take wax of different colours and melt them in separate vessels, and when they begin to cool a little, stir them all together, and form the mass into sticks.

Marbled Soap Balls.

Take ten pounds of white oil-soap and ten pounds of Joppa soap. Cut them into small square pieces, which set to dry for three days: the oil-soap, particularly, must be thus dried. Scrape, very fine, five pounds of oil-soap, which dry for one day in the open air; mix it well in the shaving-box, with five pounds of powder, and add an ounce and a half of the best vermilion.

In mixing, place pieces of soap and coloured powder in layers in the box; making in all four alternate layers of each. When a layer of each has been laid in the box, sprinkle a pint of rose-water over the cut soap; for if it be much combined with the powder it will become lumpy and hard, and consequently spoil the wash-balls. The same quantity of water is to be used for moistening each of the other soap layers. Next mix a pint of thin starch, which has been well boiled in half a pint of rain-water, with half a pint of rose-water, and distribute it, equally well mixed, among the mass, by turning it over repeatedly, and then press it down close with the hands. If a piece be now cut out from the mass the operator will perceive whether the marbling is sufficiently good: and if so, he may proceed immediately to form his wash-balls.

Marble for Leather Book-Covers.

Wash the cover and glaire it, take a sponge charged with water, having the book between wands, and drop the water from the sponge on the different parts of the cover, sprinkle very fine with vinegar black, then with brown, and lastly with vitriol water. Observe to sprinkle on the colours immediately after each other, and to wash the cover over with a clean sponge and water.

To Clean Marble.

Chalk (in fine powder), 1 part; pumice, 1 part; common soda, 2 parts. Mix. Wash the spots with this powder, mixed with a little water, then clean the whole of the stone, and wash off with soap and water.

To Stain Marble.

It is necessary to heat the marble hot, but not sufficiently so to injure it, the proper heat being that at which the colours nearly boil.

Blue.—Alkaline indigo dye, or turnsole with alkali.

Red.—Dragon's blood in spirits of wine.

Yellow.—Gamboge in spirits of wine.

Gold Colour.—Sal ammoniac, sulphate of zinc, and verdigris, equal parts.

Green.—Sap green, in spirits, with potash.

Brown.—Tincture of logwood.

Crimson.—Alkanet root in turpentine.

The marble may be veined according to taste. To stain marble *well* is a tedious and difficult operation.

Hard Mareschal Pomatum.

White wax, 3 pounds; suet, 8 pounds; mareschal powder, ½ pound scent. Mix.

Sievier's Water-proof Cloth.

Indian rubber, turpentine to dissolve. With a brush apply it to the cloth once or twice, and afterwards apply a similar solution mixed with litharge or sugar of lead, or other drying material; then sprinkle wool-floss upon the varnish, press, dry, and apply a brush to lay the nap.

Water-proof Composition for Leather, &c.

1. Boiled oil, 16 parts; yellow wax, 2 parts; burgundy pitch, 1 part, turpentine, 2 parts. Mix.

2. Linseed oil, 16 parts; suet, 8 parts; wax, 6 parts; resin, 1 part; turpentine, 5 parts. Mix.

3. *Patent.* Boiled oil, 50 parts; resin, 1 part; wax, 3 parts; boil with driers, 4 parts, until it begins to feel stringy; when cold add spirits of turpentine, 20 parts; or as much as will reduce it to a convenient consistence. Colour to taste, and apply with a sash-tool. The best driers for this purpose will be found to be litharge or red lead, finely powdered, for dark colours, and sugar of lead for light ones.

4. *Patent.* Indian rubber, 1 part; copal varnish, 6 parts; turpentine, 16 parts. Dissolve with a gentle heat, then add beeswax, 1 part, previously dissolved in boiled oil, 12 parts; lastly, add litharge, 3 parts. Bring the mixture to a boil, and set it aside for use. Colour as you please.

Water-proof Varnish for Boots, Shoes, &c.

Linseed oil, 8 parts; boiled oil, 10 parts; suet, 8 parts; beeswax, 8 parts. Mix with heat and apply hot.

To purify Putrid Water.

1. Water, 1 pound; sulphuric acid, 8 drops. Mix, and filter through charcoal.

2. Water, 8 gallons; powdered alum, 1 ounce. Dissolve with agitation, then allow it to rest for twenty-four hours, decant into another vessel, and add a solution of carbonate of soda, until it ceases to produce a precipitate.

3. Instead of alum add seven or eight grains of red sulphate of iron, then proceed as before.

4. Add a little aqueous chlorine to the foul water.

5. *Easy Method.* Arrange a suitable pipe to the end of a pair of bellows, (double bellows are best,) and continue driving the atmospheric air through the water for some time, then allow it to settle for use.

To remove the Burnt Smell from Distilled Waters.

Expose them to a temperature lower than 32° Fahr.

American Green (Factitious) Wax.

Verdigris, 1 ounce; beeswax, 2 pounds; sonorous stearine, 5 pounds scent. Apply heat till of a proper colour.

Wax Lute.

Beeswax; linseed oil to temper. Mix.

Wax Marble, for Leather Book-Covers, &c.

This marbling must be done on the fore-edge, before the back of the book is rounded, or becomes round, when in boards, and finished on the head and foot. Take beeswax and dissolve it over the fire in an earthen vessel: take quills stripped of their feathers, and tie them together; dip the quill-tops in the wax, and spot the edge, with large and small spots: take a sponge charged with blue, green, or red, and smear over the edge; when done, dash off the wax, and it will be marbled. This will be useful for stationery work, or for folios and quartos.

Soft Sealing-Wax.

Yellow resin, 1 part; beeswax, 4 parts; lard, 1 part; Venice turpentine, 1 part; colour to fancy. Mix with a gentle heat.

Wedding Cake.

Flour and butter, each, 3 pounds; sugar and raisins, each, 3 pounds, eggs, 2 dozen; currants, 6 pounds; citron, 1 pound; brandy, 1 pound; cinnamon, nutmegs, mace, each 1 ounce; cloves, ½ ounce. Bake thoroughly.

Weld Pink. (Yellow.)

Take a strong decoction of weld, to which add a little alum, then stain finely-powdered whiting with it, and dry on chalk stones.

Welsh Ale.

Pale malt, 3 quarters; hops, 25 pounds; sugar, 10 pounds; grains of paradise, ¾ pound. Mash at 170° Fahr., for first liquor, for one hour, let it rest two hours; set the tap. Turn on second liquor at 190° Fahr., then as before. Boil with the hops and grains of paradise, one hour, then add the sugar. Tun at 62°.

To prevent Mildew in Wheat.

Sulphate of copper, 1 pound; water, 4 gallons. Dissolve, and steep the grain in it for one hour.

Whipped Cream.

Whites of 8 eggs; cream, 1 quart; white wine, ½ pint; sugar to sweeten. Flavour with musk and lemon, then whip it up well with a whisk.

Antidote for Arsenic.

The hydrated peroxide of iron is said to be an antidote to arsenic, by changing the peroxide (when arsenic has been taken) into arseniate of iron; thus establishing its claims as a specific.

Another Antidote for Arsenic.

Swallow the whites of three or four eggs immediately.

Black Palmer Worm.

To destroy this worm, throw over them fresh slaked lime.

Warts in Horses and Cattle.

Wash them with a strong ley, made of pearlash and water, thrice a day

Silk-Worms in France.

The rearing of silk-worms in France is progressing with promise. M De Gasparin, in a memoir submitted to the Academy of Sciences, states his belief that the various conditions of heat, soil, light, &c. being ascertained, the mulberry tree may be acclimated in the neighbourhood of Paris, especially since it has been successfully attempted still further north. It is not the great cold of winter that does harm to this plant, since it can support a maximum of —25 of the centigrade scale, but rather the hoar-frosts that are liable to attack it at the moment of its foliation. Moisture is necessary to the good growth of the tree, and light especially so. A tree planted in a sunshiny climate has a rounder form, and the leaves are not so long and are more firm, than those of one planted in a district where the sky is often cloudy. It is known that the leaves of the mulberry-tree grown in shady situations are not so nutritious as those of a tree which has enjoyed much light. The workmen commonly state that leaves of the former kind give the silk-worms the dropsy ; and M. de Gasparin, on drying two such sorts of leaves, and then subjecting them to certain processes, has found that those of the former kind retain of solid matter only 27 per cent., whereas the latter have 58 per cent.: the difference of light, therefore, produces a difference of 2 to 1 in the value of the leaf for economical purposes. Such has been the success of rearing silk-worms in France, that in 43 departments, the annual value of the products was 42,000,000 francs.

M. Bonafons has likewise communicated to the French Academy, that the Chinese practice of sprinkling rice-flour upon silk-worms led him to ascertain whether by colouring the flour with madder, indigo, or other innocuous dyes, he could give a colour to the produce of the worm. The result has proved satisfactory, and cocoons thus tinted have been submitted to the Academy.

French Method for Embalming. (New Discovery.)

The following is M. Gannal's mixture for injecting the carotid artery, whereby all the purposes of embalming are attained :—Take dry sulphate of alumine, 1 kilogramme, (equal 2 lbs. 3 oz. 5 drs. avoirdupois,) dissolved in half a litre (a little less than a pint) of warm water, and marking 32° of the aerometer. Three or four litres of this mixture will be sufficient to inject all the vessels of the human body, and will preserve it in the summer; in the winter, from one to two litres will be enough. But to keep away insects, there should be added to the above chlorure of copper, at the rate of 100 grammes to a kilogramme of the sulphate of alumine ; or else 50 grammes of arsenious acid. This applies to all kinds of animals, birds, fishes, &c., as well as to the human subject. The above process has been introduced into the great anatomical schools in Paris ; and in nearly all the recent interments of distinguished individuals, the old and revolting mode of embalming has been superseded by this new and simple method.

Peppermint Drops.

1. Sugar, 7 pounds ; peppermint water, 1 pound. Make them into drops. Instead of peppermint water, a little oil of peppermint may be used.

2. Take confectionary drops, aud flavour with essence of peppermint.

To prevent Depredations by Hawks.

One or more guinea-hens in a flock of fowls it is said will effectually prevent molestation from hawks.

Gilding Metal.

Copper, 4 parts; brass and tin, each 1 part. Fuse together.

Bottled Ginger Beer.

Take the bottles and nearly fill them with clear water, then add white sugar, 2 drachms; bicarbonate of soda, 35 grains; tincture or essence of ginger, 2 drachms; sulphuric acid, 10 or 12 drops. Three to six drops of essence of lemon will improve this article. The acid must be added last, and the bottles immediately corked and wired.

Gingerbread.

1. Flour, 7 pounds; treacle, 3½ pounds; raw sugar, 2 pounds; butter, 1 pound, or less; carbonate of magnesia, 2 ounces; tartaric acid, 1 ounce; ginger, 1 ounce; cinnamon, 1 ounce; nutmeg, 6 ounces. Mix.

2. Flour, 7 pounds; carbonate of magnesia, 5 ounces; treacle, 4 pounds; butter, ½ pound; cream of tartar, ½ pound; spice, ½ pound. Mix with water. Ready for the oven in thirty minutes.

3. Flour, 3 pounds; sugar, ½ pound; butter, 1 pound; powdered ginger, 1 ounce; allspice corns (ground), 24 in number; cloves, 12 in number; a little cassia powdered, and molasses, 1 pint. Knead well.

Common Gingerbread.

Treacle, 3 pounds; seconds flour, 4 pounds; potass, 2 pounds; butter, ¾ pound; ginger, 2 ounces; mixed spice, 2 ounces. Water to mix. Make them into a dough and keep it until it rises, then bake it. This takes several days to ripen.

Extemporaneous Gingerbread.

Flour and treacle, each 7 pounds; bicarbonate of soda and carbonate of ammonia, each 2 ounces, more or less; spice. Water to mix. Ready for the oven immediately.

Good Gingerbread.

1. Flour and molasses, each 20 parts; carbonate of magnesia, 2 parts; spice. Water to mix. This is fit for baking in five or six hours.

2. Flour, 7 pounds; treacle, 5 pounds; carbonate of magnesia, 4 ounces; tartaric acid, 2 ounces; spice. Water to mix. This will be ready for baking in from fifteen to fifty minutes.

Poundcake Gingerbread.

Eggs, 6 in number; sugar, 1 pound; molasses, 1 pint; ginger powder, ½ tea-cupful; pearlash, 1 ounce; butter, 1 pound; a little mace and nutmeg Well mix, then beat in flour, 2 pounds.

Short Gingerbread.

Sugar, 5 pounds; butter, 3 pounds; flour, 9 pounds; eggs, 20 in number; cream, ¾ pint; pearlash, ½ pound. Bake on tins and mark it for cutting

Ginger Candy.

Ginger, finely powdered, 1 ounce; sugar-candy, 7 pounds. Water sufficient.

Ginger Cake.

Flour, 3 pounds; sugar and butter, each 1 pound; ginger, 2 ounces; treacle, 1 pint; cream, ¼ pint; a little nutmeg. Mix warm, and bake in a slack oven.

Candied Ginger.

Ginger (grated), 1 pound; loaf-sugar, 15 pounds; water sufficient to dissolve the sugar. Put them into a preserving pan over a slow fire and stir them well, until the sugar begins to boil, then add sugar (powdered), 1 pound, and keep stirring till it grows thick, then take it from the fire and drop it in cakes on a slab of marble; set it in a warm place to dry.

Ginger Drops.

1. White sugar, 2 pounds; infusion of ginger sufficient quantity. Form into drops.

2. Take finely-powdered ginger and sift it through lawn, then add it to the sugar and water in quantity as required, and follow the same plan as for confectionary drops.

Ginger Essence.

Capsicums, 1 drachm; bruised ginger, 3 ounces; alcohol, 1 pound. Macerate for ten days.

Ginger Lozenges.

Powdered ginger, 4 ounces; white sugar, 2 pounds; starch, 1 pound. Mix with mucilage.

Ginger Wine.

Water, 10 gallons; lump-sugar, 20 pounds; bruised ginger, 8 ounces; 3 or 4 eggs. Boil well and skim, then pour hot on six or seven lemons cut in slices, macerate for two hours, then rack and ferment; next add spirit, 2 quarts, and afterwards finings, 1 pint. Rummage well.

To Gild Glass and Porcelain.

1. Apply to the part a surface of gold size; when nearly dry, lay on the leaf.

2. Gold powder, 2 parts; borax, 1 part; turpentine to mix. Mix and apply to the surface to be gilded with a camel-hair pencil; when quite dry heat it in a stove until the borax vitrifies. Burnish. Platina, silver, tin, bronze, &c., may be applied in a similar manner.

Glass in Powder.

Take glass, heat it to a slight red, then throw it into cold water, take it out, dry and powder it.

Brown under Glaze.

Glass of antimony, 16 parts; litharge, 32 parts; manganese, 6 parts; blue calx, 1 part.

China Glaze.

Glass, 10 parts; lead, 2 parts; blue calx, 3 parts.

Cream Coloured Glaze.

Cornish stone, 100 parts; flint, 35 parts; white lead, 200 parts.

To Break or Cut Glass.

1. Take a worsted thread dipped in turpentine, tie it round the part, then set fire to it, and while hot wet it with cold water.

2. Apply a red-hot wire over the part, and then pour cold water on it

Purple under Glaze.

Fluxed blue, 1 part; manganese, 4 parts; red lead and flint, 4 parts.

Shining Black Glaze.

Lead, 100 parts; flint, 20 parts; manganese, 4 parts.

White Glaze.

Glass, 52 parts; litharge, 14 parts; nitre, 6 parts; arsenic, 4 parts; blue calx, 1 part.

Gum Paste for Gilding on Confectionary.

Take some dissolved gum, and make it into a paste with a little starch-powder to finish it; or it may be made with some of the prepared sugar gum-pastes, finishing it with starch-powder. Put it on the part to be gilded with a brush, let it dry smooth; then moisten with the breath, and gild.

Perfume for Gloves.

Oil of lavender, 20 drops; neroli, 10 drops; essence of musk, 5 drops ottar of roses, 2 drops; alcohol, 2 ounces. Mix.

Glue Liquid.

Glue, water, vinegar, each 2 parts. Dissolve in a water-bath, then add alcohol, 1 part. An excellent cement.

Parchment Glue.

Parchment shavings, 1 pound; water, 6 quarts. Boil until dissolved, hen strain and evaporate slowly to the proper consistence. Use a water bath if you want it very light coloured.

Portable Glue for Draughtsmen, &c.

Glue, 5 parts; sugar, 2 parts; water, 8 parts. Melt in a water-bath and cast it in moulds. For use, dissolve in warm water.

Water-proof Glue.

1. Glue, 1 part; skimmed milk, 8 parts. Melt and evaporate in a water-bath to the consistence of strong glue.

2. Glue, 12 parts; water sufficient to dissolve. Then add yellow resin, 3 parts, and when melted, add turpentine, 4 parts. Mix thoroughly together. This should be done in a water-bath.

Goldbeater's Skin

Is prepared by extending the peritoneal membranes of the cæcum, and washing them, first with plain water, and then with a solution of alum, and afterwards with a solution of isinglass and spices.

Isinglass Glue.

Dissolve isinglass over a slow fire, in a small quantity of water.

Gold-Coloured Sealing-Wax.

1. Bleached shell lac, 1 pound; Venice turpentine, 4 ounces. Melt and add gold-coloured talc as required.

2. Bleached shell lac, 3 pounds; turpentine, 1 pound; Dutch leaf, ground fine, 1 pound or less. Mix with a gentle heat. The leaf should be ground or powdered sufficiently fine without being reduced to dust.

Golden Sulphuret of Antimony.

Take the liquor left from making kermes mineral and add vinegar to precipitate the sulphuret.

Gold Cordial.

Angelica root, 4 pounds; ottar of roses, 50 drops; stoned raisins, 5 pounds; bruised coriander-seeds, ½ pound; bruised caraways and cassia, each ¼ pound; bruised cloves, 2 ounces; saffron, 2 ounces; sliced liquorice-root, 1 pound; proof-spirit, 15 gallons; macerate for fourteen days, then add sugar, 30 pounds; dissolved in water, 5 gallons. Mix and fine

Gold for Dentists for filling Decayed Teeth.

Gold, 1 part; mercury, 8 parts. Incorporate by heating them together, when mixed pour them into cold water.

To separate Gold from Gilt Copper or Silver.

Take a solution of borax in water, apply to the gilt surface, and sprinkle over it some finely powdered sulphur, make the article red-hot and quench it in water, then scrape off the gold and recover it by means of lead.

Gold in Grains.

Gold, 3 parts; silver, 1 part. Granulate by pouring it in a small stream from some height into cold water, then dissolve out the silver with nitric acid, and wash well in pure water, next heat the grains to give them a proper lustre.

Bees.

But few persons are aware how early in the season bees eat honey faster than they produce it. By not attending to this in due time, learning from experience, observation, or the experiments of others, much is lost. When the weather is dry, bees usually consume honey faster than they collect it after the middle or 20th of July, unless they have access to buckwheat or other suitable flowers cultivated for their use; in this case, they may gain honey in September.

This subject is important to bee-masters who follow the old system, and destroy the bees when they take the honey. Some let them remain till the latter part of September, eating honey two months after they have ceased to collect any of consequence. In our short seasons for collecting honey, and long ones for consuming it, the habits of the bees must be studied very attentively, and there must be the most careful and economical management in order to make them profitable.

Common Gold.

Spanish copper, 16 parts; silver, 1 part; gold, 2 parts. Melt together.

Composition Golden Showers for Rockets.

Nitre, 16 parts; sulphur, 10 parts; charcoal, 4 parts; gunpowder, 15 parts; lamp-black, 2 parts; fine saw-dust, 1 part. Mix.

Thirteen Receipts on the Formation and Crystallization of Salts.

1. If common Glauber's salt be dried and reduced to powder, and then dissolved in three times its weight of boiling water, it will not only be found to crystallize again on cooling, but the crystals will assume the identical form which they exhibited before they were pulverized. This experiment is designed to show that a determinate figure has been instamped upon every individual salt.

2. Dissolve three-fourths of an ounce of Glauber's salt in two ounces of boiling water, pour it while hot into a phial and cork it close. In this state it will not crystallize, even when perfectly cold; but if the cork be now removed the crystallization will be seen to commence and proceed with rapidity, affording an instance of the effect of atmospheric air on crystallization.

3. Repeat the experiment with a small thermometer immersed in the solution, and closed so as to exclude the atmospheric air. If the solution be suffered to cool completely under these circumstances, the thermometer will be seen to rise on the removal of the cork. This experiment is designed to show that saline solutions give out caloric in the act of crystallization.

4. Put half an ounce of quicksilver into a wine-glass, and pour about an ounce of diluted nitrous acid upon it. The nitrous acid will be decomposed by the metal with astonishing rapidity; the colour of the acid will be quickly changed to a beautiful green, while its surface exhibits a dark crimson: and an effervescence indescribably vivid and pleasing will go on during the whole time the acid operates upon the quicksilver. When a part only of the metal is dissolved, a change of colour will again take place, and the acid by degrees will become paler, till it is pellucid as pure water. This is one instance of a metallic solution by means of an acid; in which the opacity of a metallic body is completely overcome, and the whole rendered perfectly transparent.

5. Take the metallic solution formed in the last experiment, add a little more quicksilver to saturate the acid; then place it at some distance, over the flame of a lamp, so as gently to evaporate a part of the water. The new-formed salt will soon be seen to begin to shoot into needle-like prismatic crystals, crossing each other in every possible direction, affording an instance of the formation of a metallic salt.

6. Pour a small quantity of strong nitrous acid into a wine-glass, add twice its quantity of distilled water, and, when mixed, throw a few very small pieces of granulated tin into it. A violent effervescence will take place, the lighter particles of the tin will be thrown to the top of the acid, and be seen to play up and down in the liquor for a considerable time, till the whole is dissolved. This is another example of a transparent liquid holding a metal in solution.

7. Dissolve one ounce of quicksilver without heat in three quarters of an ounce of strong nitrous acid, previously diluted with one ounce and a half of water. Dissolve also the same weight of quicksilver, by means of heat, in the same quantity of a similar acid, and then to each of these colourless solutions add a solution of potash. In the first case, the metal will be precipitated in a black, in the other, in a reddish-yellow powder, affording an example of the difference of colour of metallic oxides, arising from different degrees of oxidizement.

8. Take an ounce of a solution of caustic soda, pour upon it half an ounce of sulphuric acid, lay the mixture aside, and when cold, crystals of sulphate of soda will be formed in the liquor. Here a mild salt has been formed from a mixture of two corrosive substances.

9. Take carbonate of ammonia (the common volatile smelling salt), and pour upon it muriatic acid so long as any effervescence continues. The produce will be a solid salt, perfectly inodorous, and of little taste.

10. Take caustic soda, one ounce ; saturate it with muriatic acid, both of these corrosive substances. The produce will be our common table-salt.

11. Mix in a wine-glass equal quantities of a saturated solution of muriate of lime, and a saturated solution of carbonate of potash, both transparent fluids : stir the mixture, and a solid mass will be the product.

12. Take the substance produced in the foregoing experiment, and pour a very little nitric acid upon it. The consequence will be, the solid matter will again be taken up, and the whole exhibit the appearance of one homogeneous fluid. An instance of a solid opake mass being converted by a chemical agent to a transparent liquid.

13. Take a transparent saturated solution of sulphate of magnesia, (Epsom salt) and pour into it a like solution of caustic potash or soda. The mixture will immediately become almost solid. This instance of the sudden conversion of two fluids to a solid, and that related in No. 11, have been called chemical miracles.

Cooking Cotton-Seed.

Take a large kettle, which holds from five to six bushels, set it upon a brick furnace, fill it with cotton-seed fresh from the gin, and then fill up the kettle with water, and boil something less than half an hour ; then empty the seed into troughs, and let the cattle and hogs to them. The milk and butter have none of that cotton-seed taste which the green or uncooked seed gives. Both cattle and hogs will keep in good order winter and summer, on seed thus prepared : and when you are ready to fatten pork, you have only to add an equal quantity of cotton-seed and corn, and boil as above. Experience has proved that it will fatten sooner and be equally good as when fattened on corn alone. Your cows will give an abundance of milk all winter, when fed in this manner, with but one bushel of corn to four of cotton-seed. The boiling of cotton-seed is very advantageous as food for stock. Besides, there is great economy in feeding seed thus prepared. By the usual method in feeding, there are more than double the quantity of seed wasted than are consumed by the stock.

Ants.

A small quantity of green sage, placed in the closet, will cause red ants to disappear

Soft Mareschal Pomatum.

Lard and suet, each 12 pounds; beeswax, 5 pounds; Mareschal powder, 12 ounces. Scent. Melt the first three with a gentle heat, then add the powder and perfume.

Mareschal Powder.

Starch or farina, 7 pounds; powdered cloves, 3 ounces; powdered cassia, 1 ounce. Mix.

Margavic Acid.

Take olive oil soap and dissolve it in water, then add a perfectly neutral acetate of lead; wash and dry the precipitate, and digest ether over it, decant and dry again; lastly, dissolve the lead out with hot muriatic acid; wash and dry the residuum.

Marjoram Water.

Fresh marjoram, 1 cwt.; water a sufficient quantity. Draw over twenty-five gallons.

Marking Ink.

Lunar caustic, 2 parts; sap green and gum arabic, each 1 part; distilled water. Dissolve.

The Preparation.—Soda, 1 ounce; water, 1 pint; sap green, ½ drachm. Dissolve, and wet the linen (where you intend to write) with this mordant, then well dry it.

Transparent Marmalade.

Cut very pale Seville oranges into quarters; take out the pulp, put it into a basin, and pick out the skins and seeds. Put the peels into a little salt and water, and let them stand all night, then boil them in a good quantity of spring water until they are tender; cut them in very thin slices, and put them into the pulp. To every pound of marmalade put one pound and a half of double refined beaten sugar; boil them together gently for twenty minutes; if they are not transparent, boil them a few minutes longer. Stir it gently all the time, and take care not to break the slices. When it is cold, put it into jelly and sweetmeat glasses; tie down tight.

Marshall's Cerate.

Palm oil, ½ ounce; calomel, 1 ounce; sugar of lead, ½ ounce; nitrated ointment of mercury, 2 ounces. Mix.

Marshall's Guitæ Vegetabilis.

Lunar caustic, 2 grains; isinglass, 3 or 4 grains; distilled water, 1 ounce. Dissolve the isinglass in the water, then add the silver.

Heat of Water for Mashing.

First mash. For very pale malt, turn in at 176° F. Pale and amber, 172° F. Amber, 170° F. Dark amber, 168° F. Amber, pale and brown, mixed, 160° F. Dark or charred brown, 156° F.

Second mash. Very pale, 182° F. Pale and amber, 178° F. Amber, 176° F. Dark amber, 172° F. Pale amber and brown, mixed, 166° F Dark or charred brown, 165° F. In winter turn on four or five degrees higher than the above.

Marshall's mixed Oils.

Linseed oil, rape oil, and green oil, each 2 pounds; oil of turpentine, 1 pound; oil of vitriol, 1 ounce. Mix.

Marshmallow Lozenges.

Powdered marshmallow-root, 1 pound; white sugar, 7 pounds. Mucilage to mix.

Marshmallow Ointment.

1. Yellow resin and yellow wax, each 56 pounds. Melt and reduce them to a proper consistence with rape oil, then add thick mucilage, 1 gallon; turmeric to colour if required. Stir till cold.

2. Oil of mucilages, 36 pounds; yellow wax and yellow resin, each 7 pounds; spirits of turpentine, 2 pounds. Mix.

3. Yellow resin, 56 pounds. Melt and reduce it to a proper consistence with rape oil, then add tallow or suet 28 pounds; thick mucilage, 7 pounds; water, 1 gallon. Turmeric to colour.

4. Rape oil, 28 pounds; resin, 16 pounds; spirits of turpentine, 4 pounds. Mix with a gentle heat, then add thick mucilage, 7 pounds. Stir well till cold.

Mastic Varnish.

1. Gum mastic, 5 pounds; spirits of turpentine, 2 gallons. Mix with a moderate heat (carefully applied) in a close vessel, then add pale turpentine varnish, 3 pints. Mix well.

2. Mastic, 1 pound; white wax, 1 ounce; oil of turpentine, 1 gallon. Reduce the wax and mastic small, then digest in a close vessel, with heat, until dissolved.

To protect Sheep from the Gad Fly.

In August and September this fly lays its eggs in the nostrils of sheep, where they are hatched, and the worms crawl into the head, and frequently they eat through to the brain. In this way many sheep are destroyed. As a protection, smirch their noses with tar. Lay some tar in a trough or on a board, and strew fine salt on it: the sheep will finish the operation. The tar will protect them, and what they eat will promote their health.

Smoke Protector.

Mr. Wallace has exhibited and explained to the British Association his Apparatus for enabling persons to enter places on fire without danger from smoke, by means of breathing through water. A box of tin, containing the water, is placed on a man's back with tubes connected, forming a ring round the body and straps for the shoulders. A hood of Mackintosh cloth, glazed in front, is put on the head, and being attached to the side tubes, four gallons of water will enable a person to bear the densest smoke for twenty minutes. The Protector resembles the diving apparatus in appearance.

Candles.

Prepare your wicks about half the usual size, wet with spirits of turpentine, put them into the sun until dry, then mould or dip your candles. Candles thus made last longer, and give a much clearer light. In fact they are nearly or quite equal to sperm, in clearness of light.

Odontalgic Paste.

Orris powder, 10 parts; rose pink powder, 1 part; gum mastic, 2 parts; cream of tartar, 2 parts; burnt alum, 2 parts; prepared chalk, 20 parts; honey, 40 parts; oil of cloves and roses to perfume. Mix.

Alcoholic Extract of Nux Vomica.

Rasped nux vomica, 1 part; strong alcohol, 6 parts. Digest, strain and distil off the spirit.

Perfumer's Oil of Cassia.

Finest oil of cloves, 3 parts; ground cassia, 1 part. Pour the oil warm on the cassia; macerate for three or four days or more, then strain with expression.

Odoriferous Esprit.

Oil of rosemary, 2 drachms; essence of Tonquin bean, 4 drachms; oil of originam, 12 drops; oil of cassia, 20 drops; oil of cajeput, 10 drops; tincture of angelica, 1 drachm; oil of cloves, 1 drachm; essence of lemon, 2 drachms; essence of musk, 2 drachms; essence of ambergris, 2 drachms; essence of almonds, 6 drops; ottar of roses, 6 drops; alcohol, 1 quart. Mix.

To remove unpleasant Odours.

If from a water-closet, put into it some powdered fresh-burnt lime, chloride of lime, wood ashes, or soap suds, and the disagreeable odour will be absorbed or destroyed. Aromatic pastiles may also be burnt, but it must be recollected that they do not destroy the smell, they only disguise it with one more powerful. A little powdered quicklime put into a night-pan, will effectually destroy any disagreeable odour, a purpose very important to effect in a sick chamber.

Common Oil Varnish.

Resin, 4 pounds; bees'-wax (genuine), ½ pound; boiled oil, 1 gallon. Mix with heat, then add spirits of turpentine, 2 quarts.

Oil of Tartar.

Take pearlash; put it into a flat jar or vessel, and expose it in a damp cellar until it becomes liquid; pour off the clear.

Oil Colours, in Bladders or Bottles.

As for oil-colour cakes, and increase the quantity of oil to reduce them to the proper consistence.

To Extract Oil from Boards.

Fuller's earth, 5 parts; soft soap, 1 part; pearlash, 1 part; boiling water to mix. Lay it on hot, then let it remain until dry; scour off with soap.

To Extract Oil from Stone or Marble.

Soft soap, 1 part; Fuller's earth, 2 parts; potash, 1 part; boiling water to mix. Lay it on the spots of grease and let it remain for a few hours.

The Oils.

Oil of vitriol, oil of turpentine, rape oil, equal parts. Mix with great care.

Oil-colour Cakes.

Gum mastic, 1 part; turpentine, 12 parts. Dissolve and grind the colours in it; let them dry, then place your stone over charcoal until hot, and grind your prepared colours on it, reducing them to the proper consistence with the following composition in a melted state; lastly, take a piece and mould it: Spermaceti, 3 parts; poppy oil, 1 part. Mix, with heat. These cake colours are to be rubbed down with a little poppy oil and turpentine for use.

Odor Delectabilis.

Rose-flower water, 1 pint; orange-flower water, 1 pint; oil of cloves, 3 drachms; oil of lavender, 3 drachms; essence of musk, 3 drachms; oil of bergamot, 7 drachms; musk, 8 grains; alcohol, ½ gallon. Macerate for six days.

Ointment for Chaps and Eruptions of the Skin.

Simmer ox-marrow over a fire, and afterwards strain it through a piece of muslin into gallipots. When cold, rub the part affected.

Simple Ointment.

Lard, 66 pounds; suet, 40 pounds. Melt, and add water, 2 gallons. Continue stirring until cold

To Strengthen Old Pictures.

Give two or three coats of good paint to their backs.

Onion's Fusible Metal.

Tin, 2 parts; lead, 3 parts; bismuth, 5 parts. Melt. This fuses at 197° Fahr. The addition of a little mercury renders it still more fusible.

To Pickle Onions.

Take off the outside skin and "top and tail" them, then put them into the bottles and add sufficient vinegar to cover them. Put also a few mustard-seeds into each bottle, a blade of mace, and a capsicum. It is said that a spoonful of salad oil to each bottle will keep the onions white.

Opake White Paste.

Plain paste, 100 parts; bone powder, 10 parts. Mix.

Factitious Opal.

1. Strass, 500 parts; horn silver, 10 parts; calcined magnetic ore, 2 parts; chalk marl, 25 parts. Mix in fine powder, and fuse with great care.

2. Plain paste, 100 parts; calcined bones, 6 parts.

Extract of Opium.

Opium, 1 part; water, 7 parts. Mix, digest, and strain, then evaporate to the consistence of an extract.

Homberg and Baume's Purified Opium.

Opium, 1 pound; water, 1 gallon. Boil until dissolved, strain and evaporate at a boiling heat, to the consistence of a thick extract.

Oil-colour Cakes.

Gum mastic, 1 part; turpentine, 12 parts. Dissolve and grind the colours in it; let them dry, then place your stone over charcoal until hot, and grind your prepared colours on it, reducing them to the proper consistence with the following composition in a melted state; lastly, take a piece and mould it: Spermaceti, 3 parts; poppy oil, 1 part. Mix, with heat. These cake colours are to be rubbed down with a little poppy oil and turpentine for use.

Odor Delectabilis.

Rose-flower water, 1 pint; orange-flower water, 1 pint; oil of cloves, 3 drachms; oil of lavender, 3 drachms; essence of musk, 3 drachms; oil of bergamot, 7 drachms; musk, 8 grains; alcohol, ½ gallon. Macerate for six days.

Ointment for Chaps and Eruptions of the Skin.

Simmer ox-marrow over a fire, and afterwards strain it through a piece of muslin into gallipots. When cold, rub the part affected.

Simple Ointment.

Lard, 66 pounds; suet, 40 pounds. Melt, and add water, 2 gallons. Continue stirring until cold

To Strengthen Old Pictures.

Give two or three coats of good paint to their backs.

Onion's Fusible Metal.

Tin, 2 parts; lead, 3 parts; bismuth, 5 parts. Melt. This fuses at 197° Fahr. The addition of a little mercury renders it still more fusible.

To Pickle Onions.

Take off the outside skin and "top and tail" them, then put them into the bottles and add sufficient vinegar to cover them. Put also a few mustard-seeds into each bottle, a blade of mace, and a capsicum. It is said that a spoonful of salad oil to each bottle will keep the onions white.

Opake White Paste.

Plain paste, 100 parts; bone powder, 10 parts. Mix.

Factitious Opal.

1. Strass, 500 parts; horn silver, 10 parts; calcined magnetic ore, 2 parts; chalk marl, 25 parts. Mix in fine powder, and fuse with great care.
2. Plain paste, 100 parts; calcined bones, 6 parts.

Extract of Opium.

Opium, 1 part; water, 7 parts. Mix, digest, and strain, then evaporate to the consistence of an extract.

Homberg and Baume's Purified Opium.

Opium, 1 pound; water, 1 gallon. Boil until dissolved, strain and evaporate at a boiling heat, to the consistence of a thick extract.

Fish Oil for Painting.

Fish oil, 100 gallons; ground litharge, 12 pounds; ground sulphate of zinc, 2 pounds. Boil together for two hours, then cool a little and add soap, 3 pounds; dissolved in water, 1 gallon. Mix well, then add boiled oil, 8 gallons; turpentine, 2 gallons. Well mix.

Prechtl's method of Preserving Living Fish.

Stop their mouths up with crumbs of bread steeped in brandy, pour a very small quantity of brandy into them, and pack them in clean straw. In this way it is said fish may be preserved in a torpid state for twelve or fifteen days, and when put into water will come to life again after three or four hours.

To Preserve Fish.

Salmon and some other kinds of fish are often preserved by placing them in jars and pouring sweet salad-oil over them until covered, then bunging up quite air-tight.

Ointment for Fistula in Cattle.

1. Resin, 2 pounds; oil of turpentine, 2 pounds; suet, 2 pounds; powdered verdigris, 12 ounces. Mix.

2. Tallow, 3 pounds; Venice turpentine, 3 pounds; oil of vitriol, ½ pound; sulphate of copper, ½ pound. Add the blue vitriol (dissolved in the acid) very cautiously to the melted ointment.

3. Tallow, 5 parts; lard, 2 parts; red precipitate, 1 part. Mix.

Composition for Fixed Brilliants.

Meal gunpowder, 16 parts; zinc, or steel, or cast-iron borings, 6 parts. Mix.

Composition for Fixed Stars.

Nitre, 12 parts; sulphur, 6 parts; meal gunpowder, 12 parts; antimony, 1 part. Mix. The bottom of the rocket must be stuffed with clay; one diameter of rocket composition must be then introduced, and the remainder filled with the above mixture; the case is then to be tied up, and the pasteboard pierced with five holes for the escape of the luminous rays.

Flash.

Thick sugar colouring, 9 parts; extract of capsicum, 3 parts. Mix. Used to colour, and give a false strength to spirits.

To Remove Flatulency after Eating.

Take a spoonful of the following mixture in a little water as soon after eating as convenient: Magnesia, 3 drachms; carbonate of soda, 2 drachms, sal-volatile, 4 drachms; rose-water, 7 drachms. Mix, and well shake the bottle before taking a dose.

Flesh Colour for Staining Glass.

Red lead, 1 part; red enamel, 2 parts. Mix with alcohol.

Powder to destroy Flies.

White arsenic, 1 part; white sugar, 30 parts; rose pink, 1 part. Mix Mark it poison.

To remove Flies from Rooms.

Black pepper (powdered), 1 drachm; brown sugar, 1 drachm; milk or cream, 2 drachms. Mix, and place it on a plate or saucer where the flies are most troublesome.

Poison for Flies.

Rasped quassia, sugar, equal parts. Put them into a plate or saucer, and pour on them a sufficient quantity of boiling water.

Flint Glass.

1. Nitre, 1 part; pearlash, 5 parts; litharge, 7 parts; fine sand, 13 parts.

2. Arsenic, 1 part; magnesia, 1 part; nitre, 30 parts; refined pearlash 150 parts; red lead, 320 parts; fine white sand, 490 parts. Mix.

Flint Powder.

Take flints, heat them, and throw them into cold water, dry, and grind them.

Floating Soap.

Fine soda oil soap (in shavings), 9 parts; water, 1 part. Put them into a clean copper, place it in a water-bath, melt, then agitate the mixture until its volume is doubled, or until it becomes wholly composed of froth, then pour it out to cool and cut it into cakes.

Common Flour of Mustard.

Flour of mustard (fine yellow), 28 pounds; wheat flour, 28 pounds; cayenne pepper, 8 ounces, as required; common salt, 10 pounds; rape oil, 3 pounds, more or less; turmeric to colour. Mix well together and pass it through a fine sieve.

Flour Paste.

Water, 1 quart; alum, ¼ ounce. Dissolve, and when cold, add flour to make it of the consistence of cream, then bring it to a boil, stirring it all the while.

Hard Flour Paste.

To the above add a little powdered resin and a clove or two before boiling. This will keep for twelve months. When dry it may be softened with water.

To produce Flour that will keep well.

Make the flour from kiln-dried grain.

To Improve New Seconds Flour.

Carbonate of magnesia, 45 grains; flour, 1 pound. Mix and use the flour as usual.

To Preserve Flowers in Salt.

Common salt, 3 pounds; flowers, 10 gallons. Beat them to a paste and preserve it in wide-mouthed jars or bottles. This plan furnishes the perfumer with flowers at any season of the year. The scent is not only much improved, but the flowers rendered more suitable for the purposes of distillation.

Flowers of Ointments.

Yellow resin, 64 pounds; yellow wax, 15 pounds; suet, 25 pounds; Burgundy pitch, 8 pounds; oil, 2 pounds. Mix.

To Gather and Preserve Flowers.

Collect them when in full bloom, and dry them in a gentle heat, (say not exceeding 130° Fahr.) The colours of many flowers may be preserved by dipping them into boiling water for a moment before drying them.

To Restore Faded Flowers.

Put the flowers into scalding hot water, sufficiently high to cover one third of their stems; let them stand until the water is cold, then cut off the soft part of the stems and place them in cold water.

Alloy for Flute Key Valves.

Lead, 4 parts; antimony, 2 parts. Fuse.

Cornish Reducing Flux.

Tartar, 40 parts; nitre, 15 parts; borax, 12 parts. Mix.

Cornish Refining Flux.

Nitre, 2 parts; tartar, 1 part. Powder and deflagrate together.

White Flux.

1. Nitre, 1 part; tar, 2 parts. Mix.
2. Nitre, tartar, equal parts. Deflagrate in a crucible.

Foils for Crystals, Pastes, &c.

Put two or three layers of tin foil into the socket made for the stone, heat it gently and fill it with quicksilver, let it rest two or three minutes, then pour it out, and place in the stone.

Curriers' Foot Oil.

Strained tallow, train oil, equal parts. Melt.

Ointment for the Foot Rot.

Lard, 1 pound; turpentine, 1 pound; tallow, 1 pound; sulphate of copper (powdered), 1 pound; rape oil, 1 pound; black resin, 1 pound Melt, and well mix.

Formic Acid, or Acid of Ants.

Tartaric acid, 10 parts; black oxide of manganese, 14 parts; concentrated sulphuric acid, 15 parts; water, 25 parts. Distil. Named "acid of ants" from having been formerly only obtained from the bodies of wood ants by infusion.

Fowler's Mineral Lotion.

1. White arsenic, 64 grains; compound spirit of lavender, 1 ounce; distilled water, 15 ounces. Mix.

2. White arsenic, 65 grains; salt of tartar, 65 grains; distilled water, 1 pint. Boil, and, when cold, scent with lavender, and add distilled water to make it an exact pint. Used in agues. Dose, from two to twelve drops for an adult, three times a day.

To preserve the Peels of Fruit.

The portion of the peel to be preserved should be separated from the rest, and dried in a gentle heat.

Pennyroyal Water.

1. Dry pennyroyal, 12 pounds; water, 12 gallons. Distil over ten gallons.

2. Oil of pennyroyal, 1 pound; water, 40 gallons. Draw off thirty-five gallons.

Peppermint Cordial.

1. White sugar, 1¾ cwt.; water, 15 gallons. Break the sugar into pieces, put it into a 120 gallon cask, and pour the water on it; let it stand until the next day, then put a stick into the bung-hole and rummage until dissolved; next add English oil of peppermint, 2 ounces; proof-spirit, 40 gallons. Well mix, and further add water sufficient to make up 106 gallons. Let it stand until fine.

2. Water, 50 gallons; sugar, 200 pounds. Make them into a syrup, then add proof-spirit, 40 gallons; oil of peppermint, 4 ounces. Mix well and fine. Kill the oil with a little sugar and spirit before you add it to the syrup.

Common Oil of Peppermint.

Castor oil, peppermint oil, alcohol, equal parts. Mix.

Best Peppermint Lozenges.

1. Finest lump-sugar (powdered), 2300 parts; smalts, 1 part; English oil of peppermint, 12 parts. Mix with mucilage. Be careful to turn them out of hand in proper style, as on this depends their fitness for sale.

2. *Fine Transparent.* Best powdered white sugar, 2300 parts; smalts, 1 part; English oil of peppermint, 12 parts; oil of almonds, 20 parts; mucilage to mix. Do not powder the sugar *too* fine, and roll the cake very thin before cutting.

3. *Good.* Sugar (very white), 7 pounds; blue starch, 1 pound; oil of peppermint to flavour. Mix with mucilage.

4. *Second Quality.* Good lump-sugar (powdered), 2000 parts; smalts, 1 part; English oil of peppermint, 10 parts. Mix with mucilage.

5. *Third Quality.* Powdered lump-sugar, 2000 parts; clean plaster of Paris (baked), 200 parts; smalts or indigo, 1 part; common oil of peppermint, 10 parts. Mix with mucilage. Be sure to have the plaster *white,* and sifted through fine lawn.

6. *Fourth Quality.* Common white sugar, 2000 parts; Paris plaster (fine and sifted), 755 parts; smalts or indigo, 1 part; commonest oil of peppermint, 10 parts. Mix with mucilage. More plaster may be used for a still commoner article.

Peppermint Water.

1. Oil of peppermint, 1 pound; water, 45 gallons. Draw over thirty-four to thirty-six gallons.

2. Green peppermint, 1 cwt. (or less); water, 40 gallons. Draw over thirty-five gallons.

Black Pepper Ointment.

Finely-powdered pepper, 4 ounces; finely-powdered capsicum, ½ ounce lard, 1 pound. Well mix. Very stimulant and irritating. One part of the ointment (according to circumstances) to two of lard, forms an excellent external application in cases of impotence.

Perfume Bags, for Drawers, &c.

Coriander-seeds, orris root, cassia, cloves, each, in coarse powder, 1 ounce; lavender flowers, 8 ounces; rose-leaves, 8 ounces. Mix, and put the powder into small calico bags, and afterwards cover them with silk or satin.

Marston's prepared Black Pepper.

Take black peppercorns, soak them in salt and water for three days, then dry and grind them.

Red Permanent Ink.

Vermilion, 4 parts; sulphate of iron, 1 part; drying oil to mix. Any other colour will answer besides red. This ink will resist most of the usual reagents.

Black Permanent Ink.

Nitrate of silver, 2 parts; distilled water, 28 parts; sap green, 1 part. Dissolve.

For the Mordant—Common soda, 2 parts; gum arabic, 1 part; soft water, 8 parts. Mix, and moisten the linen with this fluid, and well dry, before using the ink.

Permanent White.

Take a solution of muriate of barytes, and precipitate the earth with dilute sulphuric acid, wash the powder in two or three waters, and dry it.

Plaster of Peroxide of Iron.

Diachylon, 50 pounds; yellow resin, 12 pounds; yellow wax, 6 pounds; sweet oil, 8 pounds; peroxide of iron, 16 pounds. Mix, with heat.

A Remedy against Flies and Maggots in Living Animals.

Wash with a strong decoction of elder bark, mixed with an equal quantity of spirits of turpentine.

Ointment for Sore Eyes in Dogs.

Nitrate of quicksilver ointment, 1 part; tutty and lard, 1 part. Mix To be applied very lightly. Or, wash the eyes once a day with a very weak solution of saltpetre.

Distemper in Dogs.

Pass a red-hot iron through the skin on top of his neck, and pass through the aperture a thick woollen string; this must be drawn round once or twice a day, to promote a free discharge of matter. If the dog is bound, give him some laxative medicine; if too loose, give a little strong salt and water, once a day. In many instances the same medicines that would be recommended to man, would in like manner prove beneficial to dogs.

Perpetual Ink, for Tombstones, Marble, &c.

Pitch, 11 parts; lampblack, 1 part; turpentine sufficient. Mix with heat.

Persian Cream.

Bichloride of mercury, 5 parts; almond emulsion, 900 parts; essence of almonds, 15 parts; essence of neroli, 3 parts; spirits of wine, 60 parts Mix.

Pew's Composition for covering Buildings.

Take the hardest and purest limestone (white marble is to be preferred), free from sand, clay, or other matter; calcine it in a reverberatory furnace, pulverize and pass it through a sieve. One part, by weight, is to be mixed with two parts of clay well baked and similarly pulverized, conducting the whole operation with great care. This forms the first powder. The second is to be made of one part of calcined and pulverized gypsum, to which is added two parts of clay, baked and pulverized. These two powders are to be combined, and intimately incorporated, so as to form a perfect mixture. When it is to be used, mix it with about a fourth part of its weight of water, added gradually, stirring the mass well the whole time, until it forms a thick paste, in which state it is to be spread like mortar upon the desired surface. It becomes in time as hard as stone, allows no moisture to penetrate, and is not cracked by heat. When well prepared it will last any length of time. When in its plastic or soft state, it may be coloured of any desired tint.

Pewter.

1, Tin, 100 parts; antimony, 17 parts. Mix.

2. Zinc, 1 part; copper, 3 parts; lead, 8 parts; tin, 60 parts. Melt the copper, then add the rest.

3. *Fine.* Tin, 50 parts; antimony, 4 parts; bismuth, 1 part; copper, 1 part. Mix, as before.

4. *French.* Lead, 9 parts; tin, 41 parts. Mix

Phosphorus.

Calcined bones, 15 parts; water, 30 parts; oil of vitriol, 6 parts. Mix, and let them remain together for twelve hours, then add more water, strain, and wash the sediment with repeated doses of hot water; mix the several waters together and evaporate to the consistence of an extract, then mix it with powdered charcoal, and distil with the beak of the retort in water.

Phosphorous Bottles.

1. Phosphorus, 2 parts; powdered lime, 1 part. Mix with care and put it into a well-stopped phial, and expose it to heat for half an hour.

1. Phosphorus, 3 parts; white wax, 1 part. Melt in a closed bottle (carefully) together; and, when cooling, coat the sides by turning it round.

Liquid Pickle for Meat.

Brown sugar, bay salt, common salt, each, 5 pounds; saltpetre, 1 pound: pimento (bruised), 5 ounces; black pepper (bruised), 3 ounces; nutmegs (rasped), 1 ounce; boiling water, 5 gallons. Mix. This not only imparts a fine red colour to the meat, but also gives it a most delicious flavour.

Picalilly.

1. White cabbages (sliced), cauliflowers (in pieces), radishes, French beans, celery (in pieces), elder flowers (in clusters, unopened), equal parts. Salt them for two or three days, then drain and mix them with apples and cucumbers (sliced), equal parts, and spice with ginger, garlic, turmeric, long pepper and mustard-seed. Put them all into the bottles, and pour on them strong vinegar.

2. *Indian Method.* This consists of all kinds of pickles mixed and put into one large jar; girkins, sliced cucumbers, button onions, cauliflowers, broken in pieces. Salt them, or put them in a large hair sieve in the sun to dry for three days, then scald them in vinegar a few minutes; when cold put them together. Cut a large white cabbage in quarters, with the outside leaves taken off and cut fine, salt it, and put it in the sun to dry for three or four days; then scald it in vinegar, the same as cauliflower, carrots, three parts, boiled in vinegar and a little bay salt. French beans, rack samphire, radish-pods, and nasturtiums, all go through the same process as girkins, capsicums, &c. To one gallon of vinegar put four ounces of ginger, bruised, two ounces of whole white pepper, two ounces of allspice, half an ounce of chillies, bruised, four ounces of turmeric, one pound of the best mustard, half a pound of shallots, one ounce of garlic, and half a pound of bay salt. The vinegar, spice, and other ingredients, except the mustard, must boil half an hour; then strain it into a pan, and put the mustard into a large basin with a little vinegar; mix it quite fine and free from lumps, then add more; when well mixed put it to the vinegar just strained off, and when quite cold put the pickles into a large pan, and the liquor over them; stir them repeatedly, so as to mix them all; finally, put them into a jar, and tie them over first with a bladder, and afterwards with leather. The capsicums want no preparation.

Pickling Salt.

Brown sugar, 10 parts; bay salt, 15 parts; saltpetre, 1 part. Mix.

Fine Picture Varnish.

Fine-picked mastic, 12 pounds; clean glass, coarsely pounded, 5 pounds; colourless spirits of turpentine, 5 gallons. Put them into a suitable vessel, and agitate for four or five hours, repeat the same next day, then let it settle for several months, and pour off the clear.

Injection for Ulcerated Piles.

1. Sulphate of zinc, 1 drachm; water, 30 ounces. Mix.
2. Sulphate of copper, 40 grains; water, 1 quart. Mix.
3. Nitrate of silver, 35 grains; water, 1 quart. Mix.

Ointment for the Piles.

Ointment of nitrate of mercury, 1 ounce; extract of belladonna, ½ ounce, spermaceti ointment, 3½ ounces. Mix, and apply night and morning. This ointment is particularly useful when the disease is accompanied with much itching and irritation.

2. Spermaceti ointment, 80 parts; powdered opium, 1 part; powdered galls, 16 parts; acetate of lead, 2 parts. Mix.

Instantaneous Light Matches.

1. Chlorate of potash and flowers of sulphur, each 10 parts; vermilion, 2 parts. Oil of turpentine to mix. Dip the ends of the matches previously sulphured and steeped in turpentine into this paste and dry.

2. Chlorate of potash, 10 parts; sugar and sulphur, each 3 parts; wheat flour and vermilion, each 1 part. Spirit to mix. For use, dip them into the instantaneous light bottles.

Essence of Meadow Sweet.

Flowers, 1 pound; water, 5 pounds. Steep at a hand heat for three hours, then decant or strain, and add spirit, 1 ounce.

Meat Pickle.

1. Common salt, 7 pounds; molasses, 4 pounds; saltpetre, 1 pound. Water barely enough to dissolve.

2. Salt, 12 pounds; sugar or treacle, 2 pounds; saltpetre, ½ pound; water, 7 or 8 gallons. Mix. The same pickle will do for a long time, by simply boiling and straining it. It may, however, occasionally have a little of each ingredient added, to keep up its strength.

To preserve Meat.

1. Place the meat in an open wicker basket, and put it into a running spring; in four to six days it will begin to rise to the surface, then use it. It will be perfectly fresh.

2. Take a clean charred cask and strew over its bottom a handful each of flowers of sulphur and iron filings, then pour on the required quantity of boiling water, over which pour a thin layer of salad oil; allow the whole to cool, and suspend the meat in the water, so that it is perfectly covered; let it rest until wanted for use, then wash it in clean water. Meat treated in this way will keep fresh for a long time.

Keller's Medal Alloy.

Tin, 9 parts; copper, 89 parts; zinc, 2 parts.

Medallion Wafers.

Take good glue, and colour to fancy with vermilion, turmeric, brazilwood, &c., then pour it into moulds, or on a marble slab previously oiled, and when partly cold, cut and stamp the cake as required.

Rules to administer Medicine.

For an adult, suppose the dose to be one drachm; under 1 year will require only one-twelfth 5 grains; under 2 years, one-eighth 8 grains; under 3 years, one-sixth 10 grains; under 4 years, one quarter 15 grains; under 7 years, one-third 1 scruple; under 14 years, one-half ½ drachm; under 20 years, two-thirds 2 scruples; above 21 years the full dose of 1 drachm; 65 the inverse gradation of the above. This is an excellent table for regulating the doses of medicines: a mixture, powder, pill or draught may be proportioned to a nicety by attention to the above rules.

Melilot Suet or Ointment.

Suet or tallow, 10 pounds; melilot leaves, 2 pounds. Boil until the leaves become crisp.

Melilot Plaster for Horses.

1. Yellow resin, 7 pounds; yellow wax, 3 pounds; suet, 2 pounds, green melilot, 4 pounds. Melt and keep them on the fire until the melilot is crisp.

2. Yellow resin, 8 pounds; yellow wax, 1 pound; tallow, 3 pounds. Melilot sufficient to give it a smell. Copper to colour. Genuine wax need not be used; factitious wax will do as well.

Bistre.

This is an excellent light brown colour, prepared from wood soot; it is used for colouring confectionary.

Stimulating Drops for Suppression of the Menses.

Compound tincture of aloes, 3 ounces; tincture of black hellebore and tincture of castor, each 2 drachms; tincture of lyttæ, 5 scruples. Mix. Dose—one tea-spoonful three times a day.

For a Cough.

Roast a large lemon very carefully without burning; when it is thoroughly hot, cut and squeeze it into a cup, upon three ounces of sugar-candy finely powdered; take a spoonful whenever your cough troubles you. It is as good as it is pleasant.

For the same.

Take two ounces of syrup of poppies, as much conserve of red roses. Mix, and take one spoonful for three nights when going to rest.

For the same, with a Hoarseness.

Syrup of jujubes and althea, of each two ounces; lohoch sanans, one ounce; saffron and water-flag powdered, of each a scruple. Lick it off a liquorice-stick when you cough.

For a Hoarseness.

Take every night, going to rest, half a pint of mum, as warm as you can drink it at a draught, for three nights together.

For a Hooping-Cough, very good.

Take a quart of spring-water, put to it a large handful of chin-cups that grow upon moss, a large handful of unset hyssop; boil it to a pint, strain it off, and sweeten it with sugar-candy. Let the child, as often as it coughs, take two spoonfuls at a time.

Another for a Cough.

Make a strong tea of ale-hoof, sweeten it with sugar-candy, pour this upon a white toast, well-rubbed with nutmeg, and drink it first and last.

For a Consumptive Cough.

Take half a pound of double-refined sugar, finely beat and sifted, wet this with orange flower water, and boil it up to a candy height, then stir in an ounce of cassia-earth finely powdered, and use it as with any other candy.

Metallic Varnish, for Coach-Work, &c.

Asphaltum, 56 pounds; melt, then add litharge, 9 pounds; red lead, 7 pounds; boil, then add boiled oil, 12 gallons; yellow resin, 12 pounds. Again boil, until, on cooling, the mixture may be rolled into pills, then add spirits of turpentine, 30 gallons; lamp-black, 7 pounds. Mix well.

Metheglin.

Honey, 2 cwt.; warm water, 40 gallons, or more. Put them into a cask, let them remain together for twelve hours, then well rummage them, and add hops, ½ pound; yeast, 1 pint. Ferment.

To drive away Mice.

Strew some of the cynoglossum, or hound's tongue, bruised, about the parts where they frequent.

Microcosmic Salt.

Phosphate of soda, phosphate of ammonia, equal parts. Water sufficient. Dissolve, evaporate, and crystallize. A small excess of ammonia promotes the crystallization.

Microscopic Cement.

Isinglass, 2 parts; gum, 1 part; water, 2 parts. Dissolve, then mix in alcohol, 1 part.

Millefleurs Perfume.

Essence of lemon, 3 ounces; essence of ambergris, 4 ounces; oil of caraway, 2 ounces; oil of lavender, 3 ounces. Mix.

French Milk of Roses.

Rose-water, 5 pounds; tincture of storax and tincture of benzoin, each 1 ounces; spirits of roses, 1 ounce; rosemary water, 1 pint. Mix.

A Substitute for Milk.

Take three eggs and break them into a basin, beat them well, then add hot water (gradually) half a pint, and beat them again until quite smooth.

Milk of Roses.

1. Bitter almonds (blanched) and water, each 8 ounces; elder-flower water, 6 ounces; salt of tartar, 1 drachm; tincture of benzoin, 2 drachms. Mix and strain.

2. Oil of almonds, 4 ounces; pearlash, 1 drachm; rose-water, 12 ounces; essence of bergamot and orange-flower water, each 1 ounce. Reduce the oil and pearlash to a milk, with a little of the rose-water, by rubbing together in a mortar, then add gradually the remainder of the waters, and well mix.

3. Sweet almonds (blanched), 1 pound; oil of almonds and castile soap, each 1 ounce; white wax, 7 drachms; spermaceti, 3 drachms; oil of lavender and oil of bergamot, each ½ drachm; rose-water, 7 pints; alcohol, 1 pint. Mix.

4. Blanched sweet almonds, 7 pounds; rose-water, 5 gallons. Reduce them to a milk and strain, then add spirit of wine, 1 gallon; oil of lavender, 1 ounce; castile-soap, 1 pound; ottar of roses, about 60 drops

Millefleurs Pomatum.

Lard and suet, each 1 pound; white wax, 2 ounces, essence of lemon, ½ ounce; essence of musk, 60 drops; gum benzoin, 1 ounce. Melt the solids, then withdraw the pot from the fire; and, when partly cold, stir in the essences.

German Milk of Roses.

Sugar of lead and spirits of lavender, each 1 ounce; rose-water and almond milk, each 6 ounces; water, 16 ounces; rosemary water, 2 ounces. Mix.

Milk of Wax.

White wax and alcohol, equal parts. Mix with heat in a porcelain vessel, then pour it on a slab, grind to a paste with more alcohol, and as soon as it appears of a perfectly even consistence, add water gradually to the amount of three and a half to four times the weight of the wax; grind to a fine emulsion, and strain through canvass.

Sugar of Milk.

Take whey, clarify with white of egg, and evaporate.

A very good Pectoral Drink for Consumptive Cough.

Take quitch-grass roots, 2 ounces; eringo-roots 1 ounce; loris, 2 drachms; hartshorn, 1 ounce; stoned raisins, 2 ounces; figs, 6; one spoonful of pearl-barley; colts-foot and sage of Jerusalem, of each one handful. Boil these in three pints of water, till a third part is wasted; strain it, and dissolve therein two drachms of sal-prunella and one ounce of syrup of violets. Drink a quarter of a pint often, when you cough or are dry.

Pills for Shortness of Breath.

Take a quarter of an ounce of powder of elecampane-root, half an ounce of powder of liquorice, as much flower of brimstone and powder of aniseed, and two ounces of sugar-candy powdered. Make all into pills, with a sufficient quantity of tar: take four large pills when going to rest. This is an incomparable medicine for an asthma.

Another for the same.

Take half a pint of the juice of stinging-nettles; boil and scum it, and mix it up with as much clarified honey. Take a spoonful morning and evening.

For an Asthma.

Take hyssop-water and poppy-water, of each 5 ounces; oxymel of squills, 3 ounces; syrup of maiden-hair, 1 ounce. Take one spoonful when you find any difficulty of breathing.

A good Drink in a Consumption.

Take of St. John's-wort, the great daisy-flowers (called ox-eyes) and scabious, of each two handfuls. Boil these in a gallon of spring-water till half be wasted, then strain it, and sweeten it with clarified honey to your taste. Take a quarter of a pint of this in half a pint of new milk morning and evening.

To Cure Foxed Beer.

Add a handful or two of hops to the diseased beer, with a little powdered alum.

To Remove Freckles.

1. Alysson seeds, 1 part; honey, 2 parts. Make into a pommade.
2. Bichloride of mercury, 2 parts; hydrochloric acid, 1 part; spirit of wine, 3 parts; milk of almonds, 25 parts; rose-water, 45 parts. Mix, and apply night and morning.

Euphorbium Plaster.

Compound pitch plaster, 4 pounds; powdered euphorbium, 1 ounce. Mix with care. Used to induce suppuration in encysted tumours.

Drying Ointment for Excoriations.

Oxide of zinc, 1 drachm; spermaceti ointment, 1 ounce. Mix.

Ointment for Obstinate Excoriations.

Ointment of nitrate of mercury, 1 ounce; superacetate of lead, 2 scruples; spermaceti ointment, 2 ounces. Mix.

Expectorant Pills.

Take dried root of squills, in fine powder, one scruple, gum ammoniac, lesser cardamom seeds, in powder, extract of liquorice, each one drachm. Form them into a mass with simple syrup. This is an elegant and commodious form for the exhibition of squills, whether for promoting expectoration, or with the other intentions to which that medicine is applied. Dose, six to twelve grains, three times a day.

Extract of Nosegay.

Spirit of jasmin, 65 parts; spirit of violets, 65 parts; spirit of cassia, 35 parts; spirit of roses, 35 parts; spirit of orange, 35 parts; spirit of clove gilly flower, 35 parts; essence of amber, 13 parts; benzoic acid, 1 part. Mix.

Extract of Peach Blossoms.

Alcohol, 15 pounds; bitter almonds, 6 pounds; spirits of orange-flower, 2 pounds; essence of bitter almonds, ½ ounce; essence of lemon, 4 ounces; balsam of Peru, ½ ounce. Mix.

To make Extracts.

Take of the plant, root, or leaves you wish to make the extract from, any quantity, add sufficient water, and boil them gradually, then pour off the water and add a second quantity; repeat the process until all the virtue is extracted, then mix the several decoctions, and evaporate at as low a temperature as possible, to the consistence of an extract. Extracts are better made in a water-bath, and in close vessels, and for some very delicate articles, the evaporation may be carried on at a very low temperature, in a vacuum, by surrounding the vessel with another containing sulphuric acid Manufacturing druggists usually add to every seven pounds of extract, gum arabic, 4 ounces; alcohol, 1 ounce; olive oil, 1 ounce. This mixture gives the extract a gloss and keeps it soft.

French Marble for Books.

Provide a wooden trough, two inches deep, six inches wide, and the length of a super-royal sheet. Boil in a brass or copper pan any quantity of linseed and water until a thick mucilage is formed; strain it into the trough and let it cool; then grind on a marble slab any of the following colours in small-beer: Prussian blue, king's yellow, rose pink, vermilion, flake white, lamp-black, brown umber, green, blue and yellow, orange, red and yellow, purple, red and blue, brown, black and yellow, or red.

The lamp-black and umber must be burnt over the fire to deprive them of their greasy nature.

For each colour you must have two cups, one for the colour after grinding, the other to mix it with ox-gall, which must be used to thin the colours at discretion. If too much gall is used, the colours will spread; when they keep their place on the surface of the trough, when moved with a quill, they are fit for use.

To prevent the water entering between the leaves of the book, tie it tight between cutting-boards of the same size, and place the trough in a steady situation, to prevent the colours from moving.

Having all things in perfect readiness for marbling, supposing you begin with the blue, throw on with the brush bold spots of blue, sprinkle very fine with the white on the blue spots, fill up the spaces with red and yellow, by dipping first the quill-top into the yellow, and touching the gum therewith, then with the red. The red and yellow may be waved or drawn round the blue spots with an iron pin, or as the marbler may think proper, according to fancy.

Hold the book with its edge downwards, and press it lightly on the colours so disposed on the gum, and the edge will be immediately marbled. The colours that may remain on the gum must be taken off, by applying paper thereon, before you prepare for marbling again. In this manner you may marble the edges to resemble the end-papers, which will have a pleasing effect.

French Bread.

Take a pint of milk and put it into three quarts of water. In winter let it be scalding hot, but, in summer, little more than milk-warm; put in salt sufficient. Take a pint and a half of good ale yeast, free from bitterness, and lay it in a gallon of water the night before. Pour off the yeast into the milk and water, and then break in rather more than a quarter of a pound of butter. Work it well till it is dissolved; then beat up two eggs in a basin, and stir them in. Mix about a peck and a half of flour with the liquor, and, in winter, make the dough pretty stiff, but more slack in summer; mix it well, and the less it is worked the better. Stir the liquor into flour, as for pie-crust, and after the dough is made, cover it with a cloth, and let it lie to rise, while the oven is heating. When the loaves have lain in a quick oven about a quarter of an hour, turn them on the other side for about a quarter of an hour longer. Then take them out, and chip them with a knife, which will make them look spongy, and of a fine yellow, whereas rasping takes off this fine colour, and renders their look less inviting

Frank's Solution of Copaiba.

Is said to be made as follows: Copaiba, 1½ pound; magnesia, 12 ounces. Triturate together, then add spirit of wine, 1 quart. Filter, and add nitrous ether, 2 ounces. Keep it closely corked.

Choice of Fowls.

If a cock, choose one with short spurs, observing that they have not been pared or cut; if a hen, her comb and legs must be smooth; smell them whether they are fresh, and feel whether the breast-bone is well covered; if not, they have probably died from disease.

Lotion for Chronic Ulceration of the Eyelids.

Carbonate of zinc, 4 parts; laudanum, 2 parts; tincture of camphor, 3 parts; rose-water, 65 parts. Mix, and wash the part affected night and morning.

Ointment for Inflammation of the Eyelids.

Protochloride of mercury, 40 grains; spermaceti ointment, 1 ounce. Mix.

Ointment for Sore Eyelids.

Levigated red precipitate, 1 part; spermaceti ointment, 25 parts. Mix, and apply with the tip of the finger every night on going to bed.

Eye Ointment.

1. Sulphate of zinc (in fine powder), 6 drachms; lard, 1 pound. Mix carefully.
2. Sugar of lead, 7 drachms; lard, 1 pound. As before.

To Preserve the Eyesight.

1. Avoid sitting in the dark for any length of time.
2. Avoid straining the eyes by reading small print, or looking at minute objects.
3. Avoid reading or writing much in the dusk of the evening or by candle light.
4. Do not gaze for any length of time on bright or glaring objects, as the fire, gaslight, &c.
5. Observe to hold your book, paper, or work, at a suitable distance from the eyes.

Eye Water.

1. Sulphate of zinc, 1 part; water, 50 parts. Mix, and apply night and morning. The bowels should be kept moderately open at the same time.
2. Nitrate of silver, 4 grains, or less; distilled water, 1 ounce; nitric acid, 1 drop. Dissolve. For purulent ophthalmia in infants.
3. Acetate of lead, 4 grains; distilled water, 1 ounce. Dissolve. For purulent ophthalmia, &c. in infants.
4. Alum, 6 grains; distilled water, 1 ounce. Dissolve. For purulent ophthalmia, &c. in infants.

Grease Ointment.

1. Tallow, 3 pounds; lard, 3 pounds; white lead, 1 pound. Mix.
2. Tallow, 2 pounds; rape oil, 8 ounces; Goulard's extract, 7 ounces. Mix well.

Grecian Gilding.

Take sal ammoniac and bichloride of mercury, equal parts, dissolve in nitric acid, and make a solution of gold with this fluid, lay it on the silver and expose it to a red heat; it will then be gilded.

Greek Fire.

Asphaltum, 30 parts; sulphur, 28 parts; nitre, 42 parts. Mix.

Greek Tincture for Dyeing the Hair.

Nitrate of silver, 11 parts; nitric acid, 1 part; sap green, 3 parts; gum arabic, 1 part; distilled water, 180 parts. Mix.

Green Balsam.

Linseed oil, 14 pounds; powdered resin, 3½ pounds; verdigris, 1 pound. Mix.

Green Basilicon.

Common basilicon, 7 pounds; lard, 4 pounds; powdered verdigris, 1 pound. Mix.

Cheap and Beautiful Green.

Roman vitriol, 16 parts. Dissolve it in a kettle of water, then add yellow arsenic, 1 part; pearlash, 8 parts. Mix. For a pea-green use less, for an apple-green use more yellow arsenic.

Green Composition for Tree Fireworks.

Crystals of verdigris, 4 parts; blue vitriol, 2 parts; sal ammoniac, 1 part. Grind to a paste with alcohol, and impregnate coarse cotton rovings with the composition, then tastefully twist them round the trunk, branches, &c., of the tree, and at once set fire to them.

Green Enamel.

Frit, 1 pound; oxide of copper, ½ ounce; red oxide of iron, 12 grains.

Green Flame.

Take alcohol, and dissolve a little of one of the salts of copper, or a little borax in it.

Green Glaze.

Oxide of copper, 1 part; yellow glaze, 2 parts. Mix.

Green Ink.

1. Cream of tartar, 1 part; verdigris, 2 parts; water, 8 parts. Boil until reduced to a proper colour.
2. Crystallized acetate of copper, 1 ounce; soft water, 1 pint. Mix.

Magnificent Green.

Sulphate of copper, 6 parts; arsenic, 8 parts; potash, 8 parts. Dissolve separately, then mix, and add in a few minutes three or four parts of vinegar, or until the liquor smells slightly acid; set it aside, and after a few hours collect the crystals. Use as little water as will possibly dissolve the articles.

To take Fac-similes of Signatures.

Write your name on a piece of paper, and while the ink is wet sprinkle over it some finely-powdered gum arabic, then make a rim round it and pour on it some fusible alloy, in a liquid state. Impressions may be taken from the plates formed in this way, by means of printing-ink and the copperplate-press.

Green Marble for Leather Book Covers, &c.

The edge must be marbled with a good bright green only. When the colour is prepared with the ox-gall, and ready for use, a few drops of sweet oil must be mixed therein, the colour thrown on with a brush, in large spots, till the gum is perfectly covered. The oil will make a light edge round each spot, and have a good effect.

Blue, green, and brown may be also used separately in like manner.

Sheets of paper may be done, having a trough large enough, and the sheets damped as for printing, before marbling.

Spirits of turpentine may be sprinkled on the colours, which will make white spots.

Green Paint.

1. Whiting, 1 cwt.; road dust, 1 cwt.; blue-black, 30 pounds; ground blue, 25 pounds; ochre, 30 pounds; lime-water, 9 gallons. Grind in equal parts of linseed and factitious linseed oil.

2. Yellow ochre, 2 cwt.; road dust, 3 cwt.; blue-black, 25 pounds; lime-water, 15 gallons; blue to shade. Factitious linseed oil sufficient to grind to proper consistence.

Green Oil.

Rape oil, 1 gallon; verdigris, one ounce. Mix and boil until sufficiently coloured.

To Procure Green Peas in Winter.

Take the peas when they are plenty, shell them, wash and scald in hot water, then drain, put them into bottles, and pour strong brine on them until they are perfectly covered; over this pour a thin layer of good salad oil, and cork tight, then dip the corks into melted pitch. The bottles should be quite full and kept upright.

Green Precipitate.

Take quicksilver, nitric acid, equal parts. Dissolve and reserve the liquid, then take a similar quantity of copper and acid, and dissolve, mix the two solutions, evaporate to dryness and calcine in a shallow vessel until it ceases to emit red fumes.

Green Sealing-Wax.

Shell lac, 2 parts; yellow resin, 1 part; verdigris, 1 part. Powder and mix by heating slowly.

Green Sprinkle for Books.

1. Yellow the edge, then sprinkle with dark blue.

2. French berries, 1 part; soft water, 8 parts. Boil and add a little powdered alum; then bring it to the required shade of green, by adding liquid blue.

Green Stain for Glass.

Calx of brass (oxidized brass), 1 part; minium, 1 part; white sand, 4 parts. Mix.

Composition for Grindstones.

River sand, 30 parts; shell lac, 10 parts; powdered glass, 2 parts. Melt in an iron pot and cast in moulds. The fineness of the sand must depend on the purposes for which the stone is required.

Ground for Metallic Lustres, for Pottery Ware.

Flints, 2 parts; white clay, 2 parts; china, 2 parts; felspar, 3 parts. Grind.

Grouts.

Malt (ground), 1 gallon; water, 2 gallons. Mix and keep them at a temperature of 75° Fahr. until in a full state of fermentation, observing to stir them repeatedly, then evaporate to the consistence of an extract. This is used to make Devonshire white ale.

Grosvenor's Tooth Powder.

Prepared chalk, 10 parts; rose pink, 5 parts; bole, 2 parts; orris powder, 1 part. Mix. Scent with oil of rhodium.

Gum Lozenges.

1. Gum, white sugar, equal parts; starch glue, sufficient to mix; essence of orange, to flavour.
2. Gum arabic, starch, white sugar, equal parts. Mix with rose-water.

Compound Gum Plaster.

Diachylon, 18 parts; gum ammoniac, 1 part; gum galbanum, 1 part; yellow wax, 1 part. Mix. Stimulant.

Gun Metal.

1. Brass, 100 parts; spelter, 13 parts; tin, 6 parts. Mix.
2. Copper, 9 parts; tin, 1 part.

French Government Gunpowder.

Nitre, 75 parts; charcoal, 12½ parts; sulphur, 12½ parts. Mix.

Gunpowder, of Bâle.

Nitre, 76 parts; charcoal, 14 parts; sulphur, 10 parts. Mix.

Gunpowder, of M. Guiton de Morveau.

Nitre, 76 parts; charcoal, 15 parts; sulphur, 9 parts. Mix.

Sporting Gunpowder.

Nitre, 77 parts; charcoal, 13 parts; sulphur, 9 parts.

Waltham Abbey (Royal) Gunpowder.

Sulphur, 2 parts; charcoal, 3 parts; nitre, 15 parts. Mix.

Prepared Gut Skins.

They are cleaned and prepared in the same way as for Sausages. The blind gut is the one used.

Bougie for Piles.

Powdered galls, 1 ounce; olive oil, ½ ounce; white wax, 1 ounce. Make them into a pear-shaped bougie of suitable size.

Compound Pitch Plaster.

Burgundy pitch, 6 parts; yellow resin, 8 parts; yellow wax, 3 parts; lard, 7 parts; turpentine, 1 part; palm oil, 1 part; linseed oil, 1 part. Mix.

To transfer Engravings to Plaster Casts.

Cover the plate with ink and polish its surface in the usual way, then put a wall of paper round it, and when completed, pour in some finely-powdered plaster of Paris mixed in water; jerk the plate repeatedly, to allow the air-bubbles to fly upwards, and let it stand one hour; then take the cast off the plate, and a very perfect impression will be the result.

Defensive Plasters.

Olive oil, 1 pound; suet, 8 ounces; wax, 20 ounces; litharge, 4 ounces; turpentine, 4 ounces; resin, 8 ounces; bole, 2 ounces; wheat flour, 2 ounces. Mix, with heat, and spread it while hot.

Simple Plaster, for Horses.

1. Yellow resin, yellow wax, each, 28 pounds; suet, 10 pounds, Mix, with heat.

2. Yellow wax, 21 pounds; mutton suet, 15 pounds; yellow resin, 14 pounds. Mix, with heat.

3. Yellow wax, yellow resin, mutton suet, equal parts. Mix, with heat.

Spread Adhesive Plaster.

Diachylon, 2 pounds; yellow resin, ½ pound; common turpentine, 1 ounce. Melt, pour it upon the cloth and spread it evenly.

Plate Powder.

1. Quicksilver with chalk, 1 part; whiting, 5 parts. Mix.

2. Quicksilver with chalk, 2 parts; prepared chalk, 14 parts; carbonate of soda, 1 part. Mix.

3. Prepared chalk, 5 parts; levigated oxide of iron, 1 part. Mix. Use dry.

To clean Plate.

1. Cream of tartar, common salt, alum, each, half an ounce; water, 2 quarts. Dissolve and wash the plate in the liquor, then rub it dry. This will make the articles appear like new.

2. Alum, cream of tartar, vinegar, equal parts; water, twice as much. Mix. Add a little to the water you boil the plate in, or use it with a little hot water and a cloth.

3. Vinegar, 11 parts; water, 12 parts; alum, 1 part; unslaked lime, 1 part. Mix. Apply hot.

Platina for Springs.

Platinum, 1 part; gold, 12 parts. Add the platinum to the gold in a state of fusion.

Black Powder of Platina.

Take muriate of platina, expose it to heat until it becomes a greenish yellow chloride, then dissolve it in a strong solution of potash, in a large vessel, and add alcohol (cautiously) to precipitate the platina. Collect the black powder and boil it in alcohol, filter, and repeat the boiling and filtering, first with muriatic acid, and then with a solution of potass, and lastly with four or five times its weight of water; then wash it with pure water and dry it on a porcelain capsule.

Lotion for Piles.

Compound solution of alum, 1 ounce; laudanum, 1 ounce; rose-water 8 ounces. Mix.

Pimento Water.

Pimento, 56 pounds; water, 108 gallons. Draw off 100 gallons.

Pinchbeck.

1. Brass, 2 parts; copper, 3 parts. Melt under charcoal dust.
2. Copper, 5 parts; zinc, 1 part. Melt the copper, then add the zinc.

Pink Dye.

Washed safflowers, 1 ounce; pearlash, 4 scruples; spirit of wine, 4 ounces. Digest for three hours, then add soft water, 8 ounces. Digest for five or six hours more, decant, and add distilled vinegar, a sufficient quantity to produce a fine rose-colour.

Pink Saucers.

Safflower or certhamus (washed), 8 ounces; subcarbonate of soda, 3 ounces; water, 2 gallons. Macerate, strain, and add French chalk (scraped fine with Dutch rushes), 3½ pounds; and precipitate the colour on it with tartaric acid, a sufficient quantity.

Piperine.

Black pepper, 2 parts; alcohol, 3 parts. Digest for twelve hours, pour off the clear, and repeat the process until nothing more is taken up; then mix and evaporate the tinctures; wash the residue with hot water, then dissolve in alcohol and slowly evaporate, when crystals of piperine will be obtained.

Piquante Sauce.

Soy, 1 part; port wine, 2 parts; cayenne, 2 parts; brown vinegar, 16 parts. Mix, and let them stand for three or four days before bottling.

Pistachio Cream.

Pounded pistachio nuts, 1 pound; cream, 1 quart; yolks of 2 eggs, beaten fine. Heat and stir them well, until the mixture grows thick, then pour it into china soup-plates, and when cold stick it over with pieces of the nut.

Tapioca Jelly.

Tapioca, 1 pound, water, [illegible] pints. Put them together over night, next morning boil until quite clear and of a proper consistence, then flavour to taste.

Salt of Tartar.

Take argol, any quantity, calcine it till it becomes white, then dissolve it in water, filter, evaporate, and crystallize.

Lozenges of Tartrate of Iron.

Tartrate of iron, 9 parts; white sugar, 240 parts; essence of mint, 1 part; mucilage sufficient quantity to mix. Form into fifteen-grain lozenges, each of which will contain about half a grain of the tartrate of iron.

Tar Varnish.

Tar, 2 gallons; tallow, 1 pound. Melt, then add ground ochre, 7 pounds; spirits of turpentine, 6 pounds. Mix well. By regulating the quantity of the ochre, a very excellent chocolate paint for rough out-door work will be produced.

Tasteless Purging Salt.

Take powdered burnt bones. Nitric acid to dissolve. Add a solution of sulphate of soda as long as any precipitate is produced; filter, distil off the nitric acid, evaporate and crystallize.

Tawing.

Take the skins and soak them in the lime-pit for five or six weeks, then rinse them well in clean water, and again soak them in water mixed with bran, until they rise to the surface, and, when beaten down, do not rise again; then take them out and scrape them clean; lastly, wash them over repeatedly, or soak them in the following mixture for some time, then dry them as quickly as possible: alum, 9 pounds; salt, 3½ pounds. Dissolve in warm water, then add wheat flour twenty-one pounds, and ninety or one hundred yolks of eggs. Well mix, and dilute with a sufficient quantity of water. This is enough for 100 or 120 skins.

Tea for Icing.

Cream for icing, 2 pints; strong tea, 4 ounces; sugar, 1 ounce. Yolks of four eggs. Mix well and strain, ready for icing.

Soluble Tea.

Tea, 1 part; boiling water, 7 parts. Digest at a heat of 170° for half an hour, and evaporate at a low temperature in a vacuum. In this way can be made an excellent extract of tea, which preserves many of the virtues of the leaves, and will produce a cup of decent tea by adding a few grains to the hot water. The lower the temperature at which the evaporation is carried on, the finer the quality

Substitutes for Tea.

1. Clean chopped meadow-hay is said to make a very good substitute for tea, if used in the proportions of three to one.

2. Dried rosebuds, 5 parts; rosemary leaves, 1 part; balm, 2 parts. Mix.

3. Strawberry and black currant leaves make a very good substitute for tea when properly treated.

4. The herb spring-grass (*anthoxanthum odoratum*), when dried, forms an excellent substitute for China tea, and is more wholesome.

Tar Ointment.

Tar, tallow, equal parts. Mix. Detergent.

Tears of the Widow of Malabar.

Water, 3 quarts; proof-spirit, 4 quarts; white sugar, 4 pounds; powdered cinnamon, ½ ounce; powdered cloves, ¾ drachm; powdered mace, ¾ drachm. Burnt sugar to tinge. Macerate for ten days in a closely corked carboy.

Opiate for the Teeth.

Honey, 1 pound; laudanum, 8 ounces; oil of almonds, 1 ounce; essence of bergamot, 2 drachms; tincture of pellitory, 4 ounces. Mix well and strain. Apply with a piece of cotton or lint.

Terra-Cotta.

Potter's clay, ryegate sand, and water, each a sufficient quantity. Model and bake.

Terro-Metalicum for filling Decayed Teeth.

Mineral succedaneum, and mix with it some levigated porcelain or china. Apply it in the same manner as marmoratum.

Thernard's Blue.

Take oxide of cobalt and nitric acid. Digest, evaporate to a paste, then dilute with water and filter; pour the clear liquor into a solution of phosphate of soda, wash the precipitate and mix it with eight times its weight of pure gelatinous alumina, dry powder, and calcine at a cherry-red heat for half an hour.

Binder's Thread Marble.

Yellow the edge; when-dry, cut pieces of thick thread over the edge, which will fall on different parts irregularly, give it a fine dark sprinkle and shake off the thread.

Tin Filings.

Take grain tin, melt it in an iron vessel, and stir it, while cooling, until it becomes a powder, then sift it.

Tin in Grains.

Take Cornish grain tin, melt it, and pour it into a wooden box, well rubbed on the inside with whiting or chalk; close the cover, and continue shaking it violently until the tin is reduced to powder, then wash it in clean water and dry it immediately.

Oxide of Tin.

Take tin and dissolve it in nitromuriatic acid in a close vessel, then precipitate the oxide with an alkaline solution.

Tin Tree.

Into a suitable white glass bottle put three drachms of muriate of tin and ten drops of nitric acid, and nearly fill it with water. Suspend a piece of zinc about one inch long and a quarter of an inch thick, by means of a thread, (perpendicularly,) from the cork; set the bottle aside, where it will not be disturbed, and metallic vegetation will commence.

To preserve Milk.

1. Evaporate the milk by a very gentle heat, applied to a large surface, preserve the powder in bottles.

2. To every gallon of milk add about one ounce of calcined magnesia, or until the acid is destroyed.

3. Fill bottles with new milk and loosely cork them; then put them into cold water, in a boiler, and apply heat; as soon as the water boils, or four or five minutes after, take them out, and secure the corks down with wire or pack-thread, then replace them in the boiler, remove it from the fire and let it cool; lastly, pack them securely in the coldest place you can find. Place a little straw on the bottom of the boiler, lest the heat should crack the bottles.

To remove the Turnip Flavour from Milk.

Water, 25 parts; nitrate of potash, 1 part. Add a little to the milk, warm from the cow.

Mineral Marmaratum for filling Decayed Teeth.

Mix a little finely-powdered flint-glass with some mineral succedaneum, and apply it in the same way.

Mineral Metallic Cement for filling Decayed Teeth.

Take some mineral succedaneum, and add some steel-dust.

Mineral Succedaneum for filling Decayed Teeth.

Tinfoil and quicksilver. Melt together in a convenient vessel, and take a small quantity, knead it in the palm of the hand, and apply it as soon as possible.

Mineral Tincture of Bark.

Peruvian bark, 1 ounce; quicklime, ½ ounce; lime-water, 30 ounces. Macerate. Dose—three ounces three times a day.

Mint Water.

1. Oil of mint, 1 pound; water, 180 gallons. Draw over one hundred gallons.

2. Dried mint, 17 pounds; or, green mint, 30 pounds; water, 12 gallons. Distil off ten gallons.

Miser's Sauce.

Sliced onions, 1 pound; vinegar, 1 quart; cayenne and salt to flavour. Boil for fifteen minutes, and serve it up with a little butter.

Mixed Wine.

Red currants, 4 gallons; red gooseberries, 3 gallons; raw sugar, 16 pounds; red tartar, 1 ounce; water, 7 gallons; white spirit, ½ gallon Ferment the fruit, water, and sugar, then rack and add the rest.

Mock Turtle.

A fine calf's head, cut the meat clean from the bones, then boil the bones in water; season with cayenne, nutmeg, and mace; pour into the gravy a pint of Madeira wine, with a little parsley and thyme.

Moirée Metallique.

Heat the tin plate, then apply diluted nitro-muriatic acid to its surface for a few seconds; wash, dry, and lacquer it.

Morella Wine.

Morellas, 60 pounds, bruise the stones well; sugar, 20 pounds; water, 15 gallons. Boil and ferment, then add spirit, 1 gallon; red tartar, 6 ounces. Rack and fine it with eggs.

Solution of Muriate of Morphia.

Muriate of morphia, 8 grains; muriatic acid, 30 drops; distilled water, 1 ounce. Mix.

Solution of Sulphate of Morphia.

Distilled water, 7 drachms; sulphuric acid, 1 drachm; sulphate of morphia, 8 grains. Dissolve.

Morveau's Reducing Flux.

Powdered glass, 16 parts; calcined borax, 2 parts; charcoal powder, 1 part. Observe not to employ a glass that contains lead.

Mosaic Gold, or Molu.

Take copper and zinc, equal parts. Melt at the lowest temperature that will fuse the former; then mix by stirring, and add five per cent. more zinc.

Parker's Mosaic Gold.

Copper, 100 parts; zinc, 54 parts. Mix.

To keep Moths from Clothing.

Put a few cuttings of Russia leather in your trunk or wardrobe; or sprinkle a few pepper-corns, pimento corns, or cloves, in the same places.

For a Cough.

Take one spoonful of linseed oil, new drawn, first and last. This is good in a pleurisy, or any other cough, and may be used safely at any age.

For a Chin-Cough.

Dry the leaves of box-tree very well, and powder them small, and give the child of this fine powder, in all its meat and drink that it can be disguised in. It is excellent in that distemper.

An admirable Electuary for a Cough.

Take a syrup of hoarhound, ground-ivy, and white poppies, of each one ounce, and spermaceti, half a drachm. Mix and beat these very fine, and take a little spoonful when your cough is troublesome, and at going to rest.

For an Asthma.

Take juice of hyssop, juice of elecampane-root, of each one pound; boil these to a syrup, with double their weight in honey or sugar-candy Take one spoonful of this syrup in two spoonfuls of hyssop-water, and one spoonful of compound briony-water Take this three times a day.

Orange Colour for Marbling or Sprinkling Books, &c.

Ground Brazil-wood, 16 parts; annotto, 4 parts; alum, sugar, and gum arabic, each 1 part; water, 70 parts. Boil, strain, and bottle.

Orange Cordial.

Oil of orange, 4 ounces; proof-spirit, 50 gallons, or less. Mix well, then add sugar, 150 pounds; dissolve in water, 40 gallons. Mix and fine.

Candied Orange Flowers.

1. Orange-flowers, 1 pound; sugar, 7 pounds. Boil the sugar to a candy height, then stir in the flowers, and pour it out on a slab of marble The flowers should be deprived of their cups, stamina, and pistils.

2. Picked orange-flowers, 4 ounces; sugar, boiled to a candy height, 2 pounds. Mix, and pour them out on an oiled marble slab as before.

Orange-Flower Drops.

Take essence of neroli or orange-flower water, and flavour plain confectionary drops.

Orange-Flower Paste.

1. Plain dry almond paste, 7 pounds; neroli to flavour and turmeric to colour. Mix well, and sift through gauze.

2. Almond paste, plain, dry, 5 pounds; orange-flowers, 1 pound. Powder and sift through gauze, as before.

Pastilles of Orange-Flower.

Neroli, 1 part; nitre, 9 parts; galbanum, 13 parts; olibanum, in tears, 12 parts; storax, in tears, 11 parts; pure orange-powder, 16 parts; charcoal, 70 parts. Reduce the solids to fine powder, then make them into a paste, with gum tragacanth, 2 parts; dissolved in orange-flower water, 15 parts; rose-water, 17 parts.

Orange-Flower Soap.

Palm soap, 2 parts; tallow soap, 3 parts. Mix, as for cinnamon soap, and perfume with the following essences: Essence of Portugal, 8 parts; essence of amber, 7 parts. Mix. Colour with the following, as required: Red lead, 5 parts; yellow green, 33 parts. Mix.

Perfumer's Oil of Orange-Flowers.

Orange-flowers, 1 part; blanched almonds, bruised, 2 parts; olive oil, 1 part. Mix, and let them remain together for a week, then express the oil. More flowers may be used to increase the perfume.

Candied Orange Marmalade.

Cut the clearest Seville oranges into two, take out all the juice and pulp into a basin, and pick all the skins and seeds out of it. Boil the rinds in hard water till they become tender, and change the water two or three times while they are boiling. Then pound them in a marble mortar, and add to it the juice and pulp; put them next into a preserving-pan with double their weight in loaf-sugar, and set it over a slow fire. Boil it rather more than half an hour, and put it into pots; cover it with brandy paper and tie it close down.

Orange-Flower Water.

Water, 9 gallons; orange-flowers, 15 pounds. Distil off, at a low heat, seven gallons.

Pommade of Orange-Flowers.

Lard, 12 parts; orange-flowers and beef suet, each 6 parts. Mix, and treat them as for rose pommade.

Orange Lake.

Best Spanish annatto, 1 pound; pearl-ashes, 4 pounds; water, . gallon. Boil until dissolved, and strain, then add alum, 4 pounds; water, 2 gallons. Dissolve and add it to the first solution, so long as any sediment falls.

Candied Orange-Peel.

Soak the peels in water, which must be changed, until they lose their bitterness, then put them into syrup until they become soft and transparent; lastly, take them out and place them to dry.

Essence of Orange-Peel.

Orange-peel, 1 pound; spirit, 1 gallon. Macerate for ten days.

Orange-Peel Water.

Seville orange-peel, 7 pounds; water, 30 gallons. Distil off twenty-eight gallons.

Orange Pomatum.

Clarified lard, 7 pounds; mutton suet, 1½ pounds; yellow wax, 1½ pounds; palm oil, ¾ pound. Melt and strain, then add, while cooling, Portugal water, ½ pint; essence of bergamot, 1 drachm; neroli, 1½ drachms. Stir well in, and pour it into the pots.

For sweating in the night in a Consumption.

Drink a glass of tent, or old Malaga, with a toast, every morning early, and sleep an hour after it. This is good for consumptive persons, or such as are weak, in recovering a long sickness.

For a Shortness of Breath.

Take flower of brimstone and elecampane-root finely powdered, of each an equal quantity; mix this into an electuary with clarified honey, and take it whenever you cough, or find it difficult to breathe.

For a Cough and Shortness of Breath.

Take elecampane-roots, 1 ounce; saffron, ¼ ounce; ground-ivy and hyssop, of each one handful. Boil this in two quarts of water until it is above half consumed; strain it out, and sweeten it with sugar-candy, and take three spoonfuls often.

Another for the same.

Syrup of garlic, two spoonfuls, or the cloves of garlic preserved; either of them very good. But if the breath be very bad, it is best to lose nine or ten ounces of blood, if the patient can bear it, before you begin to take so hot a medicine.

French Orange Pomatum.

Mutton suet, palm oil, lard, beeswax, each 1 pound. Melt and, when nearly cold, stir in orange-flower water, 8 ounces; essence of lemon, 3 drachms; essence of neroli, 7 drachms, or more.

Orange Sprinkle for Books.

Colour the edge with King's yellow, mixed in weak gum-water, then sprinkle with vermilion mixed in the same manner.

Orange Stain for Glass.

Precipitated silver powder, yellow ochre, red ochre, equal parts. Turpentine to mix.

Spirit of Oranges.

Orange-flowers, 5 pounds; Seville orange-peel, 2 ounces; balm leaves, 1½ ounces; spirit, 9 pints. Water sufficient. Distil over eight or nine pints.

Orange Wine.

The same as lemon wine, only with essence of orange.

Ottar of Roses.

Steep the rose-buds or leaves in pure water, and collect the floating oil This operation is never performed in England, the ottar being all imported.

Orgeat Paste.

Blanched and pounded sweet almonds, 3 pounds; blanched and pounded bitter almonds, 1 pound, or less; powdered loaf-sugar, 3 pounds; orange-flower water to mix. Beat them in a mortar to a stiff paste, then put it into pots for use. When wanted for use, put a little into some water, mix, and strain it through a bit of gauze.

Oriental Pomatum.

Mutton suet, 7 pounds; yellow wax and palm oil, each 1 pound. Melt, then stir in orange-flower water, 8 ounces; rose-water, 6 ounces; essence of lemon, 4 drachms; essence of bergamot, 6 drachms; oil of lavender and oil of rosemary, each 3 drachms.

Factitious Oil of Originum.

Oil of originum, 10 parts; castor oil, 5 parts; oil of turpentine 3 parts. A little to colour. Mix.

Factitious Oriental Ruby.

Strass, 7000 parts; precipitate of cassius and nitric peroxide of iron, ach 165 parts; golden sulphuret of antimony, 160 parts; manganese calcined with nitre, 150 parts; rock crystal, 1000 parts. Mix in fine powder, and carefully melt.

Cadet de Gassincourt's Oriental Rusma.

Orpiment, 1 part; quicklime, 4 parts; pearlash ley, 35 parts. Boil until a feather dipped into the solution loses the flue. Keep it in close-corked bottles. For use, apply a little with friction to the part, then wash it off with water; the hair will generally come away with one application

Or-Molu or Mosaic Gold.

Copper and zinc, equal parts. Fuse at the lowest possible temperature, and stir well to produce a perfect admixture, then add more zinc until the fused alloy becomes perfectly white; lastly, pour it into moulds. The proportion of zinc to the copper is from 50 to 55 per cent., exclusive of what is lost by the heat employed.

Orris Lozenges.

Orris powder, 1 ounce; white sugar, 2 pounds: starch, 1 pound. Mix with a weak decoction of Brazil-wood.

Prepared Ox-Gall.

Fresh gall, 1 pint; alum, 1 ounce. Boil until the latter is dissolved, then fresh gall, 1 quart; salt, 1 ounce. Boil in like manner, keep both solutions in separate bottles for two or three months; pour off the clear, and mix them together; allow them to settle, and decant the pure gall for use.

Oxycroceum.

1. Burgundy pitch, 20 pounds; black pitch, 35 pounds; yellow resin, 30 pounds; turpentine, 25 pounds; dragon's-blood, 3 pounds. Mix, with heat.

2. Black pitch, resin, and yellow wax, each 20 pounds; Chia turpentine, galbanum, ammoniacum, myrrh, mastic, and olibanum, each 5 pounds; saffron, 12 ounces. Mix, with heat.

For a Looseness.

Take two drachms of ipecacuana; decoct it in an equal quantity of claret and water; let it boil more than half in half away; strain it, and add one spoonful of oil; give it in a clyster to the party afflicted. If the patient is weak, or a child, you must infuse less of the root; two drachms being a full quantity for a strong man.

For the same.

Take an ounce of cinnamon, and as much ginger; slice both small, and strew it on a chafing-dish of coals, over which let the patient sit as long as the fume lasts.

Jerusalem Artichoke.

It flourishes most in a rich, light soil, with an open enclosure. The only mode of propagation is by planting the middle-sized tubers or cuttings of the large ones, one or two eyes being preserved in each. These are best planted towards the end of March, though it may be performed as early as February, or even in October, and continued as late as the beginning of April.

Panes of Glass

May easily be removed by the application of soft soap for a few hours, however hard the putty has become.

Cure for Grubs in Horses.

Add a pint of strong vinegar to a cubic inch of chalk; when the effervescence ceases, drench the horse with the liquid from a bottle.

Orgeat.

Blanched Jordan almonds, 1 pound; blanched bitter almonds, ¼ ounce; white sugar, 23 ounces; water, 2 pints. Reduce to an emulsion and strain, then add orange-flower water, ¼ ounce.

Oxygen Gas.

Take chlorate of potass, or red oxide of mercury, expose it to the heat of a spirit-lamp, in a suitable vessel, and collect the gas.

Oyster Catsup.

Fish and juice, 1 pint. Press them through a sieve, then add white wine, 1 pint; salt, 1 ounce; spice to flavour. Boil for fifteen minutes, strain and bottle.

Oyster Powder.

Oysters and wheat flour, equal parts. Salt to taste. Reduce them to a paste in a mortar, roll into slices, dry and powder, then keep it in closely corked bottles. One ounce will make a pint of oyster sauce.

Chinese Packfong.

Copper, 5 parts; zinc and nickel, each 7 parts.

Elastic Water-proof Paint.

Hot water, 1 gallon; soap, 2 pounds. Dissolve, then add boiled oil, 5 gallons; linseed oil and turpentine, each 1 gallon. Mix well and grind, or mix your colours in it. This paint is very suitable for canvass, by omitting the linseed oil and using less water.

Painter's Cream.

Pale linseed oil, 18 parts; powdered mastic, 3 parts; sugar of lead, 1 part. Water to reduce it to the consistence of cream.

To Extract Paint or Grease Spots.

Dip a pen in spirit of turpentine, and transfer it to the paint spot, in sufficient quantity to discharge the oil and gluten. Let it stand some hours, then rub it. For large or numerous spots, apply the spirit of turpentine with a sponge, if possible, before it becomes dry.

To mix Paints.

In mixing paints, observe, that for out-door work you must use principally, or wholly, boiled oil, unless it is for the decorative parts of houses, &c., then mix as for in-door work.

For in-door work use linseed oil, turpentine, and a little dryers, observing that the less oil, the less will be the gloss, and that for *flatted white*, &c., the colour being ground in oil, will scarcely require any further addition of that article, as the object is to have it dull.

To Fine Pale Sherry.

Take the white of six eggs and three pints of skimmed milk, beat them to a froth, then mix them with the wine and rummage it well. A little pale brandy or spirit added a few minutes after the finings, and well mixed in, will also improve the wine.

To convert Brown Sherry into Pale Sherry.

Fine it with two or three quarts of skimmed milk to the hogshead. This precipitates the colouring matter.

Black Edge Paper.

Black-lead, 11 parts; common ink, 22 parts; dissolved gum arabic, 1 part. Mix. Then with a sponge lay the colour on the edge of the paper, previously placed in the cutting-press, rub it in with a piece of cloth, and burnish. The edge of the paper must be rendered perfectly smooth before applying the black.

Fire-proof Paper.

Take a solution of alum and dip the paper into it, then throw it over a line to dry. This is suitable to all sorts of paper, whether plain or coloured, as well as textile fabrics. You must try a slip of the paper in the flame of a candle, and if not sufficiently prepared, dip and dry it a second time.

French Paper of Safety.

Take white paper pulp and tinged paper pulp, equal parts. Mix, and make it into sheets as usual. Any stain easily affected by chlorine, the acids, alkalies, &c., should be used.

Paper for Draughtsmen, &c.

Powdered tragacanth, 1 part; water, 10 parts. Dissolve and strain through clean gauze, then lay it smoothly with a painter's brush on the paper, previously stretched on a board. This paper will take either oil or water colours.

To Stain Paper or Parchment.

Red.—Brazil, 12 parts; water, 70 parts; alum, 5 parts. Boil.

1. *Blue.*—Sulphate of indigo. Water to dilute.

2. Prussian blue, 2 parts; muriatic acid, 1 part. Water to dilute.

3. Logwood, 4 parts; water, 30 parts; sulphate of copper, 1 part. Mix

Green.—Crystals of verdigris, 2 parts; vinegar, 1 part. Water to dilute.

Yellow.—French berries, water, and a little alum. Boil.

Purple.—Logwood, 2 parts; alum, 1 part; water, 20 parts. Boil. The addition of a little gum to the above, renders them suitable for colouring maps, &c.

To make Catsup that will keep good Twenty Years.

Take a gallon of strong stale beer: one pound of anchovies, washed and cleaned from the guts; half an ounce of mace; half an ounce of cloves; a quarter of an ounce of pepper; three large races of ginger; one pound of shallots; one quart of flap mushrooms, well-rubbed and picked. Boil all these over a slow fire until it is half wasted, then strain it through a flannel bag; let it stand until it is quite cold; then bottle and stop it very close. This is thought to exceed what is brought from India; and must be allowed the most agreeable relish that can be given to fish sauce One spoonful to a pint of melted butter, gives taste and colour above all other ingredients. The stronger and staler the beer is, the better the catsup will be.

Hair Dye.

Nitric acid, 1 part; nitrate of silver, 10 parts; sap green, 9 parts, mucilage, 5 parts; water, 300 parts; essence of musk, one or two drops to each bottle. Mix. In all cases first free the hair from grease. All hair dyes must be applied by means of moistening a clean comb with them, and then passing it through the hair, observing not to touch the skin with the dye, and the hair first washed clean with soap and water Various other forms for hair dyes will be found in different parts of this work.

Hair for Wigs.

Roll the hair round little cylindrical pieces of wood or metal, then boil them; and, lastly, expose them at the mouth of an oven for a few hours.

Ointment to promote the Growth of Hair on Horses.

Resin, 3 pounds; tallow, 3 pounds; rape oil, 3 pounds; camphor, 12 ounces; oil of rosemary, 1 ounce; mustard (flour), 1 pound; ivory-black, 1 pound. Mix.

A la Rose Hair Powder.

Starch or farina, 1 cwt.; oil of rosemary, 1 ounce; oil of cloves, 1 drachm; ottar of roses to perfume. Mix and sift through lawn.

Ambergris Hair Powder.

Starch or farina, 1 cwt.; essence of ambergris to perfume. Mix and sift through lawn.

Bergamot Hair Powder.

Starch or farina, 20 pounds; bergamot (essence), 80 drops, or more. Mix and sift through lawn.

Brown Hair Powder.

Take flour and roast it carefully over the fire to the required colour, then sift it through lawn.

Musk and Civet Hair Powder.

Starch or farina, 1 cwt.; essence of musk, 2 ounces; essence of ambergris, 2 ounces. Mix and sift through fine lawn.

Perfume for Hair Powder.

Any of the fragrant essences of oils in small portions.

Plain Hair Powder.

Take starch or farina, and sift it through lawn.

Violet Hair Powder.

Starch or farina, 1 cwt.; orris powder, 7 or 8 pounds; oil of rhodium, 30 drops; oil of cloves, 60 drops. Mix, and pass it through fine gauze.

To Preserve the Hands Dry for Delicate Work.

Take club moss (lycopodium) in fine powder, and rub a little over your hands.

To Preserve Hams, &c. in Hot Climates.

Most grocers, dealers in hams, and others who are particular in their meat, usually take the precaution to case each one after it is smoked in canvass, for the purpose of defending it from the attacks of the little insect (the dermestes lardarius), which, by laying its eggs in it, soon fills it with its larvæ or maggots. This troublesome and expensive process may b altogether superseded by the use of the pyroligneous acid. With a painter' brush dipped in the liquid, one man, in the course of a day, may effectually secure two hundred hams from all danger. Care should be taken to insinuat the liquid into all the cracks, &c. of the under surface.

Hartshorn Blancmange.

Hartshorn shavings, 16 parts; water, 32 parts; Cape wine, 2 parts; lump-sugar, 3 parts. Boil the hartshorn in the water until you find it of he proper consistence on cooling a little, then add the wine and sugar.

Hartshorn Drink.

Hartshorn shavings, 3 ounces; gum arabic, 1 ounce; sugar, 1 ounce; water, 3 pints. Boil until reduced to one quart, and strain.

Hartshorn Jelly.

1. Hartshorn shavings, 1 pound; a small piece of lemon-peel; water, 1 gallon. Boil, clarify with white of egg, and add white wine, ½ pint.

2. Hartshorn, 1 pound; water, 1 gallon; peel of two lemons. Boil over a gentle fire until sufficiently thick, strain, and add loaf-sugar, ½ pound: whites of ten eggs (beaten to a froth); juice of six lemons. Whisk together well.

Dr. Bœrhaave's Rules for Preserving Health.

1. Keep the feet warm.
2. The head cool.
3. The bowels sufficiently open.

These rules, though short, "speak volumes."

Rules for Preserving Health.

1. Rise early, and never sit up late.
2. Wash the whole body every morning with cold water, by means of a large sponge, and rub it dry with a rough towel, or scrub the whole body for ten or fifteen minutes with flesh-brushes.
3. Drink water generally, and avoid excess of spirits, wine, and fermented liquors.
4. Keep the body open by the free use of the syringe, and remove superior obstructions by aperient pills.
5. Sleep in a room which has free access to the open air.
6. Keep the head cool by washing it when necessary with cold water, and abate feverish and inflammatory symptoms when they arise by persevering stillness.
7. Correct symptoms of plethora and indigestion by eating and drinking less per diem for a few days.
8. Never eat a hearty supper, especially of animal food; and drink wine, spirits, and beer, if these are necessary, only after dinner.

Hard White Metal.

Tin, 1 part; spelter, 3 parts; brass, 20 parts. Mix.

Harvey's Sauce.

Quin sauce, 48 parts; soy, 16 parts; cayenne, 1 part. Mix and steep for one week, then pour off the clear liquid.

Hassan's Dye for the Hair.

Nitrate of silver, 1 part; sap green, 1 part; distilled water, 77 parts ix.

To Relieve Headache in Bed.

Discontinue wearing a night-cap, and use an extra pillow.

Ointment to Stop the Feet of Horses.

1. Cow-dung, clay, tallow, equal parts. Mix, with heat.
2. Tallow, tar, turpentine, equal parts. Mix.

To Prevent Cold Feet.

Wear worsted or lambs' wool stockings, and, on going to bed at night, rub your feet and ankles with them, until they are warm.

Dr. Bally's Ferruginous Lozenges.

Powdered iron filings, 16 parts; chocolate paste, 16 parts; powdered saffron, 4 parts; mucilage sufficient quantity to mix. Divide into twelve-grain lozenges, three or four to be taken daily.

Dr. Colombat's Ferruginous Powder.

Pure sulphate of iron, 2 parts; tartaric acid, 6 parts; sugar, 12 parts. Mix in fine powder, and divide into papers containing twenty-five grains each.

Quesneville's Ferruginous Powder.

Bicarbonate of soda, 4 parts; tartaric acid, 7 parts; pure sulphate of iron, 4 parts; sugar, 8 parts. Powder each fine, then mix and keep the powder in a well-corked bottle. Dose, one spoonful in six or seven ounces of sweetened water.

To make (for Wine, &c.) Filtering Bags.

Take a square of canton flannel or other suitable stuff, and cut it into two pieces, from corner to corner, then carefully sew two of the sides together, and place strings of tape at the mouth, to tie it to a hoop, by which it must be suspended for use. Always keep separate filters for white and coloured liquors.

Beer or Porter Finings.

Isinglass, 1 pound; water, 8 gallons; vinegar, 4 gallons. Mix the vinegar and isinglass, and macerate for four days, then add the water.

Wine or Beer Finings.

Isinglass, 1 pound; sour beer or cider, 5 gallons; water, 6 gallons. Digest the first two until the isinglass is dissolved, then add the water and strain.

Fining Powder.

Take eggs, any quantity; beat them to a froth, and expose them to a gentle heat or in the sun to dry, then powder. In some cases a little fine wheat flour is added, the paste made into balls, and dried in the sun, or a warm room, and then powdered. Used for all the purposes of fresh eggs by solution in cold water.

The Art of Fire Eating, &c.

The power of resisting the action of fire is given to the skin, by frequently washing it with diluted sulphuric acid, until the part becomes sufficiently callous. It is said that the following mixture is very efficacious: Dilute sulphuric acid, 3 parts; sal ammoniac, 1 part; juice of onions, 2 parts. Mix. It is the acid however that produces the effect.

To Extinguish Fire in Chimneys

1. Throw several handfuls of flowers of sulphur on the burning coals.

2. Throw some wet straw, or horse litter on the fire, and keep sprinkling it with water. This must be neither so wet as to put out the fire, nor so dry as to burst into a flame.

To bring Horses out of a Stable on Fire.

Throw the harness or saddle, &c. over them, and it is said they will come out immediately.

French Polish.

Alcohol, 260 parts; copal varnish, 13 parts; sandarach (powdered), 1 part; mastic (powdered), 1 part; shell lac (powdered), 24 parts. Mix and digest in a moderate heat, in a strong close vessel.

To French Polish.

The varnish being prepared (shell lac), the article to be polished being finished off as smoothly as possible with glass paper, and your rubber being prepared as directed below, proceed to the operation as follows: The varnish, in a narrow-necked bottle, is to be applied to the middle of the flat face of the rubber, by laying the rubber on the mouth of the bottle and shaking up the varnish, once, as by this means the rubber will imbibe the proper quantity to varnish a considerable extent of surface. The rubber is then to be inclosed in a soft linen cloth, doubled, the rest of the cloth being gathered up at the back of the rubber to form a handle. Moisten the face of the linen with a little raw linseed oil, applied with the finger to the middle of it. Placing your work opposite the light, pass your rubber quickly and lightly over its surface until the varnish becomes dry, or nearly so; charge your rubber as before with varnish, (omitting the oil), and repeat the rubbing, until three coats are laid on, when a little oil may be applied to the rubber, and two coats more given to it. Proceeding in this way, until the varnish has acquired some thickness, wet the inside of the linen cloth, before applying the varnish, with alcohol, and rub quickly, lightly, and uniformly the whole surface. Lastly, wet the linen cloth with a little oil and alcohol without varnish, and rub as before till dry.

To make the Rubber.—Roll up a strip of thick woollen cloth which has been torn off, so as to form a soft elastic edge. It should form a coil from one to three inches in diameter, according to the size of the work.

Fire-proof Stucco for Wood, &c.

Take moist gravelly earth (previously washed), and make it into stucco with the following composition: Pearlashes, 2 parts; water, 5 parts; common clay, 1 part. Mix. This costs about one shilling and sixpence per hundred square feet. It has been tried on a large scale and found to answer.

Six Reasons for Planting an Orchard, by Edson Harkness.

1. Would you leave an inheritance to your children? Plant an orchard. No other investment of money and labour will, in the long run, pay so well.

2. Would you make home pleasant — the abode of the social virtues? Plant an orchard. Nothing better promotes, among neighbours, a feeling of kindness and good will, than a treat of good fruit, often repeated.

3. Would you remove from your children the strongest temptations to steal? Plant an orchard. If children cannot obtain fruit at home, they are very apt to steal it; and when they have learned to steal fruit, they are in a fair way to learn to steal horses.

4. Would you cultivate a constant feeling of thankfulness towards the great giver of all good? Plant an orchard. By having constantly before you one of the greatest blessings given to man, you must be hardened indeed if you are not influenced by a spirit of humility and thankfulness.

5. Would you have your children love their home, respect their parents while living, and venerate their memory when dead — in all their wanderings look back upon the home of their youth as a sacred spot — an oasis in the great wilderness of the world? — Then plant an orchard.

6. In short, if you wish to avail yourself of the blessings of a bountiful Providence, which are within your reach, you must plant an orchard. And when you do it, see that you plant good fruit. Don't plant crab-apple trees, nor wild plumbs, nor Indian peaches. The best are the cheapest.

French Pommade.

Pommade (any), 8 ounces; white wax, 1 ounce; spermaceti, ½ ounce; oil of almonds, 3 ounces. Mix.

French Rolls.

Lard or butter, 1 spoonful; flour, 3 pints; yeast, 3 table-spoonfuls; milk to mix. Before taking them from the oven, brush them over with milk.

French Salop.

Take potatoes, peel them, and bake slowly until quite dry and hard, then grind them.

French Sealing Wax.

Shell lac, 2 pounds; yellow resin, 1 pound; Venice turpentine, 1 pound; Chinese vermilion, 3 pounds. Melt with a gentle heat, and form into sticks from twelve to twenty-four to the pound.

Fresco Painting.

Apply any colours that are not injured by lime (according to taste), on a fresh mortared or plastered wall.

Frigorific Mixture.

1. Phosphate of soda, 9 parts; nitrate of ammonia, 6 parts; dilute nitric acid, 4 parts. Mix.

2. Snow, 3 parts; potass, 4 parts. Mix.

3. Snow, 3 parts; diluted nitric acid, 2 parts. Mix. The above are three of the most useful combinations selected from Mr. Walker's tables.

White Frit.

Glass, 35 parts; lead, 10 parts; nitre, 5 parts; arsenic, 2 parts. Fuse.

English Frontignac.

1. Sun raisins, 18 pounds; water, 18 gallons; lump-sugar, 40 pounds. Boil for two hours, then add of elderflowers, 1½ peck; white tartar, 4 ounces; spirit (white), 2 gallons. Set the bung loosely for fourteen days, then close tight.

2. Water, 60 gallons; white sugar, 1½ cwt.; raisins, ½ cwt.; flowers of white elder, 5 gallons; white tartar, 8 ounces; yeast, 1 pint. Ferment.

3. Six gallons of water, twelve pounds of loaf-sugar, and six pounds of raisins of the sun, cut small; boil these together an hour; then take of the flowers of elder, when they are falling and will shake off, half a peck; put them in the liquor when it is almost cold. The next day put in six spoonfuls of the syrup of lemons, with four spoonfuls of ale yeast: after it has worked two days, put it into a clean cask, and bung it up.

4. Lump-sugar, 36 pounds; soft water, 12 gallons; elder flowers, ½ peck; eggs, 2 in number. Boil the sugar and eggs, skim, then remove the vessel from the fire and add the flowers; when cool, add a little lemon-juice and yeast, and ferment, then rack it into a clean cask containing twelve pounds of raisins and some finings; bottle in six months.

To restore Frosted Beer.

Add some finings, with a few handfuls of flour, and some scalded hops.

To Gather and Preserve Fruits.

They should in most instances be collected ripe, and kept in sand or straw.

To Pack Fruit.

Fruits of the most delicate sorts are sent from Spain and Italy to England, packed in jars with saw-dust from woods not resinous or otherwise ill tasted. One large bunch of grapes is suspended from a twig or pin laid across the mouth of the jar, so that it may not touch either the bottom or sides; saw-dust or bran is then strewed in, and, when full, the jar is well shaken to cause it to settle; more is then added till it is quite full, when the supporting twig is taken away, and the earthen cover of the jar closely fitted and sealed, generally with fine stucco.

Peppermint Drops.

Moisten the sugar with peppermint water, or flavour it with the essence of neroli, and moisten it with water.

For Costive Habit of Body.

Distil a quantity of wood-sorel water in the spring, and sweeten it with syrup of violets. An ounce of syrup to a quarter of a pint of water is a dose for anybody, and may be safely taken, even in a fever or lying-in A less quantity for a child.

Another.

Roasted apples, with caraway-comfits, eaten constantly every night.

Another.

Boil a few mallows in a porringer of water-gruel; strain it out, and instead of salt, put in a pugil of cream of tartar. Let this be your morning's draught.

Paper that Resists Moisture.

Take unsized paper, lay it flat on a clean surface and brush it over with a solution of mastic in oil of turpentine; or plunge it into the solution and hang it up to dry. This paper possesses all the usual qualities of writing paper, with the advantage of resisting moisture.

To Detect the presence of Plaster in Paper.

Calcine the paper in a close vessel, and dilute the residue with vinegar, in a silver spoon; if sulphuretted hydrogen is disengaged, which blackens the spoon, the presence of a sulphate (plaster) will be shown. This adulteration has lately become very common among the paper-makers, with the view of increasing the weight.

To extract Grease Spots from Paper.

Apply a little powdered pipe-clay, on which place a sheet of paper, then use a hot iron. Remove the adhering powder with a piece of India rubber.

To Gild the Edges of Paper.

Armenian bole, 4 parts; sugar-candy, 1 part. White of egg to mix. Apply this composition to the edge of the leaves, previously firmly screwed in the cutting-press; when nearly dry smooth the surface with the burnisher; then take a damp sponge and pass over it, and with a piece of cotton-wool take the leaf from the cushion and apply it to the work; when quite dry burnish, observing to place a piece of silver or Indian paper between the gold and the agate.

Waxed Paper.

Take cartridge or other paper, place it on a hot iron and rub it with beeswax, or make a solution of the wax in turpentine, and apply it with a brush. Useful for making water or air-proof pipes, for chemical experiments, &c.

Papier Maché.

Take paper, any quantity. Boil it well, then pound it to a paste and mould. Used in making toys, snuff-boxes, &c.

Paracelsus' Plaster.

Diachylon, 56 pounds; compound diachylon, 5 pounds; gum thuris, 3 pounds; white canella, 2 pounds. Mix.

Simple Cure for Worms.

One spoonful of syrup of peach-blossoms, taken in a glass of the water distilled from the leaves, or in which the leaves and worm-seed have been decocted, is a most safe and certain medicine for the worms in children.

Parsnip Sugar.

Take parsnips, wash them clean, then put them into a powerful press, and express the juice; next take the cake out, break it up, and sprinkle it with water, and press it a second time; lastly, strain and evaporate.

Full Blue Paste.

Take plain paste, 600 parts; zaffre, 4 parts; manganese, 1 part. Fuse carefully.

Opake White Paste.

Flint-glass, 100 parts; white arsenic, 9 parts. Use as little heat as possible.

Plain Paste or Strass.

1. *Very hard.*—Washed sand, 12 parts; pearlash, 7 parts; saltpetre, 1 part; borax, ½ part.

2. *Hard.*—White sand, 24 parts; pearlash, 14 parts; nitre, 2 parts; borax, 1 part; arsenic, ½ part.

3. *Soft.*—White sand, 6 parts; red-lead, 3 parts; potash, 2 parts; nitre, 1 part.

4. *Very soft.*—White sand, 30 pounds; red-lead and potash, each 15 pounds; nitre, 5 pounds; borax, 3 pounds; arsenic, 1 pound, or less. See also Mayence base, strass, &c.

Pastilles à la Rose.

Essence of roses, 1 part; nitre, 9 parts; gum, tears of olibanum, and tears of storax, each 12 parts; powder of roses, 16 parts; charcoal, 60 parts. Reduce the solids to fine powder, then make the whole into a paste with gum tragacanth, 2 parts. Dissolved in rose-water, 35 parts.

Pastilles à la Vanilla.

Gum galbanum, in fine powder, tears of olibanum, in fine powder, tears of storax, in fine powder, nitre, in fine powder, cloves, in fine powder, each 25 parts; vanilla, 35 parts; spirit of wine, 12 parts; powdered charcoal, 115 parts. Make into a paste as above, and form into pastilles.

Manure.

Put on your land all the manure that can be scraped from your premises, or that you are entitled to from the road. Leave not a particle in the barn-yard. It matters not how coarse or long it is, if you can plough it in. All you get from it before another season is clear gain, for it will lose but little more under the ground with a crop over it, than exposed to the action of the sun and rains in the yard. If it cannot be used, place it in heaps and cover it two feet thick with earth, which will inhale and retain most of its enriching gases till wanted.

Tar-Water.

Tar, 3 pounds; Boiling water, 1 gallon. Digest and strain.

Explosive Pastilles.

As for other pastilles, and when moist, press a small stick or quill into the broad end, then fill it with gunpowder, and cover it over with the composition. Observe to dry them sufficiently.

Pâte de Guimauve.

1. Marshmallow-roots, 1 pound ; water, 4 gallons. Boil to one half and strain, then add powdered gum, 2 pounds ; powdered sugar, 8 pounds. Evaporate to an extract, and add a little orange-flower water, and the whites of twelve eggs beaten to a froth.

2. Powdered gum, 10 pounds ; sugar, 10 pounds. Water to dissolve ; strain, evaporate to the consistence of honey, then add the whites of 20 eggs, beaten to a froth, and 2 ounces of orange-flower water ; continue the evaporation, constantly stirring the mixture until it will not stick to the fingers. It should be light, spongy, and white.

Patent Malt, or Porter Colouring.

Take malt and roast it until it acquires a dark chocolate colour. One part mixed with eighty of pale malt imparts the flavour and colour of porter. The Excise laws of England allow burnt malt to be used by the brewer to colour his liquors.

Patent Yellow.

Mix triturate minium or red oxide of lead and common salt together, and then expose them in a crucible to a gentle heat. In this process the salt is decomposed, and the acid unites with the oxide of lead, and forms the patent yellow. The alkaline base of the salt remains in the compound, which is to be carefully washed and crystallized.

Muriate of lead tinges vitreous matters of a yellow colour. Hence the beautiful glazing given to Queen's-ware. It is composed of eighty pounds of muriate of lead, and twenty pounds of flints ground together very fine, and mixed with water, until the whole becomes as thick as cream. The vessels to be glazed are dipped in the glaze and suffered to dry, when they are exposed to a sufficient degree of heat to vitrefy the surface.

Peach Brandy.

Bruised bitter almonds, 3 pounds ; light proof-spirit, 100 gallons ; water, 30 gallons ; sugar, 50 or 60 pounds. Mix, and macerate for fourteen days. Colour with brandy colouring, if required darker.

Peach Wine.

Water, 12 gallons ; bruised bitter almonds, ¼ pound ; sugar, 23 pounds ; honey, 3 pounds. Boil and ferment, then add spirit, 1 gallon ; dried orange-peel, ½ ounce ; cassia and ginger, each ¼ ounce ; white tartar, 2 ounces.

Pearl Powder for the Complexion.

1. Take pearl or bismuth white and French chalk, equal parts. Reduce them to fine powder, and sift through lawn.

2. Take white bismuth, 1 pound ; starch powder, 1 ounce ; orris powder, 1 ounce. Mix, and sift them through lawn. Add a drop of ottar of roses or neroli.

Pearl Soft Soap.

Take lard, 2 parts; potass ley (36° B.) 1 part. Put the lard over the fire; and, when half melted, stir it with a spatula until it assumes the appearance of milk, then add half the ley, stir well, but avoid increasing the temperature. When soapy granulations commence forming, and fall to the bottom, add the rest of the ley; continue the stirring until the paste is formed, then transfer the pan to a bath of warm water, and let them cool together. When cold, pound it in a marble mortar until it assumes a pearly appearance. Scent with bitter almonds essence.

Pearl Water for the Complexion.

Castile soap, 1 pound; water, 1 gallon. Dissolve, then add alcohol, 1 quart; oil of rosemary and oil of lavender, each 2 drachms. Mix well.

Tincture of Pearls for the Complexion.

Blanched almonds, 1 pound; acetate of lead, 4 ounces; water, 7 pints. Reduce them to a milk and strain, then add spirit, 3 pints; essence of neroli and essence of lavender, each 1 drachm. This is used for removing freckles.

Pearl White.

Nitrate of bismuth in solution, and add it to a dilute solution of chloride of sodium until the whole of the bismuth is precipitated; collect, wash, and dry the powder with great care.

Pectoral Lozenges.

1. Lump-sugar, 50 parts; orris powder, 3 parts; liquorice, 2 parts; extract of poppies, 1 part. Mucilage to mix.

2. Orris powder and liquorice powder, each 4 ounces; saffron powder, 1 ounce; sugar, 2 pounds. Mucilage to mix.

3. Powdered opium, 1 drachm; balsam of tolu, 2 drachms; Italian juice and sugar, each 1 pound. Mix with mucilage.

To cure Deafness.

Take clean, fine black wool, dip it in civet, and put it into the ear; as it dries, which in a day or two it will, dip it again; and keep it moistened in the ear for three weeks or a month.

Another.

Take an equal quantity of good Hungary water and oil of bitter almonds, beat them together, and drop three drops in the ears, going to bed; stop them with black wool, and repeat this nine nights at least.

For a Pain in the Ear.

Take the juice of mountain sage, oil of fennel, or oil of olives, and mix well together; drop into the pained ear three drops for several nights. It will ease and draw out any imposthume, if that be the cause.

For a violent Colic Pain in the Side.

Mix an equal quantity of spirit of lavender, spirit of sal-ammoniac, and Hungary-watery; rub it in with a very hot hand, and lay a flannel on as hot as you can bear it. Repeat this often.

For a Pain in the Ear.

Take half a pint of claret and a quarter of a pint of wine-vinegar, put in sage, rue, or rosemary; let it boil up, put it into a new mug, with a bottle-mouth, and hold your ear close, so that the steam may be sure to go in. As it cools, heat it again and again; and when the strength is pretty well wasted, wrap your head very warm and go into bed.

A certain Remedy to take Fire out of a Burn.

Beat an apple with salad oil until it is a poultice, pretty soft; bind it on the part, and as it dries, lay on fresh. You must be sure to pare, core, and beat your apple well, for fear of breaking the skin of the burn. But if the skin be off, there is nothing in nature so sure to take out the fire.

An excellent Ointment for a Pain in the Side.

Beat two ounces of cummin-seed very fine; sift it, and put to it two spoonfuls of neatsfoot oil, and two spoonfuls of linseed oil; make it hot over the fire, and anoint the side with it. Dip a flannel in the ointment, and lay it on as hot as you can endure it.

Whipped Syllabub.

Take a lump of sugar and rub it on the outside of a lemon until coloured, then put it into a pint of cream and sweeten to taste; squeeze in the juice of a lemon, and add a glass of Sherry or Madeira, mill to a froth and take off the froth as it rises, and drain it well in a sieve, then half fill a glass with red wine, and pile up the froth as high as possible.

Whiskey Cordial.

Bruised cassia, bruised ginger, and bruised coriander-seeds, each 1 ounce; mace, cloves, and black pepper, each ½ ounce; saffron, 1½ ounces. Steep them for five days in whiskey or proof-spirit, 4 gallons. Then add sugar, 12 pounds. Dissolved in water, 5 gallons. Mix and fine.

Devonshire White Ale.

Pale wort, 12 gallons; hops, 5 ounces; grouts, 7 pounds. Mix and ferment, and bottle immediately.

White Cerate.

Sweet oil and white wax, each 1 pound; spermaceti, 2 ounces. Melt, then add water, 1 pound, and continue stirring until cold.

White Elder Ointment.

Elder flowers, 30 pounds; lard, 90 pounds; suet, 28 pounds. Melt and strain.

White Crystal, or Factitious Diamond.

Manganese, 1 part; rock crystal, 2800 parts; borax, 1900 parts; white lead, 5700 parts. Mix in fine powder, then fuse in a clean crucible, pour it into water, dry, powder, and repeat the process two or three times.

White Currant Wine.

Cold soft water and fruit, each 9 gallons; lump-sugar, 25 pounds; white tartar, 2 ounces; white brandy, 1 gallon; orris root, ½ ounce; bitter almonds, bruised, ½ ounce. Ferment the first three, then add the rest

White Enamel.

Tin, 2 parts ; lead, 1 part. Calcine, then take of the above oxides, 1 part ; crystal, 2 parts ; manganese, a small portion. Grind well together, fuse, and pour the mass into cold water ; dry, grind again to powder, and fuse ; repeat the process four or five times, observing great care to prevent any contamination from smoke, or iron, or copper.

Whitehead's Essence of Mustard.

Oil of turpentine, 22 parts ; flour of mustard, 5 parts ; camphor, 1 part. Digest for a week.

Clark's Process for making White Lead. (American Patent.)

A chamber of 12 to 15 feet square is furnished with a vinegar trough, through which a pipe of about one-inch calibre passes ; it connects at right angles with a large main of steam-pipe at one end, and is there commanded by a cock ; the other end passes entirely through the trough and chamber, and there discharges the condensed steam. They are also each supplied with a gas distributing-box or trunk, which is about four inches square in the clear and about thirteen feet long. These are placed an inch or so above and over the vinegar troughs, having small holes at short intervals through their sides, and at one end are connected by means of a short pipe, to which a cock is also adapted, to a main gas-pipe which is furnished by means of a blowing apparatus with the requisite supply of atmospheric air and carbonic acid gas. The sides of the chambers have cleats secured to them for supporting the rod over which the sheets of lead are suspended for conversion to white lead.

A boiler of iron or copper is heated with anthracite coal, from which the steam and carbonic acid gas are obtained for heating and supplying the chambers. The doors of the chambers fit close, so that some pressure is produced in them during the process of conversion.

The vinegar in the troughs, the sheet-lead on the rods, and the cisterns being closed, fire is applied to the furnace of the boiler, the blowing apparatus is put in motion, and the process of making white lead has commenced. Moderate quantities of coal and vinegar, and the constant attention of one man, are necessary to continue it ; and one thousand tons of lead may be operated on by this attention as well as one hundred. The largest sized chamber will contain about ten tons of the metallic sheets, and require supplies of vinegar twice each twenty-four hours. If the lead appear moist and pasty, the vinegar is withheld ; and, to these points, namely, the supply of the gases, and attention to the fires, the duty of the operative is confined. At first the vinegar was placed on the floor of the chambers and covered with a false floor, which was perforated at short intervals, so as to distribute the gases and acid vapour equally through them. In this way the sheets of lead became much more expeditiously converted to white lead, but its specific gravity was lessened, and it was less esteemed by the painters.

It is computed that from sixty to seventy-five per cent. of the expense of converting metallic lead into white lead, is saved by substituting Mr Clarke's plan for any of the old methods now in use ; or the saving by employing his method, is nearly as three to one.

Patent Bread.

Wheat flour, 7 pounds; carbonate of soda, 350 to 500 grains; water, 2¾ pints; muriatic acid from 420 to 560 grains, or as much as may be sufficient. Bake quick. See Pereira on Food and Diet, p. 152.

Another Mode.

Flour, 1 pound; sesquicarbonate of soda, 40 grains; cold water, ½ pint, or as much as may be sufficient; muriatic acid of the shops, 50 minims (drops); powdered white sugar, 1 tea-spoonful. Mix the flour with the soda and sugar, then gradually mix the acid with the water by stirring. Now mix up quick your flour into a paste with this water, divide into two loaves and immediately put them to bake in a quick oven.

British Herb Tobacco.

Thyme, 2 parts; coltsfoot, 3 parts; betony, 4 parts; marjoram, 2 parts: hyssop, 2 parts; rosemary, 8 parts; lavender, 8 parts; roses, 5 parts. Mix.

Toilet Soap.

Lard, 30 pounds; caustic ley (17° Baume), 46 pounds. Saponify with heat.

Tolu Lozenges.

Sugar, 4 pounds; starch, 2 pounds; balsam of tolu, 1 ounce. Mix with mucilage.

Tomato Catsup.

Cut tomatoes in pieces, and between every layer sprinkle a thin layer of salt; let them stand a few hours, then add a little horseradish, garlic, pepper and mace. Boil well and strain, then bottle, cork and seal for use.

Tombac.

1. Copper, 16 parts; tin, 1 part; zinc, 1 part.
2. *Red.* Copper, 10 parts; zinc, 1 part. Fuse the copper, then add the zinc.
3. *White.* Copper, 10 parts; arsenic. Cover the surface of the liquid metals with common salt to prevent oxidation.

Tonic and Alterative Draught. (*Syphilitic.*)

Bichloride of mercury, 5 grains; hydrochloric acid, 70 drops; tincture of bark, 3 ounces. Mix. Dose, one tea-spoonful two or three times a day.

Tonic Draught.

Compound tincture of cardamoms, 1 drachm; tincture of orange-peel, 2 drachms; tincture of bark, 2 drachms; cinnamon water, 11 drachms. Mix, and take every morning for debility, &c.

Toothache Oil.

Oil of cloves, 1 part; laudanum, 2 parts; camphor, 2 parts; oil of cassia, 3 parts. Mix.

Toothache Drops.

Laudanum, 3 parts; alcohol, 5 parts; camphor, 1 part; pellitory of Spain (powdered), 2 parts; cassia, 1 part; opium, 1 part. Digest for a few days, and decant the clear liquid. Apply by means of a little lint.

Remedy for Toothache.

Take a small piece of the inside of a nutgall, and put it into the tooth; replace it by a fresh piece at intervals of an hour.

To prevent the Toothache.

Clean your teeth every morning with Sibella snuff, or powdered tobacco, and well wash your face with cold water.

Tooth Powder.

1. Powdered cassia, 1 part; rose pink, 1 part; orris powder, 3 parts; burnt alum, 2 parts; powdered bark, 2 parts; powdered myrrh, 2 parts; prepared chalk, 20 parts. Mix, and sift through lawn.

2. Prepared chalk, 20 parts; powdered myrrh, 2 parts; cassia, 2 parts; orris powder, 2 parts; burnt alum, 1 part; rose pink, 1 part. Mix, and add a few drops of the oil of cloves.

3. *Excellent.* Howard's prepared chalk, 5 pounds; cassia, ¼ pound; bole, 2 pounds; Bath brick, 3 pounds; charcoal, 2 pounds. Reduce all to powder, then sift through the finest gauze.

Chevalier Ruspini's Tooth Powder.

Powdered bark, 2 parts; powdered bole, 4 parts: burnt alum, 1 part; myrrh, 1 part. Mix.

Barker's Tooth Tincture.

Tincture of pellitory, 4 parts; tincture of red lavender, 1 part; tincture of red sanders wood, 1 part. Mix.

Tooth Water.

Rose-water, 2 pints; tartaric acid, 2 ounces; burnt alum, 1 scruple; common salt, 1 scruple. Mix, and wash your teeth with it by means of a piece of sponge.

Factitious Topaz.

1. Strass, 1000 parts; glass of antimony, 42 parts; purple of Cassius, 1 part. Fuse for twenty-four hours, and cool slowly.

2. Strass, 4000 parts; saffron of Mars, 40 parts. As before.

To solder Tortoise-shell.

Bring the edges of the pieces of shell to fit each other, observing to give the same inclination of grain to each, then secure them in a piece of paper, and place them between hot irons or pincers; apply pressure, and let them cool. The heat must not be so great as to *burn* the shell, therefore try it first on a piece of white paper.

Tracing Paper.

Nut oil, 4 parts; turpentine, 5 parts. Mix, and apply it to the paper, then rub it dry with wheat flour, and brush it over with ox-gall. This will bear writing on.

Composition to heal Wounds in Trees.

Chalk, 4 parts; tar, 2 parts; brick-dust, 1 part. Melt, and apply warm.

Transparent Soap.

Good tallow soap, (in shavings and perfectly dry,) strong alcohol, equal parts. Put them into a copper still, and apply a gentle heat until the solution is complete; then allow the fluid to settle, and pour off the clear into moulds, which must be so arranged that the alcohol can be saved as it evaporates from the hardening mass. This soap may be coloured red with tincture of archil, and yellow with tincture of turmeric.

Travers's Infernal Drops.

Lunar caustic, 2 grains; distilled water, 1 ounce. Mix.

Treacle Beer.

Hops, 1 ounce; water, 1 gallon. Boil for ten minutes, strain, and add treacle, 1 pound, and when lukewarm, yeast, 1 spoonful. Ferment.

Tree Marble, for Leather Book-Covers.

A marble in the form of trees may be done by bending the boards a little on the centre, using the same method as the common marble, having the cover previously prepared. The end of a candle may be rubbed on different parts of the boards, which will form knots.

To protect Trees and Shrubs from the Attacks of Hares.

Take tar, 1 part; tallow, 3 parts. Apply hot to the bark of the tree, with a paint-brush.

Composition to heal Wounds in Trees.

Chalk, 4 parts; tar, 2 parts; brick-dust, 1 part. Melt, and apply warm.

Luting for grafting Fruit Trees.

Take train oil and resin equal parts, and melt in an earthen vessel; mix well and apply with a painter's brush. This is in general use, in the northwest part of France, and, where it is employed, it is said that the grafts *never* fail.

To destroy Moss on Trees.

Paint them with white-wash made of quicklime and wood ashes.

To preserve Truffles.

Keep them in well-corked bottles in salad oil.

Perfumer's Oil of Tuberose.

Take the flowers and treat them as for Oil of Jasmin, which see.

Tuberose Pommade. (French Method.)

The same as Jasmin, with the difference of the perfume.

Tunbridge Wells Water.

Chloride of sodium, 5 grains; tincture of steel, 20 drops; distilled water, 1½ pints. Mix.

Choice of a Turkey.

Choose a smooth leg and short spur; eyes full and bright, and feet supple and moist.

Turkish Bloom.

Gum benzoin, 1 pound; powdered red sanders, $1\frac{1}{4}$ pound; dragon's blood, $2\frac{1}{2}$ ounces: alcohol, 1 gallon. Digest for fourteen days, and filter.

Turmeric Paper.

Turmeric, 1 ounce; water, 1 pint. Boil until of a sufficient colour, strain, and dip strips of yellow wove post into the decoction, and dry them.

Turner's Brass.

Brass, 98 parts; lead, 2 parts. Mix.

Turner's Cerate.

1. Factitious wax, 1 pound; lard, 1 pound; carbonate of zinc, 6 ounces. Mix at a low heat. Healing.

2. Sweet oil, 2 pounds; yellow wax, 1 pound; powdered carbonate of zinc, 1 pound. Mix at a low heat.

Turnip Wine.

Turnip juice, 25 gallons; lump-sugar, 60 pounds; spirit, 7 quarts, or more. Put it into a cask and loosely bung it until it has done fermenting This wine is said to cure the gout.

Turpentine Liniment.

Spirit of turpentine, 4 ounces; yellow basilicon, 8 ounces. Mix. Used in burns.

Turpentine Varnish.

Resin, 1 part; boiled oil, 1 part. Melt, then add turpentine, 2 parts. Mix well.

Paste resembling the Turquoise Stone.

Eagle marine paste, 100 parts; calcined bones, 20 parts; smalts, 1 part. Fuse them together with a moderate heat, equally applied for a sufficient length of time.

Tutania or Britannia Metal.

1. Plate brass, tin, bismuth, antimony, each, 2 parts; copper, arsenic, each, 1 part. Mix, and add this alloy at discretion to melted tin.

2. *Spanish.*—I. Antimony, 4 parts; tin, 2 parts; arsenic, 1 part.

II. Scrap iron, 1 part; antimony, 2 parts; nitre, a little. Melt and harden one pound of tin with two ounces of this composition. A little arsenic improves the colour of this alloy.

Tutenag.

Tin, 2 parts; bismuth, 1 part. Fuse.

Type Metal.

Lead, 10 parts; antimony, 2 parts. Fuse.

Umber.

This is a blackish-brown colour; it is an earth found near Cologne.

Vaccine Matter.

Open the pustule with a lancet, and collect the matter.

Heartburn Lozenges.

1. Howard's prepared chalk, 2 pounds; magnesia, 2 pounds; powdered gum, 3 pounds; powdered starch, 3 pounds; powdered white sugar, 12 pounds; essence of lemon, 1 ounce. Mix with strong decoction of Brazil wood (strained).

2. Powdered lump-sugar, 100 parts; Howard's prepared chalk, 15 parts; subcarbonate of soda, 5 parts; mucilage to mix.

Heel Balls for Leather.

Tallow, 2 parts; yellow wax, 2 parts; resin, 2 parts; ivory black, 1 part; lamp-black, 1 part. Mix.

Heel Ointment, (for Cattle).

Tallow, 2 pounds; resin, 2 pounds; molasses, 2 pounds; spirits of turpentine, 2 pounds; sulphate of copper (powdered), ¼ pound; verdigris (powdered), ¼ pound; alum (powdered), ¼ pound. Mix, with heat.

Ointment of White Hellebore.

Powdered white hellebore, 4 ounces; lard, 1 pound. Mix.

Hematine.

Logwood (small), 1 part; water, 15 parts. Macerate at a heat of 135° Fahr., filter and evaporate in a steam bath, then dissolve in alcohol, evaporate slightly, and set it aside, when crystals of hematine will be obtained.

Hemlock Ointment.

Hemlock leaves, 4 ounces; simple ointment, 5 ounces. Beat together melt, and strain.

Hemmet's Tooth Powder.

Prepared chalk, 20 parts; carbonate of magnesia, 20 parts; cream of tartar, 4 parts; orris powder, 3 parts. Reduce to fine powder and sift through lawn.

To Choose Herrings.

If fresh, the gills will be red, eyes bright, and body stiff and firm.

Hiera Picra.

Aloes, 3 pounds; white canella, 1 pound; pimento, 4 ounces; turmeric, 4 ounces; liquorice powder, 4 ounces. Mix. Dose, eight to twenty grains.

English Imitations of Hollands.

Juniper berries, 2 pounds; silent spirit (proof), 83 gallons; water sufficient. Draw over one hundred gallons.

Hollands, (Schiedam Process).

Ground malt, 1 cwt.; rye meal, 1 cwt.; water, 450 gallons. Mash at 160° Fahr. for two hours, then draw off the wort and add cold water until it is of the specific gravity of 1.047. Ferment at the temperature of 80° Fahr with yeast, 6 quarts, until the gravity of the wash indicates eleven pounds per barrel, then distil into low wines and rectify them twice over a small quantity of juniper berries, and a very minute quantity of Strasburg turpentine. Sometimes the berries are bruised and put into the wash.

To Gather and Preserve Herbs.

Herbs should be gathered early in a morning, at the season when they are just beginning to flower. The dust should be washed, or brushed off them, and they should be then dried by a gentle heat, as quick as possible.

Balsam of (Pectoral) Honey.

Balsam of tolu, 16 parts; gum storax, 2 parts; opium, 2 parts; honey, 64 parts; spirit of wine, 260 parts. Dose, one or two teaspoonfuls.

Honey Butter.

Butter (best fresh), 14 pounds; clarified honey, 1 pound. Beat well together. A delicacy for children or sick persons. It generally proves mildly laxative.

To Clarify Honey.

Honey, 1 barrel. Fifteen eggs mixed with five gallons of water, pour into a cold copper, mix well, then apply heat, and skim; filter if necessary. The water may be evaporated if desired, only observing to use as little heat as possible.

To Preserve Seeds in Honey.

Seeds put into honey in bottles have been carried to great distances, and have afterwards vegetated.

Honey Water.

Essence of ambergris, 1 drachm; musk and neroli, each, ½ drachm; spirit, 1 quart. Mix.

First Quality Honey Water.

Spirit of roses, 180 parts; spirit of jasmin, 90 parts; spirit of wine, 100 parts; essence of Portugal, 3 parts; essence of vanilla, 12 parts; essence of musk, 11 parts; flowers of benzoin, ½ part; orange-flower water, 100 parts. Mix.

Refrigerant Lotion.

Muriate of ammonia, 1 ounce; vinegar, 4 ounces; water, 10 ounces Mix.

Resin Cerate.

1. Resin ointment, 16 parts; yellow wax, 1 part; yellow resin, 1 part Mix.
2. Resin ointment, 9 parts; yellow resin, 1 part. Mix.
3. Yellow resin, yellow wax, rape oil, equal parts. Mix, with heat.

Common Resin.

Tar, brown resin, resin dregs, equal parts. Melt and stir together.

Resin Ointment.

1. Lard, 65 pounds; yellow resin, 35 pounds; yellow wax, 14 pounds Mix.
2. Yellow resin, yellow wax, rape oil, lard, equal parts. Mix.
3. Yellow resin, 2 parts; lard, 6 parts. Mix. If too thick, add a little oil or more lard.
4. Yellow resin, suet, rape oil, equal parts. Mix.

Resin Plaster.

Simple diachylon, 93 pounds; yellow resin, 19 pounds. Melt, with a gentle heat.

Refined Liquorice.

Solazzi juice, 85 pounds; starch, 10 pounds; moist sugar, 17 pounds. Reduce to a thin paste with water, then strain and evaporate in a gentle heat to the consistence for rolling.

Rheumatic and Toothache Embrocation.

Sal volatile, 6 parts; laudanum, 3 parts. Mix. This may be applied to the tooth by means of a piece of lint.

Embrocation for Syphilitic Rheumatism.

1. Sulphuric ether, 1 ounce; composition camphor liniment, 1 ounce; acetate of morphia, 2 grains. Mix.

2. Opodeldoc, 1 ounce; tincture of camphor, 1 ounce; laudanum. 1 ounce. Mix.

3. Acetate of cantharides, 1 ounce; opodeldoc, 4 ounces; oil of cajeput, 4 ounces. Mix.

Factitious Oil of Rhodium.

Oil of sandal-wood, 11 parts; oil of rhodium, 1 part. Mix.

Extract of Rhubarb.

Rhubarb, 1 pound. Bruise it, and macerate for three days in spirits, 4 pints. Pour off the clear, and supply its place with water, 5 pints. Macerate for four days longer, pour off the clear, mix the two tinctures together, distil off the spirit, and evaporate to the consistence of an extract.

Rhubarb Lozenges.

Powdered rhubarb, 1 ounce; powdered cassia, 1 ounce; sugar, 1 pound. Mix with mucilage.

Rhubarb Wine.

Sliced rhubarb, 3 ounces; cardamom seeds (bruised), 1 ounce; ginger (bruised), ½ ounce; spirit, 1½ pint. Digest for three days, then add of any white wine two gallons.

Rice Marble, for Leather Book Covers, &c.

Colour the cover with spirits of wine and turmeric, then place on rice in a regular manner: throw on a very fine sprinkle of copperas-water till the cover is nearly black, and let it remain till dry. The cover may be spotted with the red liquid or potash-water, very freely, before the rice is thrown off the boards.

Rice Tea.

Rice, 1 ounce; raisins (stoned), ½ ounce; a shred of lemon-peel; water, 1½ pint. Boil to a pint, and strain.

Specific for the Rickets.

Sugar, 2 pounds; young shoots of the flowering fern, 1 pound. Make them into a conserve by beating them together in a mortar.

Factitious Riga Balsam.

Spirits of turpentine, 12 parts; oil of juniper, 1 part. Mix.

Ring Gold.

Copper (Spanish), 6 parts; silver, 3 parts; gold, 5 parts. Mix.

Ringwood Ale.

Pale malt, 1 quarter; hops, 6 pounds. Water sufficient to produce two barrels and a half. Turn on first mash at 180° Fahr. Second mash at 190° Fahr. Turn at 60°.

Rob of Elder Berries.

Take elder juice, and evaporate by a gentle heat to a proper consistence.

Rochelle Salt.

Scotch soda, 5 parts; water, 20 parts, or more. Dissolve and filter, then heat it nearly to the boiling point, and add cream of tartar, 6 parts. Filter, evaporate, and crystallize.

Compositions for Roman Candles.

For the candle, nitre, 16 parts; charcoal, 7 parts; sulphur, 4 parts. Mix For the stars, nitre, 16 parts; gunpowder, 5 parts; sulphur, 7 parts. Mix with camphorated spirit and gum-water. For use, put in one spoonful of fine gunpowder, then a star, then a measure full of the composition, and proceed in this way until the case is full.

English Roman Cement.

Take a bushel of lime slacked, with three pounds and a half of green copperas, fifteen gallons of water, and half a bushel of fine gravel sand. The copperas should be dissolved in hot water; it must be stirred with a stick, and kept stirring continually while in use. Care should be taken to mix at once as much as may be requisite for one entire front, as it is very difficult to match the colour again; and it ought to be mixed the same day it is used.

Genuine Roman cement consists of the pulvis Puteolanus, or puzzolene, a ferruginous clay from Puteoli, calcined by the fires of Vesuvius, lime, and sand, mixed up with soft water. The only preparation which the puzzolene undergoes is that of pounding and sifting; but the ingredients are occasionally mixed up with bullock's blood, and fat of animals, to give the composition more tenacity.

To Gather and Preserve Roots.

Roots should be gathered in spring, with but few exceptions, and are better for being fresh.

Roots to be dried should be well washed and sliced, unless they are preserved for the sake of the bark, when they must be merely washed and dried.

The process of drying may be simply performed by stringing the pieces together, or scattering them on paper trays, and exposing them, for a sufficient time, to a gentle heat, say from 90° to 130° Fahr.

To Cool and Ventilate Rooms.

A trough, six or eight feet long, six inches deep, and two inches wide, with a perpendicular support at each end, about seven feet high, the tops being united by means of a cross piece of wood. Arrange a few hooks at the bottom of the trough, and also on the top cross piece; then take a wet blanket or other suitable article, hook it on at top and bottom, and fill the trough with water. Evaporation will immediately commence, and keep the room cool.

To Cure Ropy Beer.

Put a handful or two of flour, and the same quantity of hops, with a little powdered alum, into the beer, and rummage it well.

Roseate Depilatory.

Powdered quicklime, 1 pound; starch, ½ pound; orpiment, 1 ounce; powdered rose-leaves, 1 ounce. Mix.

Rose Beads or Pearls.

1. Take petals of the red rose; reduce them to a paste, by beating them in an iron mortar, then form into beads. A few drops of ottar improve the quality.

2. Starch, 12 parts; gum arabic, 1 part; rose pink, 7 parts; ottar to perfume. Beat to a thick paste, with water, and form into beads.

Rose Drops.

Rose water, 6 ounces; sugar, 2 pounds. Make into drops.

Rose Lozenges.

Sugar, 6 pounds; starch, 1 pound; ottar of roses, 1 drachm; powdered gum, 12 ounces. Mix with water, pinked with cochineal.

Rosemary Water.

Rosemary tops, 21 pounds; water, 10 gallons. Draw over seven gallons.

Rose Oil.

Finest olive oil, 2 parts; rose-leaves, 1 part. Pour the oil warm on the leaves, cover the vessel up, and let it rest a week, then strain with expression.

Rose Pink.

Take a strong decoction of Brazil-wood, to which add a little pearlash, then pour it over finely-sifted whiting, and reduce it to a thick paste, and dry slowly.

Rose Pommade.

Lard, 11 parts; beef suet, 5 parts; rose leaves, 4 parts. Melt in a water-bath, and stir occasionally for two hours, then let it rest in a warm place free from dust, for two or three days, after which time apply a heat, just sufficient to liquefy the fat, and keep it in this state for two hours, stirring all the time; allow it to cool, when it must be formed into lumps of three pounds each, placed in canvass bags, and subjected to the press The pommade thus formed must be again treated with fresh rose leaves to increase the perfume.

French Rose Pomatum.

White wax, 1 pound; lard, 3 pounds; suet, 3 pounds. Melt, and, when partly cold, stir in rose water, 1 pint; oil of rosemary, 20 drops; ottar of roses, 25 drops. The appearance of this pomatum is much improved by "pinking" it slightly with alkanet.

Essence of Roses.

1. Ottar of roses, 7 drachms; spirit, 1 gallon. Mix.

2. Rose-leaves, 4 parts; water, 12 parts. Distil off one-half. When a sufficient quantity of this water has been obtained, it must be used as water upon fresh rose-leaves, and the same process must be repeated to the fourth, fifth, or even the sixth time, according to the quality desired.

French Milk of Roses.

1. Rose-water, 50 parts; extract of lead, 1 part. Dissolve, and add a little ottar of roses.

2. Oil of almonds, 1 pound; blanched sweet almonds, 5 pounds; pearl-ash, 8 ounces; castile soap, 12 ounces. Reduce to a milk with rose-water, 3½ gallons. Then add ottar of roses, 20 drops; oil of lavender, 4 drachms; spirit, 3 quarts.

3. Jordan almonds (blanched), 6 pounds; oil of lavender, 1 ounce; spirit of wine, 1 gallon; rose-water, 3 gallons; ottar of roses, 20 drops; bichloride of mercury, 4 drachms; hydrochloric acid, 3 drachms. Reduce the almonds to a milk with the rose-water, and strain, then add the other ingredients. Rub the bichloride and acid with half a pint of hot water until dissolved, before you add them to the mixture.

Honey of Roses.

Fresh rose-leaves, 1 part; water, 1 part. Steep for one week, then add honey, 3 parts. Steep one week longer, and strain with expression.

Oil of Roses.

1. Olive oil, 1 pound; ottar of roses, 50 drops; oil of rosemary, 20 drops. Mix.

2. Roses (barely opened), 12 ounces; olive oil, 16 ounces. Beat them together in a mortar, let them remain for a few days, then express the oil.

3. (Red.) Olive oil, 1 pound; alkanet, ½ ounce, or less; ottar of roses, 40 drops; oil of rosemary, 35 drops. Mix.

Rose Water.

1. Rose petals, 60 pounds; water, 26 gallons. Draw over twenty gallons.

2. Rose petals, 5 bushels; water sufficient. Draw over nine gallons. Rose-root water and yellow sandal-wood water, are often sold for this article.

Rose Wine.

Loaf-sugar, 100 pounds; water, 33 gallons; rose-leaves (red), 4 gallons. Put them (hot) into a clean cask; let them stand till cold, then ferment, and afterwards add spirit, 3 gallons; cochineal (powdered), 1 ounce; a few drops of ottar of roses. Let it stand one month and rack it

Economical Rouge.

1. Finely-powdered carmine, 1 ounce; white pomatum, 7 ounces. Mix, and pot it for use.

2. French chalk (finely powdered), 1 pound; carmine, 3 ounces; oil of almonds to mix.

Rouge for Cleaning Plate.

Precipitated subcarbonate of iron, 3 parts; prepared chalk, 3 parts; Armenian bole, 2 parts. Mix. Be sure to reduce the articles to the finest powder possible.

Rouge for the Complexion.

Carmine in fine powder, 1 part; levigated French chalk, 5 parts. Mix.

Jeweller's Rouge.

Sulphate of iron, 1 part; water, 15 parts. Dissolve and precipitate the oxide of iron with a solution of potass or pearlash; wash the precipitate, dry and calcine it until it becomes of a bright-red colour.

Liquid Rouge.

1. Carmine, 2 parts; pearlash, 1 part; water, 9 parts. Mix.

2. Rouge, 1 part; alcohol, 1 part; wine vinegar, 1 part; water, 1 part. Mix.

Pure Rouge.

Take safflowers, any quantity; wash them until the water comes off colourless, dry, powder, and digest in a weak solution of carbonate of soda; then place some fine cotton wool at the bottom of the vessel, and precipitate the colouring matter by gradually adding lemon-juice or white vinegar till it ceases to produce a precipitate. Next wash the cotton in cold water, then dissolve out the colour with a fresh solution of soda; add a quantity of finely-powdered French chalk, proportional to the intended quality of the rouge; mix well, and precipitate as before; lastly, collect the powder, dry with great care, and triturate it with a minute quantity of oil of olives, to render it smooth and adhesive.

This is the only article which will brighten a lady's complexion, without injuring the skin.

Spanish Ladies' Rouge.

Take tincture of carmine or cochineal, any quantity, wet some cotton wool with it, and repeat the operation until the wool has sufficient colour.

To solder together Rubies.

Apply them to a strong flame by means of the blow-pipe, and when sufficiently soft unite them with care; they will neither lose their colour nor weight.

Factitious Ruby.

Strass, 40 parts; oxide of manganese, 1 part. Mix, and treat as for topaz.

Rue Water.

Rue, 15 pounds; water, 18 gallons. Distil over fifteen gallons.

Rum Shrub.

1. Tartaric acid, 5 pounds; pale sugar, 1 cwt.; oil of lemon, 4 drachms; oil of orange, 4 drachms. Put them into a large cask (80 gallons), and add water, 10 gallons. Rummage until the sugar and acid are dissolved, then add rum (proof), 20 gallons; water to make up 55 gallons in the whole; colouring, 1 quart, or more. Fine with twelve eggs. If you add twelve Seville oranges (sliced), and three-quarters of an ounce of bitter almonds (bruised), it will improve the flavour.

2. Sugar, 200 pounds. Dissolve in water, 50 gallons. Put the syrup into a cask, then add rum, 30 gallons, or less; oranges (sliced), 2 dozen; lemons (sliced), 2 dozen; cassia (bruised), ½ ounce; cloves (bruised), ½ ounce; bitter almonds (bruised), ½ ounce; Guinea pepper (powdered), 2 ounces. And as much tartaric acid dissolved in ten times its weight of water as will give it the necessary acidity; let it stand for a week, frequently stirring, then add 20 eggs (whites, yellows, and shells). Rummage well and bung tight.

Prince Rupert's Metal.

Copper, 2 parts. Melt, and add zinc, 1 part.

Rushlights.

Make them in the same way as dip candles.

Ruspini's Styptic.

Sulphate of iron, 1 part; water, 50 parts; alcohol, 14 parts. Mix.

Ruspini's Tincture.

Orris root, 8 parts; rhatany, 8 parts; cloves, 1 part; alcohol, 30 parts; essence of musk to every pint, 5 drops. Mix.

Saffron Cake.

Hay saffron, 1 part; petals of safflowers, 8 parts; rape oil, 1 part, or less. Make them into a cake.

Saffron Lozenges.

Finely-powdered hay saffron, 1 ounce; finely-powdered sugar, 1 pound; finely-powdered starch, 8 ounces. Mucilage to mix.

Sage Wine.

Follow the same plan as for rhubarb wine.

Sago Jelly.

Sago, 1 pound; water, 5 pints. Wash the sago, then boil it with the water until reduced to a transparent jelly; lastly, flavour it to taste.

Elastic and Water-proof Paint for Sail Cloth, &c.

Ochre, 96 parts; lamp-black, 16 parts; boiled oil to mix. Then add yellow soap, 2 parts, dissolved in water, 8 parts. Well mix, and apply two coats of this mixture with a paint-brush, at intervals of two or three days; lastly, give a finishing coat of varnish formed of lamp-black and boiled oil, well ground together. Sufficient boiled oil must be used to reduce the mixture to the consistence of a thick varnish.

White Fire.

1. Nitre, 50 parts; sulphur, 14 parts; sulphuret of antimony, 8 parts. Mix.

2. Nitre, 75 parts; sulphur, 24 parts; charcoal, 1 part. Mix.

3. Meal powder, 80 parts; fine borings, 20 parts. Mix well.

White Gooseberry Wine.

Cold water and bruised fruit, each 9 gallons; lump-sugar, 18 pounds. Ferment, then add bitter almonds, ¼ ounce; brandy or spirit, 1 gallon, or less.

Common White Lead.

Pure white lead, 1 cwt.; sulphate of barytes, 2 cwt.; chalk, 3 cwt. Mix.

White Mead Wine.

Honey, 56 pounds; water, 18 gallons; cider, 6 gallons; sugar, 25 pounds. Boil and ferment, then add spirit, 2 gallons; bruised bitter almonds, ¼ ounce; white tartar, 2 ounces; finings, 1 pint.

White Metal.

1. Brass, 1 part; tin, 2 parts; antimony, 4 parts.

2. Lead, 20 parts; bismuth, 12 parts; antimony, 1 part. Fuse.

White Ointment.

1. Simple ointment, 1 pound; ceruse, 2 ounces. Mix.

2. Lard and suet, each 1 pound; carbonate of lead, ½ pound. Mix.

White Paint.

Whiting, 5 cwt.; white lead, 4 cwt.; lime-water, 20 gallons. Factitious linseed oil to mix.

White Pectoral Lozenges.

Sugar, 2 pounds; starch, 1 pound; flowers of benzoin, 1 drachm; balsam of tolu, 1 drachm. Mucilage to mix.

White Poppy Water.

The flowers, 20 pounds; water, 22 gallons. Draw over twenty gallons.

White Precipitate.

Sal ammoniac, 4 parts; bichloride of mercury, 6 parts. Dissolve in water, and precipitate with a solution of potass.

White Precipitate Ointment.

Lard, 15 ounces; white precipitate, 1 ounce. Mix.

White Spirit Varnish.

Strongest alcohol, 100 parts; sandarach, 25 parts; tears mastic, 6 parts; elemi, 3 parts; Venice turpentine, 7 parts. Dissolve in a closely-corked vessel.

White Stars for Rockets.

Nitre, 16 parts; sulphur, 8 parts; meal powder, 7 parts. Reduce them to fine powder, then mix up with spirits of wine and camphor.

White Hard Spirit Varnish.

Gum sandarach, 2½ pounds; alcohol (65 op.), 1 gallon. Place them in a strong, well-closed vessel, and apply the heat of warm water with occasional agitation until dissolved; next add pale turpentine varnish, 1 pint. Mix well, and let the whole rest for twenty-four hours.

To clean White Veils.

Clean them with a solution of white soap, and rinse well, then pass them through another water, to which two or three drops of liquid blue have been added; lastly, starch them and keep clapping them with the hands until dry.

Factitious White Lead.

Hard cake stearine, 100 parts; bleached resin, 90 parts; fine potato starch, 25 parts. Melt and well mix, then add mucilage, 20 parts. Stir well until nearly cold, then form into cakes. If well managed, this recipe will form a good article for all the commoner purposes for which white wax is required, especially for making ointments.

Virgin White Wax.

White wax, 3 parts; cake stearine, 2 parts; mucilage, 1 part. Melt and stir well: when nearly cold, form into cakes as before.

To convert Red Wine into White Wine.

Skimmed milk, 4 quarts; red wine, 90 or 100 gallons. Mix well.

Whiting.

Take soft chalk and grind it with water; pump off the milky fluid and let it settle, then decant the water, and dry the residue.

Wilson's Liquid Asphalt.

Bruised asphalt, 2 parts; balsam of copaiva, 4 parts; spirits of turpentine, 3 parts. Mix. This liquid, thinned with a little spirits of turpentine, forms an indestructible ink, capable of resisting all the usual reagents.

Prismatic Diamond Crystals for Windows.

A hot solution of sulphate of magnesia, and a clear solution of gum arabic, mixed together. Lay it on hot. For a margin or for figures, wipe off the part you wish to remain clear with a wet towel.

Windsor Ale. (For Private Families.)

Pale malt, 5 quarts; hops, 50 pounds; honey, 12 pounds; corianders, 1 pound; orange-peel, 10 ounces; grain of paradise, 2 pounds; ground liquorice-root, 4 pounds. To produce two barrels and three quarters per quarter.

Zinc Lozenges.

Sulphate of zinc, 1 ounce; lump-sugar, 3 pounds. Mucilage to mix. Add a little essence of lemon.

Compound Ointment of Carbonate of Zinc.

Wax ointment, 5 ounces; carbonate of zinc and Goulard's extract, each 1 ounce. Mix.

Ointment of Oxide of Zinc.

Flowers of zinc, 2 ounces; simple ointment, 1 pound. Mix. Used in ophthalmia.

Windsor Soap

1. Hard soap, 7 pounds; water to soften, then add oil of caraway, 2 drachms; finely-powdered cassia, 3 ounces. Form into cakes.

2. Hard white soap, 7 pounds; oil of caraway, 3 drachms; essence of bergamot, 6 drachms. Reduce to a paste with water, and mould.

3. White hard soap, 1 cwt.; potato starch, 56 pounds; pipe-clay, 16 pounds; pearlash, 4 pounds; oil of cassia and oil of lavender, each 8 ounces; oil of caraway and oil of origanum, each 6 ounces; oil of cloves, 1 ounce; bergamot, 7 ounces. Mix.

4. White soap, 14 pounds; oil of caraway, 3 ounces; essence of musk, 1 ounce; oil of origanum, ½ ounce; oil of lavender and essence of bergamot, each ¼ ounce; finely-powdered cassia, 8 ounces. Reduce with water, and form into cakes.

5. White hard soap, 56 pounds; white pipe-clay, 50 pounds; white pearlash, 6 pounds. Reduce them to a paste with water, then add oil of cassia and oil of caraway, each 8 ounces; oil of lavender, 6 ounces; oil of cloves, 1 ounce; essence of lemon and essence of bergamot, each 5 ounces. Mix, and form into cakes as before.

6. *Brown.*—Brown pearlash soap and white hard soap, each ½ cwt.; pearlash or soda and yellow ochre, each 7 pounds; powdered cassia, 3 pounds; powdered cloves, 1 pound; oil of caraway and oil of lavender, each 8 ounces; essence of bergamot and essence of lemon, each 12 ounces. Mix.

7. *Brown.*—Good brown pearlash soap, fuller's earth, and white hard soap, each ¼ cwt.; soda and ochre, each 8 pounds; powdered cassia, 5 pounds; powdered cloves, ½ pound; oil of caraway, 8 ounces. Mix.

8. *Brown.*—Good brown soap, 2 cwt.; white hard soap and fuller's earth, each 1 cwt.; yellow ochre, ¼ cwt.; pearlash, 25 pounds; oil of caraway and oil of rosemary, each 1 pound; oil of lavender, 2 pounds; essence of bergamot, 3 pounds; finely-powdered cassia, 18 pounds; finely-powdered cloves, ½ pound. Mix.

9. *Very fine.*—Beef suet, 9 parts; olive oil, 1 part. Saponify with caustic soda ley, then collect the paste, and add one per cent. of the following perfume: Oil of caraway, 16 parts; oil of rosemary and oil of lavender, each 5 parts. Mix well, and mould.

To clean Wine Decanters.

Use a little pearlash or soda, and some cinders and water. Rinse them well out with clean water.

Family Wine.

Black currants, red currants, white currants, ripe cherries, raspberries, and gooseberries, each 28 pounds; water, 9 gallons. Steep for three or four days, frequently stirring up the mash, then strain with expression, and add to each gallon of the liquor good moist sugar, 3 pounds; cream of tartar (dis.), 3 drachms. Ferment, cork, and lastly add good spirit at the rate of two to five per cent.

Pommade avec l'Iodate de Zinc.

Iodate of zinc, 1 part; lard, 2 parts. Mix.

Wine Test.

Expose equal parts of sulphur and powdered oyster-shells to a white heat for fifteen minutes, and when cold, add an equal quantity of cream of tartar; these are to be put into a strong bottle with common water, to boil for an hour, and the solution is afterwards to be decanted into ounce phials, adding twenty drops of muriatic acid to each. This liquor will precipitate the least quantity of lead from wines, in a very sensible black precipitate. As iron might be accidentally contained in the wine, the muriatic acid is added to prevent its precipitation. Lead will not only correct the acidity of wine, but remove the rancidity of oils, a property well known to painters.

To Allay Inordinate Fermentation in Wine.

1. To each barrel add mustard, $\frac{1}{2}$ pound.
2. Add $\frac{1}{2000}$ to $\frac{1}{1000}$ part of *sulphite* of lime.
3. Rack into a clean fresh-sulphured cask.

To Detect Honey in Wine.

The following method is said to be practised in Paris: Take a phial containing four or five spoonfuls of Spanish wine, and when quite filled, stop the mouth of the phial by placing the thumb tightly on it; plunge it into a basin of water, and, while thus plunged, withdraw the thumb. If the wine be adulterated, the honey which enters into the composition will sink to the bottom. When the precipitation has ceased, replace the thumb on the mouth of the phial, and bring it up. The liquor, deprived of its honey, frequently proves to be some meagre wine, and sometimes nothing but water, which had held the honey in solution.

To Flavour Wine.

When the vinous fermentation is about half over, the flavouring ingredients are to be put into the vat and well stirred into the contents. If almonds form a component part, they are first to be beaten to a paste and mixed with a pint or two of the must. Nutmegs, cinnamon, ginger, seeds, &c., should, before they are put into the vat, be reduced to powder, and mixed with some of the must.

Animal Matter and Peat.

There are some sources of alkali for converting peat into soluble matter. Of these, the chief is animal matter. Here we have ammonia produced. It has been actually proved, by experiment, that a dead horse can convert twenty tons (or cubic yards) of peat into a valuable manure, richer and more lasting than stable dung; a barrel of alewives is equal to a load of peat. The next great and prolific source of ammonia is urine. The urine of one cow for a winter, mixed up as it is daily collected with peat, is sufficient to manure half an acre of land with twenty loads of manure of the best quality, while her solid evacuations and litter, for the same period affords only seventeen loads, whose value is only about one-half that of the former.

To improve Poor Wine.

Rack it and add one per cent. of sugar or honey, and five per cent. of spirit, then fine it. For weak-flavoured Sherry add half an ounce or an ounce of bruised bitter almonds to every hundred gallons, with about a quarter of an ounce of cloves and cassia, also bruised. For Port deficient in astringency and flavour, add some red tartar and catechu, dissolved separately in hot water, and the cloves and cassia as for Sherry.

2. Rack the wine, then add five pounds of flour and three pounds of sugar, with four or five gallons or more of spirit to every hundred gallons; let stand twelve hours and fine.

To Mellow Wine.

Wine, either in bottle or wood, will mellow much quicker when only covered with pieces of bladder well secured, than with corks or bungs. The bladder allows the watery particles to escape, but is impervious to alcohol.

To remove Ropiness from Wine.

Add a little catechu or a small quantity of the bruised berries of the mountain ash.

To remove the taste of the Cask from Wine.

Finest oil of olives, 1 pound. Put it into the hogshead, bung close, and roll it about, or otherwise well agitate it, for three or four hours, then *gib* and allow it to settle. The olive oil will gradually rise to the top and carry the ill flavour with it.

To restore Flat Wine.

Add four or five pounds of sugar, honey, or bruised raisins, to every hundred gallons, and bung close. A little spirits may also be added.

To Polish Wood.

Take a piece of pumice-stone and water, and pass regularly over the work until the rising of the grain is cut down; then take powdered tripoli and boiled linseed oil, and polish the work to a bright surface.

To Roughen Wine.

Take bruised sloes or powdered catechu, and add to the wine in suitable proportions.

To Gather and Preserve Woods.

Woods should be gathered and exposed in a dry situation, to a heat of 90 to 150° Fahr., until sufficiently dry; the larger sorts are better chipped before drying.

Stains for Wood.

Red.—Brazil-wood, 11 parts; alum, 4 parts; water, 85 parts. Boil.

Blue.—Logwood, 7 parts; blue vitriol, 1 part; water, 22 parts. Boil.

Black.—Logwood, 9 parts; sulphate of iron, 1 part; water, 25 parts. Boil.

Green.—Verdigris, 1 part; vinegar, 3 parts. Dissolve.

Yellow.—French berries, 7 parts; water, 10 parts; alum, 1 part. Boil.

Purple.—Logwood, 11 parts; alum, 3 parts; water, 29 parts. Boil.

To restore Musty Wine.

1. Bruised mustard-seed, ½ pound; camphor, ¼ ounce; bruised cloves, ½ ounce. And add them to 90 or 100 gallons of the wine, then bung close.

2. Add a few sticks of clean fresh-burnt charcoal, and bung close for fourteen or fifteen days.

3. Put in some new bread with a few cloves stuck in it, and bung close

To Preserve Woodwork.

Take boiled oil and finely-powdered charcoal, mix to the consistence of a paint, and give the wood two or three coats with this composition. Well adapted for water-spouts, casks, &c.

Cautions to Woollen Manufacturers.

It is not generally known, that flocks mixed with, or moistened with oil, will sometimes take fire. From this cause a very extensive fire has lately occurred.

To Free Trees, &c., from Worms and Caterpillars.

Flowers of sulphur, 1 part; starch, 3 parts. Make into a paste with water, and apply hot with a painter's brush.

Worm Lozenges.

Powdered lump-sugar, 10 parts; starch, 5 parts. Mix with mucilage, and to every ounce of the dough add twelve grains of calomel, then divide into twenty-grain lozenges. Dose—two to six or eight. A mild purgative should be taken a few hours after sucking the lozenges.

Worm Oil.

Oil of turpentine, 1 pound; castor oil, 5 pounds. Mix.

Extract of Wormwood.

Prepared from the tops by decoction and evaporation.

Salt of Wormwood.

Take wormwood ashes, dissolve them in water, filter and evaporate to dryness.

To Cool Worts.

Pass them through a pipe, like a still-worm, immersed in a stream of water; the wort will flow out of the lower end cool enough for fermentation.

To Cure a Cough or Cold.

The editor of the Baltimore Farmer and Gardener says, that the best remedy he ever tried in his family for a cough or cold is a decoction of the leaves of the pine tree, sweetened with loaf-sugar, to be freely drank warm when going to bed at night, and cold throughout the day.

A certain Cure for the Piles.

Take 1 scruple of powdered opium, 2 scruples flour of sulphur, and 1 ounce of simple cerate. Keep the affected parts well anointed. Be prudent in your diet.

To Cure Hydrophobia.

Make a strong wash by dissolving two table-spoonfuls of the chloruret of lime in half a pint of water, and instantly and repeatedly bathe the part bitten. The poison will in this way be decomposed. It has proved successful when applied within six hours after the animal has been bitten. I wish these facts generally known, as they may be of service to our fellow-citizens at large.

To restore Writing Effaced with Chlorine.

1. Expose it to the vapour of sulphuret of ammonia, or dip it into a solution of the sulphuret.

2. Ferrocyanide of potass, 5 parts; water, 85 parts. Dissolve, and immerse the paper in the fluid, then slightly acidulate the solution with sulphuric acid.

Blue Writing Fluid.

1. Ferrocyanide of iron, powdered, and strong hydrochloric acid, each 2 parts. Dissolve, and dilute with soft water.

2. *Indestructible.*—Shell lac, 4 parts; borax, 2 parts; soft water, 36 parts. Boil in a close vessel till dissolved; then filter, and take of gum arabic, 2 parts; soft water, 4 parts. Dissolve, and mix the two solutions together, and boil for five minutes as before, occasionally stirring to promote their union; when cold, add a sufficient quantity of finely-powdered indigo and lamp-black to colour; lastly, let it stand for two or three hours, until the coarser powder has subsided, and bottle for use. Use this fluid with a clean pen, and keep it in glass or earthen inkstands, as many substances will decompose it while in the liquid state. When dry, it will resist the action of water, oil, turpentine, alcohol, diluted sulphuric acid, diluted hydrochloric acid, oxalic acid, chlorine, and the caustic alkalies and alkaline earths.

To Gild or Silver Writing.

Let there be a little gum and lump-sugar in the ink you write with; when dry, breathe on it and apply the leaf.

To give an appearance of Age to Writing.

Infuse a drachm of saffron in half a pint of ink, then write with it.

Substitute for Yeast.

Take wheat flour, 8 pounds, and water to make it of the consistence of cream. Boil for an hour, then add sugar, 1 pound; yeast, ½ pint. Ferment.

To improve Bad Yeast.

Add a little flour and sugar, and let them work together for a short time.

To Preserve Yeast.

1. Take a close canvass-bag, fill it with yeast, then press out the water and make it into cakes. I have tasted bread made with yeast preserved in this manner, and it has been excellent. The mode of using it is to dilute it with warm water, to which a little sugar and flour are added.

2. Whisk the yeast to a froth, and then with a paint-brush lay it on writing-paper; continue coating the paper, every time it dries, until a cake is formed, then divide it into squares with a knife.

To remove the Acidity from Yeast.

Take yeast and add subcarbonate of magnesia to it, until the acid is neutralized.

Factitious Yellow Diamond.

1. Strass, 500 parts; glass of antimony, 10 parts. Fuse.
2. Strass, 500 parts; chloride of silver, 25 parts. Mix, and fuse.

Yellow Dipping Metal.

Copper, 19 parts; spelter, 6 parts. Mix.

Yellow Enamel.

White oxide of antimony, 1 part; white lead, 2 parts; alum and sal ammoniac, each 1 part. Mix in fine powder, and apply heat just sufficient to decompose the ammoniac.

Yellow Lake.

French berries, 1 pound; pearlash, 2 ounces; water, 1 gallon. Boil for one hour, then strain and add gradually a solution of alum until it ceases to produce a precipitate; collect the powder, and form it into drops.

Cheap Yellow Paint.

Whiting, 3 cwt.; ochre, 2 cwt.; ground white-lead, 25 pounds. Factitious linseed oil to grind.

Yellow Sealing-Wax.

Shell lac and yellow resin, each 2 parts; Turpeth's mineral, 1 part Powder fine and mix with heat. Observe not to burn it.

Yellow Stain for Glass.

Chloride of silver, 1 part; burnt pipe-clay, 3 parts. Reduce to fine powder and mix. This stain must be applied to the back of the glass.

Soft Soap.

Ten pounds of potash mixed in ten gallons of warm water, over-night; in the morning boil it, adding 6 pounds of grease; then put it in a barrel, adding 15 gallons of warm water.

To Cure Criss in the Neck.

As soon as you find your neck stiff or turned to one side by the contraction of nerves, apply over the place diseased a piece of black oil-cloth, with the right side to the skin, and then with a thick handkerchief tie up the neck; in a short time the part will grow moist, and by leaving it thus during the night or through the day, the pain will be removed.

To Stop Diarrhœa.

Take half a pint of brandy and stir it with an iron nearly red-hot, previously adding loaf-sugar sufficient to make it agreeably sweet. A spoonful or two to be taken two or three times a day.

A quick Purge for Horses when Bound.

Take one pint of olive oil and half a pint of soft soap. Mix. Given as a drench.

Ultramarine.

Take lapis lazuli, 8 parts; heat it, and throw it into cold water, then grind to a fine powder, and add resin, 3 parts; turpentine, wax, oil, each, 1 part. Melt the last four with a gentle heat, then knead the lapis lazuli with it to a dough; repeat the operation in warm water, and change the water, until it is no longer coloured blue; allow the several washings to settle, and sort them as to quality.

Ultramarine Ashes.

Take the residuum from the manufacture of ultramarine, and apply a sufficient heat to drive off the wax and oil, then well wash the remainder.

M. Gmelin's Ultramarine.

Sulphur, 2 parts; dry carbonate of soda, 1 part. Put them into a Hessian crucible, cover it up, and apply heat until the mass fuses; then sprinkle into it gradually a mixture of silicate of soda and aluminate of soda; (the first containing 72 parts of silica, the second, 70 parts of alumina); lastly, calcine for one hour, and wash in pure water.

M. Robiquet's Ultramarine.

Kaolin, sulphur, dry carbonate of soda. Mix, and calcine at a red heat. The proportions should be such, that the resulting compound may be formed of silica, 35 parts; alumina, 33 parts; soda, 22 parts; sulphur, 3 to 10 parts.

Uncoloured Sealing-Wax.

Shell lac, 2 parts; yellow resin, 3 parts; turpentine, 1 part. Mix carefully by heating. This may be coloured to fancy, or used as it is.

Usquebaugh—(Escubac).

Saffron one ounce, catechu three ounces, ambergris half a grain, dates without their kernels, and raisins, each three ounces, jujubes six ounces, anise-seed, cloves, mace, and coriander seed one drachm, cinnamon two drachms, proof spirit six quarts; pound the ingredients, infuse for a week, and distil.

This spirituous preparation is generally employed as an adjunct in making liquors; it is also used for flavouring ices, liqueurs, bon-bons, &c., or anything in which liquors are introduced.

Drogheda Usquebaugh.

1. Nutmegs, cloves, cassia, aniseed, each (bruised), 1 pound; caraways, corianders, saffron, each (bruised), 2 pounds; brandy or spirit, 100 gallons; raisins, 10 pounds; powdered liquorice root, 10 pounds. Macerate for ten days, then add water according to the intended strength of the liqueur.

2. Plain spirit, 50 gallons; brandy, 50 gallons; raisins (stoned), 50 pounds; sugar, 100 pounds; cassia, cloves, nutmegs, bruised cardamoms, each, half a pound; saffron, dried orange-peel, each, 2 pounds. Macerate for twenty days.

Gargle for Relaxation of the Uvula.

Tincture of catechu, 8 parts; laudanum, 1 part; rose-water, 60 parts Mix.

Essence of Vanilla.

Vanilla (cut small), 6 pounds; cloves, 4 drachms; musk, 1 drachm; spirit of ambrette, 1 gallon; alcohol, ¾ gallon. Digest for two months in a heat of 100 to 130° Fahr.

Vanilla Lozenges.

Powdered vanilla, 4 ounces; sugar, 2 pounds Mix with mucilage.

Varnish for Toys.

Copal, 7 parts; mastic, 1 part; Venice turpentine, ½ part; strongest alcohol, 11 parts. Dissolve the copal first, with the aid of a little camphor, then add the mastic, &c. and thin with alcohol as required.

To clear. Varnish.

Use a ley of potash or soda, mixed with a little powdered chalk. Do not make the liquor too strong of the alkali.

To polish Varnish.

Take 2 ounces of tripoli powdered, put it in an earthen pot, with water to cover it: then take a piece of white flannel, lay it over a piece of cork or rubber, and proceed to polish the varnish, always wetting it with the tripoli and water. It will be known when the process is finished by wiping a part of the work with a sponge, and observing whether there is a fair even gloss. When this is the case, take a bit of mutton suet and fine flour, and clean the work.

To ascertain the Quality of Veal.

Choose the meat the kidney of which is well covered in white fat, the lean dry and white, and the suet firm. If clammy or spotted, the veal is stale. The flesh of the cow calf is whitest, but that of the bull calf firmest. The whitest veal is not the most juicy, having generally been made so by lengthened bleeding.

To decolour Vegetable Liquors.

Mix a portion of finely-powdered fresh-burnt animal charcoal (bone black) with the liquor, and shake it occasionally for a few days, then filter.

To purify Vegetable Oil.

Oil, 50 gallons: roche alum, 7 pounds, dissolved in water, 25 pounds. Mix, and rummage well for one hour, then add strong oil of vitriol, ¾ gallons. Agitate for two hours more, then let it stand, and draw off the clear in three or four days, and wash it with hot water. Either of the processes named for Rape Oil may also be followed.

Vegetable Rouge, for the Complexion.

Finely-powdered carmine, 1 part; levigated French chalk, 4 parts, clarified lard, 4 parts. Mix on a slab, and perfume with ottar of roses or lavender.

To preserve Vegetables and their Juices.

Take strong glass bottles and fill them with the article to be preserved, cork and wire them tight; then place them in a kettle of boiling water, heat it to the boiling point, and let it cool.

To make Vegetables eat Tender.

Put a spoonful or two of pearlash or soda into the water you boil them in.

To pickle Vegetables in Brine.

Take the articles to be preserved and put them into pickle bottles, fill them with a strained saturated solution of common salt, and cork immediately.

To preserve or pickle Vegetables in Vinegar.

Soak them for some hours in brine, then drain them, put them into bottles, and pour on them boiling vinegar until *quite* covered. Cork immediately.

Factitious Venice Turpentine.

Resin, oil of turpentine, equal parts. Mix, with heat.

To ventilate Rooms, &c.

Arrange the funnel over the gas or lamp by which the room is lighted, and unite it with the open air by means of a small tin pipe (say one to two inches in diameter). Experiment has proved that by means of a small pipe of the class named, the air of a room will undergo constant renovation, while the deoxidized air from the light will at the same time be carried off.

To ventilate Ships.

Air-pipes are used for drawing foul air out of ships, or other close places, by means of fire. One extremity is placed in a hole in the side of a furnace, (closed in every part excepting the outlet for the smoke;) the other in the place which it is designed to purify. The rarefaction produced by the fire causes a current of air to be determined to it, and the only means by which the air can arrive at the fire being through the pipe, a quick circulation, in the place where the extremity of the pipe may be situated, is consequently produced.

Pommade De Veratrine.

Veratrine, 4 grains; prepared lard, 1 ounce. Mix. Used in rheumatism and gout.

English Verdigris.

1. Blue vitriol, 14 pounds; sugar of lead, 7 pounds; alum, 2 pounds; plaster of Paris, 10 pounds. Reduce them to a fine powder, and grind to a thick paste with water, then dry.

2. Sulphate of copper, 12 parts; sugar of lead, 15 parts. Dissolve each separately in water, and mix the solution; collect and preserve the precipitate.

Verdigris Ointment.

Powdered verdigris, 1 pound; suet, 14 pounds; lard, 14 pounds; yellow resin, 1 pound. Mix. Detersive.

Blue Verditer.

Sulphate of copper, 1 part; sal ammoniac, 1 part; lime, 8 parts. Mix the above with a sufficient quantity of water; then dry and grind it into a fine powder for use.

Spanish Vermilion for the Toilette.

Take an alkaline solution of bastard saffron, and precipitate the colour with lemon juice; mix the precipitate with a sufficient quantity of finely-powdered French chalk and lemon-juice, then add a little perfume.

To fine Vidonia.

Rack it on the lees of Madeira, then fine it with isinglass finings.

Vinegar Black for Bookbinders, &c.

Steep iron filings or rusty iron in good vinegar for two or three days, then strain off the liquor.

Paste resembling Vinegar Garnet.

Plain paste, 1000 parts; glass of antimony, 500 parts; calcined iron, 16 parts. Add the antimony last.

Malt Vinegar.

Good crushed malt, 1 boll. Mash at three times, at 160°, 190° and 208° Fahr., so as to produce 100 gallons of wort; cool to 75°, then add three gallons of beer yeast, and ferment. In thirty-five or forty hours rack it into casks till they are two-thirds full, then keep it in an even temperature of about 70° Fahr. with the bungs out, and where there is a free circulation of air.

Vinegar of Cantharides.

Powdered cantharides, 1 ounce; acetic acid, 8 ounces. Macerate for a week, then strain. Used as an extemporaneous blister.

Sugar Vinegar.

Water, 1 gallon; sugar, 1¼ pound. Dissolve with heat, (say about 75° Fahr.) then add yeast, 1 ounce. Ferment, decant the clear, and add cream of tartar, 1 ounce; bruised raisins, 1 ounce. Let it stand until sufficiently sour.

Vinegars from Orange and Elder Flowers, Clove Gilliflowers, Musk Roses, &c.

Dry an ounce of either of the above flowers, (except the orange flowers, which will not bear drying,) for two days in the sun; then put them into a bottle, pour on them a pint of vinegar, closely stop the bottle, and infuse fifteen days in a moderate heat or the sun. Vinegars of any other flowers, as tarragon, &c., may be made in a similar manner.

Violet-Blue Glazing.

Tartar, flints, each, 116 parts; zaffre, manganese, each, 1 part.

Essence of Violets.

Alcohol, 1 pint; orris powder, 4 ounces. Mix.

Flowers of Sal Ammoniac.

Take grey sal ammoniac, powder it and sublime into a large receiver.

Plaster of Sal Ammoniac.

Simple diachylon, or wax plaster, 4 parts; castile soap, 2 parts; sal ammoniac part. Mix. This plaster is said to be useful in white swellings.

Salberg Bug Wash.

Bichloride of mercury, 2 parts; spirits of turpentine, 6 parts; muriatic acid, 1 part; water, 100 parts. Mix, and thoroughly wash the cracks and joints of the piece of furniture with this liquor.

Salt of Sorel.

1. Take sorel leaves; bruise them, and express the juice; let it settle; decant the clear and crystallize.
2. Oxalic acid, 1 part; water sufficient to barely dissolve. Add a solution of subcarbonate of potash in water, until it ceases to produce a precipitate, then filter.

Sap Green.

Buckthorn juice, 1 pound; gum arabic, 1 ounce. Dissolve and evaporate.

Factitious Sapphire.

1. Oxide of cobalt, 1 part; strass, 80 parts.
2. Paste or strass, 2300 parts; oxide of cobalt, 34 parts. Fuse carefully for thirty hours.
3. Plain paste, 100 parts; smalts, 12 parts; manganese, 1 part. As before.
4. Plain paste, 10 pounds; zaffre, 3 drachms; precipitate of gold and tin, 1 drachm. As before.

Compound Decoction of Sarsaparilla.

Sarsaparilla root (bruised), 1 pound; boiling water, 1 gallon. Simmer gently for two hours, adding a little water occasionally to make up for evaporation, then add sassafras root (sliced), 1 ounce; guaiacum root (rasped), 1 ounce; liquorice root (bruised), 1 ounce; mezerion root (bruised), 1 ounce. Boil for a quarter of an hour and strain. Dose, two to six ounces, three times a day.

Extract of Sarsaparilla.

Bruised sarsaparilla, 1 part; water, 16 parts. Boil until reduced to ten parts, then pour off the clear, and add to the residue water, 6 parts. Boil down to four parts, pour off the clear, and evaporate in a steam heat.

Sauce Aristocratique.

Green walnut juice, 1 part; anchovies, 1 part; cloves, mace, and pimento, bruised, one drachm of each to every pound of juice. Boil and strain, then to every pint add one pint of vinegar, half a pint of port wine, quarter of a pint of soy, and a few shalotts. Let the whole stand a few days, and decant the clear liquor.

Sauce au Roy.

Brown vinegar (good), 3 quarts; soy, ¼ pint; walnut ketchup, ¼ pint; cloves, ½ dozen; shalotts, ½ dozen; cayenne pepper, 1 ounce. Mix, and let them stand for fourteen days.

Saur Kraut.

Take white cabbages; slice them horizontally, and place them in a barrel with common salt, in alternate layers; cover them over with salt and press them down tight; keep them in a cool place for some weeks. Spice may be added to taste.

To Prepare Intestines for Sausages.

Take the intestines, cut off the extraneous fat and peritoneal membrane, turn them inside out and wash them clean, then soak them for twenty-four hours in a pail of water, to which a little chloride of lime or potass has been added; then tear off a part of the mucous membrane to thin them, and wash them well in two or three pails of clean water.

Savine Ointment.

Yellow wax, 1 pound; savine leaves, 1 pound; lard, 5 pounds. Mix. Applied to blisters and ulcers to keep them open.

Savoy Biscuit.

Sugar, 12 parts; flour, 7 parts; eggs, 12 parts; lemon rind (ground), to flavour. After being in the oven a few minutes, grate on a little sugar

Saxon Blue.

1. Saxon blue may be successfully imitated, by mixing with a divided earth prussiate of iron, at the moment of its formation and precipitation.

Into a solution of 144 grains of sulphate of iron, pour a solution of prussiate of potash.

At the time of the formation of iron, add, in the same vessel, a solution of two ounces of alum, and pour in with it the solution of potash, just sufficient to decompose the sulphate of alumine; for a dose of alkali superabundant to the decomposition of that salt might alter the prussiate of iron. It will, therefore, be much better to leave a little alum, which may afterwards be carried off by washing.

As soon as the alkaline liquor is added, the alumine precipitated becomes exactly mixed with the prussiate of iron, the intensity of which it lessens by bringing it to the tone of common Saxon blue. The matter is then thrown on a filter, and after being washed in clean water, is dried. This substance is a kind of blue verditer, the intensity of which may vary according to the greater or less quantity of the sulphate of alumine decomposed. It may be used for painting in distemper.

2. Sulphate of iron, 1 part; alum, 8 parts. Dissolve in a suitable vessel in water, then add ferrocyanodide of potash, 2 parts, and common pearlash (dissolved) till it ceases to produce a precipitate; pour off the clear and preserve the precipitated blue.

3. Liquid.—Oil of vitriol, 4 parts; indigo, 1 part. Dissolve with heat then add water, 12 parts.

Savine Cerate.

Savine leaves, 2 pounds; yellow wax, 1 pound; lard, 5 pounds. Mix.

To Clean White Satin and Flowered Silks.

1. Mix sifted stale bread crumbs with powder blue, and rub it thoroughly all over, then shake it well, and dust it with clean soft cloths. Afterwards, where there are any gold or silver flowers, take a piece of crimson ingrain velvet, rub the flowers with it, which will restore them to their original lustre.

2. Pass them through a solution of fine hard soap, at a hand heat, drawing them through the hand. Rinse in lukewarm water, dry and finish by pinning out. Brush the flossy or bright side with a clean clothes-brush, the way of the nap. Finish them by dipping a sponge into a size, made by boiling isinglass in water, and rub the wrong side. Rinse out a second time, and brush, and dry near a fire, or in a warm room. Silks may be treated in the same way, but not brushed.

Perfumed Powder for Scent Bags.

Orris powder, coriander-seeds, lavender flowers, rose-leaves, cassia and cloves, each equal parts. Reduce to powder, then add a few drops of oil of lavender, oil of lemon, essence of bergamot.

Scented Powders, for Drawers, Trunks, &c.

1. Orris root, in powder, 1 pound; musk, 12 grains; essence of lavender, 1 drachm; essence of ambergris, 1 drachm; essence of bergamot, ½ drachm; essence of lemon, ½ drachm. Mix.

2. Take pure starch (powdered), any quantity; colour it with a little finely-powdered rose pink, and perfume it with ottar of roses, oil of rosemary, lavender, and neroli, letting the rose predominate.

Species for Scent Powders.

Take the muscus arboreus (lichenes prunastri) and reduce it to powder; it has the property of retaining odours better than most other powders.

Schab-ziger Cheese.

Flavoured with melilot.

Scheele's Green.

Carbonate of potass, 32 parts; water, 325 parts. Dissolve, then add arsenious acid, 11 parts. Next, sulphate of copper, 32 parts; water, 480 parts. Dissolve and filter each solution separately, then add the first to the second, until it ceases to produce a rich grass-green precipitate; collect and wash the green powder in clean water.

Schiedam Hollands.

Very fine spirit, 100 gallons; juniper berries (4 years old), 2 pounds; cassia buds, ¼ ounce; water sufficient; salt, 2 pounds. Draw over one hundred gallons.

Schwanberg's Fever Powder.

Common antimony, 4 parts; hartshorn shavings, 1 part. Reduce both to powder, heat them in a crucible, and well stir them, then put on the cover and keep it at a red heat for one hour.

Schweinfurth Green.

1. Arsenious acid, 16 parts, verdigris, 19 parts. Diffuse the latter through water at 120° Fahr., and pass the pap through a sieve, then mix it with the arsenic in solution, and set the vessel aside until the reaction of the ingredients produce the required shade of colour.

2. A saturated boiling solution of acetate of copper and arsenious acid, in equal proportions. Mix, and allow the whole to rest until the precipitate acquires the proper colour.

Oil of Scorpions.

Centipedes or ants, 1 ounce; rape oil, 3 pounds; water, 1 pound. Boil until the water is evaporated.

Scotch Marmalade.

Seville orange-juice, 1 gallon; honey, 8 pounds. Boil.

Scouring Balls to remove Spots from Clothes.

Fuller's earth, 1 part; pearlash, 1 part; yellow soap, 1 part. Mix. First moisten the spot with water, then apply the ball, and then water to wash the cloth clean.

Scouring Drops.

Essence of lemons (fresh), 4 ounces; oil of turpentine, 5 ounces. Mix.

Cure for the Scurvy.

Flour of sulphur, 2 parts; cream of tartar, 1 part. Four large teaspoonfuls to be taken every morning in milk or treacle.

Seal Engraver's Cement.

Resin, brickdust, equal parts. Mix, with heat.

Scented Sealing-Wax.

1. Balsam of Peru, 2 parts; sealing-wax composition, 130 parts. Mix, with a gentle heat.

2. Sealing-wax composition, 99 parts; essence of musk, 3 parts. Add the latter when the wax is cooling, and stir well.

3. Wax composition, 96 parts; oil of lavender, 4 parts; oil of lemon, 3 parts. As before.

Artificial Sea Water.

Water, 1 gallon; common salt, 2 ounces; muriate of magnesia, ¼ ounce muriate of lime, 3 drachms; sulphate of soda, 1 drachm; sulphate of magnesia, 1 drachm. Dissolve. Where sea water cannot be procured, this forms an excellent substitute, and possesses all its virtues.

To Soften Sea Water for Washing.

Add a little potash or soda.

Sedative Lotion.

Sugar of lead, 1 ounce; vinegar, 1 quart. Mix.

To Increase the Fertility of Seeds.

Nitrate of potash, 1 part; draining from a dunghill, 15 parts. Mix, and steep the seeds in it.

Bottled Seidlitz Water.

1. Take soda-water bottles and fill them with clear water; then add, as below, and cork and wire them immediately.

2. Rochelle salts, 2 drachms; bicarbonate of soda, 35 grains; sulphuric acid, 11 drops.

Strong Mercurial Ointment.

Prepared sevum, 1 ounce or part; quicksilver, 7 ounces or parts. Mix in a warm mortar, then add lard, softened with heat, 13 ounces or parts. Mix well.

Weak Mercurial Ointment.

Prepared sevum, 1 ounce or part; quicksilver, 7 ounces or part; lard (softened), 3½ pounds, or 56 parts. As before.

Shaving Paste.

1. Oil of almonds, 2 parts; white soap, 2 parts; common soda, 1 part; rosewater, 1 part. Melt and perfume with ottar of roses.

2. White wax, 2 ounces; spermaceti, 2 ounces; sweet oil, 2 ounces; soda, 2 ounces; white soap, 2 ounces; powdered cassia, ½ drachm; powdered cloves, ½ drachm; bergamot, 35 drops; essential oil of almonds, 5 drops. Mix with rose-water.

English Sherry.

1. Loaf-sugar, 20 pounds; sugar candy, 20 pounds; pale ale wort (good), 10 gallons, or more; raisins, 8 pounds; yeast, 8 ounces. Ferment, then add brandy, 1 gallon, or less; bitter almonds, 3 to 6 drachms; orris powder, 3 to 6 drachms. Bung down.

2. English malmsey, 50 gallons; Cape Madeira, 40 gallons; cassia (bruised), ½ ounce; cloves, ½ ounce; bitter almonds (bruised), 3 ounces; spirit, 5 gallons. Mix, and let them stand for fifteen days, then add finings, 1 pint.

London Sherry.

1. Chopped raisins, 400 pounds; soft water, 100 gallons; sugar, 45 pounds; white tartar, 1 pound; cider, 16 gallons. Let them stand together in a close vessel for one month, and frequently stir them, then add of spirit, 8 gallons; bitter almonds (bruised), 3 ounces; half a dozen oranges and lemons in slices. Let them stand one month longer, and fine with isinglass.

2. Wort from pale malt four times the common strength, 100 gallons; lump or light coloured sugar, 60 pounds; honey, 50 pounds. Ferment in a loosely-bunged cask, then rack and add nine or ten per cent. of spirit, and bitter almonds (bruised), 2 ounces; cassia (bruised), ½ ounce; cloves, ½ ounce; orris-root powder, 3 ounces. Let them macerate in the wine, closely bunged for fourteen days; lastly, add one quart of finings, and rummage.

To Fine Sherry.

Mix about one quart of isinglass finings well into the wine.

To Improve Sherry.

Add a little mellow Lisbon, and fine it with milk or isinglass.

Baker's Sharps.

Alum, 1 part; flour, 2 parts. Grind and sift.

Sheathing for Ships.

Copper, 98 parts. Melt at the lowest possible heat, then add tin, 1½ parts.

To Bleach Shell Lac.

Shell or seed lac, 2 parts; pearlash, 3 parts. Dissolve with heat and strain, then precipitate the lac by means of chlorine.

Sheldrake's Oil for Grinding Colours.

Pale old boiled oil, copal varnish, equal parts. Mix. This will remain good for a long time, if kept in well-corked bottles.

Shrewsbury Cake.

1. Sugar (sifted), 1 part; flour, 3 parts. One grated nutmeg and three eggs to every pound of sugar; mix, and make into a dough with melted butter and a little rose-water.

2. Flour, 2 pounds; sugar (powdered), 1 pound; butter, ½ pound. Four eggs, a little rose-water, and a quarter pint of cream. Beat them into a firm paste and roll it thin; cut into cakes, and bake in a quick oven.

The Sighs of Love.

1. Proof-spirit, 1 gallon; water, 1 gallon; sugar, 7 pounds; otto of roses, 45 drops; cochineal to produce a pale pink.

2. Rose-water, 3 pounds; water, 5 pounds; sugar, 6 pounds; proof-spirit, 7 pounds; cochineal to tinge.

To ascertain whether a Horse has good Sight.

Examine the size of the pupil of the eye in a dull light, then gradually expose it to a brighter one, and observe whether it contracts or not; if it does, the horse can see, and according to the amount of the contraction will be the keenness of his sight.

Silica, for Filling Decayed Teeth.

Gypsum, 1 part; levigated porcelain, 1 part; levigated iron filings, 1 part. Make into a paste with equal parts of thick quick-drying copal and mastic varnish.

To render Silk and Cloth Water-proof, (Oil Cloth or Silk.)

Boiled oil, 15 parts; litharge (ground), 3 parts; colour, 3 parts; bees'-wax, 1 part. Mix, and apply with a brush, to the article previously stretched against a wall, or on a table.

To Extract Grease Spots from Silks and Muslins.

Put a little powdered French chalk on the spot, cover it with a piece of paper, and apply a hot iron.

To Gild Silks, Satins, &c.

Nitromuriate of gold, in solution, 1 part; distilled water, 3 parts. Mix. Lay out any design with this fluid, and expose it, while wet, to a stream of hydrogen gas; then wash it with clear water.

A Metal that Resembles Silver.

Copper melted with tin, (about three quarters of an ounce of tin to a pound of copper), will make a pale bell-metal, that will roll and ring very near to sterling silver.

Silver Dust.

Take silver, dissolve it in nitric acid, and precipitate it with slips of bright copper; wash the powder in spirits and dry it.

Liquid Foil for Silvering Glass Globes.

1. Tin, 1 part; lead, 1 part; bismuth, 1 part. Melt, then add mercury, 3 parts.
2. Take quicksilver, and add as much tin foil as will just allow it to keep barely fluid.
3. Lead, 1 part; tin, 1 part; bismuth, 1 part. Melt, and just before it sets, add mercury, 10 parts. Pour this into the globe and turn it rapidly round.

To Extract Stains from Silver Plate.

Sal ammoniac, 1 part; vinegar, 16 parts. Mix, and use this liquid with a piece of flannel, then wash the plate in clean water.

Silvering Powder.

1. Silver powder (precipitated), 1 part; common salt, 2 parts; cream of tartar, 2 parts. Mix, and apply with friction, then wash the article in slightly alkalized water.
2. Silver dust, 4 parts; common salt, 16 parts; sal ammoniac, 14 parts; bichloride of mercury, 1 part. Mix with water to a paste, and apply it to the copper, (previously cleaned), with a piece of soft leather.

Pure Silver.

Take silver, dissolve it in nitric acid, and add a solution of salt as long as any precipitate falls, then take the sediment and boil it in water in a bright iron vessel; wash it well with clean water and dry it.

Silver Shells.

Silver leaf, gum water, sufficient quantity. Grind to a proper thickness, and cover the inside of the shells.

Silver Solder.

1. Silver, 19 parts; copper, 1 part; brass, 10 parts. Melt together.
2. For Plating.—Silver, 2 parts; brass, 1 part. Mix.

Silver Tree.

Nitrate of silver, 1 part; distilled water, 35 parts. Dissolve and filter; put the liquid into a suitable bottle in some convenient place, and pour in mercury, 1 part. A most beautiful arborescence will rapidly be formed

Brilliant Fire for Sky Rockets.

1. If under 1 inch bore, nitre, 16 parts; charcoal, 6 parts; sulphur, 4 parts; meal powder, 3 parts; steel filings, 5 parts. Mix.
2. If over 1 and under 2 inches, nitre, 16 parts; charcoal, 8 parts; sulphur, 4 parts; steel filings, 5 parts. Mix.

Chinese Fire for Sky Rockets.

1. If ¾ inch or under, nitre, 16 parts; charcoal, 4 parts; sulphur, 3 parts; cast-iron borings, 4 parts. Mix.

2. If over 1 inch and under 2 inches bore, nitre, 16 parts; charcoal, 4 parts; sulphur, 4 parts; iron borings, 5 parts. Mix.

Composition for Sky Rockets.

1. If under ¾ inch bore, nitre, 16 parts; charcoal, 7 parts; sulphur, 4 parts; gunpowder, 1 part. Mix.

2. If over ¾ and under 1½ inch bore, nitre, 16 parts; charcoal, 8 parts; sulphur, 4 parts. Mix.

3. If larger, nitre, 16 parts; charcoal, 9 parts; sulphur, 4 parts. Mix.

To Extract Stains from Silk.

Essence of lemon, 1 part; spirits of turpentine, 5 parts. Mix, and apply to the spot by means of a linen rag.

Singleton's Golden Eye Ointment.

Nitric oxide of mercury, 1 ounce; spermaceti ointment, 8 ounces. The oxide must be in the state of an impalpable powder, and then well rubbed with the ointment to ensure a perfect and equal mixture. This ointment is in extensive demand, and is sold after the rate of more than a guinea an ounce.

To Procure Sleep.

1. Magnesia, 1 teaspoonful; water to mix. Take this on going to bed, with a few drops of hartshorn or sal volatile.

2. Take a warm bath ten minutes before lying down, or use the flesh brush for a quarter of an hour. If you do not feel disposed to sleep, commence counting one thousand; before you get to five hundred you will most probably fall asleep.

To destroy Slugs on Land.

Sprinkle over it powdered fresh slaked lime, or chimney soot.

To preserve Plants from Slugs.

Strew well-cut chaff round the plants.

Smallpox Matter.

Take a lancet and carefully collect the matter from the pustules.

Smalts.

Roasted cobalt, 1 part; potash, 3 parts; sand, 3 parts. Mix and fuse

Smelling Salts.

Take subcarbonate of ammonia, 8 parts; put it in coarse powder into the bottle, and pour on it oil of lavender, 1 part.

Smellome's Eye Ointment.

Verdigris, 2 drachms; sweet oil, 2 drachms; basilicon, 4 ounces. Mix.

Smith's Soft Solder for Tin.

Lead, 1 part; tin, 1 part; bismuth, 2 parts. This melts in boiling water.

To destroy Insects in Vines.

Soft soap, 2 pounds; flowers of sulphur, 2 pounds; powdered tobacco, 2 pounds; boil for half an hour in water, 6 gallons. Apply lukewarm.

Violet Depilatory.

Quicklime in fine powder, 1 pound; orris powder, 3 ounces; starch powder, 2 ounces; orpiment, 1 ounce. Mix.

Oil of Violets.

1. Take violet flowers, and treat them as for Oil of Jasmin, which see.
2. Orris powder, 1 part; olive oil, 13 parts. Pour the oil warm on the powder, macerate for one week, then strain with expression.

Violet Lozenges.

Orris powder, 1 ounce; gum arabic, 1 ounce; white sugar, 2 pounds. Make into a thick paste with the following—Cochineal, 1 drachm; water, 1 quart. Macerate for two days.

Violet Pomatum.

White wax, suet, lard, each, one pound; orris powder, olive oil, each, 8 ounces. Melt, and macerate for six hours, then strain, and stir in orange-flower water, two ounces.

Violet Pommade.

1. Beef suet, 1 part; lard, 2 parts. Melt and strain, then follow the same plan as for Jasmin Pommade, which see.
2. Suet, 2 parts; lard, 5 parts; orris powder, 1 part. Melt with a gentle heat, and keep it in that state for two hours; cool, let it rest over for two or three days, remelt and strain.

Violet Powder.

Starch or farina, 1 cwt.; orris powder, 7 pounds; essence of bergamot, 1 ounce; essence of lemon, ¾ ounce; oil of rhodium, ¼ ounce; oil of cloves, ¼ ounce. Mix well, and sift through lawn.

Imitation Platina.

Pale brass, 8 parts; spelter, 5 parts. Mix.

Platina-mohr.

Zinc, 2 parts; platinum, 1 part. Melt and reduce the alloy to powder, which must be treated with dilute sulphuric acid until all the zinc is washed out; then wash it with water, digest it in a ley of potash, and again wash it with water. This powder possesses the property of converting alcohol into vinegar.

Mercurial Plating.

Quicksilver, 4 parts; nitric acid, 4 parts; finely-powdered cream of tartar, 2 parts; finely-powdered salt of sorrel, 1 part. Dissolve the silver in the acid, then add the rest, and stir until dissolved. This imparts a pleasing silvery appearance to articles formed of copper, by merely applying it with the finger.

To clean Point Lace.

Stretch it in a tent, and clean it with a solution of white soap; wash off the soap with water, and sponge it with starch on the wrong side; when dry, iron it on the same side, then with a bodkin set it in order.

Pomatum.

1. Prepared suet, olive oil, each, 2 parts; lard, 1 part. Melt in a water bath, then remove the vessel, and, when it begins to thicken, stir in the following scent, in quantity at discretion:—Oil of cloves, 60 drops; neroli, 20 drops; lavender, 60 drops; bergamot, 90 drops; essence of ambergris, 50 drops; musk, 50 drops. Mix. A slight colour may be given to it, according to the fancy of the manufacturer.

2. Strained suet, 10 pounds; white wax, $\frac{3}{4}$ pound. Melt, then stir well in essence of bergamot, 1 ounce; essence of lemon, $\frac{1}{2}$ ounce; oil of rosemary, $\frac{1}{4}$ ounce; oil of lavender, $\frac{1}{4}$ ounce; rose-water, 1 pint.

Plain Hard Pomatum.

1. Lard, suet, white wax, equal parts. Mix, with heat.
2. Prepared suet, 13 pounds: white wax, one pound. Mix.
3. Suet, 15 pounds. Melt, and stir in water, 2 pounds.

Either of these forms may be scented according to taste.

Roll Pomatum.

1. Suet, 5 parts; lard, white wax, each, one part. Mix, with a gentle heat, then add lavender and bergamot to scent.

2. Mutton suet, 5 pounds; white wax, one pound; essence of lemon and bergamot to scent.

3. Yellow wax, 5 pounds; suet, 15 pounds. Melt, then add neroli and lemon to scent.

Soft Pomatum.

1. Suet, 9 pounds; lard, 10 pounds; beeswax, 8 ounces; gum benjamin, 5 ounces; perfume to taste.

2. Clarified lard, 12 pounds; clarified suet, 2 pounds; essence of bergamot, 1 ounce; essence of lemon, $\frac{1}{2}$ ounce; oil of lavender, $\frac{1}{4}$ ounce; rose-water, 8 ounces. Melt the first two, then take the pan from the fire and stir in the essences.

Plain Soft Pomatum.

1. Lard, 2 pounds; suet, one pound. Mix, with heat. This is ready to receive any perfume, as agreeable.

2. Olive oil, white wax, lard, suet, equal parts. If required softer, use a little less wax, or more lard and oil.

Pommade à la Jasmin.

Lard, suet, each, one pound; oil of almonds, 4 ounces. Mix, then add spirits of jasmin, an ounce and a half.

Pommade à la Rose.

Lard, 4 pounds; suet, one pound; alkanet, one pound. Macerate with heat to give a *faint* colour, then allow it to cool, and before it sets stir in rose-water, 5 ounces; ottar of roses to perfume.

Plummer's Alterative Powder.

Protochloride of quicksilver, sulphuret of antimony, equal parts. Mix.

Pommade à la Vanilla.

Powdered vanilla, one part; oil à la rose, 2 parts; pommade à la rose, 12 parts; bergamot, $\frac{1}{3}$ part; suet, 2 parts. Melt in a water-bath, and stir well for one hour, then let it settle for two hours, and pour off the clear.

Pommade aux Fleurs.

Lard, 4 pounds; suet, 1 pound. Melt, and stir in jasmin or orange flowers to scent; let it stand for three or four days.

Pommade de Deuto-iodure de Mercure.

Deuto-iodide of quicksilver, eleven grains; lard, one ounce. Mix.

Pommade de la Jeunesse.

1. Lard, 16 ounces; white wax, one ounce; dinitrate of bismuth or pearl white, 2 ounces; scent to taste. Used as a pommade to dye the hair black.

2. Litharge (finely powdered), lime, bicarbonate of potash, each, one ounce. Mix well in the dry state, then add melted lard, 13 ounces. Stir well until cold.

Pommade de Proto-Iodure de Mercure.

Proto-iodide of mercury, eleven grains; lard, 1 ounce. Mix well.

Pommade Divine.

1. Lard, 3 pounds; white wax, $\frac{1}{2}$ pound; balm of Gilead, 3 ounces; oil of cloves, 6 drachms; essence of bergamot, 4 drachms. Mix as before.

2. Suet, white wax, lard, each, one pound; essence of lemon, essence of bergamot, each, 6 drachms; oil of lavender, oil of origanum, each, 3 drachms. Melt the first three, with a gentle heat, remove them from the fire, and while cooling stir in the scent.

3. Clarified lard, 12 pounds; storax, benjamin, orris powder, each, 4 ounces; powdered cassia, cloves, nutmegs, each, one ounce. Melt, and keep them in that state for three hours, then strain, and add oil of lavender, 2 drachms; essence of bergamot, 3 drachms; rose-water (stirred well in), one pint. Pot for use.

4. Suet, 3 pounds; storax, benzoin, orris powder, cassia, grated nutmegs, bruised cloves, each, 5 drachms. Digest in a gentle heat for twelve hours and strain.

5. *French Rose.* Beef suet, 5 pounds; yellow wax, 8 ounces; honey, 4 ounces; rose leaves, one gallon. Melt, and before it cools add rose-water, one pint, essence of roses, one ounce. Stir well and mould it.

Pommade d'Orange.

1. Beeswax, 5 pounds; lard, 6 pounds; suet, 6 pounds; palm oil, 2 pounds. Melt, and while cooling stir in orange-flower water, 8 ounces, essence of neroli, 3 drachms.

2. Lard, 2 pounds; yellow wax, 2 ounces; palm oil, 1 pound. Mix with a gentle heat, then add essence of neroli, 2 drachms.

Pommade d'Or.

Amalgam of gold (yellow), 15 grains; lard, 1 ounce. **Mix.**

Pommade Dye for the Hair.

Nitrate of silver, one part; nitric acid, 2 parts; iron filings, 2 parts. Mix, and let them stand together for four or five hours, then pour them on oatmeal, 2 parts. Next add lard, 3 parts, and mix well together.

Pontiff's Sauce.

Veal, ham, sliced onions, carrots, celery, parsnips, each, one pound; shallots, corianders, lemon-peel, each, one ounce; white wine, one quart; vinegar, 2 quarts; catsup, one quart. Boil, adding the wine last, then strain.

English Porcelain.

1. Ground flints, 7 parts; calcined bones, 18 parts; china clay, 4 parts; clay, 7 parts. Mix.

2. Ground flints, 11 parts; phosphate of lime, 17 parts; china clay, 16 parts; granite, 13 parts. Mix.

3. *Very Fine.* Fine white sand, 30 parts; phosphate of lime, 60 parts; china, 20 parts; potash, 3 parts. Mix.

Choice of Pork.

If young, the rind will be *thin, tender,* and *easily* impressed with the finger; when fresh, the flesh is smooth and cool; if clammy, avoid it; if the fat is measly, or full of kernels, it is unwholesome.

British Port.

Damson juice, 20 gallons; cider, 20 gallons; sloe juice, 1 pound; sugar, 10 pounds; honey, 10 pounds. Ferment, then add spirit, 3 gallons; red cape, 10 gallons; red tartar (dissolved), ¾ pound; powder of catechu, ¾ pound; bruised ginger, 1 ounce; cassia, 1 ounce; cloves, ½ ounce. Mix well with brandy colouring, 1 pint, and fine with bullock's blood.

2. Bullys, 8 pounds; damsons, 40 pounds; water, 6 gallons. Boil the water, skim it, and pour it boiling hot on the fruit; let it stand four or six days at least. During that time bruise the fruit or squeeze it with your hands. Then draw or pour it off into a cask, and to every gallon of liquor put two pounds and a half of fine sugar, or rather more: put some yeast on a slice of bread (warm) to work it. When done working, put a little brandy into the cask and fill it up. Bung it up close, and let stand six or twelve months: then bottle it off. The quantity of bullys should be one pound to every five of damsons. This wine is nearer in flavour to port than any other: if made with cold water, it will be equally as good, but of a different colour.

3. Red cape, 100 gallons; sloe juice, 1 gallon; honey, 12 pounds; rough cider, 21 gallons; bruised cochineal, 4 ounces; brandy colouring, 1 pint; spirit, 6 gallons; bruised bitter almonds, ½ ounce; cloves, ½ ounce; powdered catechu, 1 pound; red tartar, 1 pound. Mix well, and fine down with bullock's blood.

4. Cider, 25 gallons; elder juice, 5 gallons; port wine, 5 gallons; brandy, 1 gallon; red tartar, 6 ounces; catechu, 2 ounces; finings, 1 quart; logwood, 1 pound. Well mix and bung close.

Yellow Ink.

1. French berries, 1 pound; alum, 2 ounces; water, 1 gallon. Boil and strain, then add gum arabic, 4 ounces.

2. Water, 30 parts; Avignon berries, 7 parts; gum and alum, each 5 parts. Boil for one hour and strain.

Farrier's Embrocation for Sprains.

Oil of turpentine, soft soap, and spirits of wine, equal parts. Mix.

To Sprinkle Books.

Take a stiff brush made of hogs'-bristles, perfectly clean, dip it in the colour; squeeze out the superfluous liquid; then rub a folding-stick across the brush, and a fine sprinkle will fall on the edge of the book, which should be previously screwed tight in the cutting-press. Repeat the operation until the colour is thrown equally on every part of the leaves. The brush should be held in the left hand, and the stick in the right.

Spruce Beer.

Cold water, 10 gallons; boiling water, 11 gallons. Mix in a barrel, and add molasses, 30 pounds, or brown sugar, 24 pounds; essence of spruce, 1 ounce or more. Add a pint of yeast and ferment; bottle in two or three days. If you wish white spruce beer, use lump-sugar.

Spruce Beer Powders.

White sugar, 1 drachm; bicarbonate of soda, 1 scruple; essence of spruce, 8 grains; essence of lemon, 1 grain. Mix and wrap it in blue paper. Then add tartaric acid, ½ drachm, and wrap it in white paper. For use; dissolve each paper in separate glasses, one-third full of water, pour the one into the other, and drink immediately.

Spruce Wine.

Honey and sugar, each 50 pounds; soft water, 25 gallons; starch, made into jelly, 2 pounds; essence of spruce and cream of tartar, each ½ pound. Boil, then add essence of lemon, ¼ ounce; yeast, ½ pound. Bung close.

Starch Lozenges.

Sugar, 1 pound; starch, liquorice-powder, and orris powder, each 1 ounce. Mix with mucilage.

Ointment of Stavesacre, for Horses, &c.

Powdered stavesacre-seeds, 1 pound; lard, 4 pounds; oil, 1 pound Mix. Used to destroy lice on cattle.

To Preserve Steel Goods.

Caoutchouc, 1 part; turpentine, 16 parts. Dissolve with a gentle heat, then add boiled oil, 8 parts. Mix by bringing them to the heat of boiling water; apply it to the steel with a brush, in the way of varnish. It may be removed when dry with turpentine. The oil may be wholly omitted.

M. Dussaussy's Steel.

Copper, 100 parts; tin, 14 parts. This alloy may be hardened and sharpened in a similar way to steel.

Starkey's Soap.

Spirits of turpentine, caustic potash, and water, of each a sufficient quantity. The potash may be rendered caustic by passing the ley over quicklime.

Steel Lozenges.

1. Sugar, 2 pounds; starch, 1 pound; carbonate or oxide of iron, 6 ounces; powdered cassia, 5 ounces. Mix with mucilage.

2. *Aromatic.*—Tincture of cantharides and finely-powdered cassia, each 2 ounces; sulphate of iron, 1 ounce; sugar, 6 pounds. Mix with mucilage.

Steel Solder.

Silver, 18 parts; copper, 1 part; brass, 2 parts.

To Gild Steel.

Apply an etherial solution of gold. This is equally adapted to lettering, as wholly covering the object. It may be applied with a pen or otherwise.

Stereotype Metal. (Small Type Metal.)

Lead, 18 parts; antimony, 4 parts; bismuth, 2 parts. Melt.

Steer's Opodeldoc.

Castile soap, 8 parts; rectified spirit, 64 parts; camphor, 24 parts; oil of rosemary, ½ part; oil of origanum, 1 part; solution of ammonia, 6 parts. Mix.

For Sore Nipples.

Aleppo galls in powder, ʒvj.; Vin. Alb. ℥vj. Digest with a gentle heat for twenty-four hours, strain, and apply compresses wet with it three or four times a day, beginning as early as the sixth month of gestation, and continue until the full time.

To make a Solution of Tin Aqua Regia.

Mix together eight ounces of filtered river water, in eight ounces of double aquafortis, and gradually half an ounce of sal ammoniac dissolved piece by piece, and two drachms of saltpetre. Then take one ounce of refined black tin, and melt it, and then let it fall gradually at the height of several inches into water, so as to render it in fine pieces. Now gradually add this tin to the above liquid, allowing one piece to dissolve before another is added. When all has been dissolved, cork up in a bottle and keep in a cool place. Used by dyers in colouring yellow.

Alteratives for Animals.

Take of cream of tartar, half an ounce, of saltpetre, half an ounce, to be given mixed in a mash. The above for a horse, a little less for other animals, according to judgment.

To Prevent the Bite of Musquitoes.

Apply a thick lather of soap to the skin of the face and hands.

A Strengthening Mixture for Animals.

Take of white vitriol, 1 drachm; ground ginger, 2 drachms; powdered quassia, ½ an ounce; ale, ½ pint. Mix, and give as a drench.

Astringent Mixture for Scours.

Suet cut fine and boiled in new milk, in the proportion of one quarter of a pound to a pint of the milk. To this must be added of boiled starch, one pint; alum, in powder, one drachm. Given as a drench. Good both for horses and cattle.

Wash for Sore Eyes in Animals.

White vitriol, 2 scruples; sugar of lead, 1 drachm; water, 1 pint. Mix.

Muriate of Tin.

This is made by dissolving half an ounce of granulated tin to 8 ounces of muriatic acid; when dissolved bottle the clear liquid. Used by dyers in scarlet colours.

Stimulating Ointment for Horses.

Yellow resin, spirit of turpentine, tallow, flour of mustard, each 1 pound; rape oil, 8 ounces; red precipitate, 4 ounces. Mix.

Stimulant Plaster.

Plaster of Spanish flies, 1 part; Burgundy pitch, 7 parts; yellow wax, 1 part; oil, 2 parts. Mix.

Oil of St. John's-Wort.

1. Leaves, 1 part; rape oil, 5 parts. Infuse for some days.
2. *Factitious.*—Rape oil, 1 gallon; root alkanet, 6 ounces; verdigris, ½ ounce. Mix, and digest with heat, then pour off the clear.

Artificial (Keene's Patent) Stone.

1. *White.*—Alum, 1 pound; water, 1 gallon. Dissolve, then steep in this liquor calcined gypsum, ¾ cwt. Next dry for eight days in the open air, and calcine at a dull, red heat; grind and sift and form into a paste with water, when hard apply a thin layer of the above paste over the surface with a brush; when quite hard, polish with pumice, &c., in the usual way
2. *Cream Colour.*—Alum, 1 pound; copperas, ½ pound; water, 9 pints. Dissolve, and proceed as before.

Stone, Fig, Thumb, or Queen's Blue.

1. Starch and whiting, equal parts. Add finely-powdered indigo to colour.
2. Take starch, and indigo to colour. Mix.

Stone Marble for Leather Book-Covers, &c.

Glaire the cover, and when dry, put the book into the cutting-press with the boards sloping, to cause the colours to run gently down. Throw on weak copperas-water with a brush; dip a sponge into the strong potash-water, and press out the colour from the sponge on different parts of the back, so that the colours may run down each side from the back. Where the brown has left a vacancy apply vitriol-water in the same manner. The book must remain till perfectly dry, before washing it.

Engraver's Stopping-out Varnish.

Take lamp-black, and turpentine to make a paste.

Stone-Colour Paint.

Road dust, 2 cwt.; ground white-lead, ½ cwt.; whiting, 1 cwt.; ground umber, 14 pounds; lime-water, 6 gallons. Factitious linseed oil to grind.

Factitious Liquid Storax.

1. Liquid storax, 1 part; balsam of tolu, 30 parts; balsam of Peru, 2 parts; spirit of wine, 7 parts. Mix.

2. *Strained.*—Storax, 7 pounds; benzoin, 15 pounds; tolu, 7 pounds; socotrine aloes, 2 pounds; alcohol, 15 gallons. Digest for one week with occasional agitation, then add balsam of Peru, 1 pound; sweet oil, 12 ounces. Mix well.

3. Balsam of tolu, 12 pounds; balsam of Peru, 2 pounds. Mix.

Storm Glasses.

Camphor, 4 parts; nitre, 3 parts; sal ammoniac, 1 part; alcohol, 32 parts. Dissolve, and keep it in a glass tube or bottle, covered with bladder.

To make a Butt of Porter Stout.

Stir in thirty pounds of brown sugar, or fifty pounds of molasses with a quart of finings. It is a common practice to add, porter extract.

To mend Cracks in Stoves.

German Method.—Take equal parts of wood ashes and common salt, and mix them to a proper consistence with water; with this fill the cracks.

Strass, or Mayence Base.

1. Pure rock crystal or flint, 8 parts; salt of tartar, 25 parts. Powder, mix well, bake and cool, then put it into a basin of water and add dilute nitric acid until effervescence ceases; collect, wash, and dry the powder; next add fine white-lead, 12 parts. Levigate and well wash it with pure water, then of the above mixture, dried, 12 parts; calcined borax, 1 part. Triturate them together, melt in a clean crucible, and pour the mixture into cold water; dry, powder, and melt in the same manner, a third time, always in a fresh crucible, observing to separate any lead that may be revived. To the third frit, ground to powder, add purified nitre ⅝ part. Remelt, and a mass of crystal will be found in the crucible, of a beautiful and diamond-like lustre.

2. Arsenic, 1 part; borax, 23 parts; pure pearlash, 180 parts; minium, 525 parts; rock crystal, 338 parts. Mix, as before.

3. Arsenic, 1 part; borax, 30 parts; potash, 105 parts; carbonate of lead, 709 parts; fine white sand, 315 parts. Mix with care.

4. Arsenic, 1 part; borax, 35 parts; potass, 325 parts; minium, 900 parts; rock crystal, 580 parts. Treat as before.

5. Rock crystal, 400 parts; pure white lead, 945 parts; pure potash, 140 parts; borax, 41 parts.

6. Pure potash, 2 parts; fine white sand, 15 parts; litharge, 20 parts. See also Paste.

Strawberry Water.

Take bruised strawberries, 1 cwt.; water, 20 gallons. Distil over fifteen gallons.

Strawberry Wine.

Bruised strawberries, 12 gallons; cider, 10 gallons: water, 7 gallons; sugar, 25 pounds. Ferment, then add of bruised orris root, bruised bitter almonds, and bruised cloves, each ½ ounce; dissolved red tartar, 6 ounces.

Strengthening Mixture.

Infusion of bark, 7 ounces; sulphate of quinine, 9 grains; dilute sulphuric acid, 30 grains; syrup of orange-peel, 2 drachms. Mix. Dose—two table-spoonfuls three times a day.

Strengthening Plaster.

1. Simple diachylon, 22 pounds; thuris, 5 pounds; dragon's-blood, 2 pounds. Mix.

2. Diachylon, 20 pounds; gum thuris, 4 pounds; peroxide of iron, 2 pounds. Mix. This is a cheap form for the emplastrum thuris of the Dublin College.

3. Diachylon, 80 pounds; gum thuris, 29 pounds; Armenian bole, 5 pounds. Mix with heat. Said to be used as a mechanical support to the muscles by public dancers.

Ale, Beer, and Porter from Sugar and Malt.

Omit one-half the malt and substitute coarse brown sugar after the rate of eighty pounds of sugar for every quarter.

Prepared Suet.

Follow the same plan as for lard.

Sugar Beer.

Bran, 1 peck; hops, ¼ pound. Boil them in water, 10 gallons. Strain and add coarse sugar, 4 pounds; yeast, 1 spoonful. Ferment. This beer will not keep many days.

White Sugar Candy.

Take a saturated solution of clarified sugar, hot, and place it in a temperature of 90° or 100° F., and promote crystallization by placing threads across the syrup.

Sugar from Carrots.

From carrot roots by the same process as for Parsnip Sugar.

Sugar from Starch.

Starch, 100 parts; water, 400 parts; animal charcoal, 7 parts; oil of vitriol, 6 parts; chalk, 10 parts Dissolve the starch in two-thirds the water, and add the vitriol, diluted with the remainder; boil for five or six hours, then add the charcoal and chalk; boil for thirty minutes more; strain, evaporate, and crystallize. Similar to Grape Sugar.

Sugar of Lead Ointment.

1. Lard and suet, each 1 pound; sugar of lead, 2 ounces. Mix. Cooling desiccation.

2. Sweet oil, 2 pounds; white wax, 6 ounces; sugar of lead, 2 ounces. Mix.

Sugar from Grapes.

Take grapes and express the juice, then add chalk to saturate the acid, allow the liquid to settle; pour off the clear, clarify with eggs, skim, and evaporate.

To Clarify Coarse Sugar.

Coarse sugar, 1 cwt.; water, 6 gallons; white of eggs, 12 in number; fresh-burnt charcoal, powdered, 7 pounds. Put them into a cold copper and well mix, then apply heat for a short time, and strain through a bag, mixing a little pulp of brown paper with the syrup before putting it into the filter; return the first runnings. Animal charcoal is the best to whiten syrups.

To Clarify Loaf Sugar.

Broken sugar, 1 cwt.; water, 8 gallons; whites of eggs, 20 in number. Put them into the copper (cold), and mash until dissolved, then apply heat and skim the syrup until it is perfectly clear, then turn the cock. Have some cold water ready to throw into the copper in case it should boil over.

To Improve Common Sugar.

Moist sugar, 1 cwt.; flour, 20 pounds. Mix well, then pass them through the mill.

To make Devices in Sugar.

Powdered lump-sugar, any quantity, make it into a paste with mucilage, and mould it to taste.

Sugar Vinegar.

To each gallon of water add two pounds of brown sugar, and a little yeast, leave it exposed to the sun for six months, in a vessel slightly stopped.

Sulphuret of Iron.

Sulphur, 5 parts; iron filings, 3 parts. Melt in a covered crucible. Excellent for taking casts of medals, &c.

Sulphuret of Potash.

Flowers of sulphur, 1 part; pearlash, 5 parts. Mix in a close vessel with heat.

Sulphuretted Tar.

Balsam of sulphur and Barbadoes tar, equal parts. Mix, with heat.

Balsam or Oil of Sulphur.

Flowers of sulphur, 1 pound; Seal oil, 1 gallon. Boil until dissolved.

Sulphur Lozenges.

Flowers of sulphur, 1 ounce; essence of lemon, 1 drachm; sugar, [illegible] pound. Mix with mucilage.

Milk of Sulphur.

Sulphur, 1 part; pearlash, 3 parts. Boil in sufficient water, filter and add dilute sulphuric acid. Collect and wash the precipitate. Quicklime may be used instead of pearlash, and hydrochloric instead of sulphuric acid.

Sulphur Ointment.

1. Sulphur, 1 pound; lard, 4 pounds. Mix.

2. Lard, 7 pounds; milk sulphur, 2 pounds. Mix.

3. Flowers of sulphur, 1 pound; lard, 4 pounds; essence of lemon and essence of bergamot, each 4 drachms. Mix.

4. *Compound.*—Sulphur, 1 pound; soft soap, ½ pound; powdered nitre, ¼ pound; lard, 2 pounds. Mix. For the itch.

Superb Liquid Blue.

Put into a small matrass or common phial an ounce of Prussian blue reduced to powder, and pour over it from one ounce and a half to two ounces of concentrated muriatic acid. The mixture produces an effervescence, and the prussiate soon assumes the consistence of thin paste. Leave it in this state for twenty-four hours; then dilute it with eight or nine ounces of water, and preserve the colour thus diluted in a bottle well stopped. The intensity of this colour may be lessened, if necessary, by new doses of water. If the whole of this mixture be poured into a quart of water, it will still exhibit a colour sufficiently dark for washing prints.

Modelling Wax.

This is made of white wax, which is melted and mixed with lard to make it malleable. In working it, the tools and the board or stone are moistened with water, to prevent its adhering; it may be coloured to any desirable tint with dry colour.

Suppurating Liniment for Horses.

Tallow, 14 pounds; flour mustard, 1 pound; camphor and oil of origanum, each 1 ounce. Mix.

Sweet Fennel Water.

Fennel-seeds, 28 pounds; water, 30 gallons. Distil off twenty-seven or twenty-eight gallons.

Sweet Sauce.

Red wine, 2 pints; vinegar, 1 pint; sugar, ¼ pound; sliced onions, 1 ounce. A little cassia. Boil for fifteen minutes, and strain.

Sweet Extract of Wormwood.

Proof-spirit, 4 gallons; water, 1 gallon; tops of wormwood, 6 pounds; roots of angelica, 1 scruple; calamus aromaticus and cassia, each 1 scruple; oil of aniseed, 2 drachms. Macerate for eight days, then distil off four gallons with a gentle heat.

Sycamore Wine.

Sap, 2 gallons; water, 20 gallons; sugar, 45 pounds; cider, 5 gallons, raisins, 5 pounds. Boil and ferment, then add six to nine per cent. of spirit, and fine with eggs.

Sydenham's Liquid Laudanum.

Opium, 12 parts; cinnamon or cassia, cloves, and saffron, each 1 part; common white wine, 100 parts. Dissolve in a close vessel, with the heat of a water-bath.

Pastry Cook's Sweet Spice.

Sugar, 2 parts; cassia, nutmegs, mace, and cloves, each 1 part. Mix.

Sydenham's Styptic Water.

Alum and sulphuric acid, each 2 parts; sulphate of copper, 3 parts; water, 8 parts. Dissolve and filter.

Solid Syllabub.

Cream and white wine, each 1 quart; juice of two lemons; peel of one lemon, grated. Sugar to sweeten. Mix, and mill them to a froth, then take off the scum as it rises, and place it to drain on a hair-sieve; half fill the glasses with the scum and heap the froth on it.

Sympathetic Ink.

Write with starch water, and when you wish the writing to be developed touch the part with a weak solution of iodine.

Lotion for Syphilitic Eruptions.

Bichloride of mercury, 8 grains; muriatic acid, 10 drops; almond milk, 1 pint; spirits of lavender, 1 ounce. Mix.

Ointment for Syphilitic Eruptions, Sore Throat, &c.

Ointment of nitrated mercury, 1 ounce; superacetate of lead, 25 grains; spermaceti ointment, 3 ounces. Mix.

Ointment to Alleviate Syphilitic Pains.

1. Iodine, 1 drachm; morphine, 3 grains; spermaceti ointment, 1 ounce Mix.

2. Mercurial ointment, 1 ounce; iodine, powdered opium, and camphor each 1 drachm. Mix.

Gargle for Syphilitic Sore Throat.

Chloride of soda, 4 ounces; distilled water, 5 ounces. Mix.

Table Beer.

Brew as for strong beer, only use an increased quantity of water. If brewed after strong beer, the process is simply another mashing, to which a few hops must be added.

To restore Tainted Meat.

If salted, wash it, and throw away the old brine, then replace it with the following composition, and let it lie in it for a few days: Fresh-burnt charcoal, powdered, 12 parts; common salt, 11 parts; saltpetre, 4 parts. Mix. This must be used the same as common salt; and when you want to cook the meat, the black colour may be removed with clean water.

To Whiten Tallow.

Take the tallow, melt it, and add a little alum and saltpetre, or a little nitric or sulphuric acid.

To improve Tamarinds.

When tamarinds become dry, or lose their taste or acidity, beat them up with a little syrup, and add sufficient dilute sulphuric acid to make them pleasant.

Snow's Alterative Pills.

Socotrine aloes, 2 drachms; rhubarb, 1 drachm; carbonate of soda (dried), 1 drachm; calomel, 2 scruples; castile soap, 2 drachms. Divide into ninety-six pills.

Soap à la Rose.

Good tallow soap (new made), olive oil, equal parts. Reduce the soap to thin shavings, and put them with the oil into a proper vessel; expose it to the heat of a water-bath, until its contents form a homogeneous paste, then add vermilion to colour; cool a little, and stir in a sufficient quantity of the following mixture to perfume: Essence of roses, 4 parts; essence of bergamot, 3 parts; essence of cloves, 1 part; essence of cassia, 1 part. Mix.

Soap au Bouquet.

Good tallow soap (in shavings), ¼ cwt.; essence of bergamot, 4 ounces; oil of cloves, 7 drachms; oil of sassafras, 7 drachms; oil of thyme, 7 drachms; neroli, 3½ drachms; brown ochre to colour. Reduce the soap to a perfectly even paste by the heat of a water-bath, adding a little water, then proceed, as for Soap à la Rose.

Soap Cerate.

Litharge, 1 pound; vinegar, 8 pounds. Dissolve with heat, then add white soap, 1 pound; yellow wax, ½ pound; sweet oil, 1 pound. Mix.

Clarified Soap

Soap, 1 pound; water, 2 pounds. Dissolve and filter, then evaporate.

Liquid Soap.

Sweet oil, 7 parts; caustic potass, 1 part; rose-water sufficient quantity to reduce it to a proper state. Rub the oil, alkali, and a few spoonfuls of the water together in a hot mortar until united, then add the remainder of the water as required.

Soap Marble for Books.

This is applicable for marbling stationery, book edges, or sheets of paper for ladies' fancy work.

Grind, on a marble slab, prussian blue, with water, and a little brown soap, to a fine pliable consistence, that it may be thrown on with a small brush.

Grind king's yellow, in the same manner, with water and white soap.

When green is intended for the ground colour, grind it with brown soap, and king's yellow with white soap. Lake may be used for a ground colour, and Prussian blue ground with white soap: brown umber for a ground colour, and flake white ground with white soap. Any colour of a light substance may be ground for marbling.

Soap Plaster.

1. Diachylon, 12 pounds; soap, 5 pounds; yellow resin, 5 pounds, sweet oil, 3 pounds; red lead, 3½ pounds. Mix. Discutient.

2. Diachylon, 24 pounds; soap, 4 pounds. Mix.

3. Sweet oil, 16 pounds; red lead, 8 pounds; soap, 6 pounds. Mix.

Shaving Soap.

Good white soap (in thin shavings), 3 pounds; palm soap, 1 pound, soft water, ¾ pound; soda, 1 ounce. Melt carefully over a slow fire, in an earthen vessel, then add oil of lavender, 60 drops; oil of lemon, 40 drops; bergamot, 50 drops. Mix well, and make it into forms.

Transparent Soap.

White soap (dry), 1 pound; alcohol, 5 pounds. Dissolve and distil off the alcohol until the soap is of the consistence for moulding, then make it into forms, place them in a proper retort, and gradually distil off the remainder of the spirit.

Easy Mode of Smoking Meat.

Take pyroligneous acid, and either immerse the meat in it for a short time, or give it two or three coats with a painter's brush; then hang it up to dry.

To Cure Smoky Chimneys.

1. Contract the draught. This is infallible, if properly done.

2. Increase the height or crookedness of the chimney. The more turns a chimney has, the greater is (usually) the draught.

To Prevent the Smut in Wheat.

Steep the grain in lime-water, or a weak ley of wood-ashes, or pearlash.

Soda Water.

Take clear water, and force into it by means of a pump, from six to ten times its bulk of carbonic acid gas, obtained from marble; cork and wire the bottles. Soda water should always be kept in a cool place, with the necks of the bottle downwards.

Best double Soda Water.

Water, 1 gallon; soda, 2 ounces. Force in gas as above.

Bottled Soda Water.

1. Take the soda water bottles, and fill them with clear water, fit corks to them, and set them down, then take one at a time, add bicarbonate of soda, ½ drachm; sulphuric acid, 10 or 12 drops. Cork immediately and wire them as before.

2. Clear water, 1 gallon; bicarbonate of soda, 10 drachms. Fill the bottles with the fluid, then add sulphuric acid, 11 or 12 drops. Cork and wire down immediately. The corks should be previously fitted in readiness.

3. Instead of sulphuric acid, use for every bottle tartaric acid, 28 grains.

Green Soft Wax.

Yellow resin, 1 part; bees-wax, 5 parts; turpentine, 1 part; green verdigris, 2 parts, or less. Mix with a gentle heat. Any other colour may be used.

Common Solder, for Tin, &c.

Lead, 2 parts; tin, 1 part. Fuse together, and pour it into moulds. Used with powdered resin.

Effervescing Soluble Tartar.

Pearlash, 1 pound; cream of tartar, 3 pounds. Dry and powder each separately, then mix them and keep them in well-corked bottles. An excellent purgative, in doses of from one to six drachms.

Lotion for Sore Legs.

Copperas (green), 6 drachms; alum, 4 drachms; verdigris (crystallized), 1 drachm; sal ammoniac, 1 drachm; water, 1 quart. Mix and dissolve.

Detergent Gargle for Inflammatory Sore Throat.

Nitrate of potash (powdered), 1 part; honey, 3 parts; infusion of roses, 21 parts. Mix. To be used every two hours.

Embrocation for Sore Throat.

Strong solution of ammonia, 3 parts; salad oil, (O. O. O.), 8 parts; tincture of opium, 2 parts. Mix. To be well rubbed in with a piece of flannel night and morning.

Soujie.

Pearl sago, 13 parts; arrow-root or pure starch, 2 parts; rusk powder, 1 part. Mix in fine powder.

German Method to Restore Sour Wines.

Put a small quantity of coarsely-powdered fresh-burnt charcoal into the cask.

Soy.

Kidney beans, 1 gallon; wheat (bruised), ½ gallon; malt, (bruised), ½ gallon; salt (bruised), 1 gallon. Mix them, and let them lay together for two or three days, then add boiling water, 2 gallons; red herrings, 1 pound; garlic, 3 ounces; Italian juice, 3 ounces. Let them stand in a jar together for three months.

Cerate of Spanish Flies.

Spermaceti ointment, 13 ounces; Spanish flies, 3 ounces. Mix.

Ointment of Spanish Flies.

1. Lard, 3 parts; powdered flies, 1 part. Mix.
2. Flies, 1 ounce; water, 5 ounces. Infuse for twelve hours, then strain with expression, and add spermaceti ointment, 5 ounces.

Plaster of Spanish Flies.

1. Simple wax plaster, 3 pounds; suet, 1 pound; cantharides or flies, 2 pounds. Mix.
2. Yellow wax, yellow resin, suet, Spanish flies, equal parts. Mix.
3. Common wax plaster, 9 parts; suet, 1 part; colour to sample. Melt and rub the rolls over with a little powder of Spanish flies. In all spread listers, it is usual to sprinkle some powdered flies over the surface, and these principally, if not solely, raise the blister. This form therefore is quite as active as the genuine plaster, and is much less expensive.

Spanish Rouge or Wool.

Colour wool with safflower rouge, and dry it.

Hard Solder.

Copper, 2 parts. Fuse, and add tin, 1 part.

Soft Solder.

Tin, 2 parts ; lead, 1 part. Fuse.

Rules for Judging when the Eyes require the assistance of Spectacles.

1. When we are obliged to remove small objects to a considerable distance from the eye in order to see them distinctly.

2. If we find it necessary to get more light than formerly, as, for instance to place the candle between the eye and the object.

3. If, on looking at, and attentively considering a near object, it fatigues the eye and becomes confused, or if it appears to have a kind of dimness or mist before it.

4. When small printed letters are seen to run into each other, and hence, by looking steadfastly on them, appear double or treble.

5. If the eyes are so fatigued by a little exercise, that we are obliged to shut them from time to time, so as to relieve them by looking at different objects.

When all these circumstances concur, or any of them separately takes place, it will be necessary to seek assistance from glasses, which will ease the eyes, and in some degree check their tendency to become worse: whereas, if they be not assisted in time, the weakness will be considerably increased, and the eyes be impaired by the efforts they are compelled to exert.

Speculum Metal.

1. Copper, 43 parts; tin, 20 parts. Mix.
2. Copper, 7 parts. Melt, and add zinc, 3 parts ; tin, 4 parts.

Spermaceti Cerate.

Sweet oil, 8 ounces; suet, 4 ounces ; white wax, 3 ounces ; spermaceti, 1 ounce. Mix, and while cooling, stir in water, 5 ounces.

Factitious Spermaceti.

White spermaceti, 10 parts ; sonorous cake stearine, 20 parts ; potato starch, 5 parts ; mucilage, 1 part. Melt the first three and unite well, then let the mass cool to the consistence of dough, turn it out on an oiled marble or lead slab, and roll it into a cake ; next sprinkle a little mucilage on it, double it, and roll again, repeat the process as often as required ; lastly, allow it to cool. If it has been properly managed, it will, when broken up, flake, and resemble spermaceti.

Oil of Spike.

1. Oil of turpentine, Barbadoes tar, of each, equal quantities. Unite with heat.

2. Oil of turpentine, 1 gallon ; Barbadoes tar, 6 ounces ; alkanet root [illegible] ounces. Macerate for three or four days.

3. (Panter's.)—Spirits of turpentine, 13 ounces ; oil of lavender, 3 ounces. Mix.

Spermaceti Ointment.

1. Oil of olives, 4 pounds; white wax, 2 pounds; spermaceti, 1 pound; water, 1½ pound. Mix, and stir until cold.

2. Olive oil, 3 pounds; suet, 4 pounds; white wax, 1 pound; spermaceti, 14 ounces. Mix, and when cooling, stir in rose-water and plain water, eight ounces each.

3. (Good and cheap.)—1. Lard, ¼ cwt.; suet, 1 cwt.; rape oil, 15 pounds. Melt, then add gum arabic, 9 pounds; dissolved in water, 2 gallons. Stir well until cold.

4. White suet, 1 cwt.; rape oil, 2 gallons. Melt with a gentle heat, then add gum arabic, 6 pounds; dissolved in water, 2 gallons. As before.

Spirit of Cytherea.

Spirit of violets, 1 part; spirit of jasmin, 1 part; spirit of tuberose, 1 part; spirit of clove gilly-flower, 1 part; spirit of roses, 1 part; spirit of Portugal, 1 part; orange-flower water, 2 parts. Mix.

Spirit of Flowers of Italy.

Spirit of jasmin, 4 parts; spirit of roses, 4 parts; spirit of oranges, 4 parts; spirit of cassia, 4 parts· orange-flower water, 3 parts. Mix.

To Sweeten Spirits.

Dissolve your sugar or syrup in the water and filter it before adding it to the other articles.

Spirit Varnish.

Strong alcohol, 32 parts; pure mastic, 4 parts; sandarach, 3 parts; clear Venice turpentine, 2 parts; coarsely-powdered glass, 4 parts. Dissolve.

Factitious Burnt Sponge.

Ivory black, 6 parts; common salt, 3 parts; powdered charcoal, 14 parts. Mix.

Sponge Lozenges.

1. White sugar 1 pound; starch, 4 ounces; burnt sponge, 4 ounces. Mucilage to mix.

2. Refined sugar (powdered), 100 parts; burnt sponge (powdered), 20 parts. Mix with mucilage.

Sponge Tents.

Dip pieces of soft sponge into melted wax, and compress them while warm. When cold, cut them into the required shapes and sizes.

Prince Rupert's Drops.

Take melted glass, and let it fall in drops into cold water. These drops possess the peculiar property of bursting into powder, with an explosion on breaking off a small portion of their tails.

Prince's Metal.

1. Copper, 3 parts; zinc, 1 part.
2. Brass, 8 parts; zinc, 1 part.
3. Zinc, copper, equal parts. Mix.

Spotted Marble for Books, &c.

After the fore-edge of the book is cut, let it remain in the press, and throw on linseeds in a regular manner; sprinkle the edge with any dark colour, till the white paper is covered, then shake off the seeds. Various colours may be used: the edge may be coloured with yellow or red before throwing on the seeds and sprinkling with blue. The seeds will make a fine fancy edge when placed very thick on different parts, with a few slightly thrown on the spaces between.

Printing Ink.

1. (Very fine.)—Balsam of capaivi, 9 parts; fine lamp-black, 4 parts; indigo, 1 part; dry yellow soap, 3 parts. Grind perfectly smooth.

2. (Extemporaneous.)—Balsam of capaivi, lamp-black to colour. Grind well together with a little soap.

3. Take linseed oil; heat it in a proper vessel until it begins to boil, then remove it from the fire and kindle the vapour; allow it to burn, till it becomes stringy when tried between the fingers, then add gradually to every quart, black resin, 1 pound. Dissolve, and add very cautiously, dry brown soap in shavings, 4½ ounces to every quart. Set it upon the fire and stir the mixture until the combination is complete; next, put into a suitable pot, finely-ground indigo, 1 ounce; fine Prussian blue, 1 ounce; fine lamp-black, 18 ounces. For every pound of resin employed pour the liquid on the colour, well mix, and lastly, subject it to the action of a mill.

To make Prints and Drawings to resemble Oil Paintings.

Canada balsam, 1 part; turpentine, 2 parts. Mix and apply it to the paper or print, previously well sized and dried.

Le Blond's Varnish for Prints.

Balsam of copaiba, 4 parts; powdered copal, 1 part. Mix and keep it in a close vessel, at a heat of 150° Fahr. until the gum is dissolved, then thin it with turpentine.

Prussian Blue.

Potash or pearlash, 10 parts; coke, cinders, or coal, 10 parts; iron turnings, 5 parts. Grind into a coarse powder and expose for half an hour to a full red heat, in an open crucible, stirring the mixture occasionally. When the small jets of purple flame cease, which will be in about the time named, allow the mass to cool; then add water to dissolve the soluble matter, and set aside the black foot that remains for a future operation. Next filter the solution, and add sulphate of iron (copperas), five parts (dissolved), and brighten the colour of the precipitate by the addition of muriatic acid. This process yields twenty-five per cent. of Prussian blue (ferrocyanide of iron) on the quantity of pure potash in the salt employed. The larger the quantity operated on, the greater the relative product.

To Dye with Prussian Blue.

Immerse the silk (previously properly cleaned with soap) in a bath of persulphate of iron, then rinse well in clean water, and plunge it into a bath of ferrocyanodide of potash, slightly acidulated with sulphuric acid Rinse. Every shade of blue may be dyed in this way by properly apportioning the strength of the baths, and the duration of the immersion.

To fine Port.

As other red wine, (see Wine.)

Southampton Port.

Cider, 80 gallons; elder wine, 20 gallons; damson wine, 25 gallons; red cape, 15 gallons; brandy, 10 gallons; catechu, 6 ounces; red tartar, 9 ounces; cochineal, 1 ounce. Mix. Silent spirit is as fit as brandy for this wine.

To improve Port.

Full flavoured port, 2 pipes; common port, 1 pipe; red cape, 2½ pipes, mountain, 20 gallons; cape madeira, 15 gallons; brandy bull or washings out, 20 gallons; red tartar (dissolved), 2 pounds; powdered gum catechu, 2¼ pounds. Mix well.

To improve Poor Red Port.

Sugar, 3 pounds; flour, 1 pound; bruised cloves, ¼ ounce; colouring, 1 quart. Mix up in two gallons of the wine, then turn it into the cask, and also add ten or twelve gallons of some full-bodied white wine, and if deficient in astringency add some powdered catechu, then fine it.

Porter.

1. Pale malt, 9 quarters; brown malt, 8 quarters; amber malt, 8 quarters: hops, 1½ cwt.; Italian juice, 30 pounds; porter extract, 5 pounds.

I.—Mash at 156° Fahr. with 52 barrels for one hour; set at 137° F.

II.—Mash at 160° Fahr. with 36 barrels; set at 146° Fahr.

III.—Mash at 150° Fahr. with 59 barrels for a quarter of an hour; set at 132° Fahr.

Boil each mash with the hops in portions, and add burnt malt to colour: cool and tun at 64° Fahr.

2. Pale malt, 8 quarters; amber malt, 6 quarters; brown malt, 2 quarters. Mash at twice, with 55 and 48 barrels of water, then boil with Kent hops, one cwt. and set with yeast, 10 gallons; salt, 7 pounds; flour, 2 pounds. Twenty barrels of good table beer may be had from the grains. If deficient in colour, add burnt malt.

3. *Good Bottling.* Pale malt, 5 quarters; amber malt, 3 quarters; brown malt, 2 quarters; patent malt to colour if required. Mash with twenty-four, fourteen and eleven barrels of water, then boil with Kent hops, one cwt., and set with yeast, 7 gallons; salt, 3 pounds. Mash the grains for table beer.

To bottle Porter.

1. Choose clear weather, if possible.
2. Leave the bung out of the cask all night.
3. Fill your bottles, then throw sheets of paper over them to keep out the dust, and let them stand for twenty-four hours, then cork and wire.
4. Pack them away in a cool place.

If for exportation to a hot climate, the bung must be left out of the cask for twenty-four hours, and the bottles must not be corked for at least three days. If for immediate use, we may ripen it in two or three days, by adding a small piece of sugar to each bottle before corking.

London Port.

Rough cider, 60 gallons; port, 10 gallons; red cape, 40 gallons; sloe juice, 1 gallon; red tartar, ¾ pound; powdered catechu, ½ pound; bruised cochineal, 6 ounces; brandy colouring, 1 pint; spirit, 10 gallons. Mix well.

Portland Powder.

Round birthwort root, gentian, leaves of germander, ground pine, tops of lesser centaury, equal parts, dried and powdered. Dose: one drachm every morning in a glass of wine, water, or tea, for gout and rheumatism.

Factitious Potash or Pearlash.

Scotch soda, 1 cwt.; quicklime, ¼ cwt.; common salt, ¼ cwt.; verdigris 2 ounces. Mix all together in coarse powder and heat them in an iron pot until they unite into one mass; then cool and break it into small pieces.

Effervescing Solution of Potass.

Bicarbonate of potass, one ounce; distilled water, one gallon. Dissolve, then put it into suitable sized bottles, and force in carbonic acid gas to *supersaturate* the potass. Keep it well stopped and in a cool place.

Pommade avec l'Hydriodate de Potasse.

Hydriodate of potass, 20 grains; prepared lard, one ounce. Mix with care. Used as an application in scrofula and syphilis to swelled glands.

Pommade de Hydriodate Iodure de Potasse.

Hydriodate of potass, 20 grains; iodine, 9 grains; lard, 1 ounce. Mix with care. Applied to scrofulous and venereal swellings.

Pure or Caustic Potass.

Powdered fresh-burnt lime, one part; pearlash, 2 parts; water, 12 parts. Mix, well agitate in a close vessel, and allow it to settle: filter and evaporate until the solution appears like oil, then pour it on an iron plate and cut it into pieces. Preserve it in well-closed bottles.

Subcarbonate of Potass.

1. Nitre, 4 parts; charcoal, 1 part. Pour or throw them into a heated crucible, then cool, wash out the alkali, filter and evaporate to dryness.

2. Pearlash, one part; water, ten parts. Dissolve, filter and evaporate to dryness.

Sugar from Potatoes.

Prepared from the washed pulp in the same manner as Starch Sugar.

Poudre Subtil, for removing superfluous Hair.

Powdered quicklime, two parts; sulphuret of arsenic, one part; starch, one part. Mix in fine powder, and keep in a well-closed vessel.

Process recommended for the Cure of Cancer.

Ashes of red-oak bark boiled down to the consistence of molasses, and cover the cancer with it. In about an hour afterwards, cover it with a plaster of tar, which must be removed after a few days; and if any protuberance remain in the wound, apply more potash and the plaster again until this shall disappear.

Potent Mustard.

Powdered Cayenne pepper, one part; flour of mustard, 15 parts. Mix

Pure Potass Water.

Powdered fresh-burnt lime, 1 part; solution of pearlash (filtered), 2 parts; hot water, 10 parts. Mix and agitate well in a close vessel; when cold, filter and reduce it to any required strength.

Imitation of Gold.

Take linseed oil, 3 ounces; tartar, 2 ounces; yolk of eggs, boiled hard and beaten, 2 ounces; aloes, ½ ounce; saffron, 5 grains; turmeric, 2 grains. Boil all these together in an earthen vessel, and with it wash the iron, and it will look like gold. If there be not linseed oil enough, you may add more.

Thenard's and Blainville's Lithographic Ink.

Soap, one-fourth; mutton suet, one-half; yellow wax, one part; mastic in tears, one-half, and as much lamp-black as necessary.

Black produced by the Mixture of Colourless Liquids.

One of the most interesting phenomena in the operations of chemistry occurs in the decomposition of the sulphate of iron by the gallic acid. Into a wine-glass, containing the infusion of galls, pour a solution of the sulphate of iron. The gallic acid, from its superior elective affinity to the iron, detaches it from its former combination with the sulphuric acid, and in a short time, these two fluids, previously colourless, become intensely black. To make this black fluid into ink, nothing but a little gum is required to retard the precipitation of the feculæ.

Preparation of Borax for the Blow-pipe.

Take one ounce of borax, coarsely powdered, put it into a clean crucible, and cover it loosely. Put the whole into a furnace, and watch it till it ceases to swell, then augment the heat, and when the whole fuses quietly, take it out, and pour it into a wedgewood-ware or metallic mortar, and when cold, reduce it to an impalpable powder, in which state it is to be used.

Method of cleaning Brass Ornaments.

Brass ornaments, that have not been gilt or lacquered, may be cleaned, and a very brilliant colour given to them, by washing them with alum boiled in strong ley, in the proportion of an ounce to a pint, and afterwards rubbing them with strong tripoli.

Frost counteracted.

As the blossoms of fruit trees are more particularly affected by early frosts, the following plan has been recommended to counteract the injurious effects of the same:—A rope is to be interwoven among the branches of the tree, and one end of it immersed in a pail of water. This rope it is said will act as a conductor and convey the effects of the frost from the tree to the water. Both hemp and straw have been recommended for this purpose.

Acetous Ether in Deafness.

The vapour of acetous ether has been recently discovered by Kramer, a German artist, to be a most effectual remedy for a species of this distressing malady hitherto considered incurable. It has recently been employed by Dr. Bolton, of Richmond, Va. with remarkable success.

Useful Effects of Iodine as a Medicine.

Dr Coindet has been employing iodine in the treatment of goitres and scrofula with a success surpassing his most sanguine hopes. It is to be introduced into the system by means of rubbing, in the same manner as other mineral ointments. Out of twenty-two patients, who had all very large goitres, half of them were completely cured in the space of from four to six weeks, and the others in a greater or less degree.

Files and Rasps.

Files and other instruments for the abrasion of various substances may be made by folding up separate pieces of wet clay in muslin, cambric, and Irish linen, forcing them by the pressure of the hand into the interstices or the threads, so that on divesting them of the covering, and having them well baked, a file is produced of a new species, said to be capable of operating on steel; and very useful in cutting glass, polishing, and rasping wood, ivory, and all sorts of metals.

Flame of Hydrogen rendered Luminous.

Dr. Hare, of Philadelphia, has rendered the flame of hydrogen luminous, like that of oil, by adding a small quantity of oil of turpentine to the usual mixture for generating that gas. The light seems greater than that of carburetted hydrogen. He also found that the addition of one-seventeenth of oil of turpentine to alcohol gives this fluid the property of burning with a highly luminous flame, and there is a certain point in the proportions when the mixture burns without smoke, like a gas-light.

Preservation of Fruits by Carbonic Acid Gas.

Cherries, grapes, pears, apples and chestnuts, (and perhaps all other fruits,) placed in glass vessels filled with this gas, obtained from carbonate of lime by sulphuric acid, are said to be preserved without undergoing any change for a long period. Cherries, at the end of six weeks, had the same appearance as when preserved in brandy.

To remove Spots from Piece Goods.

Dampen them over with a sponge dipped into a weak solution of pearl-ash and water, (from one to two ounces to the gallon, according to the strength or delicacy of the colour,) and immediately roll up the goods, so that they may remain damp for two or three hours, (sometimes a whole night is necessary;) then hang out to dry in the shade, never allowing the sun to shine on them, or they will be spoiled.

To prevent Pumps and Water-pipes freezing in Winter.

Take up the valve or sucker, and let all the water out of the trunk or pipe.

For Hydrophobia.

Take of the *Herba Angali Ruber*, or red cheek weed, that has been dried, one handful, pour two quarts of good beer on it, and boil it in a new earthen pot; cover the pot with a clean, close lid until one-half the liquid boils away; boil it over a slow fire; the vessel in which it is boiled must be kept very clean and used for no other purpose; when the herb is boiled enough it must be strained through a clean cloth and squeezed so that all the substance is taken out of it, then add to the decoction two drachms of the best *Therian Venetia* or *Venice Trioite;* it must be well dissolved and mixed with the above decoction. Of this preparation, give a man or child the following proportions in the morning, fasting: A man of a strong constitution must take a pint, and that at one time, if possible. If there be any symptoms of madness the medicine must be taken two or three mornings in succession; but if actual symptoms of madness exist, a larger quantity of herb should be used to the aforesaid quantity of beer. A woman should take less than a man. For children it should be regulated according to their age and constitution. It must be observed, that children can bear more than grown persons in proportion to their age. Take the medicine warm, and do not break the fast for 3 or 4 hours; drink no water, or serious consequences may arise. When madness actually exists, no delay should be made, but the medicine given as soon as the fit is off, and should the patient reject it it must be given in small proportions at intervals, and until the person is relieved must abstain from the following: pork of all kinds, cabbage of all sorts, peas, beans, fish or water-fowl. If the person is bit through the skin the wound must be scratched until it bleeds, with a chip, and washed with some of the decoction, should it be left. If the wound requires dressing, any simple ointment mixed with the *Therian* will answer. This must be done once or twice a day until the wound is healed.

Ginger Lozenges.

Take eight pounds of loaf sugar in fine powder, and eight ounces of the best ground ginger. Mix them into a paste with dissolved gum. If gum tragacanth be preferred, the proportion is one pint of water to one ounce of gum; when properly dissolved, it must be forcibly passed through the interstices of a coarse towel or cloth. One ounce of this dissolved gum is sufficient for four or five pounds of sugar;—or one ounce of dissolved gum Arabic to twelve ounces of sugar. Essence may be used instead of powdered ginger, colouring it with saffron. A stimulant and stomachic.

Ginger Drops.

Mix a sufficient quantity of the best powdered ginger to give it the desired taste, or flavour it with the essence of ginger, and colour it with saffron. Moisten with water, and form the drops upon moistened paper, or tin or copper plates, and place them in the stove, with moderate heat.

Indian Cure for the Heart-Ache.

Take a piece of the lean of mutton, about the size of a large walnut, put it into the fire and burn it for some time, till it becomes almost reduced to a cinder, then put it into a clean rag and squeeze it until some moisture is expressed, which must be dropped in the ear as hot as the patient can bear.

Weak Sight.

Beat up a drachm of alum in the white of an egg, and smear the eye-brow and eye-lid every night with the mixture.

Locked Jaw.

It is said that the application of warm ley, made of ashes as strong as possible, to a wounded part, will prevent a lock jaw; if a foot or hand, immersed in it; if another part of the body, bathed with flannels wrung out from the warm ley.

An Incomparable Medicine for the Scurvy in the Teeth.

Take a quart of good white-wine vinegar, heat a piece of steel red-hot, and quench it eight or ten times in the vinegar, as fast as you can heat it; then add to this liquor an ounce of powdered myrrh, and half an ounce of mastic, powdered; wash your teeth twice or thrice a day.

A very good way to Prevent the Nail growing into the Toe.

If the nail of your toe be hard, and apt to grow round, and into the corners of your toe, take a piece of broken glass and scrape the top very thin; do this whenever you cut your nails, and, by constant use, it makes the corners fly up and grow flat, so that it is impossible they should give you any pain.

To make the Hair grow Thick.

Take rosemary, maiden-hair, southern-wood, myrtle-berries, hazel-bark, of each 2 ounces; burn these to ashes on a clean hearth, or in an oven; put these ashes in white wine, to make a strong ley, and wash the hair daily at the root; keep it cut pretty short. It kills the worm which is at the root.

Compost—A Substitute for Soap-Boiler's Spent Ley.

Take of fine, dry, snuffy peat, 50 pounds; salt, ½ bushel; ashes, 1 bushel; water, 100 gallons. Mix the ashes and peat well together, sprinkling with water to moisten a little; let the heap lay for a week. Dissolve the salt in the water, in a hogshead, and add to the brine the mixture of peat and ashes, stirring well the while. Let it be stirred occasionally for a week, and it will be fit for use. Apply as spent ley, grounds and all. Both ashes and salt may be doubled and trebled with advantage, if convenient. The mixture must be used before it begins to putrefy; this occurs in three weeks. It then evolves sulphuretted hydrogen gas, or the smell of gas of rotten eggs; this arises from the decomposition of the sulphates in the water and ashes, by the vegetable matter. A portion of geine is thus deposited from the solution.

To make Blue Ink for Ruling.

Take 4 ounces of vitriol, best quality, to 1 ounce of indigo; pulverize the indigo very fine; put the indigo on the vitriol, let them stand exposed to the air for six days, or until dissolved; then fill the pot with chalk, add half a gill of fresh gall, boiling it before use.

To make Black Ink for Ruling.

Take good black ink, and add gall as for blue; do not cork it, as it will prevent it from turning black.

To make Red Ink for Ruling.

One pound of Brazil-wood to one gallon of the best vinegar; let the vinegar simmer before you add the wood, then let them simmer together for half an hour, then add three-quarters of a pound of alum to set the colour; strain it through a woollen or cotton cloth, cork it tight in a stone or glass bottle. For ruling, add half a gill of fresh gall to one quart of red ink, then cork it up in a bottle for use.

Cultivation of the Grape.

The best soil for the vine is a light, dry loam, with a slight intermixture of clay and calcareous matter, moderately rich, the ground inclining a little to the south. This should be ploughed in the fall of the year, at least one foot deep, and trench ploughing would be better, making one plough follow directly after another in the same furrow, turning up the ground if possible 15 or 18 inches deep. The utility of this is, to give a light, deep surface for the roots to strike into the earth, and thus draw the more nourishment from it, and be sufficiently low and out of the way of being cut off, when the plough is run between the rows for after cultivation.

Planting and Culture.—Early in the spring, before vegetation commences, replough and harrow the land fine, strike off the rows 6 feet apart, then take cuttings or roots, as they can be best obtained, and plant them 3 feet from each other in the rows. As the vines grow they will require staking and tying up with the stalks of long, tough grass, or green, flexible straw. The after cultivation is precisely like that of corn or any root crop, it being necessary merely to plough out between the rows occasionally, and keep the weeds down by hoeing the ground about the vines, where it may be slightly elevated from the centre of the rows, in order to keep them from standing water. Two vines only are left from each main stem of a different year's growth, the rationale of which may be thus simply defined. The branch that grew for instance in the season of '40, bears in '41, and the spring of '42 it is pruned off, and that season another grows in its place, prepared to bear in '43, while that which grew in '41 bears in '42, and is cut off in '43, and the one growing in '42, when the last gave fruit, will bear in '43.

A well-cultivated field of grapes, in a reasonable favourable season, will yield 100 bushels to the acre. One hundred bushels will produce 300 to 400 gallons wine, which is worth at least $1 per gallon, so that it will be seen, that the cultivation of the grape and making wine is quite a profitable business.

To make Wine.—Gather the grapes when fully ripe, put them into a common wash-tub, take a wooden pounder, precisely like that used by women when washing to pound out the clothes, and with light blows thoroughly mash the grapes. Then take them to a screw-press, made like those used for pressing cider, but instead of laying up the pulp of the grapes in straw, like apple-pumice, take pieces of joist 3 inches square, and cut out mortices in each end, and lock them together as high as the pulp is to be laid up, say about 3 feet. These make a firm, square box, that will endure a very strong pressure from the screw, which is quite necessary to squeeze out all the wine. Many put a double purchase on the lever of the screw, to better effect this purpose. When the bruised grapes are laid up, fit a plank top just large enough to lay inside the joist to bear down the pulp, place blocks on this, and then commence pressing. Let the wine run out into an open tub, and if it will bear an egg, that is, swim it on the same principles as the strength of ley is tried, commence filling the barrel, but if not strong enough, add from 4 to 10 ounces of sugar per gallon till it will bear the egg.

After being placed in barrels, if the weather be warm, the wine will commence fermenting in a few hours, if cool, in a few days, and if cold, not short of a week or fortnight; in fact, it is subject to pretty much the same natural rule that cider is, and perhaps the better way of producing fermentation, is to place the casks as soon as filled in a cellar, of a temperature of about 50° of Fahrenheit, and thus keep it till fermented and ready to be bottled. If not removed to a cellar previous to fermentation, it should be done as soon as this process is gone through with, and in the following February or March, let it be racked off by tapping the barrel within three inches or so of the bottom, and placing the wine thus drawn from it in another barrel. This should be repeated every year as long as the wine stands in casks, as it tends to purify and improve its quality. If the wine be not clear when the process is attempted, beat up the whites of from 3 to 6 eggs for each barrel, and pour in and mix up well, and it will soon settle and rack off clear. To still further improve the quality, add loaf or brown sugar in small quantities of the wine.

Kinds of Grapes.—The Cape, or properly, the Schuylkill Muscadel, and the Catawba, both natives of the United States, are considered the best varieties for America, that have yet been tried. The latter is the hardiest and best yielder, and makes a wine very much like the celebrated Rhenish.

The Muscadel makes a wine tasting something like a mixture of Madeira and Claret. If one pound of sugar be added to each gallon, and it has the advantage of standing 2 years in barrel, and 3 more in bottle, it can hardly be distinguished from fair Madeira.

The Isabella, and many other varieties of grape are good for the table; but the wine from them either proves too light-bodied to keep, or comes out sour, crabbed, and rough.

Bronzing.

Bronze of a good quality acquires, by oxidation, a fine, green tint, called *patina antiqua*. Corinthian brass receives, in this way, a beautiful clear, green colour. This appearance is imitated by an artificial process, called bronzing. A solution of sal ammoniac and salt of sorel in vinegar is used for bronzing metals. Any number of layers may be applied, and the shade becomes deeper in proportion to the number applied. For bronzing sculptures of wood, plaster-figures, &c., a composition of yellow ochre, Prussian blue, and lamp-black, dissolved in glue-water, is employed.

To take Mildew out of Linen.

Take soap and rub it well; then scrape some fine chalk, and rub that also in the linen; lay it on the grass; as it dries wet it a little, and it will come out at twice.

Elastic Cement for Bells.

Dissolve in good brandy, a sufficient quantity of isinglass, so as to be as thick as molasses.

Prometheans.

These useful articles consist of a fold of paper, having a solid red substance inclosed at one end, which inflames with a blow from or against any hard body.

If you soak one of the prometheans in water, and then spread it open, you will find its construction to be extremely simple. The paper is a parallelogram of two inches by one in size, with a triangle cut off at one corner to remove a projection which would otherwise be situate where the red substance is put. This red substance is a mixture of chlorate of potash and sugar, coloured by vermilion, and made into a mass with gum. If you shake it in water, the vermilion precipitates, while the other substances dissolve.

When you come to shake the red substance in water, you find that it is not homogeneous; but that, though itself of no greater bulk than a barley-corn, it contains a vessel of glass of the size and shape of a canary seed, excepting that it is round instead of being flat. This little vessel is closed at both ends, and is easily seen to contain a liquid. If you crush it and put the fragments into water, you will find, by applying a solution of chloride of barium, that the liquid which is contained in it is no other than sulphuric acid.

This is the whole secret of the promethean! When you knock the end of it, you make the imprisoned sulphuric acid come into contact with the mixture of sugar and chlorate of potash; the mixture then inflames, and the inflammation is communicated to the paper.

Directions for making Prometheans.—Take equal parts of finely-pounded chlorate of potash and loaf-sugar; add a small quantity of pulverized vermilion, and mix the whole intimately together; first in the dry state, and afterwards with a solution of gum arabic, by which you make it into a dough.

Caution.—The salts must be well pounded before they are mixed together, and after being mixed must be treated very gently. A mixture of chlorate of potash with sugar is liable to explode if struck violently, or exposed to very rude handling. You should mix only a small quantity of the compound at once.

To make the glass beads, hold a thin glass tube over the flame of a lamp, and when the glass is soft, draw it out till it is about as thick as a knitting-needle, or rather until it forms a series of little ovals. Break these asunder so as to leave each oval one-third of an inch long. Close one end by holding it in the flame, then warm the oval by holding it in a pair of pincers over the flame, and while it is hot, dip the open end into sulphuric acid, a portion of which will then rise up into the oval. The open point can finally be closed by being held in the flame, or by having the blowpipe flame directed upon it. The most difficult part of the operation is the closing of the last point, because the heat applied for that purpose is very apt, if clumsily directed, to expel the sulphuric acid from the little vessel.

The paste and the glass beads being provided, you take a slip of paper of the form above described; you spread a solution of gum arabic across that end of the paper where the corner is cut off, and then roll it up into a cylinder, leaving a hollow at the gummed end. You then take a small piece of the red mixture, put one of the glass beads in the middle of it, and force the whole into the open end of the paper roll, in which place you fix it by a gentle squeeze with the fingers. The promethean is then finished. However, it requires to be well dried before it can be made to inflame.

Puff Paste.

1. Flour, 5 pounds; butter, 4 pounds. Mix by rolling.

2. Take common dough, roll it out, then add a thin layer of butter, double it and roll again, add more butter, and repeat the process of rolling, &c., eleven or twelve times, or more.

Self-acting Nautical Pump.

Captain Leslie, of the George and Susan, in a voyage from North America to Stockholm, adopted an excellent mode of emptying water from his ship's hold, when the crew were insufficient to perform that duty. About ten or twelve feet above the pump he rigged out a spar, one end of which projected overboard, while the other was fastened as a lever to the machinery of the pump. To the end which projected overboard was suspended a water-butt, half full, but corked down: so that when the coming wave raised the butt-end, the other end depressed the piston of the pump; but at the retiring of the wave, this was reversed, for, by the weight of the butt, the piston came up again, and with it the water. Thus, without the aid of the crew, the ship's hold was cleared of the water in a few hours.

A very useful hint may be taken from this plan; when a vessel has much water, and there are not hands enough to work the pumps, one pump might be arranged on this plan, and the other fully manned in the usual way.

Punch, on the Large Scale.

Water, 3 gallons; tartaric acid, 4 ounces, or to taste; sugar (lump), to sweeten; brandy, 3 pints; rum, 3 pints; the peels of three lemons grated; essence of lemon to flavour. Rub the essence with a little lump-sugar in a mortar, adding a little of the spirit, then mix. A few drops of the essence of bitter almonds improve this article.

Purgative Draught.

Rhubarb, 10 grains; jalap, 10 grains; tincture of ginger, 1 drachm; water, 1 ounce. Mix.

Purl.

Wormwood, 10 pounds; gentian, 6 pounds; rind of oranges (dried), 2 pounds; ginger (bruised), ½ pound; cloves, 2 ounces; cardamons, 8 ounces; water, 6 gallons. Boil, then digest for fourteen or fifteen days, and decant into wine bottles. Add this to warm beer according to taste.

Purple Dye for Cottons.

Pass them through a dilute mordant of acetate of iron, and dye them in a bath of madder and logwood.

Glazier's Putty.

Whiting, 70 pounds; boiled oil, 30 pounds; water, 2 gallons. Mix. If too thin, add more whiting; if too thick, add more oil.

Purple of Cassius.

1. A solution of gold in nitromuriatic acid, dilute it largely with water, and precipitate the gold with pieces of metallic tin.

2. A dilute solution of gold, and add a dilute acidulated solution of muriate of tin, as long as any precipitate is produced.

3. (Very fine.)—Crystallized protochloride of tin, 1 part; crystallized perchloride of tin, 2 parts; crystallized chloride of gold, 1 part. Dissolve each separately; mix the first two solutions, then add the gold.

Purple Sealing-Wax.

Red wax, 2 parts; blue wax, 3 parts. Mix with heat.

Purple Sprinkle for Bookbinders.

Logwood chips, 4 parts; powdered alum, 1 part; soft water, 24 parts. Boil until reduced to sixteen parts, and bottle for use.

2. Brazil dust (fine), and mix it with potash water for use.

Purple Tablets.

Magnesia, 2 pounds; sugar, 1 pound; gum powder, ½ pound. Mix with water, strongly coloured with cochineal; or use a little purple lake. Perfume with ottar of roses.

Pyro-acetic Spirit.

1. Take acetate of copper; powder, and subject to dry distillation in a sand heat. Rectify the product from a little bone-black and chloride of calcium.

2. Take acetate of lead, and proceed as before.

3. Take acetate of potass, and proceed as before.

4. Take acetate of lime, and proceed as before.

5. Take acetate of manganese; proceed as before.

6. Take acetate of zinc, as before.

7. Take peracetate of iron; as before.

Pyro-acetic spirit forms an excellent article for burning in lamps; it gives a bright, white flame, without smoke. The preceding articles yield the spirit in proportional quantities, as follows

No. 5. = 0·939.
6. = 0·695.
2. = 0·554.
7. = 0·241.
1. = 0·171.

Pyrophorus.

1. Burnt alum, 9 parts; charcoal powder, 4 parts. Mix, and put them into a phial or matrass, with a neck about six inches long, and only three-quarters fill it; put it into a crucible surrounded with sand, and apply heat, until the whole becomes red-hot, in which state keep it for fifteen minutes, until a sulphurous vapour begins to exhale, which may be allowed to enflame, but as soon as it ceases, the heat must be withdrawn, and the phial closely stopped. When cold, transfer the mixture to a dry, warm, stoppered phial.

2. Alum, 3 parts; wheat flour, 1 part. Treat as before.

Brewer's Quassia Colouring.

Take quassia, and roast it until it acquires the proper colour.

Queen's Metal.

1. Lead, 1 part, bismuth, 1 part; antimony, 1 part; tin, 9 parts. Mix.

2. Tin, 9 parts; bismuth, 1 part; lead, 2 parts; antimony, 1 part. Mix by melting.

3. Tin, 1000 parts; regulus of antimony, 80 parts; bismuth, 10 parts; copper, 40 parts. Melt the copper, then expertly add the rest and mix well together.

Oxide of Quicksilver.

Quicksilver, 1 part; nitric acid, 1 part; water, 6 parts. Dissolve and precipitate the oxide, with the solution of an alkali.

Purified Quicksilver.

Quicksilver, iron filings, equal parts. Distil in an iron retort, into a vessel containing water.

German Method to Prepare Quills.

Suspend the quills in a copper over water, sufficiently high to touch the nibs; then close it steam-tight, and apply four hours' hard boiling; next withdraw and dry them, and in twenty-four hours cut the nibs and draw out the pith; lastly, rub them with a piece of cloth and expose them to a moderate heat. The quills prepared in this way are as hard as bone, without being brittle, and as transparent as glass.

Quince Marmalade.

Take quinces that are quite ripe, pare and cut them in quarters, take out the cores, put them into a stew-pan with nearly enough spring-water to cover them, keep them closely covered, and let them stew gently till they are quite soft and red, then mash and rub them through a hair sieve. Put them in a pan over a gentle fire, with as much thick clarified sugar as the weight of the quinces; boil them an hour and stir the whole time with a wooden spoon to prevent its sticking: put it into pots, and when cold tie them down.

Quince Wine.

Quinces (sliced), 12 in number; boil for a quarter of an hour, in water, 1 gallon; then add lump-sugar, 2 pounds. Ferment, and add lemon wine, 1 gallon; spirit, 1 pint.

Quinine Mixture.

Take sulphate of quinine thirteen grains, powdered gum arabic one drachm, loaf-sugar half an ounce, water six ounces, essence of peppermint five drops. Shake the bottle well each time it is poured out. The dose is a table-spoonful every hour.

Raisin Spirit.

Chopped raisins, 1 part; water a sufficient quantity. Mash, ferment and distil with a quick fire. Used to flavour plain spirit in imitation of brandy, in the proportion of $\frac{1}{150}$ to $\frac{1}{200}$.

Quin's Sauce.

1. Walnut catsup, 2 gallons; mushroom catsup, 2 gallons; soy, 1 gallon; garlic, 1 pound; cayenne, ½ pound; sprats, 6 pounds. Boil for fifteen minutes; strain and bottle.

2. White vinegar, 1 gallon; soy, 1 pint; mushroom catsup, ½ pint; walnut catsup, ½ pint; allspice, 8 ounces; cayenne, 1 ounce Mix, and boil or macerate, then strain and bottle.

3. Green walnut-juice, 1 part; anchovies, 1 part; vinegar, 1 part; cloves, mace, pimento, and shallots, of each 1 drachm to every pound of juice. Boil and strain.

Radley's Mixed Oils.

Oil of vitriol, ¼ pound; oil of turpentine, 4 pounds; oil of linseed, 4 pounds; Barbadoes tar, ½ pound. Mix, and when cold add oil of origanum, 1 ounce.

Rag Sugar.

Prepared from rags by the action of sulphuric acid, by a similar process to that for making starch sugar.

Raisin Tea.

Stoned raisins, 1 pound; water, 5 quarts. Boil to one gallon and strain.

Raisin Vinegar.

After making raisin wine, lay the pressed raisins in a heap to heat, then to each cwt. put ten gallons of water, and a little yeast.

Raisin Wine.

1. Raisins, 5 cwt.; water, 100 gallons. Put them into a cask. Mash for a fortnight, frequently stirring, and leave the bung loose until the active fermentation ceases, then add brandy, 5 gallons. Well mix, and let it stand till fine. The quantity of raisins and brandy may be altered to suit the intended quality of the wine.

2. Sweet cider, 120 gallons; raisins, 3 cwt. or less. Mix and ferment, then add silent spirit, 9 gallons, or less; finings, 2 quarts; white tartar, 12 ounces. Bung close until fine, then bottle.

To Purify Rape Oil.

1. Rape oil, 100 gallons; strong oil of vitriol, 2 gallons. Put them into a cask and agitate for one hour, decant the clear oil in three days, and then divide the oil into two portions and put each into separate casks, add forty or fifty gallons of hot water to each, and agitate for one hour more; in three days or more, decant the clear for use.

2. Rape oil, 50 gallons; hot water, 50 gallons. Put them into a well-seasoned cask and bung tight, then roll it about for two hours; in two or three days, decant the oil, when if not pure enough, repeat the process The water dissolves the mucilage mixed with the oil.

Raspberry Vinegar.

Red raspberries, 9 pints; vinegar, 1 gallon. Macerate, then strain with expression, and add sugar, 4 or 5 pounds; brandy, ¾ pint.

Raspberry Brandy.

The same as cherry brandy with the difference of the fruit.

Raspberry Water.

Raspberries, 1 cwt.; water, 28 gallons. Distil over twenty-three gallons.

Raspberry Wine.

Fruit (bruised), 25 gallons; cider, 10 gallons; water, 15 gallons; sugar, 50 pounds. Ferment, then add red tartar (dissolved), ½ pound; spirit, 2 to 4 gallons; orange-peel (dry), 1 ounce; lemon-peel (dry), 1 ounce; bitter almonds, ½ ounce; cloves, ½ ounce; orris root, ½ ounce.

Dr. Ratcliffe's Cough Mixture.

Syrup of squills, 1 ounce; tincture of paregoric, 1 ounce; syrup of poppies, 1 ounce. Dose, one teaspoonful.

Ratifia à la Violette.

Orris root (powdered), 1 ounce; archil, 4 ounces; spirit, 2 gallons. Digest, then add sugar, 7 pounds; dissolved in water, 4 pints. Mix and filter.

Ratifia d'Angelique.

Angelica seeds, 1 ounce; angelica stalks, 4 ounces; blanched bitter almonds, 8 or 10 ounces; proof-spirit, 10 gallons; sugar, 1½ pound to every gallon. Digest for fourteen days, then filter.

Ratifia de Brou de Noix.

Young walnuts (bruised), 60 in number; brandy or spirit, 4 pints Macerate, then add sugar, 14 ounces; dissolved in water, 1 pint. Add mace (bruised), 15 grains; cassia (bruised), 15 grains; cloves (bruised), 15 grains. Macerate for one month, and strain.

Ratifia de Cassis.

Black currants (ripe and bruised), 12 pounds; cloves (bruised), 1 drachm; cinnamon (bruised), 2 drachms; sugar, 5 pounds; water, 4 gallons. Macerate for a fortnight, and strain. Add a little spirit.

Ratifia de Grenoble.

Black cherries (kernels bruised), 25 pounds; proof-spirit, 12 gallons; orange-peel, ¼ ounce or more; lemon-peel, ¼ ounce or more; citron-peel, ¼ ounce or more. Digest for a month, then add sugar, 26 pounds; dissolved in water, 1 gallon. Mix and strain.

Ratifia de Chocolat.

Caracca cocoa-nuts (roasted and bruised), 10 pounds; West India cocoa-nuts (roasted and bruised), 5 pounds; tincture of vanilla, 1 ounce; proof spirit, 10 gallons. Digest for fourteen days, and strain, then add sugar, 20 pounds; dissolved in water, 3 gallons. Well mix and filter.

Ratifia de Café.

Ground and roasted coffee, 1 pound; sugar, 1½ pound; proof-spirit, ' gallon; water, 2 quarts. Digest for a week, and strain.

Rice Bread.

Take one pound of rice, and boil it gently to a thick paste, which, when mixed with the usual quantity of yeast, will be sufficient to make five pounds of wheat or barley meal into a dough. When risen, bake it in the usual way.

Sweet Apple Pudding.

Take one pint of scalding milk, half a pint of Indian meal, a tea-spoonful of salt, and six sweet apples cut into small pieces, and bake not less than three hours; the apples will afford an excellent rich jelly. This is truly one of the most luxurious yet simple Yankee puddings made.

Watery Potatoes.

We every day hear complaints about watery potatoes. Put into the pot a piece of lime as large as a hen's egg; and how watery soever the potatoes may have been, when the water is poured off, the potatoes will be perfectly dry and mealy.

Chickens.

A disease called *the gapes*, so destructive among chickens, may be prevented, and if not too far advanced cured, by a slight mixture of assafœtida in their food. Four ounces, costing six cents per ounce, dissolved in water and mixed once a day in food, is enough for four hundred chickens.

Cure for Cancer.

Take the narrow-leaved dock-root, boil it in soft water, and wash the ulcer with the strong decoction as warm as it can be borne; fill the cavity with the liquor for two minutes; then scrape the hulk of the root, bruise it fine, put it on gauze, and lay it over every part of the ulcer; dip a linen cloth in the decoction, and put it over the gauze. Repeat this three times in twenty-four hours, and at each time let the patient take a wine-glass of the tea made of the root with one-third of a glass of port wine sweetened with honey.

Cure for Colds.

Take a large tea-spoonful of flaxseed, with two pennyworth of extract of liquorice, and a quarter of a pound of sun raisins. Put it into two quarts of soft water, and let it simmer over a slow fire till it is reduced to one; then add to it a quarter of a pound of brown sugar candy, pounded, a table-spoonful of white wine vinegar, or lemon-juice. *Note.* The vinegar is best to be added only to that quantity you are going immediately to take; for if it be put into the whole, it is liable in a little time to grow flat.—Drink a half pint on going to bed, and take a little when the cough is troublesome.

This recipe generally cures the worst of colds in two or three days, and, if taken in time, may be said to be almost an infallible remedy. It is a sovereign balsamic cordial for the lungs, without the opening qualities which engender fresh colds on going out. It has been known to cure colds, that have almost been settled into consumptions, in less than three weeks.

Hoarseness.

One drachm of freshly-scraped horseradish root, to be infused with four ounces of water in a close vessel for two hours, and made into a syrup with double its weight in vinegar, is an approved remedy for hoarseness; a tea-spoonful has often proved effectual; a few tea-spoonfuls, it is said, have never been known to fail in removing hoarseness.

Consumption.

The following is said to be an effectual remedy, and will in time completely eradicate the disorder. Live temperately—avoid spirituous liquors—wear flannel next the skin—and take, every morning, half a pint of new milk, mixed with a wine-glassful of the expressed juice of green hoarhound. One who has tried it says—"Four weeks' use of the hoarhound and milk relieved the pains of my breast, gave me to breathe deep, long, and free, strengthened and harmonized my voice, and restored me to a better state of health than I had enjoyed for years."

Inflammations.

Chlorate of soda is an immediate and effectual cure for the sting of bees, mosquitoes, &c.; for burns, (where the skin is not broken,) ringworms, and other like inflammations.

Ringworms.

After I had the tetter nearly twenty years on my hand, and had used dollars' worth of celebrated tetter ointment, which took off the skin repeatedly without effecting a cure, a friend advised me to obtain some blood-root, (called also red-root, Indian paint, &c.) to slice it in vinegar, and afterwards wash the place affected with the liquid. I did so, and in a few days the dry scurf was removed, and my diseased hand was as whole as the other.

Asthma.

Make a strong solution of saltpetre. Dip clean paper in the solution until it is well saturated. Dry the paper in the sun or by a slow fire. Cut the paper thus dried into strips, and burn them in a vessel, so that the *asthmatic* may breathe in, or inhale, as much of the smoke as possible.

Make cigars of the paper, if you choose, and smoke them. This is the most agreeable method of application.

Sago Bread.

This light and nutritious article for invalids is made in the following manner:—Two pounds of sago, to be well soaked in water, or milk, several hours; mix it with as much flour; add sal-eratus and good yeast, (a little Indian meal, if liked;) when well raised, give it a handsome bake. It is delicious, healthy, and cheap.

Flies.

The butchers of Geneva have, from time immemorial, prevented flies from approaching the meat which they expose for sale, by the use of laurel oil. This oil, the smell of which, although a little strong, is not very offensive, drives away flies; and they dare not come near the walls or the wainscots which have been rubbed with it.

Mortar.

Much of the mortar used in building is said to be imperfectly made Four parts coarse and three parts fine sand, with one part of quick-lime, well mixed with but little water, makes mortar which soon becomes as hard as adamant; resisting all atmospheric action as durably as the material it unites; and with addition of a portion of manganese, it will harden under water.

Tar for Sheep.

A gentleman, who keeps a large flock of sheep, says that during the season of grazing he gives his sheep *tar*, at the rate of a gill a day for every twenty sheep. He puts the tar in a trough, sprinkles a little fine salt over it, and the sheep consume it with eagerness. This preserves them from worms in the head, promotes their general health, and is thought to be a specific against the rot.

To prevent Horses being teased by Flies.

Take two or three small handfuls of walnut leaves, upon which pour two or three quarts of cold water; let it infuse one night, and pour the whole, next morning, into a kettle, and let it boil for a quarter of an hour; when cold, it will be fit for use. No more is required than to moisten a sponge, and, before the horse goes out of the stable, let those parts which are most irritable be smeared over with the liquor, viz. between and upon the ears, the neck, the flank, &c. Not only the lady or gentleman who rides out for pleasure, will derive benefit from this preparation, but the coachman, the wagoner, and all others who use horses during the hot months.

Liniment for the galled Backs of Horses.

White-lead moistened with milk. When milk is not to be procured, oil may be substituted. One or two ounces sufficed for a whole party for more than a month.

Bots in Horses.

The stage-drivers on the routes leading from Albany to the western parts of the state of New York, in giving water to their horses on the road, mix a little wood ashes with their drink, which, they say, effectually preserves them against the bots.

Fattening Turkeys.

Experiments have been successfully tried of shutting up turkeys in a small apartment made perfectly dark. They were fattened, it is said, in one quarter of the usual time. The reason assigned is, that they are thus kept still, and have nothing to attract their attention.

To take Paint out of a Dress.

When fresh, (having wiped off as much as you can,) make repeated applications of spirits of turpentine or spirits of wine, rubbed on with a soft rag or flannel. Ether also will answer, if applied immediately. When the paint has been allowed to harden, nothing will remove it but spirits of turpentine, rubbed on with perseverance.

Blasting Rocks.

Saw-dust of soft wood, mixed with gunpowder in equal parts, is said to have thrice the strength of gunpowder alone, when used in blasting.

Cure for Founder.

The seeds of sunflower are the best remedy known for the cure of founder in horses. Immediately on discovering that your horse is foundered, mix about a pint of the whole seed in his feed, and it will give a perfect cure.

Boil your Molasses.

When molasses is used in cooking, it is a very great improvement to boil and skim it before you use it. It takes out the unpleasant raw taste, and makes it almost as good as sugar. Where molasses is used much for cooking, it is well to prepare one or two gallons in this way at a time.

Wounds of Cattle.

The most aggrieved wounds of domestic animals are easily cured with a portion of the yolk of eggs mixed in spirit of turpentine. The part affected must be bathed several times with the mixture, and a perfect cure will be effected in forty-eight hours.

To remove Tar, Pitch, or Turpentine.

Scrape off as much as you can; then wet the place thoroughly with good salad oil, and let it remain for twenty-four hours. If linen or cotton, wash it out in strong warm soap-suds; if woollen or silk, take out the oil with ether or spirits of wine.

If the stain is of tar, you may remove it (after scraping and wiping,) by using cold tallow instead of sweet oil. Rub and press well on the spot a small lump of good tallow, and leave it sticking there till next day. Then proceed as above.

To preserve Green Corn, &c.

Take green corn, either on the ear, or carefully shelled, peas and beans in pods, dip them in boiling water, and then carefully dry them in a room where there is a free circulation of air. Thus preserved, they will keep until winter, and retain all their freshness and agreeable flavour.

Compound Cathartic Pills.

Compound extract of colocynth, in powder, half an ounce; extract of jalap, in powder, mild chloride of mercury, each, 3 drachms; gamboge, in powder, 2 scruples. Mix; then form into a mass with water, and divide into one hundred and eighty pills.

To wash Bobbinet or Cotton Lace.

Rip off the lace, and roll it round a bottle smoothly covered with white linen or muslin. Then fill the bottle with water, cork it tightly, and suspend it in a kettle of cold soap-suds, made with Castile soap. Boil moderately, until the lace looks perfectly white, which will be in about half an hour. Then drain off the suds, and set the bottle in the sun till the lace dries on it.

Assafœtida Pills.

Take assafœtida, 1½ ounce; soap, ½ ounce. Beat them with water into a mass, and divide into two hundred and forty pills.

To wash Thread Lace.

Rip off the lace, carefully pick out the loose bits of thread, and roll the lace very smoothly and securely round a clean black bottle, previously covered with old white linen, sewed tightly on. Tack each end of the lace with a needle and thread, to keep it smooth; and be careful in wrapping not to crumple or fold in any of the scollops or pearlings. After it is on the bottle, take some of the *best* sweet oil, and with a clean sponge wet the lace thoroughly to the inmost folds.

Have ready in a wash-kettle, a strong *cold* lather of clear water and white Castile soap. Fill the bottle with cold water, to prevent its bursting, cork it well, and stand it upright in the suds, with a string round the neck secured to the ears or handle of the kettle, to prevent its knocking about and breaking while over the fire. Let it boil in the suds for an hour or more, till the lace is clean and white all through. Drain off the suds, and dry it on the bottle in the sun. When dry, remove the lace from the bottle and roll it round a wide ribbon-block; or lay it in long folds, place it within a sheet of smooth white paper, and press it in a large book for a few days.

To cure the Swelling of the Throat in Hogs.

Take half a pint of molasses and a table-spoonful of hog's lard; to these add a piece of brimstone an inch in length; melt it over the fire, and when cold, or in a liquid state, drench the hog with it, and nine times out of ten it will be found to have the desired effect.

Cure for Summer Complaint.

Six drops of laudanum to half a tumbler full of rice-water; half a tumbler of the mixture to be taken every three or four hours. This simple remedy may be given to infants, children, or at any period of life, and has never failed to give immediate relief; and, if persevered in for a few days, it invariably effects a cure, however violent the disorder.

Cure for Inflamed Eyes.

Pour boiling water on elder-flowers, and steep them like tea; when cold, put three or four drops of laudanum into a small glass of the elder-tea, and let the mixture run into the eyes three or four times a day. The eyes will become perfectly strong in the course of a week.

Copaiba Pills.

Copaiba, 2 ounces; magnesia, recently prepared, 1 drachm. Mix, and set the mixture aside until it concretes into a pilular mass, which is to be divided into two hundred pills.

The Gravel.

Boil heavy red onions down with sugar, and make a thick syrup of it; drink as much of it as you please daily. It is said to cure the gravel and stone.

Pills or Carbonate of Iron.

Sulphate of iron, 4 ounces; carbonate of soda, 5 ounces; clarified honey, 2½ ounces; syrup and boiling water, each, a sufficient quantity. Dissolve the sulphate of iron and carbonate of soda, each, in a pint of water, and to each solution add a fluidounce of syrup; then mix the two solutions in a bottle just large enough to contain them, close it accurately with a stopper, and set it by that the carbonate of iron may subside. Pour off the supernatant liquid; and, having washed the precipitate with warm water, sweetened with syrup in the proportion of a fluidounce of the latter to a pint of the former, until the washings no longer have a saline taste, place it upon a flannel cloth, and express as much of the water as possible; then immediately mix it with the honey. Lastly, heat the mixture, by means of a water-bath, until it attains a pilular consistence.

To wash Lace.

Take a square black bottle, and sew all over it a piece of thick linen or cotton rag. Wind the lace smoothly round the bottle, securing the ends, and taking care that no part of the edge is crumpled or turned inward. Sew another piece of rag all over the outside, so as entirely to cover the lace. Make a strong lather of white soap with cold clear soft water, (if filtered, the better,) and put it into a large stone jar or crock, standing the bottle upright in the suds. Put the crock on a stove or furnace, and boil an hour or more. Take out the bottle, wash the crock, and fill it with clear cold water in which you have mixed a table-spoonful of starch. Replace the bottle, and let it again come to a boil. When you take out the bottle, remove the upper covering, and dry the lace in the sun, on the under linen. Take it off the bottle, and smooth it over with a cool iron, carefully pressing out each scollop of the edge.

Compound Pills of Iron.

Powdered myrrh, 2 drachms; carbonate of soda, sulphate of iron, each, 1 drachm; syrup to mix. Rub the myrrh with the carbonate of soda; then add the sulphate of iron, and again rub them; lastly, beat them with the syrup into a mass, and divide into eighty pills.

To cure Corns.

Scrape the corn so as to nearly cause it to bleed; apply a salve composed of calomel and lard; renew the application three or four times a week; keep the feet clean, and wear loose shoes.

Remedy for Fever and Ague.

Take one ounce of yellow Peruvian bark, a quarter of an ounce of cream tartar, one table-spoonful of powdered cloves, and one pint of Teneriffe wine; mix together and shake it well. Take a wine-glassful every two hours after the fever is off.

Before taking the above, a dose of Epsom salts, or other medicine, should be administered, to cleanse the stomach, and render the cure more speedy and certain.

Itching Feet, or Chilblains,

May be relieved by rubbing them with a mixture of seven parts water and one part muriatic acid, for a few nights, before going to bed.

French Polish for Boots, Shoes, and Harness.

Take two pints of the best vinegar and one pint of soft water; stir into the mixture a quarter of a pound of glue broken fine, half a pound of logwood chips, a quarter of an ounce of finely-powdered indigo, a quarter of an ounce of the best soft soap, and a quarter of an ounce of isinglass. Boil far ten minutes or longer; then strain the liquid, bottle, and cork. When cold, it is fit for use.

Remove the dirt from the boots, &c. with a sponge and water. Then lay on the polish with a clean sponge. Should it prove too thick, hold it near the fire to warm a little, and the heat will liquefy it sufficiently.

Blacking to preserve Leather.

Take spermaceti oil, 4 ounces; molasses, 12 ounces; mix. Add by degrees 12 ounces of ivory black, mixing it in smoothly, and rubbing it well, so as to leave no lumps; then add gradually a quart of the best white wine vinegar. If too thick, add more vinegar; stir it hard, and let it stand in the jar three days, stirring frequently with a round stick. Bottle it for use. If still too thick, even when warmed at the fire, dilute with a little more vinegar.

Sting of the Bee.

Common whiting proves an effectual remedy against the effects of the sting of a bee or wasp. The whiting is to be moistened with cold water, and applied immediately. It may be washed off in a few minutes, when neither pain nor swelling will ensue.

Mercurial Pills.

Mercury, 1 ounce; confection of roses, 1 ½ ounce; powdered liquorice-root, ½ ounce. Rub the mercury with the confection till all the globules disappear; then add the liquorice-root, and beat the whole into a mass. Divide into four hundred and eighty pills.

Dover's Powder.

Ipecacuanha, opium, each, in powder, 1 drachm; sulphate of potassa, 1 ounce. Rub them together into a very fine powder.

Preserved Pumpkin.

Stew your pumpkin as usual for pies, spread it thinly upon large open tins or platters, and place them over or under your stove; where, if kept four or five days, it will become dry enough to keep in bags or boxes throughout one year. Pumpkin, preserved in this way, is far superior to that preserved in the old method of drying, making much richer and better flavoured pies, besides requiring much less labour.

Cure for Cancer.

Mr. Thomas Tyrrell, of Missouri, says he has effectually cured himself of an obstinate cancer, "by the free use of potash, made from the ashes of red-oak, boiled to the consistence of molasses, used as a poultice, covering the whole with a coat of tar. Two or three applications will remove all protuberances, after which it is only necessary to heal the wound with common salve.

To drive Bugs from Vines.

The ravage of the yellow-striped bug on cucumbers and melons may be effectually prevented by sifting charcoal dust over the plants; if repeated three or four times, the plants will be entirely freed from annoyance. There is in charcoal some property so noxious to these troublesome insects, that they fly from it the instant it is applied.

To clean White Leather Gloves.

White leather gloves may be cleaned to look very well, by putting on one at a time, and going over them thoroughly with a shaving-brush and lather. Then wipe them off with a clean handkerchief or sponge, and dry them on the hands by the fire or in the sun.

To renovate Coats.

Take one gallon of a strong decoction of logwood, made by boiling logwood chips in water. Strain this liquid, and when cool add two ounces of gum arabic in powder. Keep it in well-stopped bottles for use. After the coat has been cleaned of grease and dirt, go evenly over it with a sponge wet in the above liquid diluted to suit the colour, and hang it in the shade to dry. After which brush the nap smooth, and it will look quite new. The liquid will suit all brown or dark colours, with proper dilution.

Hive Syrup.

Squill and seneka, bruised, each, 4 ounces; tartrate of antimony and potassa, 48 grains; water, 4 pints; sugar, 3½ pounds. Pour the water on the squill and seneka, and boil to one half. Strain and add the sugar; then evaporate to three pints, and, while the syrup is still hot, dissolve in it the tartrate of antimony and potassa.

To clean White Kid Gloves.

Stretch them on a board, and rub the soiled spots with cream of tartar or magnesia. Let them rest an hour. Take a mixture of alum and fuller's earth, in powder, and rub it all over the gloves with a clean brush, and let them rest for an hour or two. Then sweep it all off, and go over with a flannel dipped in a mixture of bran and finely-powdered whiting. Let them rest another hour; brush off the powder, and you will find them clean.

Ointment of Iodine.

Iodine, 20 grains; alcohol, 20 minims; lard, 1 ounce. Rub the iodine first with the alcohol, and then with the lard, until they are thoroughly mixed.

Bearing of Apple-Trees.

A horticulturist in Bohemia has a beautiful plantation of the best sort of apple-trees, which have neither sprung from seeds nor grafting. His plan is to take shoots from the choicest sorts, insert them in a potato, and plunge them into the ground, leaving but an inch or two of the shoot above the surface. The potato nourishes the shoot whilst it pushes out roots, and the shoot gradually springs up and becomes a beautiful tree, bearing the best of fruit, without requiring to be grafted.

A Cement for Broken Earthenware.

Take 1 ounce of dry cream cheese, grated fine, and an equal quantity of quicklime, mixed well together, with 3 ounces of skimmed milk, to form a good cement, when the rendering of the joint visible is of no consequence. If mixed without the milk, it perhaps might be stronger still.

Of Japan Grounds.

Red.—Vermillion makes a fine scarlet, but its appearance in japanned work is much improved by glazing it with a thin coat of lake, or even rose pink.

Yellow.—King's yellow, turbith mineral, and Dutch pink, all form very bright yellows, and the latter is very cheap. Seed-lac varnish assimilates with yellow very well; and when they are required very bright, an improvement may be effected by infusing turmeric in the varnish which covers the ground.

Green.—Distilled verdigris laid on a ground of leaf-gold, produces the brightest of all greens; other greens may be formed by mixing King's yellow and bright Prussian blue, or turbith mineral and Prussian blue, or Dutch pink and verdigris.

Blue.—Prussian blue, or verditer glazed with Prussian blue or smalt.

White.—White grounds are obtained with greater difficulty than any other. One of the best is prepared by grinding up flock-white, or zinc-white, with one-sixth of its weight of starch, and drying it; it is then tempered, like the other colours, using the mastic varnish for common uses; and that of the best copal for the finest. Particular care should be taken that the copal for this use be made of the clearest and whitest pieces. Seed-lac may be used as the uppermost coat, where a very delicate white is not required, taking care to use such as is least coloured.

Black.—Ivory-black or lamp-black; but if the lamp-black be used, it should be previously calcined in a closed crucible. Black grounds may be formed on metal, by drying linseed oil only, when mixed with a little lamp-black. The work is then exposed in a stove to a heat which will render the oil black. The heat should be low at first, and increased very gradually, or it will blister. This kind of japan requires no polishing. It is extensively used for defending articles of iron-mongery from rust.

Tortoise-Shell Ground for Metal.

Cover the plates intended to represent the transparent parts of the tortoise-shell with a thin coat of vermilion in seed-lac varnish. Then brush over the whole with a varnish composed of linseed oil boiled with umber until it is almost black. The varnish may be thinned with oil of turpentine before it is used. When the work is done it may be set in an oven, with the same precautions as the black varnish last named.

The manner of Soldering Ferrules for Tool-Handles, &c.

Take your ferrule, lap round the joining a small piece of brass-wire, then just wet the ferrule, scatter on the joining-ground, borax, put it on the end of a wire, hold it in the fire till the brass fuses. It will fill up the joining, and form a perfect solder. It may afterwards be turned in the lathe.

Varnish for Harness.

Take half a pound of Indian rubber, one gallon of spirits of turpentine, dissolve enough to make it into a jelly by keeping almost new milk warm; then take equal quantities of good linseed oil (in a hot state) and the above mixture, incorporate them well on a slow fire, and it is fit for use.

A Varnish for fastening the Leather on Top Rollers in Factories.

Dissolve 2¾ ounces of gum arabic in water, and add so much isinglass dissolved in brandy, and it is fit for use.

To make White-Wash that will not rub off.

Mix up half a pail full of lime and water, ready to put on the wall; then take a quarter of a pint of flour, mix it up with water, then pour on it boiling water a sufficient quantity to thicken it; then pour it, while hot, into the white-wash; stir all well together, and it is ready.

To Dye Pink on Silk.

After aluming, handle the goods to be dyed in peach-wood liquor till the colour desired; then take out and put in a little alum liquor, handle the goods a little longer, take out, rinse in water, and finish. In most cases, where the shade is not dark enough, the operation must be repeated.

To Dye Brown on Silk.

Alum your silk; then take one part of fustic liquor, and three parts of peach-wood liquor; handle in these till it becomes a good brown; (a little logwood liquor will darken your shade, if required,) hedge out, and put in a little alum water; again put in your goods, handle a little longer, then take out, drain, rinse well, and finish. By varying the peach-wood and fustic, various shades may be obtained.

Flaxseed Tea—Diet for the Sick.

Take of flaxseed, 1 ounce; white sugar, 1½ ounces; lemon-juice, 2 table-spoonfuls; boiling water, 2 pints. Infuse them in a pitcher some hours, and then strain off the liquor. An ounce of liquorice, shaved, may sometimes be used instead of sugar.

Camomile Tea.

Take of camomile flowers, 1 handful; boiling water, 1 gallon. Let them remain covered about half an hour, then strain off the tea. If this tea is drunk to strengthen the somach, it should be made stronger, say about ¼ ounce to a pint.

Lemonade.

Take of the outer rind of fresh lemon-peel, about 1 drachm; lemon-juice, 1 ounce; double-refined sugar, 2 ounces; boiling water, 1½ pints Let them stand in a vessel about ten minutes, then strain off the liquor.

Orangeade.

Take of the fresh outer rind of Seville orange, 1 drachm; orange juice, 2 or 3 table-spoonfuls; white sugar, 1 or 2 ounces, or enough to make it of an agreeable sweetness; boiling water, 1 quart. Let them stand in a pitcher about ten minutes, then strain off the liquor.

Barley Water.

Take a handful of either pearl barley, or the common sort, wash it clean, first in cold and afterwards in boiling water, then simmer it in a quart of water for an hour; when half done, put into it a bit of fresh lemon-peel and a little sugar. Rice-water may be prepared as above.

Pectoral Drink.

Take of common barley and stoned raisins, each 2 ounces; liquorice-root, ½ ounce; water, 2 quarts. Boil the water first with the barley, then add the raisins, and afterwards, near the latter end of the boiling, the liquorice. The decoction then will be fully completed, when one quart only will be left after straining.

Sago Jelly.

Take of sago, washed well, one large spoonful, and water nearly a pint. Boil them gently, stirring often, till the mixture is smooth and thick; then add two spoonfuls of wine, a little nutmeg, and sweeten it to the taste. A piece of lemon-peel added to it when boiling, gives it a pleasant taste and flavour, and with some patients it agrees better when boiled in milk, for debility.

Calves'-Feet Jelly.

Boil 2 calves'-feet in one gallon of water till it comes to a quart, then strain it, and when it is cold, skim the fat entirely off, and take the jelly up clean; if there be any settling at the bottom, leave it. Put the jelly into a saucepan, with a pint of mountain wine, half a pound of loaf-sugar, the juice of four large lemons, and the white of six eggs, beat up the whisk; mix all well together, set the saucepan upon a clear fire, and stir the jelly till it boils. When it has boiled a few minutes, pour it through a flannel bag till it runs clear. Then have in readiness a large china basin, with some lemon-peel in it, cut as thin as possible, let the clear jelly run upon them while warm, and from these it will acquire both an amber colour, and an agreeable flavour. Afterwards it may be poured into glasses.

Water Gruel.

1. Take of the coarse part of corn meal or grist, two hands full; water, 3 quarts; boil it till only 2 quarts remain, then strain off the liquor, and season it to the palate with salt, sugar and nutmeg, to which may be added a spoonful or two of wine.

2. Take of oatmeal, 2 large spoonfuls; water, 1 quart. Mix them well, and boil them about ten or fifteen minutes, stirring often; then strain the gruel through a sieve, and add sugar and salt enough to make it agreeable to the taste. When it is designed as a meal, dissolve it in a little butter, and then add bread and nutmeg, as occasion requires.

To Dye Buff on Cotton.

Take as much hot fustic liquor and water, as will half fill a tub, enter three pieces, give them five ends, hedge out; take another tub of cold lime-water, enter the same pieces, and give them five ends in this, take out, and in a short time they will be buff. Renew your first and second tub, and proceed as at first This is all required for buff.

To Dye Red on Cotton.

Take three pieces, enter them into a tub with hot red-wood, or peach-wood liquor, give them five ends, then run them into your wince; have another tub, called the spirit-tub, close by, half full of cold water, put into it about three tumblers full of spirits; then run the pieces from the other wince over the wince of the spirit-tub, give them five ends in the spirit tub, then wind them on the wince of the spirit-tub, then back again to the red tub; give them five ends without having renewed the tub, they are finished. Throw away the red tub liquor, put in fresh liquor, and proceed as before; but the spirit-tub must be renewed always; even at night it may be left in a tub, and renewed the next day.

To Dye Brown on Cotton.

The first process is to give them five ends in hot sumach liquor, or let them lay all night in the large tub, same as for blacks; then give them five ends in copperas, hedge out, give them five ends in lime tub; then hedge out, lay them one side till you get enough to finish that day. You next renew your tubs and repeat the operation as before. Then comes the finishing part. Make up a tub of hot red-wood liquor; enter three pieces, give them five ends, put the pieces one side the tub, put in some alum liquor, stir up, give them five ends more, hedge out, and finish.

To Dye Purple on Cotton.

Get up a tub of hot logwood liquor, enter three pieces, give them five ends, hedge out; enter them into a clean alum tub, give them five ends, hedge out; get up another tub of logwood liquor, enter, give them five ends, hedge out; renew your alum tub, give them five ends in that, and finish.

To Dye Slate on Silk.

To make a slate, take a pan of warm water and about a teacup-full of logwood liquor, pretty strong, and a piece of pearlash, of the size of a nut; take grey-coloured goods, and handle a little in this liquor, and it is finished. If too much logwood is used, the colour will be too dark.

To Dye Olive on Silk.

By adding a little fustic liquor to the above slate, it will form an olive: it may be necessary to run them through a weak pearlash water to sadden them. Wash in two waters for the above three colours. They will keep their colour very well.

A Superior Liquid Blacking. (French.)

Take 1 pound of good ivory-black; loaf-sugar, 4 ounces; the whites of 6 eggs; beer, a sufficient quantity. Mix the whole well, and let them simmer for half an hour. Then bottle for use.

Note.—I believe that blacking is generally improved by letting the ingredients simmer a little; it makes the ivory-black softer and of a more shiny lustre. A little pearlash added will improve the black of ink or blacking, but whether it is a real benefit to them, is a question.

Iron Moulds.

Wash the spots with a strong solution of cream of tartar and water Repeat, if necessary, and dry in the sun.

Ratifia de Fleurs d'Oranges.

Orange flowers (fresh), 10 pounds; proof spirit, 6 gallons; sugar, 10 pounds; dissolved in water, 1 gallon. Macerate for fourteen days, and strain.

Ratifia d'Ecorces d'Oranges.

Fresh Seville orange-peel, 1 pound; proof spirit, 5 gallons; sugar, 6 pounds; dissolved in water, 3 pints. Digest for fourteen days, and strain.

Ratifia de Noyeau.

Bitter almonds (bruised), 2 ounces; proof spirit, 1 gallon; sugar (dissolved in 3 pints of water), 2 pounds; cassia (bruised), ¼ ounce; cloves (bruised), ¼ ounce. Mix, and macerate for twenty days, then filter.

Ratifia des Cerises.

Morella cherries (kernels bruised), 10 pounds; proof spirit, 10 pints. Macerate for twenty days, then express the juice and strain, next pour on the refuse, water, 4 pints. Strain, and dissolve in it, sugar (lump), 2½ pounds. Mix, and strain.

To clear Barns, Houses, &c., of Rats and Mice.

Spread garlic or dog's tongue—Cynoglossum—(bruised), where they frequent.

To Trap Rats.

Put a little valerian and cheese in the trap, and it will attract both rats and cats to the place.

Razor Strop Paste.

Oxide of tin (levigated), 25 parts; powdered gum, 1 part; powdered oxalic acid, 20 parts; water to make a paste. Spread this thinly over the strop. Always recollect to strop your razor on a piece of soft leather after using this paste.

To Renovate a Razor Strop.

1. Rub a little clean tallow over the surface, and then put on it the light top part of the snuff of a candle; rub it smooth. Excellent.

2. Rub the strop well with a piece of soft pewter or lead.

To Hone and Strap a Razor.

Let the razor see the hone but seldom, and then only as a "caution," and keep it quite flat on the stone. Strop your razor every time after it is used, and before shaving soak it in warm water.

Red Currant Wine.

1. Red currants, 1 cwt.; brown sugar, 56 pounds; water, 25 gallons; red tartar, 8 ounces. Mix, and ferment.

2. Soft water, 11 gallons; red currants, 12 gallons; raw sugar, 13 pounds. Ferment, then add red tartar (dissolved), 2 ounces; red beet (sliced), 2 pounds; spirit, 1 gallon. As before.

Red Fire.

Sulphuret of antimony, 4 parts; chlorate of potash, 5 parts; flowers of sulphur, 13 parts; nitrate of strontia, 40 parts. Mix.

Red Flame.

Alcohol holding in solution a salt of lime.

Red Glazing.

Antimony, 3 parts; red lead, 3 parts; red oxide of iron, 1 part. Mix.

Red Gooseberry Wine.

Cold water, 20 gallons; bruised fruit, 20 gallons; raw sugar, 35 pounds. Ferment, then add red beet (sliced), 4 pounds; red tartar (dissolved), 6 ounces; good spirit, 2 gallons; ginger (bruised), ½ ounce; cloves (bruised), ½ ounce. For a cheaper wine more water may be added.

Red Ink.

1. Cochineal, 1 ounce; ammonia, 1 ounce; water, 1 quart. Digest for two or three days in a corked bottle, then dilute with water until of the proper colour.

2. Brazil (ground), 1 pound; sour beer, 1 gallon. Boil until sufficiently coloured, then add alum, 8 ounces; gum, 8 ounces.

3. Brazil dust, 1¼ pound; vinegar, 6 quarts. Boil until reduced to a gallon, then add alum, ½ pound; gum arabic, ½ pound

Red Lacker.

Alcohol, 2 gallons; dragon's-blood, 1 pound; Spanish annatto, 3 pounds; gum sandarach, 3¼ pounds; turpentine varnish, 2 pounds. Put the whole into a suitable vessel and agitate until dissolved.

Red Mead Wine.

White mead wine, 15 gallons; cochineal (bruised), ½ ounce; brandy colouring, 2 ounces; red wine (to taste), 7 gallons; red tartar, 5 ounces. Mix, and fine down with six eggs.

Ointment of the Red Oxide of Mercury.

1. Simple ointment, 15 ounces; red precipitate, 1 ounce. Mix. Too much care cannot be taken to rub down the powder until the ointment becomes of a perfectly uniform colour.

2. Simple ointment, 1 pound; red precipitate, 2 ounces. Mix.

Red Precipitate.

Quicksilver, nitric acid, equal parts. Dissolve, decant, and evaporate to dryness, in a sand heat, until it assumes the proper colour.

Red Rose Sugar.

White sugar, 16 parts; red rose leaves (powdered), 1 part. Add tincure of carmine to colour, and a few drops of ottar of roses.

Red Salt.

Red sanders wood, 1 part; spirits of wine, 16 parts. Steep until sufficient colour is extracted, then pour it over the salt; evaporate, and when dry, rub the salt through a sieve. Cochineal or a small quantity of carmine may be used instead of the red sanders wood, but they will of course render the process more expensive.

Red Ratifia.

Take cherries, raspberries, and strawberries, each twenty pounds, bruise them and collect the juice, and add two pounds of sugar and one pint of proof-spirit to every gallon of the liquid, then flavour with cassia, cloves, and mace.

Red Sealing Wax.

1. Shell lac, 2 parts; resin, 1 part; vermilion, 1 part. Powder fine, and melt over a slow fire.

2. Yellow resin, 14 parts; Venetian turpentine, 4 parts; bees-wax, 1 part; red or orange lead, 5 parts. Mix, with heat.

3. Oil of turpentine, 1 part; lard, 1 part; vermilion, 2 parts; gum lac, 12 parts. Mix, with a gentle heat.

4. (Very fine.)—Shell lac, 4 parts; Venice turpentine, 1 part· vermilion, 3 parts. Mix.

Red Sprinkle for Binders.

Brazil-wood (ground), 4 parts; alum, 1 part; vinegar, 4 parts; water, 4 parts. Boil until reduced to seven parts, then add a small quantity of loaf-sugar and gum. Bottle for use.

Red Stain for Glass.

1. Rust of iron, 100 parts; glass of antimony, 99 parts; yellow glass of lead, 98 parts; sulphuret of silver, 3 parts. Mix.

2. White hard enamel, 100 parts; red chalk, 50 parts; peroxide of copper, 5 parts. Reduce to fine powder and mix.

Red Sulphuret of Arsenic.

White arsenic, 7 parts; roll brimstone, 1 part. Mix and sublime.

Red Tombac.

Copper, 11 parts; zinc, 2 parts. Mix.

To convert White Wine into Red Wine.

Turnsole, 8 ounces; water, 3 pints. Boil gently; when cold, colour the wine with the tincture.

To guard against Spontaneous Combustion.

It is a fact better ascertained than can be accounted for, that fixed oils, when mixed with any light kind of charcoal, or substances containing carbon, such as cotton, flax, or even wool, which is not of itself inflammable, heat by the process of decomposition, and after remaining in contact some time, at length burst into flame. This spontaneous combustion takes place in waste cotton which has been employed to wipe machines, and then thrown away and allowed to accumulate into a heap. We have known an instance of the kind in a manufactory for spinning worsteds, where the waste wool, or "slubbings," as it is termed in Yorkshire, was thrown into a corner and neglected. It then heated, and was on the point of bursting into flame, when the attention of the workmen was directed to the heap by the smoke and smell. In cotton-mills, the danger exists in a still greater degree, and it is believed that the destruction of many cotton factories has been occasioned by this means. The cause of this peculiar property of fixed oils deserves more attention than has hitherto been paid to it.

Animal Gas, or the Value of Dead Animals.

M. Seguin has succeeded in drying the muscles of animals by the action of heat, in closed cylinders, so as to admit of their being kept in store-houses with very little annoyance from the effluvium; he then employed a slight steam condensation, jointly with washing and purifying the muscle, by saturated solution of chlorure of calcium, and he has thereby preserved to the gas which he extracted all its illuminating powers, while he has completely separated it from the ammoniacal salts that might render it fetid, by converting them directly into hydrochlorure of ammonium. Such gas, thus purified, has been found to contain about 10 grammes of empyreumatic vapours per cubic metre; and its illuminating power is such, that during one hour twenty-two litres of this gas will give as much light as a good Carcel lamp. The empyreumatic vapours are not found to be condensed by low temperature, but may be liquefied by compression; and these produce a fluid resembling ether, burning with a fuliginous flame, but without any odour. M. Seguin's results may be tabularized as follows:—

One horse, average weight 220 kilogrammes,
gave Gas, ... 25682 litres, or light for 411 hours;
Sal ammoniac, ... 18·5 kilogrammes.
Ivory-black, ... 21 kilogrammes.

Value of gas at 5 centimes per hour, ...	20f.	55c.
" of sal ammoniac, ...	56	50
" of ivory-black, ...	3	15
Total value, ...	80f.	20c.

Now, the average price of such an animal for killing, or dead, is 17fr. in France; the labour, &c. of extracting these mattters, cost 4f. 25c.; cost of various accessory materials, 2f. 70c.; fuel, 1f. 60c.; total, 25f. 55c. The ordinary knackers of Paris never get out of the parts from which the gas is thus produced more than about 5fr. worth of grease; and since Paris furnishes annually from 15,000 to 16,000 dead horses, the value of this method may be easily ascertained. If to this be added the gas that may be obtained from the bodies of other animals, and from refuse animal matter in the capital, the total quantity to be derived from these hitherto neglected materials will be found to be immense.

To ascertain a Horse's Age.

Every horse has six teeth above and below; before three years old he sheds his middle teeth; at three he sheds one more on each side of the central teeth; at four he sheds the two corner and last of the fore-teeth. Between four and five the horse cuts the under tusks; at five will cut his upper tusks, at which time his mouth will be complete. At six years the grooves and hollows begin to fill up a little; at seven the grooves will be well nigh filled up, except the corner teeth, leaving little brown spots where the dark brown hollows formerly were. At eight, the whole of the hollows and grooves are filled up. At nine there is very often seen a small bill to the outside corner teeth; the point of the tusk is worn off, and the part that was concave begins to fill up and become rounding; the squares of the central teeth begin to disappear, and the gums leave them small and narrow at top.

To Blaze or Produce a Star on a Horse.

Shave off the hair with a sharp razor, then anoint the place with a little oil of vitriol; one application will be sufficient. To remove inflammation, wash with a weak solution of copperas-water.

Another.

Take a piece of coarse tow-linen, the size of the wished-for star, spread on it warm pitch, and apply it to the shaved spot, leave two or three days, when wash with a little asmart-water or elixir of vitriol two or three times a day until well. When the hair grows it will be white.

Relief for Spavin.

Shave off the hair, and apply a blister of Spanish flies to the part affected. Bathe with warm strong vinegar, and let the horse have rest.

Broken Wind.

Feed with carrots, or parsnips, or beets; or use tar-water as a drink; some say lime-water; and when the cough is bad, bleed freely.

Relief for String-Halt.

Bathe with warm vinegar and sweet oil, and rub well the part affected.

Chest Founder. (Momentary Relief for)

Bleed freely, and give an ounce of aloes in a ball.

Cure for Lampass.

Burn with a hot iron: never cut them out. If they are once burnt they will not return.

Wind Galls.

Make a strong decoction of red-oak bark; add thereto some strong vinegar and a little alum in powder. Bathe the parts with this decoction as warm as possible twice a day, and bind up comfortably tight with woollen cloths dipped in a warm decoction of the above.

Founder.

Bleed from the neck; take one quart strong sassafras tea, dissolve in it one spoonful of saltpetre and a quarter of an ounce of assafœtida, and give as a drench, but do not let him drink for five or six hours, at which time, if he is not better, repeat the bleeding, and give another drench. For slight founder, let the horse stand a few hours in water; or, still better, in very soft clay-mortar.

Laxative Injection.

Sweet oil, one table-spoonful; molasses, two table-spoonfuls; salt, one tea-spoonful. Mix in a pint of warm water. To be used milk-warm.

Purgative Injection.

Take boiling water, one pint; senna leaves, one ounce; coriander seed, well bruised, one drachm. Infuse about one hour in a covered vessel. Strain, then add salt, one tea-spoonful; molasses, one table-spoonful. Stir until the salt be dissolved. To be applied milk-warm.

Ointment for Ringbone.

Take corrosive sublimate, Spanish flies, hog's lard, and Venice turpen tine. Mix. This ointment it is said will dissolve a ringbone.

Injection made of Starch.

Starch, two tea-spoonfuls; water, one pint. Mix until no lumps ap pear. Boil. Strain and use it gently warm.

Bread Poultice.

Take stale bread in crumbs, pour boiling water over it, and boil till soft, stirring it well; then take it from the fire, and gradually stir in a little hog's lard or sweet oil, so as to render the poultice pliable when applied.

Corn Meal Poultice.

Indian meal, five table-spoonfuls; rye flour, one table-spoonful. To be gradually let through the fingers into boiling water, briskly stirring at the same time. Then add a little oil as for the bread poultice.

Apple Poultice.

Apples pared, cored, and well boiled, then well washed into a pulp, form a very good poultice.

Poultice made of Hops.

Boil a handful of hops for a few minutes in a pint of water in a covered vessel, squeeze out the juice, and strain. This liquor is now to be put again on the fire and thickened with Indian meal, and a little lard added as it becomes cool.

Starch Poultice.

Starch, any quantity; thicken with boiling water. When a little cooled, stir in a little lard or oil.

Slippery Elm Poultice.

Take slippery elm in powder, and mix with water until somewhat thick, then boil a few minutes. It is to be applied warm.

Yeast Poultice.

Wheat flour, one pound; yeast, half a pint. Mix them together over a gentle heat until the mixture begins to rise, then apply warm.

Mustard Poultice.

Flour of mustard, one part; flaxseed meal, one part. Make into a paste with water. A little oil or lard should be added to prevent it sticking.

Spice Poultice.

Cinnamon, allspice, cloves, and ginger, of each equal quantities; honey or molasses to mix.

Alum Poultice.

Put the white of a couple of eggs into a plate, and then with a piece of alum between the thumb and finger stir it into a curd. To be applied wrapped in a fine piece of linen, having but one fold next the skin.

Purgative Electuary.

Take of jalap, 1 drachm; cream of tartar, 1 ounce; syrup or molasses as much as will give the whole a proper consistence. Dose for adults, from one to two tea-spoonfuls in the morning, to keep the bowels in a soluble state.

To Dye Crimson on Silk.

Take cudbear, boil it in water; then just rinse or handle your silks in it for a few minutes, you have the shade wanted. Chamber-ley or any alkaline solution will change the colour.

Rice Milk.

Take a large tea-cupful of rice, washed nicely; water, 1 pint; boil it for about half an hour, then add a quart of new milk; let it simmer over a slow fire till it is sufficiently done, and then add to it a little sugar and nutmeg.

Panado.

1. Take of bread, 1 ounce; mace, 1 blade; water, 1 pint. Boil them without stirring, till they mix and turn smooth, then add a little grated nutmeg, a small piece of butter, and sugar enough to make the mixture agreeable. When butter is not approved of, two spoonfuls of wine may be used in its stead.

2. Set a little water on the fire, with a glass of white wine, some sugar, and a scrape of nutmeg and lemon-peel; meanwhile, grate some crumbs of bread. The moment the mixture boils up, keeping it still on the fire, put the crumbs in, and let it boil as fast as it can. When of a proper thickness just to drink, take it off.

Alum Whey.

Boil two drachms of powdered alum in a pint of milk until it be curdled, then strain out the whey. This astringent preparation is often employed with advantage in uterine hemorrhage, and in diabetes. The dose is two or three ounces, or as much as the stomach will bear, several times in the day.

To Mull White Wine.

Boil a pint of good wine with a table-spoonful of allspice; beat up the yolk of an egg with a little sugar, and add it to the wine while boiling.

Refreshing Drinks in Fevers.

Boil two quarts of water with two ounces of tamarinds, an equal quantity of currants and raisins, until near a fourth be consumed. Strain it on a piece of lemon-peel, which remove in an hour, as it gives a bitter taste if left long.

Tamarinds, currants, fresh or in jelly, or scalded currants or cranberries, with cold water, make excellent drinks; a little sugar may be added, if agreeable.

Lemon Water.

Put two slices of lemon, thinly pared, into a tea-pot, a small piece of the peel and some white sugar, pour in a pint of boiling water, and stop it close two hours.

Antibilious, or Aperient and Diaphoretic Pills.

Take of calomel, jalap, each 20 grains; tartar emetic, 2 grains; syrup or mucilage of gum arabic, sufficient to form a mass; make eight pills. Dose for adults, two at bed-time, and the dose repeated every hour in the morning until it operates sufficiently. Or take four in the morning, and one every hour until the desired effect be obtained.

Apple Water.

Cut two large apples in slices, and pour a quart of boiling water on them, or on roasted apples, strain in two or three hours, and sweeten lightly.

Purgative Infusion.

Take of senna and manna, each half an ounce; salts, one ounce; ginger, one drachm; boiling water, one pint. Dose for adults, one gill every hour or two, until it operates.

Purgative Powder.

1. Take of calomel and jalap, each 20 grains, to be taken in the morning in syrup or molasses, by adults.

2. Take of rhubarb and vitriolated tartar in fine powder, each 1 drachm. Mix well together, and divide into four powders. One taken going to bed, and another in the morning, will be found an efficacious remedy, whenever it is required to cleanse the stomach and bowels of bilious and other offensive matter.

Stimulant Purgative Pills.

1. Take of calomel and gamboge, each 1 drachm; syrup sufficient to form a mass. Beat them together, and then make twenty-four pills. Dose for adults, from three to six.

2. Take of calomel, aloes, rhubarb, and soap, each 1 drachm; syrup or mucilage of gum arabic, sufficient to form a mass. Beat them well together, and make forty-eight pills. Dose for adults from four to eight.

Diaphoretic Drops.

Take of sweet spirits of nitre and antimonial wine, each 1 ounce. Mix. Dose for adults, a tea-spoonful every two hours. If the stomach is in an irritable state, add only half the quantity of antimonial wine.

Dover's Powder.

Ipecacuanha, powdered, and opium, each 1 drachm; vitriolated tartar in powder, 1 ounce. The greatest possible pains should be taken to grind the mass to a completely fine powder. Nitre may be substituted for the vitriolated tartar, when that is not at hand. This powder is the most efficacious sudorific we possess. It is an admirable remedy for quieting the bowels, when affected by the exhibition of mercury, or any other cause Dose for adults, from ten to twenty grains every three or four hours.

Infusion of Virginia Snake-Root.

Take snake-root, half an ounce; boiling water, half a pint; infuse for two hours in a covered vessel and strain. Dose—a table-spoonful occasionally, taken warm. It is used to aid other diaphoretics, and in its effects resembles camphor.

To wash White Silk Lace or Blond.

Take a black bottle covered with clean linen or muslin, and wind the blond round it, (securing the ends with a needle and thread,) not leaving the edge outward, but covering it as you proceed. Set the bottle upright in a strong cold lather of white soap and *very clear* soft water, and place it in the sun, having gently with your hand rubbed the suds up and down on the lace. Keep it in the sun every day for a week, changing the lather daily, and always rubbing it slightly when you renew the suds. At the end of the week, take the blond off the bottle, and (without rinsing) pin it backward and forward on a large pillow covered with a clean tight case. Every scollop must have a separate pin ; or more, if the scollops are not very small. The plain edge must be pinned down also, so as to make it straight and even. The pins should be of the smallest size. When quite dry, take it off, but do not starch, iron, or press it. Lay it in long loose folds, and put it away in a pasteboard box.

Thread lace may be washed in the same manner.

Tincture of Lobelia.

Lobelia, 4 ounces ; diluted alcohol, 2 pints. Macerate for fourteen days, express, and filter through paper.

Cure for a Wen.

The following has proved to be effectual. Make a very strong brine, dip in a piece of flannel two or three times doubled, and apply it to the wen ; keep it constantly wet, night and day, until suppuration takes place.

For Sprains and Bruises.

Mix equal parts of beef-gall and vinegar ; apply it often to the part injured, and dry it by the fire.

Warts, &c.

The bark of the common willow burnt to ashes, mixed with strong vinegar, and applied to the parts, will remove all warts, corns, and other excrescences.

Peach-Trees.

Marl put round the trunks of peach-trees—say a bushel, or half that measure, to each tree—protects them from the attacks of worms, preserves the trees in health, continues them in life beyond the time of their ordinary existence, promotes the growth of the fruit to almost double its former size, and increases the richness of its flavour in like proportion.

To wash a White Lace Veil.

Put the veil into a strong lather of white soap and very clear water, and let it simmer slowly for a quarter of an hour. Take it out and squeeze it well, but be sure not to rub it. Rinse it in two cold waters, with a drop or two of liquid blue in the last. Have ready some very clear and weak gum arabic water, or some thin starch, or rice-water. Pass the veil through it. and clear it by clapping. Then stretch it out even, and pin it to dry on a linen cloth, making the edge as straight as possible, opening out all the scollops, and fastening each with pins. When dry, lay a piece of thin muslin smoothly over it. and iron it on the wrong side.

Pennsylvania Apple Butter.

To make this article according to German law, the host should, in the autumn, invite his neighbours, particularly the young men and maidens, to make up an apple-butter party. Being assembled, let three bushels of fair sweet apples be pared, quartered, and the cores removed. Meanwhile, let two barrels of new cider be boiled down to one half. When this is done, commit the prepared apples to the cider, and let the boiling go on briskly and systematically. But to accomplish the main design, the party must take turns at stirring the contents without cessation, that they do not become attached to the side of the kettle, and be burned. Let the stirring go on till the amalgamated cider and apples become as thick as hasty-pudding, then throw in pulverized allspice, when it may be considered as finished, and committed to pots for future use. This is *apple-butter;* and it will keep sweet for very many years. It is a capital article for the table—very much superior to anything that comes under the name of apple-sauce.

Burnt Sponge.

Take sponge, cut it in pieces, and beat it, that any extraneous matters may be separated ; then burn it in a close iron vessel until it becomes black and friable ; lastly, rub it into very fine powder. Astringent.

To wash a Black Lace Veil.

Mix bullock's gall with sufficient hot water to make it as warm as you can bear your hand in, and pass the veil through it. It must be squeezed, not rubbed ; and it will be well to perfume the gall with a little musk. Rinse the veil through two cold waters, tingeing the last with a little blue. After drying, put it into some stiffening made by pouring boiling water on a very small piece of glue ; squeeze it out, stretch it, and clap it. Afterwards, pin it out on a linen cloth to dry, laying it very straight and even, and taking care to open and pin the edge very nicely.

When dry, iron it on the wrong side, having laid a linen cloth over the ironing blanket.

Any article of black lace may be washed in this manner.

Absorbent Mixture.

Prepared chalk, half an ounce; powdered gum arabic, and white sugar, each, 2 drachms ; water, 4 ounces. Dose for adults, a table-spoonful every two or three hours.

Absorbent and Aperient Mixture

Is made by adding one drachm of rhubarb in powder, or half an ounce of the tincture of rhubarb, to the above recipe.

Or—Take of prepared chalk and magnesia, each, half an ounce ; sugar, two drachms. Rub them well together, then add mucilage of gum arabic, two ounces ; weak cinnamon tea, four ounces. Dose for children, from one to two tea-spoonfuls.

Tobacco Ointment.

Fresh tobacco, cut in pieces, 1 ounce ; lard, 1 pound. Boil the tobacco in the lard over a gentle fire, until it becomes friable : the strain through linen.

Cure for Quinsy.

Simmer hops in vinegar a few minutes, until their strength is extracted, strain the liquid, sweeten it with sugar, and give it frequently to the child or patient, in small quantities, until relieved. This is said to be an excellent medicine.

To wash Coloured Kid or Hoskin Gloves.

Have on a table a clean towel folded three or four times, a saucer of new milk, and a piece of brown soap. Spread a glove smoothly on the folded towel, dip in the milk a piece of clean flannel, rub it on the soap till you get enough, and then commence rubbing the glove, beginning at the wrist, and rubbing lengthways to the ends of the fingers, the glove being held firmly in the left hand. When done spread them out, and dry gradually. When nearly dry, pull them out the cross-way of the leather, and when quite dry, stretch them on your hands.

White kid gloves may be washed in this manner, provided they have never been cleaned with India rubber.

To Dye Green on Silk.

Take green ebony, boil it in water, and let it settle; take the clean liquor as hot as you can bear your hands in it, and handle your goods in it until of a bright yellow; then take water and put in a little sulphate of indigo; handle your goods in this till of the shade wanted. The ebony may previously be boiled in a bag, to prevent it from sticking to the silk.

To make Sulphate of Indigo.

Vitriol, 3 pounds; ground indigo, 1 pound. Put in a little at a time, and keep stirring till all is dissolved. Let it stand twenty-four hours.

Mild Diuretics.

Of this class of medicines, nitre, by reducing the force of circulation, will be found eminently useful in febrile cases. Dose, ten or fifteen grains, for adults, every two or three hours. Conjoined with camphor, as in the camphorated powders, its diuretic effect, in some cases, is increased.

Dulcified Spirits of Nitre.

Dose for adults, half an ounce, every three or fours. Unless this medicine be given in large doses, it will excite perspiration, rather than act as a diuretic. It is chiefly valuable in the cases of children. There is, indeed, scarcely any other medicine which, in their complaints, we can substitute in its place, and it may be given to them, in the same proportion, even in the earliest periods of life.

Diuretic Infusion.

Pound a handful of pumpkin or melon seeds, with a small quantity of hard white sugar, to a smooth paste; then add a quart of boiling water, and a quarter of an ounce of saltpetre, or half an ounce of sweet spirits of nitre, and rub them well together. This is a pleasant and mild diuretic, particularly useful where the discharge of urine is attended with heat and pain. A tea-cupful may be taken every hour or two by adults.

Stimulating Diuretics.

The Spanish fly promotes as well as restrains the urinary discharge. Exhibited in a state of excitement, or in small doses, it most usually occasions strangury. But taken in a reverse state of the system, or in large doses, it as constanty proves diuretic. Thus, in the weaker forms of dropsy, two, three, or four drachms of the tincture, given in divided doses during the twenty-four hours, will produce the most copious evacuations of urine.

Nitric Lac Ammoniac.

Pour very gradually two drachms of nitric acid, diluted in eight ounces of water, on two drachms of ammoniac, and triturate them in a glass mortar till the gum is dissolved, forming a milky fluid. Of this a table-spoonful may be taken every two or three hours in sweetened water. Laudanum, in some cases, may be usefully added. Expectorant.

Pectoral Mixture.

Gum ammoniac, 2 drachms; syrup of squills, half an ounce; laudanum, 50 drops; spring water, 6 ounces. Reduce the gum to powder in a marble mortar, and gradually add the water and triturate till the gum is dissolved. Then strain from the impurities and add the other articles. Dose, a table-spoonful every two or three hours, for adults.

Or—Take sweet oil, 1 ounce; rain or soft water, half a pint; salt of tartar, 5 grains; white sugar, half an ounce. Dissolve the salt of tartar and the sugar in the water, and afterwards add the oil, when, by agitating the phial, a mixture will be formed of cream-like appearance. To this add paregoric elixir, half an ounce. Dose, a table-spoonful every hour or two.

Pectoral Emulsion.

Oil of almonds, or pure sweet oil, 1 ounce; barley-water, 6 ounces; best white sugar and gum arabic powdered, each, ½ ounce; laudanum, 40 drops. Incorporate the sugar and gum arabic together in a mortar, with a small quantity of barley-water, then gradually mix the oil, and afterwards add, by little at a time, the remainder of the water with the laudanum. One or two table-spoonfuls of this emulsion may be taken frequently.

Or—Take of the best purified honey and pure sweet oil, each, 2 ounces; fresh lemon-juice, 1 ounce; syrup and paregoric, each, ½ ounce. Mix, to form an emulsion. Dose, a tea-spoonful whenever the cough is most troublesome.

Cough Mixture.

Paregoric elixir, 1 ounce; powdered gum arabic, 1 ounce; simple water, 2 ounces; sweet spirit of nitre, 2 drachms; antimonial wine, 1 drachm Mix and dissolve. Dose, one table-spoonful to be taken whenever the cough is troublesome. But, in the first stage of catarrh, when inflammatory symptoms are present, this and all opiates are improper.

Or—Paregoric elixir, 1½ ounce; antimonial wine and syrup of squills, each, 1 ounce; lac ammoniac, 4 ounces; syrup of balsam tolu, 1 ounce. Dose, half a table-spoonful every two or three hours for adults.

Or—Tincture of opium, 1 drachm; wine of ipecacuanha, ½ drachm; oxymel of squills, ½ ounce. Mix. Dose, for adults, a tea-spoonful every two hours while the cough is severe.

Cure for Whooping-cough.

A tea-spoonful of castor oil to a tea-spoonful of molasses; a tea-spoonful of the mixture to be given whenever the cough is troublesome. It affords relief at once, and in a few days effects a cure. The same medicine relieves croup, however violent the attack.

Cure for Cough in Horses.

Take half a pound of nitre, a quarter of a pound of black regulus of antimony, and two ounces of antimony; mix them well in a mortar, and make up into doses of one ounce each. Give the horse one in a cold mash every night, in mild weather, for three nights; then omit it for a week. If he does not get better of his cough, repeat it. Care is necessary that the animal should not be exposed, while warm, to stand in a cold wind; otherwise exercise him gently, and heat him as usual.

To clean Wash-Leather Gloves.

First take out the grease-spots with magnesia, cream of tartar, or powdered Wilmington clay. Then wash and squeeze them through a lather of white soap and lukewarm water; hot water will shrink them. Squeeze them through a second suds; rinse them first in lukewarm and then in cold water, and stretch them to dry before the fire or in the sun.

Another Way.—Having removed the grease-spots, take the gloves, one at a time, on your hands, and rub them with a clean sponge wet with lukewarm soapsuds. Wash off the suds with a sponge and clear water, and stretch the gloves to dry. When almost dry, put them on your hands until finished, which will prevent them from shrinking.

Nitrous Lozenges.

Purified nitre, 2 drachms; refined sugar reduced to fine powder, 6 drachms; powdered gum tragacanth, 3 drachms. Beat these together with a small portion of water, till they are intimately mixed, and form a coherent mass, which may be divided into moderate sized lozenges, and dried by a gentle heat. In cases of quinsy or sore throat, one of these lozenges frequently put in the mouth, and suffered gradually to dissolve, will be found very beneficial.

Stain Mixture.

Sal ammoniac, 1 ounce; salt of tartar, 1 ounce. Mix well, put them into a pint of soft water, and bottle for use, keeping it very tightly corked. Wash in a little of this liquid those parts of a white article that have been stained with ink, mildew, or red wine. Having removed the stains, wash in the usual manner.

Another mixture for removing ink-spots, is half an ounce of oxalic acid dissolved in a pint of soft water; bottle and cork for use, shaking it well. When used, stretch the ink-stain over a bowl of hot water, and rub it with a sponge dipped in the solution. Then wash and dry it.

Cordial Draught.

Volatile tincture of valerian, one drachm; simple syrup and water, each, four tea-spoonfuls. To be taken at once by adults.

Diuretic Pills.

Dried squills (in fine powder) and calomel, each, half a drachm; mucilage of gum arabic, sufficient to form a mass, and then make twenty pills; two of which are to be taken at bed-time. These pills powerfully promote urine, and are very efficacious in carrying off cold phlegmatic humours, in all dropsical swellings. When the squill alone is given, it may be taken in doses of two or three grains, in the form of pills, three or four times a day, by adults.

Remedies for Whooping-Cough.

Dissolve 30 grains of salt of tartar in a gill of water, and add to it 10 grains of cochineal finely powdered; sweeten this with fine sugar, and give an infant a tea-spoonful four times a day; to a child of two or three years old, two tea-spoonfuls; from four years and upwards, a table-spoonful or more may be taken. The relief is said to be immediate, and in general within five or six days.

Or—Take equal portions of new milk and the ley obtained from hickory ashes, of which one table-spoonful may be given every hour through the day, to a child of seven or eight years old. This remedy is also strongly recommended.

Pectoral Lozenges.

Purified opium, 2 scruples; tincture of balsam tolu, 2 drachms; syrup, composed of one part of water and two parts of white sugar, 4 ounces; refined Spanish liquorice (previously moistened with a little warm water, so as to make it soft), and gum arabic in fine powder, each, 2½ ounces; emetic tartar, 8 grains. Rub the opium and emetic tartar with the tincture and syrup until the former is perfectly dissolved, then add the liquorice, and whilst beating them together, gradually sprinkle in the gum arabic. Divide the mass into lozenges, each weighing ten grains, and exsiccate them gradually in the air. One may be put in the mouth and gradually dissolved, every hour or two, when the cough is troublesome.

Opiate Pills.

Pure opium and powdered cinnamon or ginger, each, 12 grains; mucilage or syrup to make twelve pills. Dose, for adults, one or two at bed-time Anodyne.

Compound Spirits of Lavender.

Dose for adults, a tea-spoonful on a lump of sugar, to be dissolved in the mouth, and gradually swallowed.

Cordial Mixture.

Aromatic spirit of hartshorn, two drachms; compound spirit of lavender, three drachms; cinnamon water, two ounces; spring water, three ounces Mix. Dose for adults, a table-spoonful.

Cordial Drops.

Paregoric elixir, volatile tincture of valerian, of each equal parts. Mix them well together, and give, to adults, a tea-spoonful in a glass of water.

For children—the best cordial is white wine whey.

Remedy for the Asthma.

Slake half a pound of quicklime with two quarts of hot water, and stir in two spoonfuls of tar. Let it stand and settle. Take half a pound of wild turnip, half a pound of milkweed roots, and a small handful of lobelia; bruise them and infuse in two quarts of wine; place the whole in a warm place for twenty-four hours, then press and strain, add to it the lime-water, and bottle it for use. Take a wine-glassful three times a day. An excellent remedy for asthma, coughs, consumption, hysterics, &c.

For Baldness.

Fill a bottle with powdered lobelia, then pour in as much as it will contain of equal parts of brandy and sweet oil. In a few days it will be fit for use. Bathe the head once a day with this, and it will prevent the loss of hair. It is said to restore it when lost.

Canker.

This is an acrid humour, excoriating the most tender parts, particularly the mouth. Frequent application of the decoction of cranesbill, wild lettuce, white lily, or gold-thread, affords relief.

Corns.

Dissolve a little caustic potash in water, and wet the corn with it every night.

Or—Bathe the feet frequently in warm water with a little salt and potash dissolved in it, and apply a plaster made of two ounces of gum ammonia, two ounces of yellow wax, and two drachms of verdigris. Rasp away with pumice-stone as much of the corn as possible, and apply the plaster spread on thin soft leather. It must be renewed once a fortnight till cured.

Cholera Morbus.

At the commencement of the disease, give plentifully of thin broths, teas, or other diluting drinks, to promote the vomiting until the offending cause is expelled; clysters of the same may be given every hour. After these evacuations have been continued some time, a decoction of toasted bread may be given, to stop the vomiting; or, take lemon-juice, loaf-sugar and a little brandy, pour hot water to it, and drink it after puking. As the stomach and intestines are much weakened after this disease, an infusion of some tonic bitters in wine may be taken for some time.

Chapped Hands.

Wash with Castile soap and water a little warm, rubbing it in with flannel; then rinse them in clean water, and while they are wet rub them with a little honey, and dry them with a clean coarse towel. This should be done twice a day, and always before going to bed.

Chilblains.

Bathe the feet with a strong solution of alum, or a mixture of equal parts of oil of turpentine and balsam copaiva. Or, dip a piece of white chalk in vinegar, and frequently rub the chilblains with it. Or, bind on thin white skin which comes from suet.

Capons.

Place the fowl on its left side on the table, with its back to the operator, a strap round the wings, and the legs in a noose. Pluck off the feathers between the first and second ribs, and with the thumb and finger of the left hand draw the skin tense, so as to ascertain positively the space between the ribs. With a sharp knife make an incision through the skin only, an inch long, measuring from the point of the first rib backward. This will expose the two ribs and the margin of a large muscle running down the thigh. This muscle is in no danger of being injured, if the incision be made at the proper point; but if otherwise, an injury to it will cause lameness. Divide the muscle between the ribs, by introducing the knife at the point of the first rib and cutting backwards about an inch. In this way the pleura is avoided, and of course an escape of air.

Now, by introducing two small hooks, or any other suitable apparatus, draw apart the ribs so as to expose a bundle of fibres called the intercostal muscle. Should the incision be too small, it may be enlarged by passing the knife round the point of the second rib. Divide the belly of the intercostal muscle lengthwise, and you will perceive a semi-transparent membrane, called the peritoneum. This must likewise be divided, keeping the knife as far off as possible from the pleura. A branch of the cœliac artery traverses this membrane, and may be injured by a bungling hand, or by inattention. On cutting through this membrane, the upper testicle is brought into view. This lies on the margin of the lateral spinous processes, surrounded by nerves and blood vessels. It is a small yellow body, its colour somewhat darkened by the membrane covering it. In pushing downward and forward the intestine, the second testicle is brought into view, lying centrally between two large blood-vessels. This must be removed with great care, so as not to injure any of the neighbouring veins. For further information, see American Poultry Book, p. 115, by Micajah Cock.

Chlorosis, or Green Sickness.

This complaint requires relief immediately, otherwise dropsy, delirium, or consumption might follow. After taking a gentle emetic and cathartic, let the patient take a tea-spoonful of the powder of red cohush, in a gill of hot water, every half hour, or half a tea-spoonful of white birth-root powder, in a gill of warm water, every hour. Also, a tea of angelica seeds or roots, green wheat, cedar boughs, hemlock boughs, pennyroyal, mugwort, or winter clover. Before retiring to bed at night, the patient should stand or sit over a steam of hemlock boughs, or some bitter herbs; and have draughts applied to the feet. The general health should be improved by a strengthening diet and exercise in the open air.

Dysentery.

Make a strong tea of crows-foot or mouse-ear, add half a pint of brandy to a quart of the tea, and molasses sufficient to make a syrup. Drink it freely as often as the pains or gripings come on. Taken early, it seldom fails of curing the disorder.

A tea of witch-hazel bark, with boiled milk and loaf-sugar, drunk freely, is an excellent remedy.

INDEX.

30

THE END.

www.ingramcontent.com/pod-product-compliance
Lightning Source LLC
LaVergne TN
LVHW010152110826
845151LV00002B/497

* 9 7 8 1 4 2 5 5 3 7 2 8 9 *